THE MAYOR
Who Mastered New York

Also by Lately Thomas

THE FIRST PRESIDENT JOHNSON

THE VANISHING EVANGELIST

A DEBONAIR SCOUNDREL

SAM WARD: KING OF THE LOBBY

DELMONICO'S: A CENTURY OF SPLENDOR

BETWEEN TWO EMPIRES

William J. Gaynor, Justice of the Supreme Court of New York State and Mayor of New York City. Portrait by Pach.

THE MAYOR
Who Mastered New York

The Life & Opinions

OF

William J. Gaynor

BY

Lately Thomas

NEW YORK

William Morrow & Company, Inc.

1969

Printed in the United States of America
by American Book-Stratford Press, New York, N.Y.

Library of Congress Catalog Card Number 70-83690

TO
ALL POLITICIANS—
PLEASE COPY

Contents

Photographs appear between pages 96–97

The novelty . . . consists in the city having a mayor able to go into a closet with the revised statutes and the charter, and without a telephone, and reach a decision of, by, and for himself.
—NEW YORK TIMES, APRIL 19, 1910

Place: The City
Time: September, 1913

THE MAYOR WAS DEAD—abruptly, mysteriously, at a distance—and the news sent a thrill of shock through New York's four million. So pervasive of the very air of the metropolis had this mayor been, the first sensation was one of a sudden, suffocating vacuum. Then came the tributes, gushing from press, from pulpit, and from the lips and hearts of countless everyday citizens—lawyers, bootblacks, housewives, teachers, clerks, students, and many a girl and boy—as all realized that something vital, something provocative and bitter-agreeable, something comforting and cantankerous, but something atingle with gaiety and wit and hope, had gone out of their lives—something best summed up in a word, a name that had taken on a multitude of meanings—GAYNOR.

The city was moved as it seldom had been, and the newspapers strove to express the essence of that elusive vitality which had been so abruptly snuffed out. The causes of William J. Gaynor's hold on the imagination, confidence, and affection of the public were admittedly complex and the New York *Sun* traced them to the mayor's personality—"far enough from a saint, and right down near the passions, prejudices, hatreds, affections, the sympathies and the laughter of common men. He had a constituency," said the *Sun*, "—a public that took in most of these United States."

The *World* paradoxically dismissed much of Mayor Gaynor's conduct in office as defying rational explanation, but concluded:

"In the long line of commonplace and slate-colored mayors of New York, Gaynor towers, a giant among pygmies."

Yet his deficiencies had been so formidable, and he had displayed them with such unconcern! The mere enumeration sounded like a list of merits.

"He was irritable," catalogued the *Sun*. "He fought without gloves . . . he liked to swat; he was more than a 'good hater,' he was

11

a pitiless scorner of many; he turned not the other cheek but the other fist to those who assailed him; he was hot-tempered, like many generous and placable natures; he saw his enemies in hell's own black, his friends in rose colors."

Hardly ingratiating qualities, these, yet oddly the indictment rang like a citation for valor. So did the panegyrics on that implacable and adamant independence of the mayor which had balked and infuriated both his friends and his foes time and again. Said the *Nation*:

"In his public career courage was the dominant note. He never flinched from attacking what he wished to attack, or defending what he wished to defend. Whatever position he made up his mind to maintain on any subject, that position he was never deterred from maintaining by fear of either criticism or of consequences."

How, then, had a man of such rare pugnacity, who affronted friends and discomfited enemies with equal aplomb, managed to establish so warm an intimacy with the mass of people that his loss fell upon them like a personal blow?

One clue to the riddle was perceived by the magazine *Outlook*, which pointed to Gaynor's success in convincing the people of the city that "they had access to him, could get his ear, could appeal to him, when they felt his subordinates were acting unjustly or arbitrarily. . . . He was like an Oriental judge at the gate, to whom people with a grievance flocked."

As no other mayor ever had been, William J. Gaynor had been the father of his city; the people had trusted him. Instinctively the throng of voiceless, uninfluential, disregarded citizens, periodically flattered and regularly exploited by those elected to power, had recognized that in Gaynor they had a mayor who was always, unequivocally and unalterably, *on their side*.

This was unique. This was GAYNOR.

A VERY PRIVATE BEGINNING

———————■◦◯◦■———————

*There was a star danced, and under that
was I born.*

—MUCH ADO ABOUT NOTHING

A MAN'S PRIVATE LIFE, William J. Gaynor believed, is his own
affair, starting with the time and place of his birth. Not that he made
a secret of where and when he was born; but by telling it differently
on different occasions he made it a mystery.

He said he had been introduced to the world that would find
him as strange as he found it on a farm in Oneida county, New York
state. Such may have been the case, although not if the most plau-
sible date he gave for his birth was the right one. This date was
February 2, 1848, and he placed it in a written record, at an age
and under circumstances which would seem to preclude the successful passing of a fib. Later the date would unaccountably shift to
February 23, 1849, to 1851, and even to 1853. But there was a
method in this apparent scramble.

If the 1848 date is correct, and the weight of evidence points
to that conclusion, Gaynor was not born on a farm but in the semirural surroundings of the village of Whitesboro, township of Whitestown, Oneida county, central New York state.

His father, Keiron K. Gaynor, was an Irish immigrant. In the
History of Oneida County Keiron Gaynor is said to have been born
in Ireland in 1815; but in the obituary notice that appeared in the
New York newspapers when he died—data for which had been furnished by his son—his birth date was moved back to 1807. All that
is certain is that Keiron Gaynor came to the United States around

13

1832, and settled at Joliet, Illinois. From there he soon moved to the Mohawk Valley in New York state, and was employed as a blacksmith and ironworker in Whitesboro.

There in 1843 he married Elizabeth Handwright, daughter of James Handwright, a pioneer settler in the town of Marcy, across the Mohawk River. The Handwrights' ancestry was English; a great-uncle of William Gaynor, Richard Handwright, had died fighting at Quebec in 1775 under General Richard Montgomery. The religion of the Handwrights is not stated, but whatever it may have been, Elizabeth subscribed to the faith of her Roman Catholic husband, and the Gaynor children were all reared in that church.

There were seven of these, three sons and four daughters. Of the boys, Thomas Lee was the eldest, born in 1844; then came Joseph E., followed by William, born, presumably, in 1848. The girls were Mary, Helen, Theresa, and Emily. All the children surmounted the hazards of infancy and reached adulthood. All except Joseph and Helen would survive William. Joseph would leave home early, graduate from the school of medicine at the University of Michigan at Ann Arbor, and die prematurely in 1874.

The youngest son was baptized William James, and he was weak and puny until six years old. Then although his health improved, he continued to be scrawny and slight-muscled. Partly because of Will's delicacy, and partly to provide more space for his growing family, Keiron Gaynor moved in 1850 to a farm three miles west of Oriskany, beyond Utica, about five miles from Rome. The road running past the farmhouse into Oriskany was called Cider Street, and the district roundabout was dubbed "Skeeterboro"—from the clouds of mosquitoes that bred in the river bottoms. Skeeterboro was not a village, Gaynor made plain; although its inhabitants "lived close enough together for peace sake," nobody was less than half a mile away from his nearest neighbor.

This Skeeterboro farm held a romantic fascination for Gaynor as he looked back on it. To its wholesome influence he ascribed whatever success he had in life. The picture he painted in after years was both brighter and bleaker than the facts would seem to warrant. He once told an audience at the Syracuse state fair:

"We had an awful hard time to live. The best that grew on the farm was not eaten at all. We scarcely ate butter, and never drank milk except skimmed milk. We seldom ate fresh meat except pork, and seldom eggs. . . . Those were the things that brought in the only ready money we had, and we saved our butter and such things until the agent came around to buy them and turn them into ready cash to pay the bills of the year. The rest of the year we just lived the best we could on the skimmed milk and what was left, and then in the winter—I won't exactly undertake to tell you how we lived. We lived somehow or other . . . and we came out of it also with some preparation for life."

This vision of penury amid plenty did not jibe with the recollection of sister Theresa, then Mrs. Anthony V. Lynch, living in Utica. Said she:

"We always had the very best the farm afforded. In summer, early apples, berries, vegetables. . . . In the fall father put all kinds of vegetables and dried fruits in the cellar, besides beef and salt pork. We had hams smoked in the smokehouse in the old-fashioned way, with corn cobs. The corn was taken to a small village and ground into meal for johnny-cakes and other purposes. We always had at least twelve cows and about fifty chickens and had plenty of butter, milk, and eggs."

Gaynor's first encounter with education took place in the one-room district schoolhouse a mile from the farm. Its clapboards he was convinced never felt a paintbrush in their whole existence. The school in Marcy, which his mother had attended, was painted red, and every time Will saw it he was struck with awe. In his schoolhouse, he said:

"The desks slanted down from the four walls inward, and then the benches were along in front of the desks, and we studied our lessons sitting on the benches with our faces to the wall, and then when we were going to recite we threw our heels over the bench and faced about to the teacher, and at the same time faced the big stove in the center of the room that burned the cordwood. And many a day in winter have I tramped to that schoolhouse. And sometimes to get home they would have to turn out and dig out the snow. And how often we had our ears frozen on the way to school or while out playing, or our faces frozen even, and when our ears thawed out sometimes they hung over so that they came down flat almost."

Sister Theresa's version was that "in winter father used to take the children to school in the sleigh and go for them at four o'clock," but Will was having none of such namby-pamby recollections.

Gaynor conceded that in this primitive schoolhouse the pupils learned little except the "fundamentals," but what they did learn stuck with them for life.

The winters were not long spells of unalloyed hardship either.

Christmas he recalled as the happiest day of the year, and the story of the birth of Jesus was vivid to him because "we children in the country saw the cow and the ox and the manger. . . . We lived with the cattle and loved them. That Jesus was born among them made us feel that he was really one of us."

Santa Claus was another real personage in his intense inner world. "We believed in his sleigh, in his reindeer, in his coming down the chimney. . . . I do not remember ever having seen the little chap, but I am certain that he used to come around in the country when I was a boy. I think I have seen his footprints in the snow, and also the tracks of his reindeer and sleigh."

The joys of summer Gaynor recalled just as vividly. He liked to fish, and half a century later would repeat lovingly the names of the streams into which he had dropped a line. "The Unadilla. Did you ever hear a prettier name than Unadilla? And the Saquoit, and the Oriskany, and the raging Mohawk, of course." He knew the way to the swimming hole in the Erie Canal, but often instead of jumping in with the other boys he would sit on the bank and watch, thinking. He did a lot of thinking, about how things were and what made them so. Games he liked, but he seldom played them. His chief interest was to ramble the countryside, watching nature at work, prying into things, observing, with boundless curiosity. He would surprise his schoolmates with bits of curious lore, but they were not really interested in what occupied him. Often he would be seen to walk away from the other children, disgusted, to follow his own bent.

On the farm the lighter chores fell to him; brother Tom helped with the heavy work. The barnyard animals Will treated like members of the family, having pet names for favorite cows and pigs. Pigs especially fascinated him. "Is there anything more interesting than a sow with her litter?" was to become a famous rhetorical question of his. But although active and energetic, William lacked manual dexterity. Tom would say that if he tried to do anything he was bound to get hurt. If he tried to chop wood, sooner or later he would nick his foot, and if he "went up in the hayloft to see if the old black hen had hidden a nest there, he would fall and gash a leg."

The only chum Will admitted to intimacy was Bill Griffiths. There were many Welsh families in the neighborhood, and in running around with Bill, Gaynor picked up a smattering of their language. Bill had a sister, Jane Griffiths, and long after she was dead Gaynor alluded to her in a way that indicated she had been his boyhood love, and probably not a happy one. "It didn't happen, but it might have happened," was his way of intimating the situation.

But Will Gaynor was not a moody or dreamy lad. He was practical and earthy in spite of contemplative tendencies. In school he was both quick and diligent, taking to books naturally, soaking up their contents, reading some until they fell apart. What he read he retained with precocious tenacity of memory, and he pondered what he read; he was no mere neutral receptacle for a jumble of information. The streak of independence that led him to pry into things also tempted him sometimes to question, and in behavior it found expression in impish mockery and prankishness.

A boy on a nearby farm had the job of taking corn to the mill in Oriskany, riding a horse with the sacks of grain dangling down either side of the saddle. He came to expect an ambush by young Gaynor as he jogged along; a stone would zip past his ear from a thicket, and, turning quickly, he would espy a shock-headed, "barefooted urchin, slender, thin-faced, long-nosed, and sassy"—dressed in "linen breeches, coarse cotton shirt, and battered chip hat"—making off across the fields as fast as his skinny legs would carry him. The culprit was never caught.

Keiron Gaynor approved of his son's studiousness, and from the district school sent William on to the Whitestown Seminary. Being good church people, the Gaynors drove into Utica every Sunday when the roads were passable to attend mass at St. John's Church. As he entered his teen years, William developed a religious fervor that caused his parents to suspect that he might have a vocation. Partly to test this, and also because it was the best school available to one of his limited means, Keiron entered the boy in Assumption Academy, conducted by the Christian Brothers (the Brothers of the Christian Schools) in Utica.

This teaching order of the Roman Catholic church, although founded in France in 1680, was just making headway in the United States. It differed from some orders in that its members, though pledged to poverty, humility, and celibacy, were not priests, and while they took vows, these were not irrevocable. Their special work was the education of the sons of workingmen in useful and practical pursuits, eschewing the showier branches of learning.

Young Gaynor responded to the spirit of sincerity, service, and helpful devotion that permeated Assumption Academy. He was an exemplary student, quick to learn, and soon felt that he was indeed called to teach in the order. Brother Justin, the director of the academy, recognized the latent capacities of the eager, sensitive country boy and encouraged him. Brother Justin was a natural leader, a man of action as well as spirituality, filled with missionary zeal for the order, and some of Brother Justin's practical idealism rubbed off on Gaynor.

The Civil War was in progress while Gaynor was at Assumption Academy, but apart from sharing in the predominant antislavery feeling there is no evidence that he was greatly touched by the popular excitements of the time. Not only was he isolated in school, he was at an age when youth is more concerned with its own problems than with outside events. Yet Oneida County was in the thick of the storm. A former mayor of Utica, Horatio Seymour, was elected Democratic governor of New York in 1862, and as such would lead a responsible opposition to President Lincoln and the Republican national administration. The War Democrats, as Seymour's faction was called, ardently supported the war in order to preserve the Union, but just as ardently denounced many extralegal actions taken by the President.

The turbulence was at its height when Gaynor took a step toward realizing his intention: on December 17, 1863, he was accepted as a novice in the order and entered the novitiate of De la Salle Institute, at 44 East Second Street, New York City. His birth date on that occasion was recorded as February 2, 1848, showing that he was several weeks short of sixteen years old. He was given the name Brother Adrian Denys.

Tom Gaynor, meanwhile, had caught the war fever, and two weeks after his brother entered the novitiate Thomas enlisted as a private in the Union army. He was sent to a training camp on Staten Island, where William visited him in February, 1864. Shortly after that Tom's regiment was moved to the front, where he would take part in every battle fought by the Army of the Potomac from the Wilderness to Appomattox.

On August 11, 1864, while Tom was skirmishing around Petersburg, Brother Adrian Denys was enrolled as a teacher in the Christian Brothers. He took no vows, nor could he, under the rules of the order, until he was twenty-one.

For roughly the next four years, as Brother Adrian Denys, Gaynor followed his vocation. He wore the cassock and clerical bands that were the habit of the Brothers. It may be that for one year he taught in St. Louis, and it is certain that early in 1868 Brother

Justin selected him as one of a group of seven to go to San Francisco and take charge of newly founded St. Mary's College there.

On July 16, 1868, the party set out from New York aboard the steamship *Ocean Queen*. The band of Manhattan College gave them a send-off serenade. Their ship made port at Aspinwall, Panama, where they took the train across the Isthmus, and then secured passage northward on the Pacific side. The journey was long and arduous, and San Francisco, when they reached it, seemed to the pilgrims like a tenuous outpost set on the edge of an endless wilderness.

Somewhere along the route of this journey a great change occurred in the life of William Gaynor. During the years of his preparation for a religious career he had continued to read omnivorously, and as his reading widened, so did the horizon of his perceptions, his aptitudes, and his sympathies. The mainstay of his reading had been serious works of history and philosophy, though he also read much in classical and modern literature, and reveled in mathematics. It was his habit to read with a pencil in hand and make notes in the margin of the book or elsewhere, wrestling with the ideas presented.

One book that came as a revelation was the *Autobiography* of Benjamin Franklin. Its winning common sense, profound tolerance, and homespun philosophy seemed to echo Gaynor's very thoughts; the book would be a companion to him for life.

He read the Bible assiduously, preferring it to works of the Fathers or exegesis. He was attracted by the ideas of the Stoics, Seneca and Epictetus, especially by their delineation of the virtuous life as the highest attainable good. *Don Quixote* aroused his liveliest enthusiasm; that book he ranked second to only the Bible in the whole world. In another direction, the *Autobiography* of Benvenuto Cellini mirrored his taste for action, temporarily repressed.

Reading of this sort, and meditation upon what he read, was not conducive to the unquestioning piety expected of a member of a religious order. Slowly and subtly his acceptance of Christian theology was undermined, although he did not lose faith in God, or in any way lessen his veneration of Jesus and His teachings. But formal creeds and dogmas had become untenable for him. He was still religious, deeply so, but had lost contact with his church.

Just how or when this process, which had been building up over a long period of time, came to a climax Gaynor never said, nor did anyone else leave a record. The only certain fact is that shortly after

reaching San Francisco, Gaynor and the Christian Brothers parted.
The separation was open and amicable. The official reason given was
the state of Gaynor's health, which made a teaching career under
the conditions of the order inadvisable. There was no question of
receiving dispensation from any vows, because he had taken none.
Gaynor himself never spoke of the episode, and not even his wife
or his children ever heard him mention it.

Such reticence in regard to experiences personal to him stemmed
basically from his natural tendency to silence and reflection, and
also from his intense pride. At no period of his life did he ask favors;
he was touchy on that point; overly, even belligerently independent.
His pride could not bear the thought that he "owed" an explanation
of his private actions to anyone, so long as his conscience was clear.
Privacy, the sanctity of the individual, was with him in itself a
religion, and he would not violate that sanctity even to convince a
critic of the injustice of misjudging him. As for his public actions,
he would consistently point to the open record and say that if that
did not convince people of his honesty, nothing could, and he would
have to bear with it.

Although it was no longer formalized, Gaynor's religious sense
if anything deepened after he was thrown upon his own responsibilities of conscience and aspiration, without the communal support of
the brotherhood. He believed implicitly in the all-pervading goodness
and justice of God, not for any logical reason but, as he would say,
simply because he could not help it. He *knew* there was a God, instinctively, and he believed there was a divine purpose in everything.
Jesus he often termed "the greatest figure that ever came upon this
earth, the greatest teacher"; but theological doctrines henceforth
would mean little to him. With those who found comfort in such
matters he had no quarrel, but the least trace of bigotry would arouse
his fighting resentment.

Just how Gaynor made his way east is not known, although at
least once he hinted that it had been a rough experience.

"I was stranded in San Francisco when I was eighteen," he said
on this occasion, characteristically lopping a couple of years off his
age, "and I can tell you, I had a hard time of it."

By late 1868, however, Gaynor was back in Utica, where his
father had moved from the farm and was working as a machinist in
a textile mill. The family home was on Cooper Street. That no stigma
attached to his leaving the Christian Brothers was made clear by
the reception Keiron Gaynor gave his son: as a stanch Catholic, at

a time not given to tolerance in such situations, he would hardly have welcomed William back into his home had there been anything disgraceful or improper about his aborted religious career. But not only did Keiron Gaynor open his home again to William, he helped him materially in making a start on a new career. Keiron Gaynor was well and favorably known in Utica, and his help was instrumental in enabling William to enter the office of Horatio and John Seymour to read for the bar. We may be sure that the Brothers at Assumption Academy also placed no obstacle in the path of their former novice, for against their objection the Seymours would never have taken him. Horatio Seymour was Utica's most honored citizen; he had just run for President of the United States against Ulysses S. Grant.

Gaynor remained with the Seymours about a year, then transferred to the office of another distinguished Utican, Judge Ward Hunt, who later would become a justice of the United States Supreme Court. While with Hunt, in 1871, Gaynor was admitted to the bar. He was twenty-three years old. His law-reading days Gaynor himself summed up in two sentences:

"And I stayed there and studied and kept as still as I could for about a year and a half or two years. I thought Utica was a wonderful place."

But he did not think it a good place to try to practice law against the men who had taught him. Carefully he canvassed the field of possible locations, and in his choice displayed originality.

ON TO BABYLON

I have a key in my bosom, called Promise,
*that will, I am persuaded, open any lock
in* Doubting Castle. *Then said* Hopeful,
*that is good news, good brother; pluck it
out of thy bosom, and try.*

—PILGRIM'S PROGRESS

H E HAD SOUGHT advice on this step from the highest authority—a
source that never scrupled to ladle it out copiously and erratically—
Horace Greeley, editor of the *New York Tribune* and counselor-
general to generations of ambitious country boys. Gaynor wrote to
Greeley ("everybody wrote to Horace Greeley in those days," he
recalled) seeking guidance, and back came an answer in Greeley's
notoriously illegible scrawl, which required "the combined intelligence of the neighborhood" to decipher. Then it was found that the
oracle in New York recommended Florida, New Mexico, and several
other remote localities as good places to move to, but "whatever you
do, don't come down to this modern Babylon."

Assuming that Greeley had sound reasons for proffering this
counsel, Gaynor passed over the metropolis of his own state and fixed
his choice on Boston. There was the center of the nation's intellectual
life, and his tastes were intellectual; reason enough for selecting
Boston. Buoyed up by jejune hopes and airy illusions he prepared
methodically to set out. As he told the story:

"So I went down to the trunk store and bought me a good big
trunk. I never expected to come back to Utica either. And I had my

name painted on one end of it, and in big letters under it, 'Utica, N.Y.' 'Skeeterboro' was out of the question. I wanted everybody to know that I came from Utica as the intellectual hub of the country after Boston. I thought that would give me recognition wherever I went. But I only got a little way off from Utica before nobody knew who I was, and I didn't get much farther away before nobody knew or cared anything about Utica. So I shook the dust of Utica off my feet."

Gaynor's stay in Boston was brief and unproductive. He said he went there "to take up my life and study," and while there is no doubt that he studied, for he never stopped studying as long as he lived, he made no progress toward getting a foothold as a lawyer. He boarded at 90 Waltham Street, in the South End, and was employed at least part of the time by a law firm having offices at 8 Pemberton Square, mainly in running down delinquent accounts. He was admitted to practice in Massachusetts in the Superior Court of Suffolk County on September 13, 1872, but never handled a case.

Yet the atmosphere of Boston, orderly, staid, scholarly, and respectful of solid achievement, pleased him. He liked the decorum, the cautious liberalism, the private geniality and appreciation of good living, and the avoidance of vulgarity and show. And when he concluded that the chances in Boston for a tyro who possessed neither friends nor position were about zero, he chose another community in which to make a start, a community that shared many of Boston's characteristics. This was the city of Brooklyn, across the East River from rich-poor, rackety, pulsing, parvenu Manhattan, and as far from New York City in spirit as it was independent of it in government.

Brooklyn in the Seventies was a city of quiet and seclusion, with tranquil, tree-lined streets thickly interspersed with churches. Solidly respectable, it was dedicated to domesticity; its symbol to outsiders was the ubiquitous baby buggy. A recent census had showed there were more persons of New England descent living in Brooklyn than in Boston, and from New England these families had brought the virtues of thrift and sobriety. On Brooklyn Heights, overlooking the harbor, was a serene community of wealth, whose prosperous bankers, brokers, and shipping magnates ferried to Wall Street every morning, closed their desks at four in the afternoon, ferried home, dined leisurely, and on fine twilight evenings took their recreation in long drives through Prospect Park. Around the base of the Heights, spreading north, east, and south, was a less affluent population but vital and expanding, close enough to New York to benefit from its constant overflow but isolated from its more feverish life.

In 1873, when Gaynor arrived in Brooklyn, the great bridge that would connect it with Manhattan was just being built; it would not be opened to traffic for another decade. Gaynor came armed with letters of recommendation from Judge Hunt and Francis Kernan (another prominent Utica lawyer and Democrat, soon to be elected to the United States Senate) addressed to St. Clair McKelway, chief editorial writer for the *Brooklyn Daily Eagle*. Until recently this brilliant journalist had been the Washington correspondent of the *New York World*, at a time when it was known as "the best written and least read" newspaper in New York.

McKelway was favorably impressed by young Gaynor; but 1873 was a panic year, jobs were scarce, and there was no hope of getting a start on a legal career. Nevertheless McKelway found a place for Gaynor as a reporter for the *Brooklyn Argus*, a newspaper on its financial last legs but willing to pay the lad from Utica the handsome salary of fifteen dollars a week.

Gaynor lost no time in renting a room in a shabby but decent boardinghouse at 38 First Place, in downtown Brooklyn, and set to work. He still had not plunged into the whirlpool of Greeley's "modern Babylon," but he was skirting its borders. He was twenty-five years old.

A coincidence marked his first day as a reporter. The lad at whom, years before, Will Gaynor had shied stones on his way to the grist mill in Oriskany, also was a reporter for the *Argus*, drawing a salary of twenty-five dollars a week. On the first day Gaynor appeared in the city room this old hand was present. Gaynor gave no sign of recognition, went straight to the assignment book and got his assignment, then turned about and left without speaking a word to anybody. Later he handed in his report, written with businesslike competence, still without fraternizing with the rest of the staff.

This taciturnity puzzled his Oneida acquaintance, who also could not understand how Gaynor got his facts down accurately without either pad or pencil to take notes, so far as anybody could see.

One day Gaynor entered a lunchroom and took a seat near his Oneida friend. The latter patronizingly thought a little sociability would be in order; but as he watched Gaynor, "with a faraway look, drink his whole bowl of milk and eat his dry crackers," the bearing of the young man seemed to signal, "I am going it alone in this town."

Go it alone he did, and frugally, not from standoffishness, but because he had no time to fritter in companionship. Studiousness, settled habits, and "a purpose to persevere," he told himself, were the keys to accomplishment; the only genius he would recognize was the genius of being prepared. Toward the close of his life he put into words for the benefit of a group of college students the credo that had shaped his professional life:

"Never was a talkative fellow a great lawyer. Not even one. The saying is that no lawyer came to fame with a straight back or without a pale face. That tells the whole story. To be great in anything you have to toil terribly. Some of the people in the rear of the courtroom think that fellow with the immense diamond in his shirt bosom and with a very loud voice is the greatest lawyer there. But there is another chap there that they hardly hear, and who may look quite insignificant; but the judge and the jury know that he is the great lawyer. He knows something."

Hard-working, silent, and solitary, Gaynor was compiling the table of personal values that would govern all his future actions. Among these was a belief that free government can endure only as long as the citizens, individually and collectively, cooperate conscientiously in observing the laws. Let citizens who are law-abiding themselves long neglect or refuse to become involved in maintaining public order, and free government will soon give way to despotic rule. This principle he put into action with an originality that stirred up considerable comment in the press.

The episode started on July 28, 1874, when Gaynor appeared before Justice of the Peace Thomas M. Riley in Brooklyn's Willoughby Street police court and swore out a warrant for the arrest of Theodore Tilton, prominent Brooklyn resident and nationally known publicist and reformer. Gaynor's complaint charged that Tilton had uttered a libel against the Rev. Henry Ward Beecher, pastor of Plymouth Church and America's most celebrated pulpit orator. The libel consisted in Tilton's saying that over a long period of time Beecher had systematically debauched Tilton's wife. Tilton's charge had been published one week previously in the *Brooklyn*

Eagle, and it had brought into the open a scandal that had been smoldering for a couple of years in private circles, and that would rock the nation for months to come.

Gaynor knew none of the principals and had no personal connection with the case. His sole interest, he told the flabbergasted justice, was that of a law-abiding citizen, who, becoming cognizant of a violation of the law, was performing a civic duty by taking steps to bring the offender to trial. He was acting, he insisted, solely "in the interest of public morality. . . . If this man is guilty of libel, he has violated the law of the state," and he should be punished.

This doctrine stumped the justice of the peace; but he could hardly ignore Gaynor's complaint, which was in proper legal form, alleging that "the said Tilton" had published his libel "with intention to scandalize and disgrace the said Henry Ward Beecher, and bring him into contempt, infamy, and disgrace; wherefore deponent prays that the defendant may be apprehended and dealt with according to law."

More in quandary than in acquiescence, Riley dispatched a bailiff to request Mr. Tilton to come into court. The officer found his man stretched out on a sofa with his shoes off, talking with reporters. Laughing at the whole thing as a joke, Tilton obligingly put on his shoes and accompanied the bailiff to court, the reporters trooping after him. There he entered a plea of not guilty and was granted an overnight postponement in order to secure counsel.

The next day when Tilton and his lawyer appeared the courtroom was crowded. The court, the lawyer, and Tilton all joined in trying to persuade Gaynor to withdraw his complaint. Nobody wanted it, least of all Henry Ward Beecher, who was doing his utmost to hush the scandal. But, pale and intense, Gaynor stubbornly refused. Tilton affirmed that he had never seen or heard of his accuser before, and Gaynor likewise affirmed that he had no personal interest in the matter. But nothing would budge him from carrying out his duty as a citizen.

There were several postponements, and each time the courtroom crowd got bigger. All sorts of guesses were made as to Gaynor's real motive; his stated reason for the action was dismissed as utterly incredible. His sincerity was everywhere doubted. The court said so, and the *Eagle* charged that the *Argus* was behind the bizarre farce. This Gaynor denied emphatically:

"I am not in collusion with anybody," he told the court. "I have

not consulted anybody. I am a member of the community, and as
such I have a right to come forward and see that justice is done. . . .
If anyone commits a murder, or steals a horse, and I know it, it is my
duty to bring him to justice, for he is a violator of the law. . . . It
may be unusual, this proceeding, but I had a perfect right to have
this person arrested."

Nor would he consent to a private hearing, but insisted that
"the public is entitled to know what is going on."

Cynics scoffed and the ribald jeered; Gaynor stood his ground.

The truth was that not his stated motive, but the scope of his
naïveté, was what was unbelievable. Retired and withdrawn, Gaynor
had had little experience of the workaday, nonidealistic world. He
was just beginning to learn its ways, and he had tumbled into the
pitfall that trips many a youthful theorist: having formulated a
principle, Gaynor was trying to live by it literally—justice though
the heavens fall. The world, which does not live by principle but by
rote and self-interest, could not comprehend this quixoticism and
reacted with disbelief.

Discerning observers (of whom there appear to have been none
in Brooklyn in 1874) might have drawn a clue to Gaynor's basic
attitude by noting his repeated use of the words "public morality."
With the private morality of the Beecher-Tilton scandal he had
nothing to do; that was outside his sphere as a citizen and he was not
a regulator of private lives. But by publishing a libel, Tilton had
breached the peace and decorum of the community as defined in the
statutes. The distinction was crucial in Gaynor's theory of involvement, in both its legal and its moral aspects. It would be the basis
of some of his most important and startling actions in the years of
his power. And despite the public skepticism, his sincerity in 1874
could not be successfully impugned, for he told his motive and
reasoning clearly several times, and he would hold the same views
thirty years later.

The action dragged along until finally the exasperated Riley
announced that he would dismiss the case unless Gaynor obtained
an order from a higher court compelling him to proceed. No such
order was secured, and eventually the case was lost sight of in the
greater furor raised by Tilton's suit against Beecher, seeking one
hundred thousand dollars' damages.

Again Gaynor had made a false start; but he was quick to

learn, and would not soon again allow the cart of principles to run upon the plodding horse of worldly practice.

The *Argus* expired, and Gaynor became a reporter of Brooklyn doings for the New York *Sun*. He also opened a cubbyhole office in a building on Fulton Street that housed congenially a saloon in the basement, a dance hall on the first floor, and law offices above. His first legal fee was earned by drawing five deeds for the price of one. His first appearance as a trial lawyer was in behalf of three boys accused by an irascible neighbor of disturbing the peace. Gaynor heard about the boys' plight on his news-gathering rounds and offered to appear in their defense.

"Are you a lawyer?" they asked, and when he assured them he was, their next question was, "How much will you charge?"

"Nothing," answered Gaynor, "and what's more, I'll get you off."

The corps of City Hall reporters was on hand to see their taciturn and unsociable colleague match wits with a lawyer of known ability who was appearing for the complainant. Gaynor won the case, and his grateful clients chipped in and bought him a walking stick.

After that, bit by bit he began to pick up business, and in the autumn of 1874 he took another step toward joining the ranks of solid citizenship by marrying Emma Vesta Hyde, of Truro, Nova Scotia, and moving into a small frame house in outlying Flatbush. The Hyde family had gone to Canada from the district in upstate New York where the Gaynors lived; Emma's father had been associated with Cyrus Field in laying the Atlantic cable.

A significant action at the time of this marriage was Gaynor's altering, in the official record, his father's given name from the Irish "Keiron" to English- or Dutch-sounding "Kendrick." And he changed his own middle name from "James" to the more distinguished "Jay," a patronymic of prestigious luster in the history of New York jurisprudence. Later he would change "Jay" to the simple initial "J." and with Spanish gravity disclaim ever having used the form "Jay." Gaynor was continuing to build a private life to suit his tastes, and a discrepancy with facts outside did not bother him.

The first steady client Gaynor secured was the bad egg of Flatbush, Hughie McCarthy. Shifty Hughie was always in trouble, suspected of everything and usually guilty. He would deliver a load of wood in the morning, and after dark steal it back. Gaynor did what he could with this hopeless delinquent, but as soon as he felt he could afford to, he gave up on Hughie.

Flatbush was a placid community of some ten thousand inhabitants lying on the southern flank of Brooklyn and independent of it. It was peaceful and contented. It had been settled by Dutch farmers, and many of their descendants still lived in the town and had inherited their bucolic temperament. Beyond Flatbush, to the south, lay Gravesend, and beyond Gravesend was Coney Island.

The burghers of Flatbush cherished above all their traditional Sunday repose. The Coney Island road ran through Flatbush and during the Seventies roadhouses sprang up that catered to weekend parties on their way to Coney. The travelers would stop to water their horses, and at the same time stoke up on more stimulating liquids. This weekend revelry disturbed the tranquillity of Flatbush, and the right-thinking citizens formed a Law and Order Society to stem the invasion. Gaynor was retained as counsel.

With unflinching determination and merciless disregard of his own comfort he prepared a case against one of the objectionable resorts which the local constabulary was suspected of having under its sheltering wing. For a whole day Gaynor lay prone in the bushes opposite the offending roadhouse, noting every policeman who went in and when he came out. The results were printed in the local newspaper, and the Law and Order Society succeeded in putting a damper on that particular nuisance at least.

Gaynor defended drunks with equal vigor. He defended saloonkeepers accused of violating the excise laws, and represented the local excise boards in prosecuting saloonkeepers. He sued to recover a servant girl's wages, and served as adviser to boards and commissions in the towns roundabout. A few days after he had appeared as counsel for the Law and Order Society in the arrest of seven roadhouse owners, he defended sixty-three saloonkeepers of East New York, a semirural town east of Brooklyn, who were accused by the crusading wife of a crusading clergyman of illegally selling beer on Sunday. Gaynor had the prosecution thrown out on a technicality, then in thirty of the individual arrests he secured costs against the complainant, dampening her ardor for reform. Any case that turned up that was legitimate was grist to Gaynor's mill. He did not win all his cases, especially those dealing with the jumbled and really unenforceable excise laws. As he told an inquisitive reporter:

"I have been engaged in litigation on all sides of this question—

for liquor dealers, for excise boards, and for temperance organizations—and the excise law is a sort of puzzle out of which you can work any combination except one—the combination that will please everybody."

As his practice widened he took on commercial accounts in Brooklyn, and won a reputation as a good collection lawyer, not too burdened by sentiment.

In another direction he received an education in the operations of a political boss, the picturesque, pudgy John Y. McKane, supervisor, chief of police, and absolute dictator of the town of Gravesend. As counsel for the Gravesend land commissioners Gaynor had a ringside seat for everything that went on. Gravesend was small, but Gravesend owned Coney Island, and that was McKane's island of gold.

At this period Gaynor began to contribute to law journals. His article on "Chattel Mortgages Upon Stocks in Trade" appeared in the *Albany Law Journal* in 1874, the year of his marriage, and was followed by others in which he discussed with learning and often with originality debts, taxation, and wills, among other subjects. Gaynor enjoyed writing these papers; they provided an opportunity to utilize his wide reading and his analytical powers, and they drew attention to him in legal circles.

A photograph of Gaynor at this time shows him characteristically bent over a book, serious and intent. His cheek rests against one hand in an attitude of concentration and some weariness, but the lips under the flowing mustache are firm-set. There is no sign yet of the beard that would become so famous. The hair, reddish-brown, has been parted precisely in the middle, but is somewhat ruffled. The jacket, bow tie, and starched round cuffs are prim and neat. The eyes are concealed under the lowered eyelids; they were Gaynor's least attractive feature. Blue and cold, they were most of the time expressionless, conveying no emotional message at all. Their gaze was not indrawn, and though meditative, was curiously blank. Now and then, but rarely, they would light up with the malicious twinkle of a laughing leprechaun, but there was no warmth in them. Altogether not a friendly or mobile face, but one that might inspire respect and trust.

In 1881, after seven years of married life, Emma Vesta Hyde Gaynor divorced her husband on the only grounds for which a divorce was granted in New York state—adultery. Gaynor entered no defense. The union was childless and no alimony was asked. Mrs. Gaynor returned to Halifax and remarried there.

For Gaynor this divorce had unpleasant consequences, although when the episode was raised against him politically, years afterward, he declined to discuss it. He never spoke of it publicly in any way, although he did authorize friends to say that the real grounds had been nothing more than incompatibility; in fact, these friends, who believed they knew the circumstances, insisted that the "other woman" figuring in the suit was entirely imaginary. Gaynor, they maintained, merely made it easy for his wife to obtain the desired legal separation with a minimum of fuss. If this is true (and Gaynor's demonstrated virility might raise the shadow of a doubt) it would convict him of a chivalrous act of perjury. But this would not be inconsistent with his private valuation of many actions that conflicted with conventional standards. At any rate, he allowed friends to quote him as saying flatly that any fault attaching to the failure of the marriage was his alone; his wife was not to blame.

Professionally, Gaynor's reputation for a while was clouded, and he incurred hostility in church circles. Until now he had remained a nominal Catholic; but the predominantly Irish Catholic clergy of New York and Brooklyn in 1881 were unsparing of divorced persons, and Gaynor was severely censured. From this treatment stemmed Gaynor's antipathy to ecclesiasticism, especially as exemplified in the Roman Catholic hierarchy. The prejudice was never publicly expressed, but among his family it was no secret. From this time also Gaynor would minimize his Irish antecedents and lean more and more to English habits and preferences.

But though the divorce injured him to some extent, he persevered and prospered. So much so that in 1886 he felt sufficiently established to make a fresh start domestically, and he married again and left Flatbush to move into a comfortable brownstone dwelling in Brooklyn itself.

Now "Babylon" was just across the newly opened bridge that led directly to New York's City Hall, and Gaynor was a man of growing importance on its periphery.

A RESTART AND A COMMITMENT

There are truths which are not for all men, nor for all times.

—VOLTAIRE

THE PARTNER of Gaynor's new venture in marriage was Augusta C. Mayer, daughter of a well-to-do carriage maker in Belleville, New Jersey. Hopeful of an operatic career, she had received voice training in Italy, but after her marriage abandoned that prospect and never sang in public except occasionally at a charity concert. She was gracious, domestic, and fond of good society; her children accused her of being too softhearted to shut out a stray cat, and they had no appreciation of her singing operatic snatches around the house—badly, they thought. But then, there is no evidence that any of the family possessed a nice discrimination in music. Certainly Gaynor did not; he could hum popular airs and he liked band music, but that was about all.

The Gaynors settled into a comfortable home at 212 St. Johns Place, in the Park Slope section of Brooklyn, then coming into fashion. Gaynor also signalized his changed status by opening a law office in Montague Street, hard by Brooklyn's City Hall and the Kings County courthouse. He formed a partnership with Edward M. Grout, a prominent Catholic layman and Democrat, and Paul F. De Fere, and the firm soon became one of the busiest in the city.

During these years Gaynor maintained touch with his family in a desultory way. His soldier brother, Tom, after being mustered out of the army in August, 1865, drifted to Ohio and settled down as proprietor of a cigar store in Springfield. Joseph Gaynor had died a year after William left Boston. The parents were still living in Utica, as were three of Gaynor's sisters, Theresa, Helen, and Mary. Theresa had married, and so had Emily, the youngest sister, who with her husband was living in Brooklyn. Sometimes long intervals of silence intervened, but the family kept informed about each other, despite the wide disparity of their interests.

Professionally Gaynor established himself as a hard worker and relentless fighter. He had an ample knowledge of the law, and views that were sometimes unorthodox but always based on common sense. One striking faculty he possessed was the ability to get to the heart of a lawsuit quickly. In the courtroom he avoided theatrical tricks and emotional appeals to juries, relying on thorough preparation and the impact of cold logic. His speech was terse and colloquial. A slow speaker, he became dangerous when aroused, and his grasp of legal principles was matched by a deep understanding of the vagaries of human nature. Pompous orators he delighted in cutting down with sarcasm, and woolly thinking, whether by friend or adversary, set his teeth on edge. He was scornful of everything pretentious. He did have his weaknesses. One was a fondness for parading his erudition by introducing esoteric literary and philosophical allusions that were largely lost on judge, counsel, and jurymen.

One thing he never succeeded in doing was to bridle his unruly temper. It often ran away with him, and on such occasions he would let fly with a power of profanity that was positively awesome. One upcountry lawyer said Gaynor could "scorch the hide off a catamount forty feet away." His keen mind rebelled against stupidity, and he had no use whatever for small talk and gossip. In personal contacts he was brusque and often rude, although in the company of those whom he admitted to his intellectual level he could be genial and a fascinating talker. With plain people he was always breezily at ease, and would discuss such subjects as farming and politics with the least educated with complete compatibility.

When engaged in a task requiring concentration he would brook no interruptions, and his reaction often was bizarre. One day a clerk told him that a man of considerable influence was on the telephone wishing to speak with him. "Tell him to go to hell," snapped Gaynor. The caller persisted, and three times Gaynor repeated, more angrily each time, "Tell him to go to hell!" At last the clerk did as he was told, said into the receiver, "Mr. Gaynor says to go to hell," and hung up.

Such eccentricity did not necessarily work to Gaynor's disadvantage; on the contrary, it gave him a reputation for being incorruptibly independent and actually brought him some accounts. And he did not recoil from official plain speaking, either, when he deemed that necessary. As a referee in a divorce action in 1881 he said bluntly:

"I repeat that the allegations of the complaint are not proven, and that the plaintiff is not entitled to a divorce. . . . Nor is it proven that the summons and complaint were served upon the defendant. I am plainly of the opinion that the two witnesses produced by the plaintiff are hired perjurers. I can not believe a word they testify to. . . . I speak thus plainly because I feel it my duty to use words which express my opinion exactly."

In the course of his practice he met and measured up to some of the best legal talent of the generation. Appearing for the plaintiff in a petty case of assault arising out of the ejection of a floorwalker from a competitor's store, Gaynor won the verdict, although counsel for the defendant was Elihu Root. In his first murder case, in 1885, Gaynor was associated in the defense with General Benjamin F. Tracy, a foremost Brooklyn attorney, noted prosecutor, and future Secretary of the Navy. The plea was self-defense and public interest was high. When an acquittal was brought in, the crowd in the courtroom sang, danced, and cheered both defense counsel, but it was Gaynor who was chaired on the shoulders of jubilant admirers and carried in triumph through the building.

During this period there were setbacks, and at one point his career almost came to shipwreck.

Reports of frauds in the transactions of the Gravesend board of land commissioners had grown so noisome that a legislative committee was sent to investigate. Since Gaynor, as attorney for the board, was in charge of title closings, he knew all about the commissioners' dealings, and he had never criticized them. But he became involved when the investigators attempted to trace a check for $3,500 that had passed through his hands and his bank account.

A witness had testified that he had given the check to Gaynor in the latter's office, and in return had received a deed to a plot of ground in Coney Island. The deed stated that the consideration was $2,500, and the investigators wanted to know what had happened to the extra $1,000. Who had pocketed it? Gaynor was called. Upset that his integrity should be questioned, he told all the circumstances of the transaction without hesitation.

"I have nothing to conceal," he said. "I have been here twelve years at this bar and it is painful to me even to come here and explain this matter, because I have never been asked to explain anything I did before. I will tell you all that I had to do with it so as to get to the end of it."

A client of his had made a bid of $2,500 on a Coney Island lot, the minimum price set by the land commissioners. Another man wanted the property, and told Gaynor that he would be willing to pay $3,500 for it. Gaynor referred the offer to his client, who decided to take the $1,000 profit and transfer his bid. The deal was worked out in Gaynor's office, and a check for $3,500, payable to the first bidder, was forwarded by Gaynor to him. But this man did not deposit it. Instead, he handed the check back to Gaynor in payment of legal services which Gaynor had rendered previously. Gaynor deposited the check to his personal account, and "the money was spent by me and never went one inch beyond; that is all there is to it."

His frankness saved him. But other evidence implicated McKane and the land board so deeply that the Democratic organization of Kings County deemed it advisable to read McKane out of the party temporarily.

The autocratic boss took umbrage at this and by way of revenge threw the entire Gravesend vote to Benjamin Harrison in the 1888 Presidential race, thereby shutting Grover Cleveland out of the White House for four years; Cleveland lost New York state by a thousand votes and by that lost the election. McKane marched his machine voters, garbed in gray frock coats and gray toppers, to Washington and took part in Harrison's inaugural parade. And soon after this he was back in the Democratic fold, and Gaynor had ceased to function as attorney for the trustees of Gravesend's common lands.

By the mid-Eighties, the firm of Gaynor, Grout & De Fere was representing some of the most influential interests in Brooklyn. Gaynor himself was consultant to Abraham Abraham and aided him in setting up (with Nathan and Isidor Straus) the great retail house of Abraham & Straus. A warm personal friendship developed between Gaynor and Abraham.

At this period, too, Gaynor acquired his most valuable single client, William Ziegler. This onetime pharmacist's helper had built up the Royal Baking Powder Company into an enormously profitable enterprise, but he was at odds with his associates over control of the business. Gaynor took charge of the litigation, which pivoted on the rights of minority stockholders and attracted wide attention in legal circles, and after a hard fight won for Ziegler. That restless tycoon thereupon sold his interest in the company, bought two minor firms, merged them with still others, and in a short while was able to gobble up the Royal company and create the so-called baking-powder trust, a multimillion-dollar industry. Ziegler and Gaynor hit it off perfectly in temperament and basic views, and it was through Ziegler that Gaynor's interest in politics was aroused.

Up to this time he had shared the prevalent notion that politics was a "dirty game," not fit for gentlemen. He had not shirked civic responsibilities, and had occasionally put into practice the theory that had motivated him in the Tilton affair, namely, the moral obligation of involvement by the citizen in maintaining public decency and order. In national politics he was a Democrat like the mentors of his youth, the Seymours, Hunt, and Kernan, and in the 1880 Presidential campaign he spoke in Flatbush Town Hall on behalf of Winfield Scott Hancock, the Democratic nominee against James A. Garfield. In 1882 he campaigned for Grover Cleveland for governor of New York state and had the satisfaction of seeing him elected. And from time to time he had taken part in the parochial politics of Flatbush, in the town-meeting tradition. But he had joined no political group and declined to submit to the governance of any political organization, large or small. In that area, as in all others, he insisted on exercising his own judgment, and he desired that others should do the same, especially in local elections.

At least once he had intervened aggressively in Flatbush affairs. That occurred soon after he moved there. Municipal government generally was at the low-water mark of morality and efficiency during those years. It was the heyday of the political boss, and nearly every city had its corrupt machine and the attendant hordes of parasites and privilege seekers. New York City was still reeling from the Tweed ring disclosures, and Brooklyn had a boss who, although a model of domesticity and a pillar of sobriety, was just as plunder-minded. His name was Hugh McLaughlin, and he ran the town from the back room of Kerrigan's Auction Rooms on Willoughby Street. In McLaughlin's shade flourished petty bosses, two of whom had long controlled Flatbush. Their dishonesty and incompetence were blatant, and one day Gaynor remarked that the conditions were a disgrace and a reproach to every person in Flatbush. He was met with smiles and shrugs of helplessness.

A few days later every voter in Flatbush received a circular, printed and distributed by Gaynor, inviting them to a meeting in the town hall to nominate a "clean government" slate of candidates for the town offices. The turnout packed the hall. Both bosses were on hand, unperturbed; they had taken measures clandestinely and the chairman of the meeting was in their pocket.

A motion was presented naming a slate hand-picked by the bosses. Gaynor handed up a resolution substituting different names from top to bottom. The chairman refused to put this resolution to a vote; whereupon Gaynor, stepping up on his chair in order to be both seen and heard the better, told the chairman that if he did not put the resolution to a vote, it would not be difficult to pitch him out the window and put somebody else in his place.

This brought a cheer, and the chairman wilted, presented the substitute resolution, and it was carried overwhelmingly. Although the two bosses a few days later nominated their rival slate, they were beaten in the election by three to one.

In another instance, a man who would become a close associate of Gaynor, William A. Prendergast, was witness to Gaynor's grim tenacity at a meeting in Brooklyn in 1886 to choose a candidate for judge. When Gaynor tried to speak against the machine's selection, he was hissed, booed, and catcalled. But he stood his ground, until at length a disgusted voice was heard, "Oh, let the counselor speak!" and he was allowed to proceed.

But these spasmodic brushes with the political establishment were different from an active participation in the political turmoil. They led nowhere, yet Gaynor relished them. Long afterward he would recall with obvious satisfaction:

"Flatbush is where I started and did some of my best work in the way of reforming and lifting up the government."

By discharging his civic duties Gaynor was merely trying to emulate his admired Stoics; one of their rules had been never to flinch from performing a necessary action publicly, simply because the public might misconstrue it. Did not Epictetus instruct in his *Discourses*:

"When you do a thing because you have determined that it

ought to be done, never avoid being seen doing it, even though the world should misunderstand it. For if your action is wrong, then avoid doing it altogether; but if it is right, why fear those who censure you unjustly?"

Both the principle and the logic of this precept commended it to Gaynor's principled and logical nature. The arrest of Theodore Tilton had been an inept and exaggerated application of the principle, while the logic had forced Gaynor to stick to his position, even when the public misunderstood and condemned him.

Gaynor would constantly strive to attain to the condition of the self-fulfilled philosopher, and all his life would keep assuring himself that he was succeeding, when he was not. He said and perhaps believed that he never acted on impulse, but only after long reflection and deliberation. But the fact was that his very deliberation at times was impulsive, or gave rise to pure impulsiveness. When called upon to make a decision, he would review all the alternatives coolly and deliberately—and then embrace with passionate impetuosity the one he chose. His was that rare combination of qualities—vigorous powers of cerebration and red-hot impulses, sometimes side by side and sometimes interfering with each other. The result inevitably was repeated frustration and apparent inconsistency—a nature storm-driven and a prey to cross-purposes.*

Gaynor's participation in political matters came at a moment when a strong reaction against degenerate municipal government was gathering headway on numerous fronts. A few pioneers had started the movement—men like Grover Cleveland when mayor of Buffalo, and Abram S. Hewitt, elected mayor of New York in 1886, and Seth Low, a product of Brooklyn Heights, high-minded, high-toned, rich, and able, who was elected mayor of his own city for two terms in 1881 and 1883. These men had introduced reforms which a succeeding generation of city executives, of whom "Golden Rule" Jones and Brand Whitlock in Toledo and Tom L. Johnson in Cleveland were notable examples, would carry to fruition.

Oddly, such men, with their ideals of simple honesty and intelligence in the public service, found an ardent sympathizer in the self-aggrandizer Ziegler.

Lincoln Steffens called William Ziegler a rare businessman

---

* A close associate would say years afterward: "Gaynor never acts except on reflection—but sometimes he reflects like lightning."

because he had imagination outside his specialty of money-getting. Ziegler would, of course, live to finance Arctic explorations, and also to be indicted for bribing the Missouri legislature; but he would survive to comprehend the enormity of his methods and the threat they carried to free institutions.

Ziegler lived in Brooklyn, and in the Eighties and Nineties he took a keen interest in the subject of civic corruption. He hated to be cheated and bilked by the sticky-fingered politicians who ran the town under Boss McLaughlin, and as a taxpayer he took steps to stop them when he could. He had the means, and he engaged Gaynor as his counsel; in his own words, Gaynor provided the brains and he provided the money.

The first action came about as an afterthought. An attempt was being made to palm off on the city a virtually worthless water-supply company. The company—the Long Island Water Company—held a charter to supply water to the town of New Lots, one of the small communities just outside Brooklyn. The growing city was swallowing up these separate villages one by one, and it was desirable to provide a uniform water system throughout, so that even before New Lots was annexed it was evident that the city should either control or acquire outright the Long Island company. As early as 1886 a deal had been rigged to sell the company to Brooklyn for $2,500,000, but the scheme was premature and the purchase was not made.

Thereafter the stock of the company sank lower and lower until it was almost valueless. The holders of the stock included clients of Gaynor's, so he was acquainted with the situation.

About 1889 a promoter named Cyrus E. Staples, joining forces with a clique of Brooklyn politicians, quietly bought up this depreciated stock at bargain prices, and soon a rumor arose that the company was to be unloaded on the city for $400,000. Ziegler became interested, for he knew Staples' methods, and he asked Gaynor to investigate. The latter wrote to Brooklyn's mayor, Alfred E. Chapin, courteously requesting a clear statement of the facts.

Chapin was maladroit. Instead of returning a frank answer, he pettishly directed his secretary to send a curt acknowledgment of Gaynor's communication, but no information.

This caused Ziegler to smell a large-size mouse, and he instructed Gaynor to bring a taxpayer's suit to block the purchase.

During protracted hearings, Gaynor brought to light facts

that were more damaging than the rumors had been. A secret agreement already had been entered into with the city fathers to sell the water company to the city not for $400,000 but for $1,250,000; yet Gaynor produced figures to show that the installation could be duplicated for $195,000.

A howl of protest went up, and Ziegler and Gaynor became civic heroes. The syndicate's lawyers tried to ride out the storm by procrastinating; but in the end the court ruled that the city was powerless to buy the company on any terms, because it had not acted within the time limit set by statute after New Lots had been annexed.

This was a technical victory, but it had far-reaching consequences. It brought Gaynor before the public in a congenial role, and it turned his own thoughts into fresh channels.

During the long tussle he had displayed inventiveness, originality, and independence of a sort that delighted the press. He made "good copy." For instance, when asked to discuss the law in the case, he had declined, but offered to discuss with reporters the laws of the Medes and the Persians, or those of the Jewish Mishnah and the Pentateuch, subjects on which he was well informed. He declined to waste time on mere maneuvering, such as angling to get his case before a friendly judge. The day before the temporary injunction came up for argument, reporters asked him whether he had any preference as to which judge should conduct the hearing. A matter of indifference to him, Gaynor replied:

"I don't care what judge will be there. I have never made a choice of judges in my life. If I should go into court of a morning and find the Devil on the bench, I should get up and open my case."

But this first successful public-spirited litigation gave a new trend to his thoughts and set in motion that process of cool deliberation succeeded by passionate action that characterized him. There reverted to his mind an incident of his early days in Flatbush, when, in the religious sense of the word, he had experienced a "call" to serve the unregarded people of the community—the hard-working, undistinguished, uninfluential, weak and voiceless "people," on whom the burdens of life weigh the heaviest and who reap the fewest of its rewards. In Gaynor the religious sense was never far from the surface, and though he was sensitive he was anything but visionary; nevertheless he was vouchsafed moments of striking clairvoyance. That distant "call" had been pushed aside, and it would be yet some while before he would tell of the experience at all. When he did, it was in a letter to his brother Tom.

Excerpt of a letter written by William J. Gaynor to Thomas L. Gaynor, at Springfield, Ohio:

"My attention one day was called to a long line of people extending from the City Hall a block away. I was then a reporter on the newspapers. I found it was the first day for the payment of their taxes. I walked along the line on the other side and looked at them. There they were, the men and women whom you and I knew as boys, and have known ever since: good, intelligent people, whose lives are a continuous struggle to bring up their children and make both ends meet from month to month. Their bony hands and bent bodies gave evidence of their life of toil, and most of their faces were anxious. As I looked at them my mind became filled with the awful baseness of men, who having got into office by the votes of these people turn around and betray and rob them of their hard-earned money paid in as taxes. I made a covenant then and there that from that time onward, however much or little I might advance in life, I should devote some time every year against low, base, and corrupt officials and government, and to lift government up."

HE LOVES ME, HE LOVES ME NOT

Between the yea and the nay of a woman, I would not undertake to thrust the point of a needle.

—DON QUIXOTE

Gaynor had paid his disrespects to peculating politicians even before Ziegler's and his own frontal assault on the water-supply swindle. Years before, in defending a contractor named McCann, accused of libel, he had spoken with bitter contempt of the plaintiff in the case, a supervisor of Kings county named O'Brien. The county poor farm, St. Johnsland, was administered by the supervisors, and whenever they felt in need of spending money there was always some improvement to be voted for St. Johnsland. McCann was put out when he failed to get the contract for a new wall at the farm, and he lashed at O'Brien with remarks that constrained that dignitary to sue for $50,000 damages to his fair name and reputation. Gaynor told the jury:

"Here is a statesman without any visible means of support— without a stake in the hedge—living so far as appears by his wits—a supervisor of Kings County. How he got into that office is not for me to say. Who is he? Has he given any account of himself which would entitle him to one cent of damages, let alone $50,000? . . . O'Brien is a public scandal and a public disgrace."

The jury agreed.

Gaynor was never a man of one idea or one pursuit at a time. While he was conducting an extensive legal practice he kept up his scholarly researches, and in 1887 he contributed to the *Albany Law*

Journal a paper on "The Arrest and Trial of Jesus" which would continue to attract interest for years; he would use it as a lecture topic, and a publisher brought it out in pamphlet form. The article, displaying much curious learning, was a review of the legal aspects of Jesus' arrest, his trial before the Sanhedrin, his condemnation, and his later hearing before Pontius Pilate. Such an analysis demanded a thorough acquaintance with both Hebraic law and Roman law and procedure. His conclusions, some of them original and all ably argued, were that the arrest was unlawful; that the charge constituted a crime under the law and was in form; that the court, although lawfully constituted and possessing jurisdiction, was unlawfully assembled; that the judgment, although supported by evidence "the sufficiency of which the court had a right to pass upon," was rendered in violation of established procedure; and that Jesus' judges were so prejudiced against him as to be "unfit to try him." Pilate's conduct was rated "contemptibly weak and vacillating."

Such avocations, however, did not deflect Gaynor from diligently strengthening his financial position. His income was large, and he invested his earnings shrewdly, preferably in guaranteed first mortgages. In furtherance of his public duties, in 1890 he traveled to Albany with a delegation to oppose the annexation of Flatbush by Brooklyn, without success, and in 1892 he sat as a delegate in the Democratic National Convention at Chicago and thrilled to Bourke Cockran's great speechmaking feat at two o'clock in the morning, made in a vain, last-ditch attempt to head off Grover Cleveland's nomination for the Presidency. That speech Gaynor called the most astonishing exhibition of sheer rhetoric in his lifetime; yet he would point out that he could remember not a single thing that the speaker said except one sentence, and that one false, namely, that Grover Cleveland was popular every day in the year except on election day. Gaynor would use this speech as an illustration of the difference between mere rhetoric and true oratory.

In 1890 the Republicans toyed with the notion of nominating Ziegler to run for mayor of Brooklyn, but he sidestepped and suggested Gaynor; there was a man, he said, who not only possessed the keenest insight into political affairs, but would never be subservient to any political boss or machine.

The bosses agreed with this last, and though Gaynor intimated that he might run if Chapin were the Democratic candidate, both parties were unresponsive. McLaughlin decided to replace Chapin with David A. Boody on the Democratic side, and having named Boody he elected him.

Ziegler and Gaynor thereupon became the gadflies of the new administration, and in 1892 they scored resoundingly twice.

The elevated railroads of Brooklyn, contending that their street-rights franchises had been grossly overvalued for tax purposes, had withheld payment of their franchise taxes until they were $1,300,000 in arrears. The dispute at last went to a referee by mutual consent. Now Gaynor had been promised, he said, an opportunity to intervene and show the real value of the franchises, and he was therefore outraged when, after hearing almost no testimony, the referee rendered judgment of $283,321. Charging collusion, he said the figure had been agreed upon privately in advance. Mayor Boody retorted that before assigning the case to the referee he had called in Gaynor to get the "benefit of his advice and experience," and that Gaynor himself had suggested that precise figure.

In wrathful rebuttal Gaynor released a series of facts and figures which indicated that the city had been cheated. Although in the end the settlement stood, Gaynor's reputation was enhanced by the public's belief that but for him there would have been no settlement at all.

His next tilt at impudent government extravagance was directly productive. In order to celebrate fittingly the four-hundredth anniversary of Columbus' landing in the New World, the city fathers voted $50,000 for such outlays as $6,000 for a reviewing stand that might have been built for $1,700; $2,050 to decorate the courthouse, when a few hundred dollars would have been ample; and thousands of dollars for "sundries" (liquor and cigars) and "special sundries" (crates of champagne). Feasts and fiestas proliferated, and even the superintendent of schools, a man of exemplary probity under ordinary circumstances, felt obliged to help himself to several thousand dollars to assist the children in commemorating Columbus' historic landfall. All bills submitted were approved by the city comptroller without question, and paid by the city auditor with the same complaisance.

Again Ziegler and Gaynor rode to the rescue of the abused taxpayers. They sued to recover the moneys paid out, on the ground that the expenditures had never been authorized by the common council, and that the council had no power in the first place to authorize such appropriations of public money. In the upshot, some thirty officeholders and city employees were indicted, and the City Hall crowd rushed to Albany in desperation, appealing to the legislature to pass a bill legalizing the whole business. This the legislature did; but when the bill was sent to Governor Roswell P. Flower for signature, Gaynor submitted a long memorandum denouncing the measure as "a license to commit larceny from the public treasury," and then, catching a train to Albany, was in consultation with the governor for two hours. Roswell vetoed the bill and Gaynor's popularity rose.

By now he was spending some of his own money to ferret out rascals, and of course he was being tagged as the best man to become Brooklyn's mayor. Understandably, the leaders of both parties fought shy of a man who spoke so harshly of machine politicians, but among independent voters the boom gained momentum. Gaynor himself began to give intimations of the trend of his own wishes and his thoughts about what could be achieved by a really vigorous and reliable mayor.

There was the speech he gave in Greenpoint, an industrial suburb of Brooklyn lying along the banks of Newtown Creek, that noisome drainage ditch which separates Kings from Queens counties. A Democratic rally to ratify the nomination of Cleveland and Adlai Stevenson for President and Vice-President was being held in the Academy of Music in Brooklyn that evening, but Gaynor was not there; he was talking about a municipal problem. Referring to the stench arising from Newtown Creek, he told his audience that the nuisance could be abated, and that he in fact had been offered a retainer to undertake the task; he had declined, he said, because he was earning enough money in Brooklyn so that he was able to refuse any retainer offered. But "with seven men I can close down the Newtown Creek factories within a week so that they will never open again," he assured the Greenpointers. And so could their elected officials, he advised, if they would choose men of action.

"You want a mayor who will look at, and if necessary smell, everything," he said. "Then let him call his officers about him and see that they execute the law."

His philosophy of executive responsibility already had taken form.

A month after this speech Gaynor appeared on behalf of the Democratic national ticket before independent voters and delivered a speech that was out of the ordinary but thoroughly effective. His opening allusions to *Gil Blas* and the Bishop of Toledo were lost on the crowd, but they responded when he reverted to slangy English:

"We know no anti-snappers, mugwumps, Dolly Vardens, or people of the most variegated opinions in this campaign. We are all Democrats. . . . From the twilight of fable, from that borderline in the world of time when fable hardly yet ceases, and history scarcely begins, all down through the generations and centuries, from the human owl's perch of stupidity, has been hooted the same old hoot: 'To whit, to whoo, don't disturb the existing order of things.' The existing order of things may be a very poor order of things."

But in general Gaynor turned a deaf ear to all entreaties that he himself run for public office. With his independent wealth (he was now estimated to be worth three-quarters of a million dollars, and had an annual income of about one hundred thousand) there was no reason why he should not devote himself to public service and the excitements of politics attracted him. And he did begin to act like a man who eyes the scene of local action with more than meditative aloofness. In the spring of 1893 the agitation for nominating him as mayor increased, and in May of that year a resolution was laid before the Republican county committee proposing his selection as that party's candidate in the forthcoming election. The resolution recited glowingly Gaynor's public services, and a reporter for the *Brooklyn Eagle* hurried to get Gaynor's reaction.

It took the form of a firmly expressed wish to be left alone.

"I am not a candidate for mayor," he said with literal accuracy, inasmuch as he had not been nominated by anyone, "and moreover there is no political party in Brooklyn which has the slightest desire to make me mayor. I will be thankful if all political organizations will leave me alone. I should be happy to have their good will, but I ask nothing of them."

The knocks he had received in the course of rendering the public unsought services had left bruises that still smarted, and he indicated that recognition of the value of his work was coming a little late.

"This resolution," he said with feeling, "enumerates certain things which I have done. In the struggle and hard work of doing them, I felt lonesome enough more than once, and a very little encouragement from some organized body would have been more than welcome to me, I can tell you. I do not complain," he went on, assuming the toga of the Stoic, "but it is not improper for me to say that no organized body of men in Brooklyn ever sent me a word of encouragement."

This was perfectly true. Gaynor, an outsider bristling with nonconformity, was a standing threat to the established order, and the men of the political establishment were wary. They did not trust this advocate of civic righteousness who excelled in exposing civic chicaneries and who spoke so often and so tiresomely of his own achievements.

"If it be true," Gaynor went on in this candid and at the same time typically uncandid interview with the *Eagle* reporter, "that I have done something for good government in Brooklyn, I have done it with no object in view except to promote good government. This may seem incomprehensible to persons incapable of conceiving that anyone should do anything except for selfish motives, but I can not help that. I mingle so little with my fellow citizens that I do not know what they think of the little I have done. I only know that I have been actuated by a desire to bring about intelligent, honest, and prudent government in Brooklyn and Kings County and by no personal object whatever."

The Republicans tabled the nominating resolution, while Gaynor went on spreading the gospel of honest government. He spoke without distinction of parties, for, like Seth Low and other up-lifters of the time, he believed that one of the causes of municipal corruption had been the prostitution of the cities' vote to the rival parties' national interests. Municipal issues had nothing to do with national issues, he preached; the two should be kept entirely separate.

Before the Young Men's Democratic Club of Brooklyn, at their annual Jefferson Day dinner, Gaynor again stressed that his motive in attacking civic wrongs was not selfish but moral, saying:

"If it is necessary for a man in Brooklyn to sit down in what seems to be deemed respectable silence, while his friends and neigh-bors, the people of Brooklyn, are being openly robbed, in order to save himself from the imputation of acting from personal motives, then I beg for one to say that I will not bow to that necessity. . . .

"The treasury of Brooklyn is made up in by far its greater part of taxes paid out of the hard earnings of hard-working, industrious people, whose lives are a constant struggle to bring up their children and make both ends meet. The larceny or waste of their money by public officials, acting as the mere tools of others, is a heartless crime. It is not a wrong against one, but against all."

Referring to the Columbus celebration frauds, he said:

"When a messenger brought these bills into the mayor's office for approval and payment, the best thing the mayor could have done was to throw them out the window. These bills were not itemized because they could not be itemized. . . . The mayor and all the officials in Brooklyn combined had not the power to incur a single one of these bills, and they know it."

Lest Mayor Boody plead lack of authority, Gaynor quoted the charter under which Brooklyn functioned, and which gave the mayor power to appoint all department heads except two, with the right to supervise them in office and dismiss them at will.

"The mayor is the absolute ruler of the city," he summed up, "and the people can hold him responsible."

A few days after this speech, he read a lesson in the basics of representative government to the Long Island Republican Club. His theme was the parlous financial position of Brooklyn after years of corruption and misrule.

"The greatest evil," he told this group, "is that most people think themselves incapable of understanding questions of government and law. There is nothing in our government which you can not understand as well as the statesmen at City Hall.

"For instance, there is a clause in the state constitution which says that no city shall contract a debt greater than ten percent of its assessment rolls. . . . The assessment rolls of Brooklyn show a valuation of \$477,000,000, which means we can contract a debt of \$47,000,000. We are now very close to that limit. The great bulk of taxation comes out of the middle class and not out of the rich. The waste of our high taxes, let alone the theft of them by public officials, is a crime. Being at the limit of taxation, we need prudent government. You people can get it if you want it. . . . Public opinion can do everything. The people, by an intelligent understanding and discussion of the situation, can make their government anything that they want to make it."

It was by addressing juries in this tone, in simple language, with inescapable logic, that Gaynor won lawsuits.

The response to this educational work Gaynor at times found disheartening. He told a Board of Trade dinner at Delmonico's in Manhattan that "in New York *men* are concerned in politics; in Brooklyn, only fools." New York was run from Tammany Hall, whereas Brooklyn was run from "a junk shop"—a reference to Boss McLaughlin's hangout in Kerrigan's Auction Rooms.

To the *New York World*, which was becoming curious about him, Gaynor expressed himself less pungently:

"What little I have done for good government in Brooklyn I have done openly. I have proceeded steadily, abusing no one. Though I have succeeded every time, I appreciate that I am only one feeble individual, but at the same time I realize the power and goodness of Almighty God."

Such oracular piety caused the *World* to wonder, and it kept an interested eye on Gaynor.

One tribute that touched Gaynor deeply was a banquet given in his honor by the Knights of Labor at the Hotel St. George. Terence V. Powderly, head of the Knights and a powerful figure in labor and political circles then, came from Philadelphia for the dinner, and engraved resolutions praising Gaynor's contributions to the public welfare were presented. In accepting them he could not hide his emotion.

"I hesitated about accepting your invitation," he told the diners, "only because I feared it possible that your motives and mine might be not only misunderstood, but misrepresented to your injury. Yours was the very first recognition I had ever received from any body of men. For myself I do not care so much, although I am not as unfeeling as some seem to think. If I were, I should have been spared a good deal of pain during the last two or three years. . . .

"These resolutions I shall treasure as priceless to my last hour. I shall hand them down to my children with the admonition never to forget that they came to me at a time when I felt painfully that I stood almost alone, and made me realize anew what all history attests—that all that is noblest and purest and deepest in human aspirations throbs first out of the great heart of the plain people of the world. . . .

"My friends, I know you and you know me. When Cervantes, at the age of seventy, came to write the preface of his great book, one of the five or six greatest emanations of the human mind, he set it down as his most glorious reminiscence that he had served as a private and lost a hand in the great sea fight at Lepanto which decided that Europe was to remain Christian and not become Turk. Happy is any man, as life draws to a period and becomes reminiscent, if he be able to recall that, though he held no public place, he yet did his part as a private citizen for good government and the benefit of all."

Eloquence and feeling apart, Gaynor did not cease to tilt against iniquities in government, and now he took on one of the most prolific sources of public corruption, the traffic in franchises to operate streetcar lines. With the expansion of cities, the need for inexpensive, convenient public transportation had become imperative, and daring promoters had turned their attention to this source of immense wealth for themselves. Huge fortunes, some of the largest in the nation, were being erected on the manipulation of franchise rights in collusion with corruptible politicians. Notable were the great fortunes built up in New York City by Thomas Fortune Ryan and William C. Whitney. To attack this hydra of exploitation even in one small branch was considered foolhardy and certainly futile. But Gaynor moved in without misgivings, in the case of two street railroads with deceptively similar names. This was a device resorted to frequently to confuse stockholders and the public. The two companies were the Union Rail Road Company and the Union Street Railway Company. The former, whose stock had been spread judiciously among key officeholders, wished to take over the latter's franchise, and offered to pay the city $30,000 for it, plus compensation to the property owners affected.

The Board of Aldermen, however, decided that they had no right to sell the franchise, but they could give it away, and this they did. Mayor Boody vetoed the gift, but the aldermen voted it again, over his veto. Then Gaynor brought a taxpayer's suit to void the transaction. The court ruled that the aldermen did not have power to give away city property (and the use of the public streets was that); whereupon the aldermen turned around and sold the franchise to the petitioning company at a ridiculously low figure, without a public hearing. Gaynor challenged this disguised giveaway, but the grand jury reported regretfully that it could find no legal basis for indicting the aldermen. The courts upheld the fraudulent sale, but though Gaynor's suit failed technically, it opened the public's eyes to the goings-on at City Hall in a dramatic way.

The demands that Gaynor run for mayor of the city stepped up in intensity and persistence; Gaynor was easily the most popular man on his side of the East River. Edward M. Shepard, a civic-minded Brooklyn attorney of Gaynor's age and leader of a faction of antimachine Democrats, drew attention to the crusading lawyer's attacks on municipal abuses as "a curious development—popular government by lawsuit," and on May 15, 1893, the agitation came to a head at a gathering of independents in Acme Hall. Gaynor was cheered when he appeared and spoke briefly, committing himself to nothing, merely reminding his listeners that "government can rise no higher than the people who create and support it." As for himself:

"In a busy life I have not been unwilling to do a citizen's part; and that is as much as I am willing to admit may be truthfully said of my conduct. Eternal vigilance is the price of honesty as well as liberty. I have been actuated by no motive except to bring about honest, prudent, and intelligent government in Brooklyn."

Two months after this, with the issue still unresolved, Gaynor prepared to leave on a vacation trip to Europe. Two opposite impulses warred in him: on the one hand, his inclination toward a studious life; on the other, an itch, a craving, for activity, coupled with a genuine desire to carry out certain reforms in the city government which would make Brooklyn a model for municipalities all over the nation. He had a real fondness for the city, and to serve it worthily would give him much satisfaction. And since the wind was setting in that direction, was it right to whistle against it? During the course of that preliminary reflection which had become habitual with him before embarking on a definite program, he went over the assets and the drawbacks of his position and his wishes. He had evolved a concrete philosophy of public responsibility and public behavior, and one tenet of that code was that the office should seek the man, not the man thrust himself forward in pursuit of a place of honor and emolument. His pride revolted at seeming to put himself on a level with the self-serving politicians he so scorned. And despite his readiness to rough-handle an opponent in a lawsuit, Gaynor was sensitive to criticism; there was something feminine in his need for sympathy and concurment. Besides, he would hate to lose; so he would enter no contest unless the auspices were right, and mere independent support was a weak prop to rely on for winning an election.

Reluctant yet responsive, too proud to ask and yet not quite refusing, in July Gaynor sailed for Europe on his annual vacation trip. As the liner *Paris* steamed down New York Bay he wrote a letter to his best friend and collaborator, William Ziegler, in which, in terms of firm decision, he revealed his indecision. This letter, penned in a bold, rapid hand, read:

"You have always understood me, though doubtless many have not. I aspire to no place. I have had and have no motive but to bring about intelligence, honesty, manliness, and fidelity to the people in the politics and government of Brooklyn. I could not be silent in the face of gross wrongs to the rent payers and taxpayers of Brooklyn with whom my lot is cast. That is all. If this is to hurt me in the end, I am content. I leave you to speak for me now. You may show this letter to all who may inquire, so that it may be absolutely and finally known that I did not and do not want anything. There are pitiful little souls who cannot understand this, but I can not help it. If my future has been hurt by the course which I took, again I am content. I shall, at all events, have ever abiding with me the sense of right. When I started out in life in Brooklyn I had a reverent faith in Almighty God and was content to leave myself in His hands. I have not lost that faith yet, and trust that I never shall. And now, friend of friends, good-by. Your loyalty to me I can never forget. Nor can I ever forget that from the very start I was understood by the industrious people of Brooklyn."

Among Gaynor's feminine traits, one was a teasing tendency, when pressed too hard, to retreat into mystery.

During his vacation abroad Gaynor toured Wales, and hearing Welsh spoken carried him back to his boyhood in Oneida County. And he was charmed to find that he could still "make a pretty good fist at the language," he told friends on his return in September, flashing one of his rare, sly twinkles.

In Brooklyn the political pot was bubbling. The time for nominating candidates was near, and reform was the watchword. This reflected a predictable trend. In flush times, buffoons in office may be tolerated and even enjoyed, but when business stagnates and hard times pinch, the impulse is to "turn the rascals out." (In the giddy 1920s James J. Walker was an entertaining mayor of New York, but after the crash of '29 his performance became a disaster.)

Brooklyn offered a handy target for crusaders against corruption and waste, and the *New York Herald*, which catered to a large circulation in Kings county, launched a well-documented attack on the deplorable conditions prevailing there. Brooklyn was the "worst governed city in the United States," said the *Herald*, its people "restless under years of fraud, peculation, and legislation for private gain." These were evils which Gaynor, in his own right as well as when acting for Ziegler, had been combatting with singular success. But his victories had not altered the basic situation; only control of the city government could do that. He read with interest the *Herald*'s portrayal of Brooklyn's low estate:

"The stranger who sees Brooklyn for the first time would never think that he was in a municipality which in point of wealth and population is the fourth on the continent.* The streets, wretchedly paved, uncared for, full of dreadful odors, and deep with mud and accumulated nastiness, are the streets of an exaggerated prairie village. The public buildings are small and poor; the sidewalks in ill repair. Pandemonium reigns all day in the principal thorough-fares, where under a dismal elevated structure a procession of jolting trolley cars rushes to and fro, sounding deafening gongs. The few policemen look spiritless and ineffectual from very loneliness. . . . The credit of the city is at the lowest ebb in its history. Its treasury is empty. Public improvements demanded for many years halt while favored persons associated with or friendly to public officials divert public funds for their own profit."

Gaynor was not alone in detecting inadequacies in the rule of Boss McLaughlin and his staff of adjutants.

For twenty years, caustically continued the *Herald*, the people of Brooklyn had apathetically accepted McLaughlin and his coterie of five or six cronies. The only break had been the two short terms of Seth Low as governor, and much of the good which he accomplished had been swallowed up in the misrule of later administrations. Said the *Herald:*

"The whole government rests with six men, who hold no office, and have no responsibility except to themselves and their pocket-books. The public payrolls are padded and contractors grow fat. McLaughlin names the mayor and all other officials, and controls all nominations made by the Democrats."

The background of the men who ran Brooklyn was traced in pitiless detail. Uneducated, and in some cases stupid as well as ignorant, they had acquired fortunes by means that did not appear on the surface. All, or nearly all, had started in the lowest ranks of labor, got into politics, and thereafter "did nothing and amassed fortunes." McLaughlin, once a carpenter at $2.50 a day, was reputed to be worth $1,500,000.

Citing the recent indictment of thirty city and county officials for malversation of public funds and other crimes, and pointing out that Mayor Boody himself had escaped indictment "only by inter-position of questionable advice from the district attorney that the offense with which he was charged is not indictable," the *Herald* concluded that "the story of events . . . is probably the most remark-able chapter in municipal history since Tweed rule in New York."

* Its population was close to a million.

This laying it on the line of what Gaynor had been saying—and not he alone—added impetus to the movement among Republicans to select Gaynor for their mayoral candidate. Independent voters of all shades of opinion were overwhelmingly for him. When the *Herald* reporter interviewed Gaynor on the prospect, he found him dignified, austere, and epigrammatic.

"I do not enter into any perfunctory compliment to the *Herald* when I applaud it for putting into consecutive form the most glaring abuses of Brooklyn during the past few years," he began.

"Are you a candidate for the mayoralty nomination?" asked the reporter.

"I am not," came the answer, "and I should be glad to have the *Herald* make that clear. There seem to be some people in the city who do not know it yet, though I have often said it."

Would he favor a coalition or fusion ticket to run against the Democrats?

He had never been a partisan advocate in municipal elections, Gaynor replied. "I should like to see politics so elevated in Brooklyn that the motto at City Hall would be, not party and individual gain first and the people second, but the people first, party second if at all, and individual gain not at all."

This was sententious, but hardly an answer. The fact was that with the outlook so propitious for breaking the Democrats' grip on the city, Gaynor was beginning to hanker for the Republican nomination. He would not admit this even to himself; his pride forbade. He knew that the McLaughlin machine would not nominate him, and independent support was inadequate; he had no intention of sacrificing himself to the starry ideals of men who had no organization but hoped for a political miracle. But the Republican leadership was reluctant to head their ticket with a known Democrat, and Gaynor would not repudiate his nominal affiliation, although he belonged to no Democratic group. During heated debates, Gaynor's temper and temperament were raised against him by the wary leadership, and in the end he was bypassed and the mayoral nomination went to a businessman, Charles A. Schieren, who was popular with the German element and the brewing interests. But in a move to draw the independent, reform vote, the Republicans named Gaynor for justice of the state Supreme Court. Even here, so suspicious were the "regulars" of his motives and real intentions, he would not have won the nomination except for the determined fighting of a lawyer who was so little in Gaynor's favor that the latter had not spoken to him for years; not since the man, acting as opposing counsel in a lawsuit, had filed a brief with the court taking exception to Gaynor's "spectacular and unbridled" language.

Gaynor's first impulse was to reject the judicial nomination.

"I can not help feeling moved that such a nomination should come to me," he told reporters, "but I can not accept it. I can not. I can not. If I were to accept, every little fellow in Brooklyn would say I sought it, and their number seems to be disproportionately large to our population. I could not bear to have it thought by anyone that I had been looking for a nomination. That is sufficient reason for declining it."

Friends begged him to reverse his decision. Delegations representing all sorts of splinter groups crowded his Montague Street office, urging him to run for mayor independently. Under the aegis of the well-financed Citizens Union these elements staged a demonstration at the Academy of Music and by acclamation nominated Gaynor themselves for the mayoralty. A committee was named to notify him of the meeting's action.

When the committee called the next day, they were welcomed courteously, but Gaynor was not to be decoyed. It was still a case of no political organization wishing him to run for mayor, he said, and he could not afford to campaign on his own. He felt that he could not be elected without the backing of at least one of the regular parties.

The pressure on him to accept the judgeship candidacy was kept up, and he weighed the alternatives for several days. Then he sat down and composed a letter definitely declining. His friend Abraham Abraham chanced to come in while Gaynor was penning this announcement. In tears, Abraham begged him not to send it. Finally Gaynor, himself moved, handed the letter to his friend and said, "You decide." Abraham did not send the letter, and the next day the *New York Herald*, which was exploiting its "clean up Brooklyn" crusade to the limit, reported with satisfaction that "another thorn was thrust into the torn and bleeding side of the Democratic ring yesterday by the acceptance by lawyer William J. Gaynor of the Republican nomination for justice of the Supreme Court."

Gaynor in his acceptance made clear that he was "yielding to the urgent advice of my distinguished personal friends," and that the nomination had come to him "unsought and unexpected. I had no intention of accepting it, but now that I have done so my mind is easy. It is the right thing to do, and therefore the wisest and the best. The final result will be an encouragement, or a warning, to others who feel it a duty not to acquiesce in public wrongs."

OF SODOM-BY-THE-SEA

*Now the men of Sodom were wicked and
sinners before the Lord exceedingly.*

—GENESIS *13:13*

GAYNOR'S ENTRANCE into the contest brought no satisfaction to
the opposition. McLaughlin and his crowd had taken the only course
open to them and renominated Boody for a second term; to have
repudiated him in the face of the mounting accusations would have
been a virtual confession of guilt. But an attorney close to the
Democratic machine opened a bitter attack on Gaynor in the press,
charging that he was simply a "hired lawyer" who had climbed to
prominence on Ziegler's back, and after having been paid handsomely for his self-vaunted services to the public, was bleating about
his unselfish motives. All this the critic found "a little tiresome. Mr.
Gaynor," said he, "is always solemn, occasionally statuesque, and at
intervals there is something theatrical about him. . . . By his own
estimate he is never anything but scrupulously unselfish and pro-
foundly disinterested." Yet the suspicion would not down that he
had his eyes "less on Brooklyn's welfare than on Ziegler's pocket-
book."

Gaynor's habit of presenting himself "in an attitude of self-
sacrifice" also irritated the *Brooklyn Eagle*, whose St. Clair McKelway had known Gaynor since the latter's arrival in the city.

"Mr. Gaynor is unquestionably a man of convictions," said the
Eagle. "That he is fully persuaded that he has done much for
Brooklyn he makes quite obvious whenever opportunity affords."

That many Brooklynites shared his notions on that subject the

Eagle would not deny, but another facet of Gaynor's temperament
caught the *Eagle*'s eye: Gaynor, it remarked, was "nothing if not
severe. His more recent utterances have been solemn, austere, caustic,
and uncompromising. When he is in a critical mood, which is frequently the case, he is always unsparing and more than apt to be
bitter." And because of this frankness, he should "hardly be surprised if his fusillades provoke return fire. It is rarely the case that
critics take kindly to criticism."

And this was so. Gaynor was irritated by the disparaging comments made in some quarters about his appropriation to himself of
the whole reform movement in Brooklyn. Other men had worked as
long or longer, and some of them with tangible results, to purge the
municipal shambles, and Gaynor, it was complained, had merely
joined the parade when it was already well under way. But there was
a difference between the other reformers and Gaynor. While he
would have welcomed assistance from the start, and did not receive
it, he worked best alone; he was not a teammate or collaborator; he
was too self-centered to work in harness with others bent on achiev-
ing the same goals. And because of his arresting personality, and
above all his gift of simple expression, using words in a way that any
man could understand, and that stuck and struck home, there was
no denying that to the average Brooklynite he had come to personify
the cause of honest government. Others spoke fluently, but their
words did not sting and ring like Gaynor's. And he had the rare
faculty, also, of being able to keep silence when there was nothing
he wished to say particularly. He was not long-winded and was
never a bore.

The campaign was given the customary grand send off at the
Academy of Music, under the auspices of the Committee of 100.*
This was a group of business and professional men determined to
overthrow ring rule. Gaynor was the principal speaker, and many
were turned away. He struck at "the one-man or five-man power of
Willoughby Street," and again called "the waste of public money by
public officials, acting as the tools of others, a heartless crime." He
also dwelt on another of his recurrent themes:

"The first thing we have to consider tonight is that as regards

---

* Politically minded New Yorkers of that time, especially the amateurs, seem to
have had a superstitious faith in the magic of numbers. There were Committees of
1,000, of 100, of 15, of 14, of 7, and of numbers in between, all *ad hoc* improvisations,
brought hopefully into existence to meet some temporary crisis or to achieve a special
goal.

city affairs, national questions are of no importance. We have come to discuss municipal issues, and municipal issues alone."

These ideas he hammered upon in subsequent speeches. Schieren proved dull on the platform, although he was effective in addressing German-speaking groups, and the main speechmaking fell to Gaynor and fellow campaigners like Shepard, another Democrat fighting Willoughby Street rule.

Gaynor's speeches flouted the conventions of stump oratory. There were no spread-eagle appeals to large if vague sentiments, and they abounded in so many Biblical quotations and invocations of the Almighty ("by the Eternal!") that his associates suggested he was overdoing it. (Lawyers who knew his volcanic profanity in private were amused.) And just as he quoted the Bible, he abounded in quotations from *Don Quixote*, Shakespeare, Benjamin Franklin, Frederick the Great, and other works and authors little perused by the average voter of Brooklyn. But he always had something to say, and said it tellingly.

When Mayor Boody challenged Schieren to debate, knowing the latter's weakness on the platform, Schieren wisely declined; but Gaynor took up the challenge and dared the mayor to meet him in debate.

"If he really wants to debate, let him meet me," was Gaynor's defiance. "I know about the Columbus celebration scandal and the franchise frauds, and those fire hydrants in cabbage lots and potato patches over in East New York, with the plot to rob the city of a million dollars. I know about them and can discuss them with the valorous Mr. Boody. I will meet him and I will pay for the hall."

When Boody also chose the better part of valor and sensibly declined, Gaynor gave him no higher marks for rectitude than he had given to former Mayor Chapin. Boody, he told audiences, had been elected on a reform ticket, but "he got your vote and he got mine under false pretenses. Instead of being an independent man, he put on the old clothes of Chapin, and they have grown older and dirtier from day to day." His own candidacy, he said, was fraught with possible unhappy consequences for himself, for if he were defeated he stood to lose much; "but I have not prostituted my manhood for the sake of the future." And he was determined not to be defeated. This brought on the real fireworks of the campaign.

These began when the election was less than two weeks away, and they centered on a man whom Gaynor knew well, and to whom

Gaynor was not an unknown factor—John Y. McKane, the swash-
buckler boss of the quiet town of Gravesend.

The settlement of Gravesend had been laid out south of Brooklyn in the seventeenth century by Lady Deborah Moody, a domineering, dissident exile from Puritan Massachusetts, on a novel plan. To
afford protection against maurauding Indians, the town hall and
other public structures were enclosed by a stockade, and each of the
original thirty-nine settlers was allotted an equal segment of the
enclosed space, with farm lands radiating outward all around, like
the slices of a neatly divided pie. Coney Island, a sandspit on the
ocean side, was reserved as common lands, although the town officials were not debarred from alienating it.

This historic pattern of land ownership was put to ingenious
use in the Nineties by Gravesend's overlord, short-legged, pudgy,
barrel-chested, belligerent McKane. With the intention of safe-
guarding the purity of the ballot, the legislature had passed a law
requiring each election district in the state to have at least one polling place within its own boundaries. Gravesend, with six districts,
had one polling place, serving all six, located in the town hall, where
McKane could keep an eye personally on the voting. Dutifully com-
plying with the new law, he redrew the boundaries of the districts so
that they converged at a point inside the town hall, thus enabling
him to oversee the balloting at all six boxes simultaneously.

McKane was full of resources. He had been brought to this
country by his parents from County Antrim, in Northern Ireland,
and had grown up in Gravesend. After a start as a Coney Island
clam digger, he had become a carpenter. There was a story that during the Civil War, when he spelled his name McCain, he had dodged
the draft by taking oath that he was a subject of the British crown,
and he never deigned to deny this, terming it "too malicious to
dignify by a denial." One way and another, from building bathhouses and hot-dog stands during Coney Island's boom in the Seventies, he had progressed to general contractor, until almost all the
building at the resort was in his hands.

What he hungered for, however, was not so much wealth as
adulation and power. Edging into politics, within a dozen years he
made himself undisputed master of his bailiwick—town supervisor,
land commissioner, chairman of the water, tax, and excise boards,
and chief of police. In this last role he enforced the law personally at
Coney Island. There McKane *was* the law. The thousands flocking
to what was becoming the world's gaudiest carnival were accustomed

to see him patrolling the beachfront, his diamond-studded badge glinting in the sunlight, and his luxuriant imperial and mustaches (modeled on those of the Emperor Napoleon III, McKane's contemporary), quivering in the breeze. His rotund, dumpy figure in no way detracted from the awe he inspired in card sharps, confidence men, pickpockets, and blasphemous drunks. Under McKane Coney Island was wide open in some respects; no Bible class, but decorous. The Bible business he kept for his private edification; he was a good Methodist and superintendent of his Sunday school. Married, he was the proud parent of two sons and three daughters, and did not drink, smoke, or engage in games of chance, although he was a darb at dominoes.

Those were his personal preferences in the way of conduct, but he saw no reason why the people who came to Coney Island to have fun should be denied their special tastes. For the family trade, which was large, there were merry-go-rounds, hot-corn pots boiling appetizingly, chowder palaces, popcorn stands, peepshows, taffy booths, photographers' tents, fortunetellers, weight guessers, and a variety of rides, slides, and dips, besides bathing and toasting in the sand. For those fuller-blooded, there were prize fights, horse racing, faro wheels, and general harlotry. All McKane required was that public decency be respected.

Free with his money in Gravesend, he was accepted there as the benevolent despot he was. With a certain charm of manner, all he demanded in return for his largesse was instant and absolute obedience, and he got it. True, he had some unamiable failings, such as his sadistic chastising of interlopers who tried to horn in and "give Coney a bad name," by beating them with a scourge of his own devising—a thin steel rod bound with cord, that in use whistled like a banshee and cut cleaner than a knout. Such was the man who, by shifting the votes of his domain from party to party as he pleased, could, according to his complacent boast, make and unmake Presidents of the United States. Nominally and most of the time, McKane was a Democrat, and a puissant ally of the McLaughlin machine.

Of course there had long been complaints about McKane's highhanded ways. In the Gravesend election returns, for instance, there were no runners-up; there was a winner, and that was all. The lax moral tone of Coney Island periodically stirred up less tolerant citizens, and the newspapers found that a congenial theme again and again. By 1893 McKane was under a sustained fire of criticism; but even though the *New York Times* editorially shuddered over the iniquities of "Sodom-by-the-sea," and spoke with loathing of "the fermenting plague spot in which the blowflies of Brooklyn breed," McKane retained his power and his aplomb. He took the criticism good-naturedly—indeed, he called newspapers and their reporters the best friends he had—and was perfectly content to let the press stimulate the lubricity of their readers; it was good for the papers, and good for Coney, too. But when Gaynor began to be seriously boomed for mayor of Brooklyn, McKane developed sufficient uneasiness to look to his defenses. For ten years Gaynor had been counsel to the Gravesend lands board, and he was aware of McKane's deviousness. Taking counsel of prudence, the latter angled to get Gaynor and himself on the same side, unknown to Gaynor.

During the summer of 1893 junketing Brooklyn politicians kept encountering each other at Chicago, where the World's Fair and Little Egypt were coeval enticements to look and loiter. One day, in the lobby of the Palmer House, McKane buttonholed John H. McCooey, Boss McLaughlin's lieutenant, and urged that the organization nominate Gaynor for either mayor or judge. He admitted self-interest, knowing that was the only motive McCooey would believe in.

"You know my close relations with Gaynor," he said, "and if he isn't nominated I'll be ruined."

Thus ironically McKane's voice was the only one raised among the regular Democrats in favor of Gaynor. But the party nominated Boody, and after thinking the situation over McKane decided to stick with the machine.

This decision he made known about two weeks before election day, and then the fireworks started. Speaking to a large crowd in Arion Hall, Gaynor adverted to the way in which, year after year, thousands of fraudulent votes were stuffed into the ballot boxes at Gravesend, often in batches of a hundred or two hundred at a time. Appealing to the "moral sense of Kings county," he asked whether his listeners were willing to stand by and see six thousand fraudulent votes cast in Gravesend. He was not.

"I demand fair play," he announced. "Six thousand men do not vote in Gravesend, but the names of waiters, gamblers, and thieves from all over the country are checked off. I say to these people that I defy them."

This brought into the open the stories that had been told and retold to explain why McKane wielded so large an influence in Kings county. It was by delivering a bloc vote far in excess of the likely or even possible voting population of Gravesend. This was done by registering the large summertime population of Coney Island as permanent residents, and casting votes in their names on election day.

How the system worked was told by a Coney Island bartender. One day a policeman showed up, he said, and herded the restaurant's entire staff into the kitchen—cooks, waiters, barkeeps, and cleaners-up, plus a couple of stableboys who happened to be in the place— took down their names and addresses, then told them they were registered to vote in Gravesend, and warned them to report on election day or they might find themselves unwanted in Coney Island the next summer. This warning was mutually understood to be window dressing; the waiters knew and McKane knew that the sudden appearance in Gravesend of thousands of floaters on election day would be embarrassing all around.

Gaynor did not intend to be cheated in this way. He determined to check the voter lists himself, and for this purpose sent clerks from his office to copy the registration books. Apprised in advance, McKane set his own men to copying, and Gaynor's clerks were not allowed to get near the records; when they tried to, McKane's men covered the pages with their arms.

Then McKane sent his secretary, John Wesley Murphy, a Methodist Irishman like himself, to find out why Gaynor wanted the lists. To verify the names and addresses as those of bona fide residents, said Gaynor. Back came a telegram from McKane saying that if Gaynor intended to get the lists by his own methods, he would have "a very hard time of it." He offered to send Gaynor a true copy, but the latter took no stock in that. Instead, he went before Supreme Court Justice A. M. Cullen and asked for a mandamus ordering the Gravesend voting registers to allow Gaynor to copy the rolls.

The hearing on the application drew much public attention. Seconding Gaynor were his partner, Grout, and United States Attorney Jesse Johnson. Counsel opposing the application nominally represented the Gravesend election officials, but actually spoke for McKane. Technicalities were invoked to drag out the proceedings, until Justice Cullen swept these aside and Gaynor was permitted to state his case. He produced the population and voting figures on Gravesend as palpable evidence of fraud.

The 1890 federal census had put Gravesend's population at 6,931. The state census taken two years later showed it to be 8,418.

But there were 6,218 names on the voting lists, although neither women nor minors could vote. The normal ratio of voters to population would be 1,628, Gaynor showed. The election was only five days away and speedy action was sought.

An affidavit by McKane was read, in which he protested that he had nothing to do with the registration lists, and denied that he had ever tried to prevent access to them. On the contrary, he swore, he had sent Murphy to assure Gaynor of his readiness to supply him with a true copy, only to have the offer spurned with "vile language and oaths." As for the population of Gravesend, it had swelled amazingly, he averred.

Gaynor's application was made on Thursday, November 2.

On Friday Justice Cullen declined to issue a mandamus, saying the voting inspectors had been notified that they must produce the lists, and he doubted that they would disobey the law. Interest in Gaynor's action meanwhile had spread beyond the county, and newspapers in other cities were taking note of it. In New York the *Herald* speculated that although McKane had met and defeated "all who have hitherto opposed his ways and means of government in his little state by the sea, he has never arrayed himself against a greater and brainier man, and by all odds a more clever man, than he has ever met before—lawyer Gaynor of Brooklyn."

On Friday, after Judge Cullen's denial of the application for a mandamus, Gaynor sent his men back to Gravesend. At the same time he sent letters of fair warning to persons illegally registered at Gravesend whom he knew about. These letters read:

"In fairness to you, I beg to inform you that your connection with the registration and voting in Gravesend is known to me, as well as the number of men which you handle. Being advised, you may take whatever course you see fit. W. J. GAYNOR."

In Gravesend, Gaynor's men met with hoots of derision. None of the election registers could be found. A warrant had been obtained for the arrest of one, but no deputy could be found to serve it.

On Saturday morning Gaynor appeared again before Justice Cullen and requested a writ of mandamus. McKane's attorney stalled and threw up roadblocks, but at five o'clock Cullen issued the writ, peremptorily ordering the Gravesend board of voter registration to make the list available at any time except on Sunday.

The election was to be held on the coming Tuesday. Gaynor assembled a force of twenty-one copyists and hurried them to Gravesend, armed with the writ, under instructions to work on the lists until midnight, then suspend, and resume copying at midnight Sunday.

What happened reverberated across the country.

The group reached Gravesend after dark. As they stepped off the little steam train that ran from Brooklyn to Coney Island they were pounced upon by a posse led by McKane. Pushed, prodded, and kicked, fourteen of them were hustled into a waiting prison van and carried at a gallop to the Coney Island police court. There Justice of the Peace Kenneth F. Sutherland (McKane's right-hand man, known as "The Little Corporal" because of his diminutive size) booked them as vagrants and locked them in the jail, some of them four to a cell. The leader of the group, John P. McNamara, a law student in Gaynor's office, was charged with being drunk and disorderly. The seven men who got away carried the news back to Brooklyn.

The hapless fourteen were held, without anything to eat or drink, until nine o'clock Sunday morning. Then they were taken again before Sutherland, who remanded them for trial in General Sessions court on Monday. He set no bail, and after the hearing he vanished. The disheveled group was herded back into the van and taken to Raymond Street jail in Brooklyn.

Things were humming at that end. Grout got word of the men's plight early Sunday morning, and hurried to Coney Island to obtain their release on bail, taking along half a dozen wealthy Brooklyn men, collectively worth several million dollars, who were prepared to provide bail. Sutherland could not be found. Another of McKane's justices of the peace, R. V. B. Newton, was located, but he refused to touch the case.

"For all I know these men may be murderers," said he.

"Won't you go to police headquarters and satisfy yourself as to the facts?" Grout urged.

"No, I won't. I'll have nothing to do with it. Get Sutherland if you want to get your friends out of the hole. You can't use me."

"But Sutherland has disappeared."

"I don't give a damn."

With that Newton walked away.

Grout hastened back to Brooklyn and appealed to Justice Cullen, but the latter could act only by having the man brought before him on writs of habeas corpus. He was willing to issue such writs, but while these could be issued on Sunday, they could not be served until Monday. Sutherland's strategy was airtight: by failing to set bail, he had made sure that the men would remain in custody at least over the weekend. One newspaper observed with grudging admiration that if it had been the President of the United States who was in jail under the circumstances, no power in the land could get him out without the consent of the vanished Sutherland.

Grout and still another Gaynor law partner (who charged that the Brooklyn police were in cahoots with McKane) spent Sunday afternoon preparing fourteen writs of habeas corpus, and on Sunday evening Cullen signed them.

Meanwhile the affair was being talked about all over town. Mayor Boody thought it a capital joke.

"How do I know why those men were sent down there?" he asked, laughing heartily.

District Attorney James W. Ridgway took the high ground of official disinvolvement. "Inasmuch as I do not know officially what the charges are I can not express an opinion on the subject," was his only comment.

Gaynor himself had received the news at his home in St. Johns Place, and for several moments was so angry he did not trust himself to speak. The humiliation of young McNamara affected him poignantly.

"I would not have had that boy subjected to this degradation for a hundred thousand dollars," he exclaimed. "No, not for my life! He is of fine parentage and family, of finished education, and the finest qualities. His father entrusted his legal education to me. I didn't know he was going to Coney Island; my time is so occupied that I had to turn the matter over to counsel. I am beset and buffeted by a thousand difficulties, and now comes this brutal outrage! If the fathers and sons of Brooklyn can stand it, I can't!"

What did he intend to do? His answer was grim:

"I intend to send someone to state's prison."

On Monday morning the street outside the Kings county courthouse was thronged with indignant citizens when the haggard, hollow-eyed fourteen men arrived from Raymond Street jail. Judge Cullen's courtroom was packed. The district attorney tried to make out a case for the arrests, contending that several of the men "had a stubby growth of beard" and two were ex-convicts, but his effort was lame. Judge Cullen looked over the commitment papers and found them defective.

"The men committed might be held in jail forever on these commitments," he remarked, and dismissed the lot.

A cheer went up from the spectators.

Nevertheless, with the election only one day away, the consensus was that McKane had won the trick. And when reporters interviewed the boss in his Sheepshead Bay home, they found him confident, and ready to give them his version of the affair.

"The reason why these men were arrested was because they looked and acted like suspicious persons," he said, leaning back easily in his chair. "They arrived at the Gravesend town hall on the midnight train. I was there with several officers. We had been notified that an attempt would be made to steal the records in the town hall and we were taking no chances. The large number of men who left the train attracted attention, and being strangers and unknown they were arrested. The majority of them were drunk. The man McNamara, whom I arrested myself, was very drunk and disorderly. One of them was a crook, and two were known to be petty thieves. I think Mr. Gaynor stooped pretty low. He said all Gravesend was filled with illegal voters, and then he sent a gang down there at midnight."

The Sunday school superintendent in McKane was pained by the thought of such baseness. Shaking his head, he repeated, more in sorrow than in anger: "All hands were drunk and disorderly."

Anger and not sorrow was the reaction of the public in Brooklyn and elsewhere. McKane had overstepped the limit of endurance, it was felt, and the *New York Herald* looked forward to Gaynor's next move. McKane's "impudent arrogance" had climaxed the "brutal disregard of the rights of citizens" that had marked his whole career, the *Herald* thought. "He may continue his defiance until election day, but after that there will be an accounting. Lawyer Gaynor is a hard fighter, and he [has] promised to send someone to state's prison. The chances seem to be in his favor."

While McKane's victims were being restored to liberty, lively scenes were being enacted in Gaynor's law office. The seven men who had escaped were there, making affidavits Monday morning, and those freed by Cullen joined them in the afternoon. Visitors streamed in and out, prominent citizens volunteering to serve as poll watchers in Gravesend the next day, and the crush became so dense reporters could hardly squeeze through. They wanted to know what Gaynor planned to do. He said:

"I shall have twenty-five detectives in Gravesend tomorrow, and the polls will be watched as they have never been watched before. Every move of McKane and his henchmen will be noted, and if there is any wrongdoing it will be seen. In addition, I have commissioned two watchers to be inside each polling place. McKane may throw them out, but if he does he will provide a means of redress."

To make sure that his watchers functioned, Gaynor obtained from Supreme Court Justice Willard Bartlett an injunction forbidding McKane and his eighteen election inspectors to interfere.

McKane also was laying plans. In talking with reporters in his Court Street office in Brooklyn, where Sutherland had suddenly materialized, he showed little of his usual urbanity, but fairly snarled when referring to "Gaynor's gang."

"I am informed that the Gaynor mob has been discharged," he said. "Well, we'll arrest them on warrants containing other charges for their actions of Saturday night. Why, a man would have been justified in shooting them on sight on suspicion of their being burglars! When the train arrived, these thugs, sneak-thieves, and crooks walked into the arms of the police, whom I had ordered to be drawn up in front of the town hall to preserve the peace. They were asked to give an account of themselves, and when they refused to do so, I ordered them taken before Justice Sutherland. They couldn't give bail and were remanded in default."

"It is said that Justice Sutherland did not fix the amount of bail," a reporter interposed.

"Oh, yes, he did," was the emphatic retort. "It was $100 in each case."

"What about the watchers whom Mr. Gaynor says he will send to watch the Gravesend polls?"

"We'll give them the same kind of reception we gave the ruffians that came down on Saturday night! We'll be able to take care of everyone who has no business in Gravesend. They say a hundred and fifty are coming. Well, they can make it fifteen hundred or fifteen thousand for all I care. We'll take care of them all. We are law-abiding people and we don't propose to have our voters intimidated by anybody."

The little blond boss was not himself that day. Perhaps the indignation spreading among his Methodist brethren was accountable, for at a meeting of two hundred clergymen of that church over in Manhattan, a minister had won applause with his righteously sarcastic:

"It would have been too bad if that pious gentleman had jailed himself on Saturday night, for then he would have been unable to superintend his Sunday school classes and lend his highly moral support to the propagation of highly moral church ideas in his district."

Gaynor was placing his reliance on that thorough preparation in which alone he had confidence. At the close of the day, he issued a final word to the electorate, scrupulously careful to keep his own stand perfectly clear:

"If I have a hearing in Brooklyn and Kings county, it is not that I have ever asked for it. It came to me unsought. I did not even beckon to it. No politicians or set of politicians brought me forward. . . . I have tried for four years to do something for the people. If the people are now to condemn my efforts I shall bow to it, but I demand fair play. I only add that I am able to deal with this infamous business at Gravesend."

At 4:30 A.M. on Tuesday the official Republican watchers assembled at Gaynor's home in St. Johns Place. Colonel Alexander S. Bacon, a prominent lawyer and West Point graduate, somewhat pompous in manner, had undertaken to lead the assault on McKane's stronghold. In six carriages the party set out, driving rapidly through Prospect Park, and headed for Gravesend. Colonel Bacon carried Justice Bartlett's injunction.

Overnight Gaynor had sent a contingent of detectives to Coney Island. These were supposed to fan in on Gravesend from different directions at dawn, but somehow they either got their orders crossed, or lost heart, for none of them appeared in the town. For various reasons only three of the six carriages in Bacon's command got through to Gravesend, reaching there just before daybreak.

McKane had been informed of every move by his spies in Brooklyn, and he was ready. He had issued orders that at the blast of the siren on the firehouse, every man in town was to hasten to the town hall, and to come prepared for trouble. At 5 A.M. the siren sounded the alarm, and when Bacon's carriages hove into view, the town hall was surrounded by a cordon of motley-garbed policemen, carrying clubs and revolvers. Beyond these stood a promiscuous mob. McKane, dressed in his regalia as chief of police, was in command.

As Colonel Bacon stepped out of his carriage with the injunction in hand, McKane strode forward and snapped:

"So you are here at last. You might as well understand that we don't want you here. Now get out."

Bacon stated his mission and stretched out his hand to serve Justice Bartlett's injunction, but McKane drew back, put his hands behind his back, and said:

"I'll take no papers. Injunctions don't go today."

Then as Bacon managed to touch the boss's arm with the document, thereby legally establishing service, a voice came from the semidarkness, "To hell with the Supreme Court!"

"Hustle that party out of here; run 'em in quick," McKane ordered, and moved away; whereupon the mob closed in, and Bacon and his companions were knocked down and kicked, and their hats and coats were trampled in the mud. Bacon and four others were hauled off to Coney Island and locked in the jail privy.

There were reporters on hand who witnessed this fracas and what followed, but McKane had no words for them at the moment.

"Today we vote; tomorrow we talk," he said, waving them aside.

The cordon around the town hall was maintained all day. Nobody was allowed to pass unless vouched for by McKane, who remained on the scene throughout, cool, alert, and in complete control. Pickets were thrown out along the roads and no wagon was allowed to pass through the town unless surrounded by a crowd of "guards" who saw to it that there was no stopping. A few of Gaynor's detectives who reached the outskirts were driven back with threats. Arriving trains were surrounded, and anybody who could not prove his business in Gravesend was run out immediately or arrested if he resisted. Two Republican watchers who did manage to slip through the cordon were spotted and beaten severely. Reporters known to the boss were allowed to approach the police barrier, but not to go inside the hall, and two out-of-town newsmen, representing papers in Baltimore and Philadelphia, were jailed for a while. When the routed watchers applied to the sheriff for protection, exhibiting their credentials signed by the party authorities and by United States Attorney Johnson, he refused to help them.

"Who the hell is Jesse Johnson?" he demanded. "Why should they order me around?"

Meanwhile, wagons kept rolling up and dumping out certified voters all day, and inside the town hall tranquillity prevailed. There actually were properly accredited Republican watchers in each booth. McKane had obtained blank certificates from the Republican county committee and had filled in the names of reliable henchmen; so the balloting went on legally and unmolested, while in Brooklyn and New York the afternoon newspapers trumpeted that "there is no law in Gravesend except the law of the club on election day."

The *Brooklyn Eagle* hit the streets by midday breathlessly proclaiming: "This is civil war! It is successful rebellion! It is treason triumphant!"

The city was thrown into intense excitement. People were shocked as they would have been by word of a great natural disaster. Ordinary business virtually stopped. Mayor Boody was told the news as he emerged from the voting booth; he turned pale. Gaynor got word at his home.

"This great outrage succeeding ten days of outrage speaks for itself," was his angry reaction. "I wonder if the people will sustain it at the polls."

During the afternoon it became apparent that the people were not condoning it; there was a rush to vote, and the Republican nominees obviously were being helped. When the returns were counted, Schieren proved an easy winner as mayor, while Gaynor polled 93,774 votes to his Democratic opponent's 66,432. Even Gravesend was jarred out of its monolithic pattern; despite all McKane's efforts, Gaynor got 115 votes there, against his opponent's 3,506.

The day after election McKane's contemptuous "injunctions don't go here" was on every lip. In the streets, in shops and offices, and in clubs where influential men gathered, the talk was all of bringing the Gravesend boss to retribution. In one club a member brought his fist down on the table and exclaimed:

"I tell you, gentlemen, William J. Gaynor must not be left to fight this battle out by himself! This is no fight of any individual; it is the concern of the people. We should rally around him and back him up!"

A movement was started then and there to organize a citizens' committee to raise money for a relentless prosecution.

Gaynor's office was filled with congratulatory visitors, and to all he said that he had been elected simply because the people understood him and knew he had tried to serve them. He was swamped with telegrams and letters urging him to see that McKane did not escape punishment. He needed no urging.

"I have already formulated in my mind what is to be done," he said, "and it will develop very soon."

But he refused to disclose his strategy, saying:

"I propose to prosecute this enormous criminal in the courts, and not in the newspapers. McKane will understand what that means."

If the debonair boss had any premonitions of disaster he did not show it. On election night he had come into Brooklyn to get a Turkish bath and remove the grime of his hard day's work, and he appeared rosy and sleek as he chatted with friends and reporters in his Court Street office on Wednesday. He was dressed in sober black, with a neat lawn tie knotted over a large diamond stud, and wore his slouch hat cocked at a jaunty angle. Now that the election was past, he was prepared to accept the defeat of his party with good grace; he bore no grudges. True, he was somewhat concerned over the way the newspapers were misrepresenting the events at Gravesend; that certainly was reprehensible from the standpoint of simple honesty. Not that he exactly blamed the press; their readers demanded sensations, and when there weren't any, why, the papers simply had to invent some or get left behind.

A reporter reminded him that he had said, "Today we vote; tomorrow we talk." The boss was perfectly willing to tell what "really had happened" with the candor of a straightforward man.

"I'll tell you what occurred in a very few words," he began. "The citizens of Gravesend are a quiet, law-abiding people, but they are capable, like all other good-natured and honest souls, of getting stirred up when their rights are threatened. Now it was currently reported in Gravesend on the night before election day that Colonel Bacon and three hundred armed men were coming to town on election morning to make a violent assault on the ballot boxes. This stirred up the people's souls, and they got up early on Tuesday morning and naturally gathered around the town hall.

"Well, when Bacon arrived in his carriage, the people naturally thought this was the vanguard of the armed force, and they gathered around the carriage. I was there, of course, as chief of police, and seeing the excitement around the carriage I walked over to find out what was going on. It was not entirely light at that hour in the morning, you know, and I didn't recognize Colonel Bacon. I asked him what he wanted. He replied that he had come in the interests of law and order and that he had an injunction from the Supreme Court. But he didn't have any papers in his hand and I saw no papers. He said that another man had the injunction, and called to someone to come up, saying, 'Here's the man.'

"But all this didn't interest me, and I turned around and walked off. That is all there is to this story so far as I personally am concerned.

"But after I left, the crowd gathered around him and there was some little disturbance. I believe he and those with him created a disturbance around the polls, for the police arrested several of them, and I took them to police headquarters at Coney Island, where unfortunately a couple of them were locked up in cells. There was no necessity for locking them in cells; there was a room upstairs where they might have been lodged just as well. Afterwards I sent Judge Newton to look after them and he released them.

"Now, that is the whole story of a small disturbance at the polls that has been distorted into simply an amazing sensation. As far as any Supreme Court injunction was concerned, no papers were served on me and I saw no papers of any kind. But see here, I find by the papers that without knowing about the injunction I unwittingly obeyed it to the letter."

Picking up a newspaper he read the text of Justice Bartlett's writ. All right, there *were* accredited Republican watchers in the booths, and he had been enjoined from interfering with them, and he had not interfered with them.

"So there you are. There is your whole story. There was nothing illegal or unusual about it."

As for the claim that Gravesend was responsible for the Democrats' losing Kings county, why, hadn't the Democrats lost all over the country?

"Do you suppose the Gravesend matter caused the Democratic losses in Massachusetts and Ohio? Nonsense!"

He was sure the affair would blow over, once tempers cooled, and when a reporter said he didn't think so, McKane looked at him in surprise.

"Well, the Republicans have won," he said ingenuously. "They surely won't push this thing further against me? They ought to be satisfied with their victory. If they prosecute me it will be out of sheer ugliness."

But one week after election day, at a mass meeting of citizens in the Academy of Music, plans were initiated to support by popular subscription a vigorous prosecution of the boss. Many Brooklyn notables sat on the platform, William Ziegler among them; he had already wired Gaynor a pledge of $100,000 to punish "the Gravesend scoundrel." Seth Low, Brooklyn's onetime reform mayor and currently president of Columbia University, sent a check and a letter saying:

"Our whole system rests upon the rule of the majority, and until Americans lose the instincts of free men, they will not suffer rascality at the polls to offset with impunity the suffrages of honest citizens."

Gaynor sat in a box with his family and was greeted with an ovation. He did not speak, but a letter from him was read, explaining that his election as a justice disqualified him as a prosecutor.

"But I can not forget the citizens of Brooklyn who went down to Gravesend on election day as volunteers and were cruelly mistreated," he said. "I write their names down here, for they stand for the highest moral force and the most splendid citizenship."

He went on to remind the gathering that the district attorney had not taken one step toward bringing McKane to justice. This was a follow-up to the protest he had already lodged with Governor Flower against the district attorney's lethargy, with a request that special prosecutors be appointed to take the case out of the district attorney's hands. In conclusion, he cautioned his listeners against overoptimism, saying:

"In no case does success depend so much on preparation and foresight as in a trial in the courts. I do not even except military engagements."

This uprising of an aroused citizenry impressed the newspapers as something unique. Commented the *Eagle:*

"For a city to demand in mass meeting the punishment of criminals is an unusual and startling proceeding. If it occurred on the Cherokee Strip, or in one of the silver mining towns, it would not be a surprise. . . . In Gravesend, where every natural prospect pleases, only man is vile."

Gaynor, the champion who had dared to grapple with boss rule, found himself talked of everywhere. When he paid a fleeting visit to Chicago his fame had preceded him, and the Union League Club there gave him a rousing welcome.

McKane meanwhile was not alarmed by the prosecution talk. Suits for false arrest were piling up against him, but he countered with a few lawsuits of his own, for libel, against newspapers. Then, with a retinue of retainers, he departed on a hunting trip to Virginia. This was the relaxation he permitted himself after every hard-fought campaign. Lest anybody think he was absconding, however, he left his address with the authorities, saying that he could be found "at any time."

In his absence he was cited for contempt of court for ignoring Judge Bartlett's injunction; but he dallied in the South until Jere Wernberg, Brooklyn's cleverest criminal lawyer, whom Gaynor had retained to work up the evidence, got a warrant for his arrest and that of four of his underlings, including the "Little Corporal."

Then McKane began to take the matter seriously. He returned and dug in to escape incarceration for thirty days and payment of a $250 fine, the sentence passed for contempt. He managed to stay out of jail over Christmas, but on January 12, 1894, he was indicted on six counts for misconduct as an election official, oppression, conspiracy, and assault. By that time Gaynor was on the bench, a justice of the Second District, Supreme Court of New York state.

During the campaign, when the public's curiosity was intense, the press had carried various brief accounts of Gaynor's life and career. Some of these would take on significance as time went by because of their calculated omissions. From the commencement of his official life, Gaynor dictated all interviews given to the press, as well as all biographical notices of himself, even writing some in long-hand and insisting that they be reproduced verbatim, without changing a word. He was the source of almost every scrap of information about his personal life, especially his early years, that appeared in print; and he took pleasure in misleading and throwing the inquisitive off the scent. At the same time he betrayed growing prejudices and built up a picture of himself that he was resolved the public should accept.

Directly after his nomination, the *Kings County Journal* published a laudatory sketch, using data supplied by the candidate. Gaynor had been "born and brought up on a farm at Whitestown, Oneida County, New York," the *Journal* said, and at an early age had been "inured to hard work and independence." His father's name was nowhere mentioned, Keiron being alluded to only as "a prominent man in that section for many years." Of Gaynor himself, the *Journal* said, among other praiseworthy things:

"Besides having a classical education, he is a rare mathematician and still delights in that branch of study. Mr. Gaynor came to Brooklyn in 1873. . . . He almost immediately took a prominent place at the bar, and his practice has grown to very large proportions. He has accumulated a fortune out of his practice, though he has done a great amount of work for nothing for people unable to pay. He is ordinarily reticent, and in appearance usually severe and not easily moved, but when occasion calls for it he displays great animation and brilliancy of speech. . . . He is equally at home in any kind of a case, civil or criminal, and . . . is well known all over the country as a law writer. . . . He is also a student of general literature. He is fond of horses, dogs, and hunting. In politics he is a Democrat but an extremely independent one. . . . In December, 1890, he was appointed judge advocate general on the staff of General McLear of the Second Brigade of the National Guard of the State of New York with the rank of major, and still holds that position."

Conspicuously omitted from this résumé was any mention of Assumption Academy, of Gaynor's youthful connection with the Christian Brothers, of his religious faith, of his Irish parentage, of his previous marriage and divorce, and of his age.

The *New York Herald* told its readers that Gaynor was "of slight build, rather light complexion, and about forty years old," and alluded to his modest-looking but "elegantly furnished" brownstone house at 212 St. Johns Place, but hastened to add that he was "by no means extravagant in his style of living."

The *New York World* said flatly: "William J. Gaynor was born in 1853 at Whitestone [sic], Oneida County, New York, where he spent his youth upon a farm. He attended the public school in his native district and went from it to the Whitesboro' Academy. He then taught school in St. Louis, Mo., and in Boston, continuing his studies at the same time. In 1873 he came to Brooklyn."

The dubiety hovering about his age was a deliberate mystification. When Gaynor accepted the nomination for justice, he looked forward to the possibility of serving two terms. He was wealthy, domestically settled (four children had been born to him and his wife and others would follow), and the position of justice of the state Supreme Court was one of usefulness and high honor; it would round out his career fittingly. But justices were elected for terms of fourteen years, and the mandatory retirement age was seventy. Gaynor was forty-five (assuming that 1848 was his birthdate), and should he be reelected his second term would be shortened by three years. This he did not wish to consent to, so he solved the difficulty by moving the year of his birth ahead three years. From that time on, both orally and in writing, he would give the date of his birth as 1851. Both his law partner, Grout, and his secretary knew about the change, and so did another close legal associate, Charles M. Hyde. This young man was a cousin of Gaynor's first wife. He had entered Gaynor's office as a clerk in 1889, and in time would become perhaps Gaynor's closest intimate and one of his greatest embarrassments, also.

The prosecution of McKane went forward rapidly, coached by Gaynor behind the scenes and conducted by the special prosecutors named by the governor, chief of whom were Edward M. Shepard and Benjamin F. Tracy, both leaders of the Brooklyn bar. Justice Bartlett was the presiding judge. As the evidence piled up against him, McKane grew grayer and grayer; he began to foresee social disgrace and financial ruin. He had called off the libel suits and was trying desperately to compromise the damage claims. He sensed that his was not an ordinary prosecution, but one demanded by an out-raged community.

At one point Gaynor was called as a witness. He followed the captain of police at Gravesend, John T. Hinman, a well-preserved Dogberry who squirmed on the stand and admitted that he did not know the names of the seven men he nominally had in his squad, and didn't know whether they took orders from him or not.

"To whom do the policemen of Gravesend report?" asked Judge Bartlett.

"I don't know."

"You don't know! To the chief, I suppose?"

"I don't know."

Hinman said he had nothing to do with the police payroll except to draw his own salary, and that he got from John Y. McKane, in the form of McKane's personal check, whenever McKane chose. In bumbling earnestness trying to make the matter clear to the jury he explained:

"Well, now, the way it is, when I want money I go to him and ask him and get it."

As Hinman concluded Gaynor entered the courtroom and took the stand briskly. He looked steadily at McKane, but the crestfallen boss, sitting dejectedly between his lawyers, never lifted his gaze from the table.

Gaynor testified calmly how McKane had sent John Wesley Murphy to find out why Gaynor would not accept copies of the registration lists made by McKane. He told Murphy, Gaynor said, that he wanted his own copies made, "not leaving out even a blot that appeared on the page, so that if I had to go into court with these lists I could know and could prove that they were accurate."

This was what Gaynor meant by thorough preparation.

Grout testified that McKane, when informed of the injunction, backed away, saying, "I don't give a damn for all the judges and courts in the state of New York. You can go no further."

In due time opposing counsel made their closing arguments and the jury retired. It remained out for nineteen hours, while the boss's liege men kept vigil, confident that their chief would be acquitted.

When a messenger brought word to Judge Bartlett's court-room that a verdict had been reached, Gaynor happened to be trying a negligence case there. A second chair was placed for Bartlett, the jury and the defendant were brought in, and the verdict was an-nounced—*guilty*. While Judge Bartlett pronounced sentence of six years' imprisonment at hard labor, the fallen king of Coney Island felt Judge Gaynor's cold gaze fixed upon him.

"God still reigns and the people are supreme," said Gaynor dryly as McKane was led away.

Appeals failing, McKane was taken from the Raymond Street jail to Sing Sing prison on March 1, 1894, and for four years he remained there, a friendless, listless inmate known as Number 119. He would not allow his family to see him in prison stripes. He went about his tasks apathetically, and when released, his term having been reduced for good behavior, he returned home broken in health and crushed in spirit. He could not bear to visit Coney Island; the pity he encountered there was unendurable; and in a short while he died, destroyed by his own egotism and childish vanity.

From the day of McKane's conviction, the star of Gaynor, the knight-errant who had slain this one dragon of boss rule, rose steadily higher.

O UPRIGHT JUDGE! O LEARNED JUDGE!

"A lucky seeking and a lucky finding," said Sancho Panza at this; "especially if my master has the good fortune to redress that injury, and right that wrong, and kill that son of a bitch of a giant your worship speaks of: as kill him he will if he meets him, unless, indeed, he happens to be a phantom, for my master has no power at all against phantoms."

—DON QUIXOTE

STANDING ROOM was at a premium when Gaynor took the oath of office as Supreme Court justice in Queens county courthouse in Long Island City on January 2, 1894. There had been a reception beforehand in the rooms of the Queens County Bar Association, when the new judge was presented with a massive chair composed of roses, and on his desk, as the greeting of the mayor of Long Island City, was a huge bouquet.

There was much curiosity as to how Gaynor would comport himself, but by the end of the day he was acting as if he had been on the bench for years. His mild manner surprised those who had expected something more dictatorial from the man who had toppled McKane, but the reticence was deceptive. His first act was to ask the clerk to read the roll of the grand jury. He then named the foreman and charged the panel for about a quarter of an hour, instructing them to see that no person was oppressed, but that all who deserved punishment got it, and in conclusion he directed their particular attention to the statutes governing grand juries.

A week later he presided for the first time in Brooklyn, and the courtroom was crowded with lawyers. The brisk pace he set caused raising of eyebrows among the oldsters.

The first case was an application by an oysterman and cattle raiser of Canarsie, on the ocean side of the island, for an injunction to restrain the police from seizing his carts, horses, and loads of cattle fodder as they passed through Brooklyn. He had been arrested and his property sequestered if not confiscated, he complained. The corporation counsel, representing the police, was vague about the circumstances and sought a postponement. Then a lawyer who said he represented the Citizens Association asked leave to intervene, to which the oysterman's counsel objected, contending that he had no interest in the case.

"If he represents the Citizens Association he comes very near representing the people," the bench remarked.

The delay was granted and the next case was called.

A lawyer, passing up a batch of papers to be signed, was asked: "Are they all right?"

"I believe they are," was the reply.

"That is a matter that concerns you more than it concerns me," Gaynor advised dryly as he scratched "W.J.G." on the documents.

A boy handed up a paper, which Gaynor glanced over, then peered down at the stripling.

"Are you a lawyer?" he inquired.

No, the boy said; the lawyer in the case had just stepped out of the courtroom.

"It is a grave matter to order the arrest of a man on the application of a boy," said the judge. "If the lawyer can show me any reason why I should do this, I will do it. Human liberty is not so cheap as to warrant it without."

And he handed back the paper.

Business was light, and Gaynor dispatched it with such promptitude that court was adjourned at noon. Prosy counsel never had a chance.

Thereafter it became an almost daily exhibition of speediness, thoroughness, unerring perception of the issues at stake, and sure application of legal principles leavened with common sense.

For Gaynor, law (though not necessarily the law) was codified common sense. With pettifoggers, wasters of time, and slovenly pleaders he had no patience, and when these irritated him sufficiently he could grow rude and even insulting. His temper was uncertain. He worked prodigiously, and expected everybody else to do so. He never adjourned court for mere convenience, and the quantity of work he got through was impressive, yet his decisions stood up on appeal better than those of any other Supreme Court judge.*

There was none of the stuffiness and awesome dignity of the bench usually associated with courts of law in Gaynor's courtroom; everything was brisk and businesslike. Any man could have his say before Judge Gaynor, provided he kept it short. Although a martinet on the bench, the judge was always accessible to lawyers, either in chambers or at his home, and he was always ready to listen to a worthy suggestion. He helped to establish a consultation room in the courthouse, and years afterward would say, "And I can't recall ever getting a word of thanks for it." Old-timers might grumble about "hurry-up tactics," but after one month there was nobody to be found in Brooklyn who called Judge Gaynor unfair: his reputation as a judge of extraordinary caliber was acquired almost overnight.

A few days after taking office he returned the free railroad passes which the New York Central handed out routinely to all judges. His letter to Chauncey Depew, president of the railroad, read:

"I thank you for the . . . passes for me to ride over your roads and all leased lines of your company, but being disinclined to use them because of the public office which I hold, I herewith return them."

The gesture was called by some discourteous, and it certainly was unprecedented; but Gaynor knew and Depew knew that litigation affecting railroads came regularly before the Supreme Court, and that valuable free passes were not distributed without some hope of benefits in return.

Before he had been on the bench six weeks, the New York *Sun* decided that Gaynor had fulfilled every expectation of those who had elected him, and already commanded "more dignity, and earned

---

* The Governor's Commission on the Law's Delays in 1902 reported that during the 1895–1902 period Judge Gaynor tried more than 39 cases a month, compared to the average work load of 23.12 cases. And while the average of affirmations on appeal in the Second Judicial District was 68%, Gaynor's was 86%, the highest in the New York area.

more striking respect from the attorneys" than any of his colleagues. His sayings were finding their way into the press, so that soon his *obiter dicta* were repeated by bus drivers and stevedores with as much relish as they were handed around among counselors at law. Compressed into a style peculiar to himself—clear, concise, and colloquial, racy yet judicious, breezy but exact—they achieved wide currency.

A reporter for the *Eagle* spent a day in Judge Gaynor's court and recounted what he saw and heard.

As the judge entered, with "a firm and rapid step," in the rear of the room a young lawyer was confiding to an older colleague that he hoped he could get an adjournment; he was ready to go on, he said, but "Judge Gaynor is so severe, and I'm not much of a talker."

"Talk won't do you a particle of good before him," his companion reassured him. "Slice down what you have to say to the barest possible statement of facts; that's what he wants; then tell him what you want as you would your father, and you'll get it if you are on the right side of the argument."

The reporter thought Gaynor's "clear and clean-cut" features typified his requirement that lawyers stick to the point. It was "a pointed face, long . . . and the length is heightened by the pointed beard"—reddish-brown in hue, lightly streaked with gray. "The nose is long and slender, and the broad high forehead is growing higher by the thinning of the hair above. The eyes—but they are hard to describe." Cold, some people might call them. "It is a face not given to smiling, save in a quiet and dry fashion."

A stack of papers awaited the judge on the desk. Dropping into his high-backed chair, Gaynor went through these rapidly, now and then calling up an attorney for a word of explanation. His questions were short and sharp, and he expected the answers to be the same. A paper was presented by a clerk who knew none of the details. The judge sent him away with the document unsigned and a suggestion that his employer send someone who knew what the action was about.

Not a few lawyers objected to the way Gaynor called the calendar, so rapidly and in a voice so low, almost a whisper, that it could not be heard distinctly throughout the courtroom. But their objections did not induce Gaynor to increase the volume by a decibel, and of necessity the lawyers remained attentive and alert.

Few judges were so animated and restless on the bench as

Gaynor. He moved about in his chair, swung it back on its squeaking hinge, and twisted a pencil or some other small object in his hand. He might grab a pen and write with a quick hand for a moment, or call for papers and examine them at a glance. But he never lost track of the witness, and he seemed to anticipate questions and answers. Often he took a witness in hand and plied questions "with the rapidity of a Gatling gun."

But even while he was doing this, or when rebuking some lawyer for haphazard blunders, clients were never injured by his actions. "Oftentimes the most lame and halting presentation of a litigant's claim for justice finds ready disentanglement and just decision at the hands of Judge Gaynor, after a plain and unvarnished opinion of the manner in which the counsel has presented the case is expressed. . . . Very often Judge Gaynor points out to erring lawyers the proper course to pursue for the best interests of a client. Oftentimes, also, the court will argue at some little length a doubtful point with counsel at the bar, but through it all there will always shine the clear light of a just legal perception of the rights of all parties concerned."

For with all his bullying of counsel and crustiness toward witnesses, Gaynor kept one thing foremost in his mind—the interests of the litigant.

"It isn't the lawyer I see in court, it's the litigant behind him, pale with anxiety and eating up his substance in dragged-out legal expenses," he wrote. "It is for his sake that I use all my authority to compel a rapid determination of cases."

His preachment over and over again was:

"A trial is a search for the truth. A lawsuit is not a game for sharp advantage."

This preoccupation, to the point of singularity, with the man or woman seeking justice, together with his overriding desire to safeguard the rights of the individual against official oppression or the encroachments of private wealth and privilege, was the underlying theme of many of his decisions. One of his first upheld the right of citizens to vote. The village of Freeport was to hold an election on whether to install a public water system, and the town officials had decreed that only resident taxpayers could vote. Not so, Gaynor overruled them: nonresidents who owned taxable property in the village were entitled to vote, since their interests, too, were at stake, and so were all citizens who were qualified to elect the town officials.

Possessed of a prodigious memory, Gaynor knew the sources of English law literally by heart, yet he scorned the device of shoring up a weak cause by a multitude of precedents more or less relevant. His quick mind could dart to the center of a knotty legal problem after a mere glance at a brief or a law book, and he brooked no meandering by wool-gathering witnesses or voluble counsel.

The *New York Tribune* was struck by Judge Gaynor's severity toward everything he held to be inimical to the taxpayers:

"One of his strongest assertions is that the taxpayers' money is used to ill advantage when justices permit lawyers needlessly to delay the work of the court. Justice Gaynor believes that the public money is being squandered unless the courts work under full pressure all of the time. Rather than postpone a trial, Justice Gaynor often sits beyond the regular time for closing."

The *Sun* found Gaynor "particularly impatient with stupid lawyers, as he is with stupid people, and on them he vents beautiful sarcasms. These sayings are not the result of studied effort, nor do they come off only on days when dyspepsia might be suggested as the cause. Every day the judge fires sharp and caustic remarks to lawyers who have not prepared their cases, to witnesses who are slow beyond endurance or tricky in their answers. . . . As a consequence, the seats in the courtroom are filled every day with people who have heard of these interpolations into dry objections and answers."

Gaynor's concern for the class of citizens who in the jargon of later times would be called the "underprivileged" was often expressed with a directness that many considered unbecoming in a judge; but nothing could deflect his sympathy from the mass of common people—the people of whom he was one despite his oddities, accomplishments, and quirks of character. The business depression was causing much misery, and at a rally for the benefit of Brooklyn's unemployed he spoke out boldly in favor of a better deal for the laboring man.

"The stupid cry has come down through the ages, and we hear it yet," he told the crowd: " 'Don't disturb the existing order of things, leave matters alone.' Well, there can be no advance of the human race without a change in the existing order of things. . . . Can it be that in the wisdom of the Godhead there is not some social and political system under which it would be impossible for any man to starve to death simply because he could not get work to do with his hands, when the earth possesses and produces much more than an abundance for all? Let us not doubt it, but assist in moving forward to it. Let us not be content to believe that everything is just as it ought to be."

This lofty tone was a far cry from his snappishness in court, when dealing with lawyers. If handed a sloppily drawn brief, he would be likely to fling it on the floor, or back at the offending attorney.

"Woe betide the lawyer who tries to bolster up a poor cause by recourse to a minor technicality afforded by some error or mistake by his opponent," commented a reporter. At such times the lawyers in the room might be seen to lean forward in anticipation of what was coming, and "when it came, it usually came hard." In a dozen words Gaynor would strip away the technicality and leave the discomfited lawyer with nothing to stand upon but the bare, cold facts. This "dipping directly to the primal grounds upon which a motion or case was based" accounted in part for the volume of business Gaynor disposed of, for it lopped hours from the time usually consumed by verbal gymnastics.

Those in the know could read the signs which showed how close to an eruption a long-winded, prosy, or hair-splitting speaker was coming. Let a spellbinder launch into a thirty-minute exposition of a motion that could be dealt with adequately in three, and for a few moments Judge Gaynor would listen attentively, hands resting on the desk. Then, as light began to filter through the fog of words, he would grow restless, swivel back and forth, and let his gaze wander to the ceiling. Next, facing his droning tormentor, he would tug at his mustache with his right hand, press down one or two hairs in the middle and bite them off nervously. Then his hand would sweep across his forehead wearily, and perhaps his nose would be given a downward pull. This was the critical sign. Suddenly bringing both hands down hard on the desk, the exacerbated judge would lean forward and ask, in icy tones:

"Will you tell me just what you want, counselor?"

Brought up short, the lawyer would stammer the gist of his request, and Gaynor would fling back:

"Well, why didn't you say so? I'll hear the other side."

Another reporter who dropped into Gaynor's courtroom found a trial in progress that had to do with the settlement of an estate.

Gaynor's patience snapped when defense counsel submitted accounts that he had not troubled to add up.

"I'm tired of this," the judge exclaimed. "I won't sit here and listen to these cases that have not been prepared."

The lawyer flushed, and Gaynor told the witness to go ahead. The man was an honest-looking farmer, who tried to testify regarding the accounts but was constantly interrupted by his lawyer. The judge listened for a while, then turning to the lawyer inquired acidly:

"If I can't take this man's own evidence, perhaps you had better get on the stand?"

Again the lawyer blushed, but Gaynor's features never changed.

A little later, prompted by a turn in the evidence, the judge observed that no lawyer "would consent to receive two payments for the same debt . . . not at this bar."

One of two lawyers for the defense next took the stand and was examined by his partner, with Gaynor firing in a question now and then. At length the examining lawyer objected to these interruptions, only to be told:

"You needn't object. I am tired of this failure to prepare your case. We have been helping you all day."

"But I do object," the lawyer protested, "and I also object to your honor's remarks—"

"Are you all through?" Gaynor cut in.

"Yes, but—"

"Well, go ahead."

When objections were raised again, a little later, the judge brought down his gavel with a bang.

"Now," said he, turning to the lawyer witness, "you needn't testify any more after these criticisms. I only allowed you to testify as a matter of courtesy because you are a lawyer."

"I want an objection entered," began the witness, rising.

Snapped Gaynor:

"All right. Bring on your next witness."

Later Gaynor brought out that the lawyer's testimony was of benefit to neither side.

But it was inattention and dilatoriness on the part of counsel that most exacerbated Judge Gaynor. One day business in his court came to a standstill, because though case after case was called, one side or the other was not ready. Finally Gaynor lashed out:

"I don't see why lawyers can't step up here and try their cases like men! They say they are ready for trial and then come here with excuses! There is a great deal of talk about the need for greater judicial force in the courts, when the fact is that half the judicial force is ample for all the cases that honestly come to trial!"

After waiting an hour for cases, he adjourned court in a towering rage, and his law clerk that day heard some powerful profanity.

Actions marked by unusual or arresting circumstances always got Judge Gaynor's full attention; he was interested in anything out of the way or novel. A wife applied for alimony and counsel fees pending trial of her suit for absolute divorce. She alleged that her husband had obtained a divorce in South Dakota two years before, and had since remarried without her knowledge. (South Dakota divorces were not recognized in New York State.) The husband charged that she had been living with a Brooklyn schoolteacher. Gaynor listened attentively to the testimony, and granted alimony to the wife, but with a philosophical observation that went the rounds:

"There is something wrong with a woman who can't manage a man."

When a motion was presented to set aside a summons in a suit against the Truck Drivers Benevolent and Protective Association on the grounds that the title should have contained the words, "of the City of New York," Gaynor professed to be puzzled.

"If it did not mean you, why did you take any notice of it?" he asked. "How could the association know that it meant it?"

"It would have gone by default," the lawyer explained.

"Well, that wouldn't have hurt you if you were not the defendant. I would rather have a judgment against another than against myself, and I deny the motion."

Another lawyer applied to have the trial of an action transferred from Kings county (Brooklyn) to New York county (Manhattan). He got nowhere.

"I never grant such a motion," said Gaynor curtly. "The bridge is the same whichever end you start from."

Tap went the gavel, and his grave, unsmiling countenance gave no inkling of his elfin humor.

Judge Gaynor treated all lawyers alike; great legal reputations meant nothing to him. Members of prestigious Manhattan law firms who were inclined to be condescending toward the courts of Kings county were frequently called to order by the peppery judge. A lawyer from New York who believed his case would not be called that day left the courtroom, but unexpectedly the case was reached, and the lawyer's clerk asked for an adjournment until the next day. The judge asked why. With a significant glance at the clock the clerk replied that he thought a postponement wouldn't make much difference as it was within half an hour of closing time.

"Closing time!" shouted Gaynor. "I want it understood that this court does not adjourn in the middle of the afternoon! We are just beginning to work in earnest at this time of the day. If a lawyer is not willing to look after his business he should not undertake it. They think we are sleepy and behind the times over here. I want to impress upon Manhattan lawyers, who call it a day's work when they begin at eleven o'clock in the morning and get through at three o'clock in the afternoon, that there is nothing slow in this town!"

The Second Judicial District comprised the counties of Kings, Queens, and Richmond (Staten Island), in the New York City area, and seven counties beyond, lying within a radius of some ninety miles. As he traveled this circuit, Gaynor brought the fresh air of efficiency, alertness, and dispatch into the suburban and rural courts. And he did not hesitate to rebuke counsel when they erred by insufficient consideration for the bench in his person.

In a Westchester county case involving a recount of votes for mayor of the town of Mount Vernon, he exploded when he discovered what he construed as an attempt to circumvent or hoodwink him.

"I don't care who is elected," he shouted angrily. "I don't want to know. In the order which I signed several weeks ago there was a clause in relation to fines. [Fines on the members of the common council for failure to do their duty.] That clause was put into the order without my knowledge."

Glaring at both counsel, he whipped out:

"When counsel are reputable I sometimes sign orders without reading them."

The lawyers flushed and started to speak at the same time. Gaynor silenced them.

"I will not consider the motion for a resettlement of that order, and I will write no more letters to counsel in this case. It is a pity that I can not write to counsel without the letters getting into the newspapers."

Down came the gavel and the incident was closed.

While presiding at Poughkeepsie, seat of Dutchess County, seventy-five miles north of New York City, Gaynor fired another shot at dilatory and supercilious Manhattan lawyers. Appearing on behalf of a New York attorney named Harrison, a local lawyer requested that a case in which Harrison was defending counsel be put over to next term. Snapped Gaynor:

"You telegraph Mr. Harrison to be here tomorrow morning at ten o'clock, and if he is not here judgment will be taken against him. These people from the city have no regard for anybody. They are never ready for trial until you make them get ready. I find it the same way everywhere. They hinder the work of the courts in every county of the district."

The next lawyer, himself from New York, asked for a postponement on behalf of a Manhattan attorney named Waldo. Retorted Gaynor as the lawyer blushed:

"You are from New York, too! I will mark your case ready and it must stand ready. Now, you have your witnesses here tomorrow morning, and if necessary we will send a committee to bring Waldo up."

There being no more cases ready to try, court was dismissed.

A sound argument always received Judge Gaynor's close attention, but a slovenly pleading in his eyes was an abomination unto the Lord. Young lawyers, who intended to base their pleas on some novel application of a legal principle for which precedents were lacking, soon learned to seek out Gaynor's court, because he would be interested, and in ruling he would not hesitate to break fresh ground for fear of reversal on appeal. On the other hand, Gaynor refused absolutely to do the work of indolent attorneys for them.

Counsel moving for settlement of a case handed up a big bundle of papers which Gaynor briefly tried to unsnarl, gave up, and handed back the next morning with this note penciled on the reverse of one document:

"The attorneys have made no attempt even to comply with rule 32, but seek to throw upon the trial judge all the drudgery of settling this case. I refuse to have anything to do with it."

His judicial decisions, because of their broad humanity and avoidance of mechanical, rigid concepts of the law, and because of their pungent style, were quoted in the daily press from the very beginning of his term as judge. In treating of general principles, his writing was epigrammatic and deliberately aimed at a popular audience. He called things by their plain names, and declined to be swayed (let alone stampeded) by "moral uplift" cant; meddlers with other people's affairs he hated and fought at every turn.

Shortly after becoming a judge he delivered a notable opinion holding that a horse race is not a lottery, and therefore organized activities of the turf were not illegal. The opinion was widely quoted for years to come.

Philip Dwyer, one of the two "butcher boy" brothers who had built up racing in Brooklyn (Hamburg was their great stakes winner, the "iron horse" of his era), was arrested as the president of the Brooklyn Jockey Club for allegedly promoting a lottery by organizing the Brooklyn Handicap—a race that is still run on the New York tracks. Gaynor in his decision went elaborately into the history of the New York lottery law and the successive changes made by constitutional conventions, then described the conditions of the race, and concluded:

"This is not a lottery either in common speech or within legal definition. A lottery depends on lot or chance, such as the drawing of lots, the throwing of dice, or the turning of a wheel. In the scheme of this race the horse owners do not pay a sum in order to win a larger sum by lot or chance, but to enter into a contest of skill, endurance, and speed, upon which the stake depends. With the matter as a debatable moral question I have nothing to do. I can not make laws; I am bound to administer the laws as I find them. The complainant is free to urge the moral considerations urged in his behalf to churches and religious societies, or wherever he may get a hearing, with a view of elevating the moral sense of the public to his standard, out of which will come an equally improved legislature to make the law as he seems to want it. . . . Racing horses for stakes may be bad, but unlawful arrests are worse. . . . History teaches us that we have more to fear from despotic power than from all species of gambling combined."

This was an opening gun in the battle he would wage against two monstrous evils, in his eyes: the well-meaning but dangerous activities of zealots who would purify public morals by force, and the encroachments of government upon the dignity and freedom of the individual. He was ruthless in his flagellation of the police for usurping powers that had never been given to them.

Memoirs of that period abound in testimony to the highhanded arrogance of New York City policemen, and those of Brooklyn were only a shade better. The police were armed then with clubs longer and heavier than the modern nightsticks, and they swung them indiscriminately. Let a citizen watching a parade overstep the police line and he would not be told to get back, he would be more apt to get a sharp rap on the shins. If he protested, he would be likely to feel the policeman's club on his skull, and spend a night in a verminous jail cell meditating on his presumption. With simple forms of lawbreaking like drunkenness, burglary, and wife beating, the New York patrolman of the Eighties and Nineties was able to deal handily and with rough justice; but the "force" was no glamorized friend of the ordinary householder. The police were suspected of iniquities, on the one side, and they were guilty of some; and while maintaining order in their own way, on their side, the police kept the public at club's length.

This condition of affairs infuriated Judge Gaynor, and he constantly strove to arouse the public to the dangers inherent in condonation of the system. An arrest without a warrant he considered in most cases a crime of the utmost gravity. When a sidewalk ticket speculator was seized by a police captain without a warrant or written complaint, and was brought before Judge Gaynor on habeas corpus proceedings, the arresting officer was given a dose of judicial wrath, while the speculator was set free.

"I don't know by what authority a police captain can make such an arrest," Gaynor fumed. "There are too many police captains arresting persons without warrants. It would not be tolerated in any country of the world except here. There is no pretense of any criminal offense whatever, yet the petitioner is arrested and locked up overnight like a common felon. As the liberty of the citizen has been in a large measure entrusted to me as a judicial officer, I feel it my duty to characterize the arrest of the petitioner as a gross outrage. I do not think I should refrain from saying so, for such occurrences are becoming so frequent as to leave no citizen safe.

"Some police officers do not seem to know that they have no right to arrest except for crime. But the case is even worse than it appears on the police blotter. It was conceded before me on argument that the petitioner was selling tickets on a public street. At most there was nothing but a dispute between petitioner and the president of the corporation [owning the show] concerning their respective rights. There was no pretense or charge that any crime was being committed. The place to settle the dispute was the civil courts; but the police captain, at the request of the corporation, arrests the petitioner and locks him up. The occurrence to me is of the gravest character. No civilized people ever submitted to such acts of arbitrary power and long preserved their liberties. Not one inch can be safely yielded to arbitrary power. When we employ police officers and tax ourselves to pay them, we do not make them our masters."

This sermon from the bench Gaynor would repeat tirelessly in his determination to educate the people to be vigilant against the ineradicable propensity of officials temporarily entrusted with the powers of government to overstep their authority and act lawlessly. Wherever such lawlessness appeared, Gaynor would have at it, full tilt, and if possible bring it crashing down.

Another case of arbitrary arrest early in Gaynor's judicial career moved him to an outburst that would set a pattern for many, many others. Several South Brooklyn boys had been arrested for playing ball in Prospect Park on Sunday. Their bats and balls were confiscated, and they were locked up until midnight Sunday, when a friend procured their release on bail. They appealed to Gaynor, who freed them and ordered the police to restore their playing gear. Then he wrote a long letter to the Brooklyn police commissioner, saying:

"The police assumed to imprison these boys at will, and even to confiscate their property, things which even the most august courts and officials in the land have not the power to do. These are good boys, the sons of good parents, who contribute to pay policemen, and should not be subjected to such degradation. If they committed a criminal offense they were entitled to be accused of it before a magistrate, and to be bailed, instead of being cast into cells and imprisoned at the pleasure of the police. But they had not committed a criminal offense. They had not begun to play ball, and if they had, it was not a public but a private game, which is no more a criminal offense on Sunday than on a weekday, unless it attracted a noisy throng and disturbed the peace. And something is due to boys who work through the week. A ball game is better for them than the temptations and allurements I need not mention to you."

At about this same time Gaynor ordered Mayor Schieren to issue a license to the Seaside Athletic Club at Coney Island, after the mayor had refused, owing to reported violence that had occurred there under previous licenses. Certain church groups claimed that the club was an illegal prize-fight ring. Gaynor's order read:

"To license this place will do no harm. The license is not to violate the law. If in any exhibition there be any violation of the law, any citizen, which includes any policeman, may summarily arrest the offenders in the act. The laws are ample for the prevention of immorality or of illegal acts of any kind in places of public amusement."

Off the bench he said indulgently:

"As to whether they really did fight down there at Coney Island I don't know. The police commissioner was there, and he says there was no fighting. Our fine young men from athletic clubs in New York and Brooklyn do box and knock each other about pretty hard, and, God bless them, let them do it. People with little chests and little lungs and sometimes little hearts and souls should not bother too much about other people."

A case of aggravated police oppression in Westchester moved Gaynor to furious anger. In Yonkers a woman's barn was burned. She told a policeman that she had seen several boys "hanging around the barn," one of whom came running to tell her that the barn was on fire. She wanted the boys arrested. The policeman routed three boys out of their beds at midnight, took them to the station house and locked them up until the next morning. Two of the boys were seventeen and one was fifteen. In the morning the policeman took all three before a magistrate and entered a complaint of disorderly conduct, saying he had found them wandering in the street and they had refused to give an account of themselves. The magistrate held them for further examination.

A lawyer appeared and offered the customary bail of two hundred dollars each, but the magistrate refused it. The boys' parents then appealed to the magistrate, and they, too, were rebuffed. They then turned to Judge Gaynor, who was holding court in nearby White Plains, with a petition for a writ of habeas corpus. On return of the writ it was found that a new charge had been entered, namely, arson in the second degree. After listening to all the testimony, Gaynor set the boys free, and in a decision that would long be cited said:

"Who called on them to give an account of themselves does not appear; presumably the policeman; but the magistrate leaves whoever it was to be the judge of whether they could give a good account of themselves. It would be difficult to conceive of anything more outrageous. It leaves everyone at the whim of the police, and to be judged as to his manners and his reasons for walking along a public highway by the first policeman he meets.

"Never has anything like this been tolerated by the Anglo-Saxon race. Human liberty never was so cheap. The charge of vagrancy was trumped up. After this writ to produce the petitioners here, however, the policeman made a further charge in writing, but wholly on information and belief, that the petitioners had set fire to a barn. The information, which he says was given him, concerns one of them, and contains not a scintilla of evidence against him. The law is that no one may be arrested and deprived of his liberty on mere information and belief, and everyone concerned in such an arrest, from the magistrate down, is liable to action for damages for a trespass.

"This is a police case the like of which have grown to be altogether too common. . . . The conduct of the magistrate in refusing bail for the petty charge of disorderly conduct should be brought to the attention of the tribunal having the power to remove him. If such outrages are to pass quietly, it will come to pass, that no citizen is safe at the hands of the police."

Such blasts, addressed as much to the public as to the record, caused people generally to feel that in Gaynor they had a friend at court, and they turned to him for help in all sorts of difficulties. And he helped them. No subject was too out of the way for his searching analysis and sometimes his sportive learning. Certainly no decision he made was read more widely and enthusiastically than one concerning dogs, which he issued shortly after ascending the bench. The newspapers printed it with relish, and every dog owner and dog lover read it with approval—even enjoying the learned judge's including among the authorities cited Homer's *Odyssey*, Motley's *Rise of the Dutch Republic*, and Moore's *Life of Byron*.

The case was straightforward enough. A police justice had ordered a dog belonging to William Shand destroyed because he had bitten Thomas Croke. Shand refused, and the police justice said he would have to impose the penalty provided in the city ordinance of a fine of $10 for failure to comply with the order within forty-eight hours, and $5 thereafter for every forty-eight hours the dog might remain alive. A writ was sought of Judge Gaynor to prevent the carrying out of this intention. Gaynor granted the writ in a display of dog affection and legal erudition that bore the stamp of his uninhibited originality.

After quoting the ordinance, which provided for police action "if a dog attacks a person," the judge delivered himself as follows:

William J. Gaynor on Dogs—September 1, 1894

"This court is asked to issue a writ of prohibition in the name of the people commanding the police justice to desist. It will be observed that the ordinance only professes to confer jurisdiction on a justice in a case where a dog 'attacks a person.' The complaint alleges no attack by the dog; and when I come to read the evidence given by Croke upon the examination into the proceedings against the owner, I find that he swears the dog was on the street with the owner's boy, and that (to use his exact words) 'I got hold of the boy, and the dog bit me'; so that instead of the dog making an attack, Croke seems to have attacked the boy, and the dog defended him. No complaint being made to the justice that the dog had made an attack, he was without jurisdiction to do anything in the matter, conceding the ordinance to be valid.

"Property may not be taken, affected, or destroyed except by due process of law, which requires notice of hearing to the owner, and opportunity to be heard (State Constitution, Article I, Section 6, Stuart *vs.* Palmer, 74 New-York, 183). Under the common law of England a dog was not property. It was not larceny to steal a dog, though it was larceny to steal a dead dog's hide. But the world moves, and these crudities no longer exist, and in this state a dog is property (Mullaly *vs.* The People, 86 New-York, 365). The dog from the beginning has been the friend and solace of man; and the law has only recognized the testimony of human nature, history, and poetry in withdrawing him from outlawry. (Mot. *Dutch Republic*, 398; *Odyssey*, b. 17; Moore's *Byron*, Volume 7, 292.) It may be well to remember in excuse of the courts, however, that when they declared that a dog was not property, it was in order to decide that it was not larceny to steal him, for the prescribed punishment at that time for larceny of property of the value of 12 pence or more was death, and they thought it not fit that a man should die for a dog. (Coke, *Inst.*, 3d, 109, etc.) And yet it was larceny to steal a tame hawk, and, as I have said, a dog's hide. But trying to forget these oddities, suffice it that a dog is property in the fullest sense in this state; and therefore, the order of the justice to kill this dog was absolutely void, because he gave judgment without a hearing, and, as has been seen, that is no judgment at all, and can affect nothing and nobody. It follows, of course, that the justice has no jurisdiction to punish the owner for not having obeyed this void order or judgment.

"As to the ordinance itself, it is one of those absurdities which we often encounter. It is void. It professes to authorize judgment without the constitutional prerequisites of a judicial hearing upon due notice. (74 New-York, supra.) And, besides, I do not find any authority going so far as to suggest that a statute authorizing a common council to pass an ordinance to 'regulate and license' dogs, or swine, or cows, confers power to pass an ordinance to kill them. The common law is that a ferocious or dangerous dog running at large in a public street is a public nuisance, and may be killed by any one. The intervention of a police justice is wholly unnecessary. This ordinance is a fair sample of too much law and government, like many others enacted in Brooklyn, one of which is that no house-holder shall allow his chimney to take fire. I think it proper to say that I do not see that the police justice is open to blame. He only did what had been done by his predecessors for a long time. Let the writ issue."

PRIDE AND POLITICS

*How hard it is to hide the sparks
of nature.*

—CYMBELINE

Within two months of taking office as a Supreme Court justice,
Gaynor was being boomed by the newspapers for governor of the
state. The *Brooklyn Eagle* was sure that a man of his ambitious
nature and restless temperament would not long submit to the restrictions that hedge about a judge. Across the river, in New
York, the *Sun* looked forward to the same development. The speech
Gaynor had made just after his election, at the dinner given in his
honor by the Montauk Club (a dinner not attended by either the
incoming mayor, Schieren, or the outgoing one, Boody, although
both were club members) had not passed unnoticed. Nor his indicating then his chagrin at not himself having been elected mayor. He
had hoped, he said, to "do something for Brooklyn—to lift up its
government and make it an example of honest and intelligent administration to the whole world."

In that same speech he had put into words other aspects of his
political faith—a philosophy which rejected barren partisanship.
He had said:

"The safety of our institutions depends upon having a sufficient number of voters who make voting a case of individual thought
and conscience, and fall back upon their own sense of right and
wrong, instead of being the mere obedient units of party organization."

Gaynor as a studious youth in Brooklyn in the 1870s.

Justice Gaynor relaxing on the porch of his country home, Deepwells, at St. James, Long Island, about the time he was nominated for mayor. *Credit: Brown Bros., New York, for this and all subsequent photos in this volume.*

Gaynor being officially notified of his nomination for the mayoralty by the Democratic party in the fall of 1909, in the parlor of his Brooklyn home. After a frigid speech he declined to be interviewed by reporters, saying, "I have made news enough for one day."

Official photograph of Mayor Gaynor, Mrs. Gaynor, and seven children, taken on January 1, 1910, the day Gaynor was sworn into office as mayor of New York City, in the Governors Room at City Hall.

The mayor's daily walk to work across Brooklyn Bridge from his home at 20 Eighth Avenue, Brooklyn, near Grand Army Plaza, to the City Hall, a distance of nearly four miles. At the close of the business day Gaynor walked home again, undeterred by the stormiest weather.

Mayor Gaynor taught the police force to be polite. Here on Brooklyn Bridge he waves a greeting to a patrolman standing rigidly at attention.

Arriving briskly at City Hall, Mayor Gaynor and his police escort jauntily ascend the steps for another day's work.

Carrying out mayoral inspection of the city's first motorized fire-fighting equipment, trim in frock coat, striped trousers, and silk hat. Behind Gaynor is his fire commissioner, Joseph Johnson.

Baseball was a passionate interest of Gaynor, and as mayor he religiously opened the season at the Polo Grounds or Ebbets Field in Brooklyn. Here, meticulously attired, he crosses the field on the way to his box with his devoted bodyguard, Police Lieutenant Kennell.

Throwing out the first ball at the Polo Grounds with the smile that rarely lighted his face. Gaynor pitched straight and hard in making this traditional gesture.

Close-up of Mayor Gaynor at the ball park, belying the reports that he never smiled and his expression was always grim. His shrewd Irish wit is clearly shown in his eyes as he relaxes, having a thoroughly good time.

Two noted mayors together — Mayor Gaynor of New York and Mayor John F. ("Honey Fitz") Fitzgerald of Boston, crossing the ball park. For once Gaynor has replaced his high hat with a high-crowned derby, but his wing collar is as natty as ever.

Patience, infinite patience, punctuated by violent bursts of temper that sent his staff scurrying for cover when patience gave out, was a characteristic of Gaynor often commented upon. Here, as he sits at his desk in City Hall, occupied with his mountain-high correspondence in line with his policy of listening to everyone who had a grievance, Gaynor's patience under stress is evident.

It was on his farm at St. James that Gaynor, brought up on an upstate New York farm, had his pleasantest days. Farm animals he loved, and pigs were his passion. (He thought politicians could learn a lot from pigs.) His favorites had names, and here he hands a tidbit to Nancy, a prized sow.

Gaynor worked in the fields at Deepwells with his farm hands, and reporters coming to interview him on municipal problems would sometimes find him pitching hay or driving a wagonload of his own potatoes to market.

Photograph snapped aboard the liner at Hoboken on August 10, 1910, as Mayor Gaynor prepared to sail for a vacation in Europe. The camera caught him chatting good-humoredly with friends about five minutes before he was shot.

Famous action photograph of Mayor Gaynor just after he was shot by a discharged dock worker, James A. Gallagher. The bullet entered the back of his neck just below the right ear. Supporting the stricken mayor is Benjamin C. Marsh, a by-stander, while rushing up from the rear is Edward J. Litchfield, a Brooklyn neighbor of the mayor. The assassin, Gallagher, had instantly been swept back along the deck out of range of the camera by the football tackle of Gaynor's street-cleaning commissioner, "Big Bill" Edwards.

Another view of Mayor Gaynor, struggling to breathe as blood poured from his mouth just after the shooting. The wound was at first thought to be fatal, but Gaynor recovered, though the bullet was never removed and he never fully regained his health.

The assassin, James A. Gallagher, being led away from the pier. Behind him follows Street Cleaning Commissioner Edwards, who overpowered him and was lightly wounded by another shot from Gallagher's pistol. Found to be insane, Gallagher was confined in an asylum and died shortly before Gaynor's own death. Gaynor never prosecuted.

Crowd assembling outside City Hall in September, 1913, for the ceremonies connected with Mayor Gaynor's acceptance of an independent nomination for reelection. The marchers carry shovels, the party's emblem to symbolize the start of new subway construction. The signboard bears Gaynor's proud assertion, made on his last working day at City Hall.

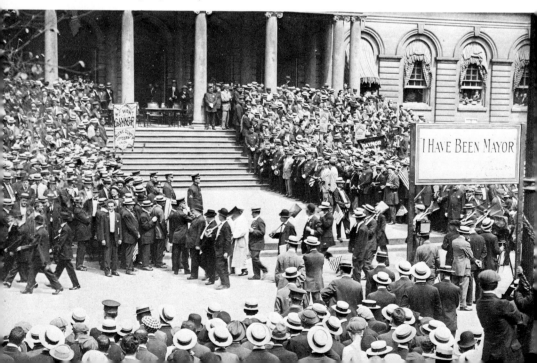

Gaynor wields a shovel in accepting the nomination for reelection, promising to "shovel all these miserable grafters into the ground." It was his last public appearance. The next day he sailed for Europe and died at sea.

Scene looking down Broadway as Mayor Gaynor's coffin, preceded by troops of mounted police, is borne from City Hall to Trinity Church for funeral services. Former President William Howard Taft and two former mayors of New York, George B. McClellan, Jr., and Seth Low, marched at the head of the honorary pallbearers. All traffic had been stopped, and the density of the crowds and the fervor of mourning were greater than at the funeral procession of Abraham Lincoln in 1865, according to witnesses of both events.

On the way from Trinity Church to Greenwood Cemetery in Brooklyn, the dead mayor was carried across the bridge for the last time, and the funeral procession went out of its way to pass his home, 20 Eighth Avenue, Brooklyn. Here the head of the escort of mounted police is passing the empty stoop of the Gaynor home, with the two lamps traditionally lighting the residence of New York City's mayor on the newel posts of the railings.

He also had hinted at some discordances left by his educational experience in his remarks about public schools:

"While the government of our great cities has been corrupt beyond anything ever known before, our common schools have been steadily assimilating the different nationalities into one harmonious citizenship, and lifting up the morals and the mentality of the nation. We may safely stake the future on our common school system. If the plain people stand by it, it will stand by them, and keep the scepter of government in their hands. It has already caused the center of political thought to pass from the few to the many. It ought to be and will be preserved in its entirety, and especially free from all sectarianism."

Coming from a man with Gaynor's background of sectarian religious training, this avowal was pregnant with meaning.

By July, 1894, the autumn election for governor was a leading topic, and Gaynor was singled out by many observers as the one man who could win for the Democrats. The Republicans were confident, and the Democrats were quarreling among themselves, a strong reform element under Shepard being in opposition to Tammany and the McLaughlin machine. Oddly, Gaynor now was the choice of the bosses whom he had so recently excoriated; but Shepard refused to endorse any candidate who was pleasing to Willoughby Street. Shepard's group was made up of enthusiasts and idealists with no real organization and little practical experience, and such forces, Gaynor knew, seldom win political victories. He looked on Shepard as a bit of a dreamer—too much a "do-gooder" for his taste—and he had no desire whatever for political martyrdom.

He really was not anxious to become governor, and he said so. His view, then and always, was limited to a narrower political horizon; there he felt at home. At the end of July the *New York World* sent a reporter out to the judge's summer home at Bellport, on Long Island's Great South Bay, with instructions to get an authoritative statement. He got one.

He found Gaynor sitting on the verandah smoking a cigar, having just come in from a drive with his wife and children. Although he greeted his caller affably, the judge shied away from an interview. At length, however, he said:

"Well, if you have got to interview me, let's step inside and go to work on it like mechanics."

"Inside" meant with a drink at one's elbow; Gaynor took his whisky straight and made no bones about it.

"People want to know whether you will be a candidate for governor," the reporter began.

"Well, well, if we are going to work on it like mechanics that's not the way," Gaynor demurred. "A mechanic never strikes till the iron is hot. No, I am not a candidate for governor, and I don't think that any of the persons who are supposed to make governors in the state of New York have any idea of asking me to be a candidate."

But the Democratic party leaders really did want Gaynor to accept the nomination for governor. Not only McLaughlin, but a strong faction at Tammany Hall favored the judge, although another element in Tammany bore Gaynor a grudge for his flings at bossism and party corruption.

Gaynor refused to yield to the pressure, for several reasons. In the first place, he did not think the Democrats could win; all the signs were against them. Then he enjoyed his current position, and the $17,500 salary of a Supreme Court justice, assured for fourteen years, was not to be disregarded.

When interviewed again in his office, Gaynor repeated that he was not, never had been, and did not expect to be a candidate for any office. He was under no delusions, he said:

"I hold a great office in which I can be useful. But I would be satisfied to hold none and be a plain citizen if I could assist in moving my day and generation forward even one foot, for in the slow progress of the human race even that is something."

Such idealistic sentiments were discounted by the politicians; it never dawned on them that Gaynor might be sincere as well as eccentric. They also failed to take into account that, as a man of extraordinary contradictions of character, he was subject to moods.

When the Democratic state convention was only a week away, a *New York Herald* reporter hied out to Bellport in an effort to obtain clarification. Gaynor felt kindly disposed toward the *Herald* because of the support it had given him during his judicial campaign, and after fending off the reporter's questions for a while he abruptly said that he would like to be frank and tell why he didn't wished to be forced to say flatly that he would or would not accept the nomination, should it be tendered, and it had not been formally tendered yet. His reasons were, so to speak, on the one hand sacred, on the other hand profane—realistic and mystical. He said:

"The fact is, I have no idea that there is any intention to even consider my name in connection with the nomination, for none of those whose influence controls in that matter—not one—has com-

municated with me about it, directly or indirectly. So you see, I am
not even in it, as the saying is. I believe now that I am glad I told
you this, for I want my friends to know."

He paused, then went on earnestly:

"There is another reason why I do not want to say whether I
would accept a nomination which I have no idea will be offered to
me. A man in the end wants to act in grave matters in accordance
with God's will, for we are mere instruments, and I do not, therefore,
see how we can act in advance."

God's will was scarcely in the minds of the convention delegates
as they gathered at Saratoga. The top party leadership still toyed
with the notion of naming Gaynor, and through intermediaries intense pressure was brought to bear on the judge. David B. Hill,
former governor and United States senator and the party's leader
in the state, took a hand. The *Brooklyn Eagle*, which was the voice
of Brooklyn, became almost dithyrambic in picturing Judge Gaynor
as "the something new and the something brave and dashing which
appeals to the hearts and brains of the Democratic party, and to
the confidence and hope of independent men."

Perhaps so, was Gaynor's reaction; but since Shepard's wing of
the party stubbornly refused to endorse any candidate who failed to
dissociate himself from the machine, and to win without a united
party backing seemed impossible, the judge declined to make himself a sacrifice.

The pressure told on him, however, and he was obviously
troubled in spirit. One day he said, "Yes, I should like to be governor in order to do some of the things for the people that have
burned in my head like a live coal." But the next day in a written
statement he took it all back. This pronouncement read:

"I said weeks ago that I was not and did not intend to become
a candidate for governor. I meant it then, and I will only say that
my intention is the same still. There are possibly many good, honest
people who think that I could have the governorship at will. Little
do they know the leaders who control such things. They don't want
me for governor. I have been in some conflicts in my time, and some
people seem to think that I am adapted to a life of political strife,
but the truth is that I never entered willingly into strife in my life.
Like Sidney Smith, I daily pray that my life may not fall into a
rut, for there is nothing more dreadful, in my opinion, than that;
but all the same, I do not like strife."

This, from one of the fightingest public men of his time, caused a blink of surprise. Gaynor was acting like the maverick that he was and that he knew he was. Now, in a political party nobody wants a maverick, and on the eve of the balloting for the nomination something happened at Saratoga. A whisper suddenly arose regarding Gaynor's 1881 divorce and his falling away from the church of his youth. The correspondent for the *New York Morning Advertiser* telegraphed his editor excitedly that "Saratoga is a great whispering gallery tonight and everybody is shaking his head and . . . asking his neighbor: 'Have you heard about Judge Gaynor?' . . . All sorts of wild and improbable reports are put into circulation . . . there are dark hints that the truth is not all known."

Who started the rumors, the correspondent did not know, although he suspected the anti-Gaynor element of Tammany Hall.

Gaynor refused to comment on the rumors himself, but he sent a personal friend, Mirabeau L. Towns, to Saratoga with a letter which Towns was authorized to show to newspapermen there. On July 24, at the United States Hotel, Towns handed out this statement marked "for publication":

"Judge Gaynor wants me to say to the gentlemen of the press that all rumors in circulation reflecting upon the character of the lady to whom he was first married he condemns and pronounces unfounded and false. Not for all the offices within the gift of the people will he permit her good name to be assailed and sit silent. Whatsoever of blame may be attached to that divorce he claims for himself, and begs his friends, his enemies, and his traducers to spare the woman."

As a result, most newspapers ignored the incident and never printed the malicious attack, but among the delegates the damage had been done. Advised of this, Gaynor wired from Riverhead, in eastern Long Island, where he was holding court, taking himself definitely out of the running.

"My present office was given to me by the people unsought and unlooked for," read the message. "I feel it my duty to continue to hold it. . . . I can not again so soon appeal to the splendid individual intelligence and integrity which stood behind the ballots cast for me last fall."

The next morning, when he arrived in court, he found a stack of telegrams on his desk imploring him to reconsider. Instead, he fired off a long message to Towns, expressing his resentment at the attempt to scandalize his good name, and lecturing the convention delegates on their proper course:

"I know the people of this state and they know me. I was born among them, went through the common schools with them, worked hard with them, and grew up with them, and I know that I now speak to you with their voice.

"It is that every one among you stop inquiring, and making it a subject of condemnation or of praise, whether this one or that one has chosen to live in the religion or way of his grandfather or great-grandfather, instead of that of his father, and that you proceed to nominate someone who, when elected, will stand for you and with the people—someone who will not when elected straightway betray the people. . . . This do, and, mark you, the people will not suffer your nominee to be beaten. . . . I would change my mind and gladly try to be the voice of the people this fall, but after the disposition betrayed toward me by some of your fellow delegates I can not."

Gaynor did not leave court that evening until eight o'clock, and then he went directly to his Bellport summer place.

The next day Hill was nominated for governor, and the convention named Gaynor for the Court of Appeals, New York state's highest tribunal.

For ten days Gaynor remained silent; then, in a long letter to the state party chairman, he declined the nomination. This extraordinary letter, compounded of wounded pride and an exalted sense of public responsibility in about equal parts, bore evidence of emotional agitation and political farsightedness. It read:

"The voice of the plain, everyday people is today, for cause, an actual living voice, and in a contest in which it should be summed up I could not be a candidate for office and sit silent, as usage and etiquette would require me to do in my present case. The center of thought has passed from the few to the many, and a great, peaceful political struggle is now impending in this country, which is to decide whether the center of power is to be and remain there also. It has more than once seemed to me that I should have some part in that great struggle when it came, but if that is not to be I still hope I may be able to feel that I have done, not much, it is true, but yet something to move my day and generation forward a little, and to better the condition of the community in which my lot is cast.

"It is now nearly five years ago that I openly objected, as an individual citizen, to political methods which I deemed loose, base, and unmanly, and to official acts which I deemed heartless crimes, involving as they did the spoliation of the people's hard-earned money for the enrichment of the few, who followed politics as a trade, and made public officials their mere tools. . . .

"I felt that I had a right to speak, for in the face of gross wrongs to the people among whom I lived I had remained silent, and silence often gives the right to speak; but furthermore, from an impulse which I can not define, or a reason which is too inscrutable to assign, I found myself unable to sit silent longer. . . . In this hour, when I have broken asunder the bonds of my perplexity, I see my duty clear."

This thunderbolt spread consternation in the Democratic ranks; but Gaynor's resolution held, and the outcome showed that his reading of the political weather signs had been correct. Hill was beaten ingloriously by the Republicans' Levi P. Morton, and the Democratic ticket went down with him.

Never again (with two exceptions) would Gaynor depart from the position taken in that self-revealing, prescient letter. Over and over again, sentiment would build up to draft him for this or that office—including the Presidency of the United States—which he neither sought nor at heart desired. Momentarily he might be tempted, and might play the coy reluctant, but these flirtations never went far. Jilted politicians might wail that he left them at the church, and perplexed friends might and would charge him with timidity, insincerity, and irregularity (that horrid word in politics) ; but being conventional themselves (and no human activity is regulated by stricter conventions than politics), they were ill equipped to grasp that William J. Gaynor could not conform to any convention long. The two opposing motives—the bent toward solitude, study, serenity, contemplation, everything he summed up in the word "contentment," and the joy in combat—were still at war and would continue to be at war in him. They would lead him into utterances that were contradictory ; and he could mischievously enjoy misleading others, especially self-important and pompous people; but in the main, his plain speaking and his cryptic silences alike would be sincere. And if they were inconsistent, well, who and what in life are not?

When Gaynor returned to Bellport from Riverhead, after finally rejecting a doomed nomination, he was noticed to be "considerably worked up." There was good cause for this; he had been holding court from nine o'clock in the morning until eight and nine o'clock at night, with an hour's break for lunch and another for dinner, and at the same time was being continually badgered to enter the political free-for-all again. The nervous strain had told, and the first thing he did on reaching his summer home was to throw himself astride a horse and gallop along country lanes for a couple of hours to clear the fumes from his brain. In consequence he was in a fairly approachable mood when a *New York World* reporter showed up, bent on finding out more about this enigmatic judge.

Already the news sleuth had gathered that while Gaynor was greatly respected in the neighborhood, he was not exactly a popular man socially; his manner was too cool. The reporter set him down as "approachable, but not desirous of being approached." Gaynor seemed to be indifferent to what people might be saying about him, though he was curious in a good-natured, offhand way.

One thing the reporter learned with surprise was that although renowned for his legal erudition, the judge read only as much law as was necessary for the discharge of his duties, and never read law at night. Once the lamps were lighted, he read philosophy, history (especially Hallam and Gibbon), Homer in the original, Shakespeare, Milton, Cervantes—anything, in fact, except law books. That was the way to escape the narrowness that comes from constant application to a single subject, he said.

The judge shrugged aside questions about his attitude to the police, whom he had recently called "greatly overrated." Yes, he conceded, he preferred the police systems of the great cities of Europe; there was too much of the "move on" sentiment among the police in New York. As for "position," Gaynor scorned it.

"The best thing we can hope for is to do something for the betterment of mankind," he philosophized. "In the end there is only a hole six feet by two. I would rather be the author of a good book than the mightiest ruler in the world."

The next day Gaynor went fishing with his eldest son, Rufus, a bright boy of seven or eight. The reporter was invited to come along in the boat rowed by an old sailor. Gaynor's hunger for information about everything that came under observation was apparent. He asked about the topography of the shore, about local folklore, traditions, the tides, navigation, the habits of fish, what fishermen earned, and a dozen other subjects. He put his questions rapidly and pointedly, and sometimes anticipated the boatman's replies. Then he recast the answers in simple, interesting terms for the benefit of the child. All this was done in the most natural way, for the teacher impulse in Gaynor was always strong, and he was at his best with very young children. Already he had four of his own—Rufus and Norman, and two daughters, Gertrude and Edith.

An incident in court illustrated how children took to Gaynor despite his forbidding air; they could read something in those inscrutable eyes that grownups could not. A negligence case was being tried. A small boy had sustained severe injuries, including the loss of the use of one hand. The boy was put on the witness stand to show the jury the extent of his injuries, and to make the matter clear he took off his coat. But when he came to put it back on, he had difficulty. Turning to the bearded man in the big chair, the child said quite naturally, "Will you please help me on with my coat, mister?" Instantly Gaynor was on his feet, and the coat was adjusted with his hands.

Family matters with the judge were taboo for publication. Stories were circulated about the Gaynor eccentricities at home, and these increased when, shortly after his election, he moved from 212 St. Johns Place to a commodious four-story brownstone at 20 Eighth Avenue, across the street from the Montauk Club's adaptation of the Cà d'Oro of Venice and a stone's throw from the entrance to Prospect Park. The house had an air of gentility and solid respectability, as had that whole stretch of Eighth Avenue; it was sometimes called "Sportsmen's Row" because of the number of residents who were prominently connected with horse racing.*

Mrs. Gaynor was a woman of considerable beauty; President Taft's military aide, Archie Butt, who had an eye for loveliness, spoke approvingly of her. In the Eighth Avenue house four more children would be born, three of whom—Ruth, Marion, and Helen— would reach maturity. As time passed, however, Gaynor grew withdrawn from his family; their interests were foreign to his, and he was more and more preoccupied with his work and intellectual pursuits. His temper was like a barrel of gunpowder in the basement, likely to blow the establishment sky-high at any second. The second floor of the Eighth Avenue house became his exclusively; there he had his library, which he also used as an office, and his bedroom, with connecting bath and dressing quarters. No one was allowed to intrude there except the housemaid who cleaned up. A niece of Mrs. Gaynor would recall visiting at Eighth Avenue as a child, and how

---

* That block of brownstones still stands, little changed outwardly and handsomely maintained although devoted now to doctors' offices.

when going up the stairs she would tiptoe past the judge's door on the second landing, quaking in terror lest it fly open and the formidable bearded figure come charging out demanding who was making unnecessary noise. None of the Gaynors, besides the judge, had intellectual tastes, the children inheriting their mother's social instincts and lightheartedness, and her interest in sports and society.

Gaynor's private secretary from 1897 to 1905 was James P. Kohler, and after he and the judge parted, his son, Philip Kohler, succeeded to the position. Many were the tales they told of Gaynor's peculiarities at work and at home. The Kohlers spent much time at Eighth Avenue and knew the family well, and both said that while the children admired their father, once they reached their teens they had hardly any vital contacts with him.*

Gaynor had strange ways of showing his affection for them. During the Nineties, when bicycling was a craze, he took it up, and as a special indulgence would allow Helen, then still very small, to accompany him on her little bicycle. Off they would start, Gaynor pedaling at a steady clip that forced Helen with her short legs to pump furiously to keep up. If they hit a downgrade, she would spurt to get far enough ahead to stop a minute and catch her breath. Her father would come on, overtake her, and sail past without a glance at where she stood flushed and panting, and she would jump back on her bike and pump frantically to catch up again.

In personal transactions the judge was scrupulously honest, and he expected others to be the same. But he was neither fair, courteous, nor considerate toward his close associates. His secretary was expected to know what to do without being told; if he did the right thing, it passed unnoticed, but if the wrong thing, he was likely to have a book hurled at his head. In all their years of serving Gaynor, the Kohlers maintained, he never once gave them a "good morning" or "good night," though young Kohler would sometimes be dismissed with a growled, "Get out of here, you goddam puppy!" Gaynor repeatedly told James Kohler, who was a graduate of Columbia Law School, that he would never amount to anything as a secretary and could do better for himself practicing law. Yet in spite of daily abuse, both the Kohlers stuck; the prestige of working for a Supreme Court justice—and a famous one at that—in part held them, and the salary was fair; but the main attraction was Gaynor himself: peculiarities and grossnesses aside, he fascinated them. In a

* The youngest of his children, Ruth, would say in 1968: "What little I know about my father is mostly from hearsay."

vague way they sensed in him a streak of unique superiority, a nobility, a breadth of outlook and magnanimity of purpose that were clouded and modified but never quite hidden under the overlay of willful contrariety. For some reason, they could not exactly say why, every time they were driven to the point of resigning they held back; and their impression of the man never left them.

Gaynor's relations with his wife were alternate periods of storm and calm. That the marriage lasted at all was due to her immense forbearance. According to the secretaries, Gaynor often humiliated his wife, and his terrible temper was a trial to the whole household. Late one winter's night (their story ran) the judge came home and found a gaslight burning. In a rage he awakened the servants and turned them into the street in bitter cold, and it took all Mrs. Gaynor's persuasiveness to get them inside again. Mrs. Gaynor told a friend that the judge once turned her out of the house in a blizzard. Her patience was infinite, and she needed all of it, although the younger Kohler insisted that there was a slug in the woodwork of the front hall that had been meant for the judge and missed.

The family lived comfortably though not ostentatiously, yet Gaynor was capable of cutting off money for household expenses for days at a time. Every month his secretary would place a check for the monthly bills on the judge's desk, and if he was in the signing mood he would sign it; if not, he would brush it off onto the floor with a curse. To tide the family over such periods of drought, Mrs. Gaynor had an arrangement with the butcher, an understanding man and great admirer of the judge. He would advance her money, which later he would add to the bill disguised as purchases of meat. Gaynor never caught on.

Because he disdained to use a wastebasket, the floor of the library was always littered with papers, to the despair of the servants, who, Gaynor complained on his side, fiendishly messed up his files. Most of his meals he took alone on the second floor, and he spent long hours there, dictating, reading, and conversing on serious subjects with clergymen of the neighborhood and friends. For scholarship, wherever manifested, he had profound respect. Mirabeau L. Towns, a lawyer who won cases by making up rhymes to make his opponent look ridiculous, lived next door on Eighth Avenue, and he and the judge had similar literary tastes. Often they would discuss philosophy over a congenial glass far into the night.

Other erudite friends were the Rev. James F. O'Donohue, pastor of the Catholic church of St. Thomas Aquinas nearby, and Dr. William Morrison, rector of St. John's Protestant Episcopal Church, where the Gaynor family worshiped, although the judge never formally became a communicant.

In only one respect was Gaynor conventional, and that was in his dress. He took pride in being well turned out, and his costume was always correct for the occasion. In the city his usual garb was a frock coat, dark gray striped trousers, dark tie with high wing collar, and a silk hat. For the country he favored a tweed suit, light vest, and a cap or flat-topped derby. His beard was neatly trimmed and his walk was graceful and springy. His hands and feet were noticeably small and delicately formed. An enthusiastic pedestrian, he thought nothing of hikes several miles long. He once challenged Recorder John W. Goff, a hearty Irishman, to a mile-and-a-quarter walking match and was put out when Goff, in a last-minute spurt, won by less than a length. During the Nineties Gaynor gave up smoking, but he liked his whisky; his secretaries were used to seeing him come in from a long walk on a cold day, pour half a tumblerful and down it, making appreciative noises.

Now and then Mrs. Gaynor and the judge took in the theater or a concert, and some summers they went abroad together; in other years he took his vacation alone. He was intensely fond of England and English ways, and English jurisprudence he venerated. His favorite recreation during working periods was a "wine supper"—a late dinner with a few cronies at Delmonico's or some other good restaurant, and then long, lively talk over a bottle of wine (he liked champagne), on politics, history, literature, the law, whatever subject came to mind. During such sessions he had a habit of stroking his beard, under the chin, upward, in great contentment. His capacity for spirits seemed bottomless, and the only effect one of these outings had on him was to sharpen his tongue, give a little more bite to his sarcasm, and make him more prompt, more exacting, and perhaps more irascible in court the next day.

Ira L. Bamberger was a Brooklyn lawyer whom the judge liked to take along on these drink-and-talk fests. One evening Bamberger, fighting a nasty cold, had just got into bed after a hot bath when the telephone rang. Judge Gaynor was on the line, insisting that Bamberger join him in uptown Yorkville for a wine supper. Bamberger tried to beg off, but Gaynor refused to listen; and not wishing to offend the judge, the invalid dragged himself out of bed, dressed, and made the long ride to the appointed restaurant. Their talk lasted well into the night, and more than one cork was popped.

Bamberger was due to argue a case in Gaynor's court the next morning. Gaynor arrived promptly, spruce and businesslike, but Bamberger was not on hand when his case was called. When he did totter in, late, the judge beckoned him to the bar and lectured him on his remissness, winding up with:

"From your appearance you would seem to have fallen among bad companions."

Bamberger retired, furious. Gaynor's unsmiling playfulness was not always appreciated by its victims.

But in contrast to his private failings, the judge's "public image" (as the cant of a later day would have it) waxed steadily more sternly benign. At the start of 1895 he figured in a celebrated strike of Brooklyn streetcar workers that brought out the National Guard to suppress rioting and caused lasting bitterness. The company, after several bloody battles, abandoned all pretense of running their cars, and application was made in the name of a taxpayer to force them to resume service. Another judge, Justice Cullen, had refused to grant a writ of mandamus ordering the Brooklyn City Railway Company to reopen its lines immediately, and Gaynor's action was awaited with tense expectancy by both sides in the dispute. He issued the mandamus, laying down the rule that a public service corporation's duty to the people transcends its obligation to its stockholders.

"This railroad corporation is not in the position of a private individual or company carrying on business for private gain, which may suspend temporarily or permanently at pleasure," the decision read. "On the contrary, it has a dual relation, a public relation to the people of this state, and a private one to its stockholders. It must not be forgotten here, though it may seem to be growing dim if not wholly forgotten elsewhere, that in its chief aspect it is a public corporation, having its duties to perform to the public. . . .

"It has received franchises of great value from the state, and has conferred upon it the state's transcendent power of eminent domain. In return it took upon itself the performance of public duties and functions, in the performance of which it is in law and in fact not an independent individual or entity, but the accountable agent of the state. Though these principles are old and inherent in the idea of the sovereignty of the people, it would seem that, due to the rapid growth of corporate power and of the tendency to use franchises for the aggrandizement of individuals first and for the service and benefit of the public second, they have come to be somewhat overlooked and need to be restated. . . .

"The duty of the company now before the court is to carry passengers through certain streets of Brooklyn and furnish men and cars enough to fully accommodate the public. It may not lawfully cease to perform that duty for even one hour. . . . The directors . . . are not merely accountable to the stockholders; they are accountable to the public first and the stockholders second. They have duties to the public to perform and they must perform them. If they can not get labor to perform those duties at what they offer to pay, then they must pay more, and as much as is necessary to get it. Likewise, if the conditions in respect of hours and otherwise which they impose repel labor, they must adopt more lenient and just conditions. They must not stop their cars for one hour, much less one week or one year, to thereby beat or coerce the price or conditions of labor down to the conditions they offer.

"To do so," the conclusion read, "would be a defiance of law and government, which, becoming general, would inevitably, by the force of example, lead to general disquiet and the disintegration of the social order and even the downfall of the government itself. Experience shows the wisdom of our fathers in retaining at least some control of corporations to whom are given public franchises for the performance of public services. . . . It must not be forgotten that this corporation is entrusted with the running of these roads as the servant of the people of the state."

The decision overjoyed the strikers, but to the *New York Times* it suggested that Justice Gaynor was a firebrand of radicalism. In a scandalized editorial, the *Times* said that what was said of Gladstone in the time of the Crimean War might be said of Gaynor, namely, that he was "in the worst sense a good man. . . . There is in his mental operations a tendency which can only be fairly designated as anarchistic." In fact, he was giving signs of "yielding to influences which, if followed to their logical conclusion, would break up society."

The *Brooklyn Eagle* reprinted the *Times*'s strictures and a reporter showed them to Gaynor.

"Well, I can't help it," was his rejoinder. "If my having joined with the best people of Brooklyn, without regard to politics, and done some little in helping them to lift things up here, and to make government better here, and to prevent gross wrongs upon the people of Brooklyn, and to destroy the anarchy which existed so long in Gravesend and scandalized us all, leads to my being characterized in this manner, I can't help it. I can only stand and take it."

Then, in the feline way in which he would strike at an adversary from an unexpected direction, he added:

"However, I am not unaware of the present control and inspiration of the *Times*. Many people in Brooklyn might be astonished to learn it."

The *Eagle* itself had cause for astonishment early in that fall of 1895, when Gaynor was boomed for mayor of Brooklyn. This position he had come to covet sincerely; he had so many ideas he longed to put into effect to bring about a reformation of the municipal government from bottom to top. "To make Brooklyn so clean and forward-looking that the political tone of the whole state would be placed on a higher level," was the way he repeatedly defined this ambition.

He seemed the logical candidate for the Republicans to nominate. The independents rallied to him at a mass demonstration at the Academy of Music. The Democrats were split between the reform faction and the regulars, neither of whom wanted Gaynor. The regulars, while they would gladly have helped to kick him upstairs to Albany, shuddered at the prospect of having him cock of the walk in their own backyard. And the reformers suddenly discovered that Gaynor was politically minded. At *their* rally Shepard tore into him as that monstrosity, a political judge, who, "either openly, silently, or by mystical utterances," was permitting lawyers practicing before him to urge his claims.

"You have no right," Shepard lectured, "while on the bench, directly or indirectly, to make partisan or political appeals or personal attacks, or to permit your friends, no matter how you may hedge about your acquiescence, to make you a candidate for a local nomination not judicial."

Again the Republican leadership hung fire, until County Chairman George Foster Peabody, a vestryman of Holy Trinity Church, balked at naming a Democrat and said so. Gaynor's reaction was bitterly sarcastic:

"May I say that in the four years in which I was trying to do something to make government in Brooklyn decent . . . I was never offered either aid or encouragement by Mr. Foster Peabody? . . . The people of Brooklyn know that I am not a candidate for the great office of mayor, and if I were, I should be looking to them . . . and not to Mr. Foster Peabody for a nomination. . . . I have noticed that Mr. Foster Peabody has picked a committee of four or five to meet with some other committee of four or five to pick out a mayor for the people of Brooklyn. I thought we had done with this sort of business in Brooklyn."

Well, *was* he a candidate, even if only in hope and expectation? wondered the *Eagle*. Solemnly Gaynor assured them:

"We are all in the hands of Providence, and Providence put me where I am without any seeking or effort on my part."

This seemed to be carrying Sybilline crypticism too far. The plain meaning of the oracle to the *Eagle* seemed to be that "Providence, having made him a judge, can also make him a mayor. He seems almost to be persuaded that the lottery of his destiny bars him from the right of voluntary choice. . . . Custom has not familiarized us with anything of the kind."

But Providence was not in the giving mood. The Republicans nominated Frederick W. Wurster, and the Democrats stayed split, the reform element nominating Shepard and the regulars naming Edward M. Grout, Gaynor's former law partner. Gaynor backed Grout, and Wurster was elected.

Gaynor allowed the hurt inflicted by this disappointment to be seen. Had the united Democrats offered the nomination, he confessed, he would have felt obliged to accept, though "I am thankful that I have always been disinclined to run for public office. I saw early that it was not those in public office who do the most good. The unknown writer of one little book, claimed and read by every denomination of Christians, has done more for mankind than all the men who ever held public office.

"I might as well say," he went on, "that I had in mind something more than bringing about good government in Brooklyn. I had in mind a lifting up of government in Brooklyn that would be an object lesson in New York City and all over the state. I had in mind that government on a high plane in Brooklyn meant, as inevitably as the rising and setting of the sun, the downfall of bad government in the City of New York. The mayor of Brooklyn, with practically all the power vested in his hands, has a greater opportunity to illuminate the traditions and philosophy of free and enlightened government, as it directly touches the people at every point, and concerns individual liberty and right, than the governor of any of our states, or the President of the United States."

The lost chance was dismissed with a sigh:

"It may have been an exaltation or a dream. But I think not. I think not. It will all be in God's time."

So he drilled himself to wait, impatiently patient, while resuming the judicial round with vigor undiminished and principles unimpaired. The setback did not in the least lessen his hold on the imagination of the public, and his sayings and decisions were quoted more widely than before.

The circulation given to one ruling that he handed down shortly after his snubbing by the political nabobs of Brooklyn may have helped to salve his injured pride. Written in the simplest language, and, as one admiring newspaper pointed out, "singularly devoid of the usual meanderings of the law," it concerned two boys, orphans. They had been living with their maternal grandmother, and their stepfather was suing to get custody. Gaynor, having studied the evidence and seen for himself the conditions under which the children were cared for, ruled as follows:

"These two little boys, eight and seven years old, having lost their father and mother, have since lived with their maternal grandmother, Mrs. Bessie G. Reed, of Stapleton, Staten Island. Her unmarried son and daughter are also of the household. The grandmother owns the modest house in which they all live. She is the housekeeper, and the son and daughter earn wages as skilled workers in Appleton's book bindery, and besides, these little boys have an income of about $30 a month from property left by their parents. The household is thus comfortable and it is happy, also.

"The little boys are going to the public school. The daughter (their aunt) is a refined and attractive young woman. She is very fond of them. She is now deaf and dumb, though not born so, and they have become part of her life. She has taught them the sign language, and I saw them all talking together.

"I have not been able to bring myself to take these little boys away from this family. It would be like two deaths in the house. I find it easy to refuse them to the stepfather. He is, in fact, trying by this writ to get them only to deliver them over to their paternal grandmother. I have not found it so easy to refuse her. She has quite an estate and offers to make her will in their favor if their custody is given to her. But money is not everything in this short life. Those who have it know how delusive is the notion that it brings peace or happiness. I think it best to leave these children where they are; but their paternal grandmother ought to visit them and they ought to visit her. She is an intelligent, good woman. The writ is dismissed."

Accessible to the public, fearless in their defense but refusing to prostitute justice to partisanship, Gaynor as a judge reflected the tastes of the ordinary people, the common man and woman. He showed an easygoing sympathy with their day-by-day anxieties and aspirations that was sometimes shocking to the strait-laced and Puritanical. His understanding of human nature was extensive, and his toleration of merely bothersome backsliders from the stricter moral codes was large. He did not believe that men could be transformed into angels, certainly not in his time, and he had clear notions about the respective and separate roles of the educating forces (school and church) and the governing forces (law and custom) in the community.

While his opinions were written with utmost care, and corrected in copy again and again, his *obiter dicta* were sparks thrown off between taps of the gavel. He enjoyed these sallies, salty or sly, and played to the gallery with relish; there had always been a tinge of the actor in Gaynor, as there is in most successful trial lawyers. He brought the fascination of the law home to laymen, and made it interesting and comprehensible to waiters, clerks, and housewives. He might be laughed at, and often was, for his quaintness, and he frequently was damned for his despotic ways, but he was inordinately respected and, above all and by all, trusted.

The judge's critics averred that he was *too* human and broad-minded, but as the years moved into the new century his step remained spry and his mind elastic while he went about championing the underdog, calling for social progress, and berating the block-headedness of judges who tried to stop it, crying up the rights of the common man, and enjoying every minute of his crowded days.

His charge to the jury in a suit for divorce in 1899 stirred up a typical gale of criticism, which he took in stride. Boldly stating the law governing the case, he said:

"The church should not meddle with the laws of the state. No matter what your religious belief may be, you are drawn as jurors, and asked to give a verdict according to the laws of the state. The

marriage question is a question with the state, and refers only to
property obligations, and can be secured only by law. The religious
question does not enter into it. The only thing to be considered is
the question of property obligation. The church should not interfere
with the laws regarding marriage. After a marriage has been annulled, if the church wants to say the parties are still married, that
is its own business. But we do not wish the church to meddle with our
laws. It matters not what your religious opinion or religious belief on
the question of divorce is, in deciding this case you must consider
only the law, which allows a marriage to be annulled when the contract has been broken by either party."

This doctrine was politically perilous in Brooklyn in 1899, and
it undoubtedly harked back, in part, to his own experience, and the
stand he had taken and the stand taken by his church at the time of
his divorce in 1881. His charge, delivered eighteen years later, was
still fervid but just.

Gaynor cared no more for the public's response to his anti-
clericalism than he did for the animosity aroused by his frequent
blasts at corporate greed, especially as manifested in the exploiting
of public-service franchises for private gain, and his actions to at
least curb some of those iniquities. When the Ramapo Water Company angled to get control of the Brooklyn water system, he fought
it, although offered the presidency of the company at a salary of
$50,000 a year. He investigated the notorious Ice Trust formed by
Charles Morse—a scheme to exploit the poor of New York's slums
by controlling the price of ice during the torrid summer months.
Morse eventually went to prison, and it was revealed that the mayor
of New York, Robert Van Wyck, as well as Tammany boss Richard
Croker, and Charles F. Murphy, soon to succeed him, and a long
list of other politicians, all had large blocks of stock in the business.

An attempted robbery of the people that Gaynor twice knocked
on the head by judicial action was the scheme of Patrick Jerome
Gleason, mayor of Long Island City, to supply that city with water
by a company in which he owned almost all the stock, besides directly
and personally owning the land from which the water supply was
drawn.

"The said mayor and commissioners," Gaynor recited, "have
discontinued pumping stations in the city and removed machinery
and created a water scarcity and alarm for the benefit of [Gleason's]
company. The said contract was made without the consent of the
common council, though the city charter requires such consent. By

the charter of the city all officials of the city are prohibited from
being interested directly or indirectly in any contract with the
city. . . . The facts present a scandalous case of official dishonor,
corruption, and betrayal of trust, and the denials presented impair
them very little if at all."

Gleason at the time was offering himself as a candidate for
mayor of New York City. Gaynor's blast failed to induce him to
retire from the race.

But the theme that occupied the judge more than any other
was the callous disregard shown by the police for the elementary
rights of the citizens, and the long-continued passive acceptance of
police usurpations by the abused public. He struck again and again
at the special iniquities of violent police raids on gambling places
and suspected disorderly houses without warrants, and the arbitrary
jailing of people for supposed infractures of the Sunday blue laws.
Both practices infuriated him.

In regard to Sunday observance, he was liberal. He believed
that people had a right to spend Sunday as they wished, as long as
they did not disturb the religious repose of the community or engage
in work forbidden in the statutes. Again and again he released boys
and young men who had been locked up by officious policemen for
Sunday ball playing. In setting one such group free, Gaynor delivered a long opinion in which he said:

"This is one of a class of cases in which it is the duty of the
judiciary to speak out plainly, after the manner of judges in times
past. I therefore deem it not at all outside of my judicial office to add
to what I have already said that it is practically the unanimous
sentiment of the religious and God-fearing people of this community
that it is far better for grown boys and young men who have to
work indoors all the week for a living to go into the fields on Sunday
afternoon after attending church and participate in, or witness,
good, elevating, healthy physical exercise, than to be driven instead
to go to dance gardens, drinking places, poolrooms, and worse
places. . . .

"The real sentiment of the community has to be consulted in
the enforcement of certain laws. . . . It is a maxim of the law that
you can not indict a whole community. The Anglo-Saxon sheds
statutes which grow obsolete and obnoxious the same as a snake sheds
its skin. He has seldom bothered to repeal them, as everyone acquainted with the history of laws very well knows. No citizen any
longer makes a complaint under them, and thus they become dead-

letter laws. It is not the business of the police to revive them. They are not employed and paid by the citizens for any such purpose."

Gaynor would point out that especially in New York was an attempt to impose a Puritanical Sabbath as senseless as pressing a stale claim. New York and its environs formed the most cosmopolitan city in the world, its population drawn from every quarter of the globe. Each of its many nationalities and races had customs and traditions of their own, and Gaynor invoked historical examples to demonstrate that "Christians of no nation, church, or sect, except the British Isles (and not there until recent centuries) ever entertained the Old Testament notion of a still Sabbath, but favored and practiced healthy exercises and amusements after church on Sunday. John Knox visited John Calvin on a Sunday afternoon at Geneva, and found him out back at a game of bowls on the green. The man who works stripped to the waist at a blast-furnace all week knows what he wants on Sunday. The anemic boy who slaves in a store all week knows what he wants on Sunday. It is not for the police, who have no more authority than other citizens, to say whether innocent and wholesome sports shall be forbidden on Sunday."

The police captain who arrested the boys in the case was pilloried:

"He sets himself above the law, a thing grown very common with the police of this city of late years. . . . It can not be too often said . . . that our government, like all free governments, is a government of laws and not of men. Those who try to turn it into one of men and not of laws are more dangerous to society than any other class of lawbreakers, or all lawbreakers combined."

Nor did Gaynor object to a little gambling, provided it was conducted decorously and public order was maintained. He held a mortgage on the Brighton race track that had come to him in a related business transaction, and he never foreclosed. He defended the merry-go-rounds and Ferris wheels at Coney Island, and when his children were little took them there. And he believed thoroughly in not interfering with people who were disturbing nobody, while living as they wanted to, whether their way happened to be that of their next-door neighbors or not.

The violent antipathy Gaynor held toward police raids on disorderly resorts—the smashing in of doors and windows and wrecking interiors and making arrests promiscuously—all without war-

rants, on mere suspicion and hearsay—culminated in a paper contributed to the *North American Review* in January, 1903. This
courageous attack on a widespread abuse of police power—just
then being carried to sensational extremes by New York's crusading
district attorney, William Travers Jerome, a man of talent but not
much balance—made Gaynor known all over the nation. Pro and
con, it was debated with heat. The title, and the theme, of the
article was "The Lawlessness of the Police of New York," and in it
he coined phrases that would become watchwords of the period, including this famous declaration:

"A policeman (to speak so plainly that everyone may understand) is only a citizen dressed in blue clothes and brass buttons
(and sometimes with a club in his belt or pocket), with no right or
lawful power of arrest without a warrant which all his fellow-citizens
do not possess; and he should be taught by those in authority over
him never to forget this fact. His fellow-citizens have not made him
their master, but only their honorable servant."

And the maxim which he repeated so often it became a refrain:

"The principal duty of the police is to preserve the public
peace, and keep outward order and decency."

Invasion of private property by police on mere suspicion of
wrongdoing inside, without a warrant, made Gaynor see red. He
inveighed against it, and against the apathy of the citizens who
submitted to it.

"Such oppression is a grave criminal offense," he wrote. "That
such outrages are not forcibly resisted by our people does not so
much testify to their well-known peaceable character as to the extent
to which they have lost that keen sense of personal right which char-
acterizes a free people. . . . The genius of a whole people, instinct
with love of liberty and constitutional government, was quick . . .
to declare what now sounds in the City of New York as an empty
boast, though it became and remains a great constitutional maxim,
with a history and a literature of its own, viz., that every man's
house is his castle. Its declaration was a revolution in government
and in human liberty. It is still as pregnant of the individual rights
and liberties of a free people as when it first emanated from what
Coke called the unpolished genius of the people. It is as vital now
as when Chatham said of it, in his speech against the practice of
issuing general or roving warrants for searches and seizures:

" 'The poorest man may in his cottage bid defiance to all the forces of the Crown. It may be frail; its roof may shake; the wind may blow through it; the storm may enter; the rain may enter; but the King of England may not enter; all his force dares not cross the threshold of the ruined tenement.' "

Because the danger was insidious was the more reason to guard against it.

"Cicero said of Julius Caesar that as he looked at him adjusting his hair so nicely and scratching his head with one finger, that it never occurred to him that such a man could conceive so vast and fatal a design as the destruction of the Roman commonwealth. . . . It is often of little consequence, and seldom of great consequence, whether an individual suspected or actually guilty of a criminal offense be arrested or convicted of it; but it is always of transcendent importance that he be not arrested or convicted except in accordance with those restrictions and safeguards which the people, taught by dire experience, and guarding against a recurrence of arbitrary power, have by their constitutions and laws prescribed. . . ."

Directing his fire at those "societies, and private enthusiasts, for the 'suppression of vice,' " who urged the necessity of extralegal methods to combat crime and vice effectively, Gaynor advised that they "read history, and learn the supreme danger of trying to do all at once by the policeman's club what can be done at all only gradually by the slow moral development which comes principally from our schools and churches. . . .

"The notion that the morals of the community can be reformed and made better, or that government can be purified and lifted up, instead of being debased and demoralized, by the policeman's club and axe, is so pernicious and dangerous in any government, let alone a free government, that no one can harbor it whose intellectuals are not, as Macaulay says, 'in that most unhappy of all states, that is to say, too much disordered for liberty, and not sufficiently disordered for Bedlam.'

"It would be difficult to speak with forbearance of the strange pretense that the police could not enforce the law if they kept within the law themselves. . . . Crimes and vices are evils to the community; but it behooves a free people never to forget that they have more to fear from the growth of the one vice of arbitrary power in government than from all the other vices and crimes combined. It debases everybody, and brings in its train all of the vices."

This article he followed, in the same magazine, the next month, with another entitled "A Government of Laws, Not of Men," in which he laid down the rule:

"When a prosecuting attorney, or a police official, says, 'I can't detect crime, I can't discover gamblers or wayward women, in their privacy, by keeping within the law,' the emphatic answer of the law is, 'Then don't.' "

These outspoken articles provoked censure in some quarters on the grounds of impropriety; but Gaynor plainly avowed his conviction that "though a judge, off the bench, may not say everything, he may say very much more than that his soul is his own, without violating any rule of etiquette." Judges generally, he added, agreed with him.

He backed his belief by action. In a celebrated case in which a policeman named Glennon was convicted before Gaynor's friend, Recorder Goff, of neglect of duty in failing to suppress a house of ill fame in his district, Gaynor granted a certificate of reasonable doubt; reluctantly, he said, because of his great respect for Goff; but he simply could not understand parts of the recorder's charge to the jury. The section under which Glennon was indicted he called a "crude experiment" and an "extraordinary law," and pointed out that because the term of imprisonment imposed was only six months, the unfortunate man would be without redress, should his conviction be in fact erroneous, because he would have served the full time before an appeal could be disposed of. Gaynor's opinion, written with care, read in part:

"The indictment accuses the defendant, a patrolman of the police force, of the misdemeanor of willfully neglecting to detect and arrest the woman keeper of a house of ill fame; the keeping of such a house being a misdemeanor. The indictment is loose and verbose, but this is the principal accusation it contains. . . . It contains such empty accusations as (in substance) that the defendant did not 'repress' or 'suppress' the said house. What this means I do not know, unless the draughtsman entertained the dangerous notion that policemen have the right to go about at will invading, raiding, and 'suppressing' houses and arresting persons without a warrant, acting at once as accuser and judge. If they had such power, then anyone could be 'suppressed' and the government would no longer be free, but a despotism."

Then remarking that the trial judge had recognized that the patrolman had no right to arrest the keeper of the house unless he knew that the place was being kept for immoral purposes, he inquired how the policeman might obtain this knowledge, and quoted Goff's answer to this riddle:

" 'The knowledge of the existence of the house [this is the recorder speaking to the jury] may be acquired by the defendant in different ways. It is not necessary that there should be evidence before you of some one having told him that such a house was a house of ill fame; nor is it necessary that there should be evidence before you which would prove that the defendant saw disorderly and indecent practices in the house, in order to charge him with knowledge of its existence.'

"I find myself unable to understand this," Gaynor confessed. How could the defendant learn about the house otherwise than by hearing or seeing? "Man has but five senses. Excluding the two (seeing and hearing), the only ones left for the defendant to acquire knowledge by were smelling, tasting, or touching. How he could have obtained knowledge of the house and its inmates by these means was not explained.

"The learned judge then instructs that they could find that the defendant possessed what he termed a 'conscious knowledge' of the character of the house, though he did not actually acquire it by either hearing or seeing. I am at a loss over this. What is this 'conscious knowledge' that one may get possessed of without the aid of the senses? Such an inquiry seems to lead us into the occult realm and mysteries of psychology. You would not like to have it possible that every or any policeman could imagine he is conscious of something being wrong in your house, and invade it and arrest you. What would a magistrate say to a policeman applying to him for a warrant on such a theory as that?"

In another notable case, when the police vice squad smashed into a poolroom on Park Row, arrested sixteen men found there, seized records, and chopped up furniture and valuable equipment, all without a vestige of legality, without a warrant, Gaynor scored the action as "mob violence" and "criminal lawlessness," set the men free, and told them they would have been justified in resisting the invasion "to the last extremity."

Naturally the police authorities were dazed and resentful of this august voice of dissent coming across the river. Their frustration was plainly, though drolly, expressed by the New York police commissioner, William McAdoo, at the banquet of the Friendly Sons of St. Patrick at Delmonico's. Directly after every raid, said McAdoo, "the owners rush out affidavits, and then a well-known firm of lawyers [Gaynor's former partners], who make a specialty of this work, are called in; a bundle of papers is taken over to Brooklyn; the judge instantly grants the writs, denounces the police commissioner, shrieks for personal liberty, talks about Russian despotism, and threatens the governor if the police commissioner is not removed at once."

With a Gaynor on the rampage, surely a policeman's lot in New York City was not an enviable one. The public, however, cheered on the judge, and at the same time the mass of citizens was set to thinking about the unwholesome situation. Gaynor was educating, educating, the teacher urge in him never still. His common-sense rulings pleased the crowd and his freewheeling erudition tickled the intellectuals. Even his severity was relished, when the shoe was on the other foot; and though some solemn-sides maintained that the irritable judge had no spark of humor, how otherwise could one construe his blithe basing of an important opinion on so lugubrious and recondite an authority as Burton's *Anatomy of Melancholy?* A woman was suing for divorce, accusing her husband of adultery, and the point was raised that while opportunity for the adulterous act had been shown, inclination to commit it had not.

Gaynor recited the facts briefly. The husband had met a woman not his wife at Grand Central Station; had taken her and her luggage to a hotel in a cab; had registered there as man and wife in his own handwriting; had gone to a room with her; and had not come down until midnight. Reviewing this fairly obvious sequence, Gaynor wrote:

"Although opportunity was shown, inclination, it is said, was not. But seeking such bedroom privacy was evidence of inclination stronger than any act of affection between them at the station or in the cab. What did they register in a hotel as man and wife and retire to a bedroom for? We have it of old that it is presumed 'he saith not a paternoster there.' (Burton's *Anat. of Mel.*, Vol. 2 (1st Amer. Ed.), P. 446, Part 3, Lec. 3, Mem. 1, Sub. 2.)"

This opinion, ticketed the "Paternoster Case," speedily found its way into the textbooks of law schools over the country. One of Gaynor's last official acts as a judge, it was issued in the midst of a wilder hullabaloo than any he had raised before, and just as he was about to embark on the great adventure of his life.

THE LONG, SLOW GROWTH

*A time-server, sir, is a swimmer who heads
downstream under the impression that he is
assisting the current.*

—AMBROSE BIERCE

FOR SIXTY-ONE YEARS W. J. Gaynor led what would come to seem
a relatively sequestered and tranquil existence. True, for certain of
his targets it had contained hair-raising moments; but through
these irruptions he had moved with a self-awareness, confidence, and
dignity suited to his judicial role. And gradually, through the turn-
of-the-century years, a wider and wider public found in the learned
judge's asperities and quixotic humor a source of entertainment, instruction, and sometimes soul-searching disagreement.

"In nothing commonplace and in few respects conventional, the
mind of Justice Gaynor is an attractive study," was the *Brooklyn
Eagle*'s opinion, in which thousands concurred. Although eclectically
embracing almost every human concern in its purview, that mind
never meandered. It might deflate the extreme claims of clericalism
by assuring a church audience that "there is nothing in religion
which laymen can not experience and understand as well as a theolo-
gian"; and the next day assail railroad rebating as "the greatest
crime of the age." His meaning was always precise, and his aim on
the whole was accurate. Week by week, year after year, the headlines traced his multifariousness and his unrelenting warfare on
ineptitude, posturing, and error.

"Gaynor Scores an Illiterate Lawyer"—"Shuts Up a Woman
Witness"—"Threatens to Punish Obstinate Juror"—"Criticizes

Grand Jury"—"Rebukes District Attorney"—"Scores Justice Kramer"—"Scores Justice Law"—"Severely Rebukes Judge Aspinwall" . . . these reflected his mood acerbic. So, too, did "Gaynor Belittles Woes of Woman Seeking Divorce." Benign was "Gaynor Holds Sunday Baseball No Worse Than Golf," to be followed by "Gaynor Attacks Overcrowded Cars"—"Rebukes Lawyer's Long-Winded Rigmarole" and "Tells Litigant He Lies"; in the midst of which sputtering from the bench would appear the paterfamilial "Gaynor Takes Daughter to Europe to Be Educated." Comic relief was provided by "Drunken Man in Court Nominates Gaynor for President."

In demand as a speaker, the judge appeared before all sorts of groups. He addressed the Society of Medical Jurisprudence at the Waldorf-Astoria in New York and the Philosophical Association in Brooklyn. He spoke in Boston, Buffalo, and Kansas City on political and economic topics; favoring equal pay for men and women teachers, and "taking down" the self-righteous who were agitating to prohibit moving-picture shows as a "demoralizing influence."

Society and social flummeries had no attractions for him. When Mrs. Gaynor entertained at a musicale for the benefit of St. John's Church, the judge was not on hand. But when he held court at Goshen, in rural Orange county, and boarded with the farmer who was foreman of the grand jury, he got up at 5 A.M. and helped his host milk the cows; a treat for him, he said; it took him back to his boyhood.

His passion for country life led him in 1905 to acquire a farm at St. James, a village on the north shore of Long Island about fifty miles east of New York. He had rented the place for three summers, and then characteristically had a dispute with the owner and through a dummy bought the property. There Gaynor would spend probably the most satisfying days of his life.

Setting up as a practical farmer—not for profit but for his health, he said—he had the place well stocked with horses, cattle, and pigs, the last his special joy; he would walk miles to see a prize porker. There were about sixty acres of land, on both sides of the highway, a mile from town. He took part in the farm work, and reporters often found him out in the fields. At harvest time he would lend a hand to a neighbor, and he drove a wagonload of his own potatoes to market with pride. The house was big and square, with a wide front porch overhung by lofty shade trees. There Gaynor liked to sit in a rocking chair through the drowsy summer evenings, usually with a glass of refreshment at hand. Deepwells was the name given the estate, but Gaynor knew it better as "the farm."

He had given up the saddle by the time he acquired Deepwells, but he continued to drive, and had a fine calming hand on a mettle-some horse in harness. Walking, however, was his principal exer-cise. A common sight around St. James, no matter what the weather, came to be the judge, with a motley escort of dogs, hiking along, hands clasped behind him, wearing baggy pants, a jacket with bits of straw and hayseed sticking to it, and a cap. He was always ready to stop and chat with a farmer, and he knew them all for miles around, or to compliment a farmer's wife on her eggs and butter.

His friends at St. James were not the wealthy summer residents, whose lawn parties and preoccupation with horsiness set the tone during the season. Gaynor preferred the company of the villagers—W. H. Monaghan, the blacksmith, and Melville Smith, who ran the livery stable, and a clam digger named James J. Snook. With these the judge would argue politics and philosophy for hours, sometimes sharing with them from a bottle of what he called "White Mule." A close friend was the town drunkard and ne'er-do-well, "Captain" Frank De Mott. The "Captain" had once been prosperous (he originally owned the Gaynor farm), but after the death of his young wife had gone to pieces. He lived during the summer by doing odd jobs, and each fall committed some petty thievery that would insure his being sent to the Riverhead jail for the winter. De Mott was well educated, and Gaynor respected his intelligence. The two would tramp the byways together, moralizing on history, literature, and human foibles, in complete harmony. It was on returning from one of these philosophical rambles that Gaynor remarked:

"What a strange world! By that I mean, how strange the people in it!"

Gaynor's fits of temper were not prorogued at St. James. It was evident that there were tensions in the family, and the townsfolk noticed that sometimes the judge and his wife, arriving from the city, would alight from separate cars at the railroad station. The villagers believed that nothing pleased the judge so much as "raisin' hell"; yet on the whole the farm was a safety valve for Gaynor's high-pressure vitality. So firmly was he drawn to this country home that during the winter, when the house at Deepwells was closed, he would come down for weekends, staying with Mel Smith, and hold-

ing long talk-sessions in the kitchen with his cronies over ginger-
bread and cider.

In the city, too, he had unorthodox companions with whom he
could discuss intellectual subjects in freedom. These were odd but
discreet. They included a defrocked priest, a disbarred lawyer, and
a newspaper reporter of dubious honesty. All were scholars, and
could take part in animated discussions with the scholar judge.
Sometimes, when a question was raised about these associates, Gaynor would turn it aside with a jaunty:

"Fortunately the Almighty has given me good ears, and I trust
I have a jovial disposition."

As the years accumulated, Gaynor's growing family presented
the usual problems confronting parents, and some of these he undertook to settle in his novel way. Rufus was his favorite, and for him
the judge had ambitious hopes; he wanted Rufus to follow him in
the law, though the boy showed little inclination in that direction.
In 1908 Rufus vanished from Amherst College, where he was a
student, and threw the family into an agony of apprehension for
nearly two weeks. Then word came that Rufus was alive and well,
but married. He had eloped with a girl described as a student at the
Boston Conservatory of Music, and improbably named May Queen.
The elopers had landed in San Francisco broke, and to tide things
over the bride was dancing in the chorus line of a musical show there.

When the first word of Rufus' whereabouts reached Eighth
Avenue, the judge's relief found expression in a profane reading of
his son out of the family. Gaynor was cruelly hurt when a newspaper
printed this as seriously meant. Actually, he had immediately wired
funds to the newlyweds and, once the shock was over, could chuckle
about the escapade, recalling his own hard time in San Francisco
when he, too, "went out to see the world." Parental indulgence
ceased, however, when it was revealed that May Queen was really
Maria Guiffre, and that she had omitted to mention a previous husband from whom she was not divorced. The marriage to Rufus Gaynor
was annulled; but from that time on Rufus seemed to develop a
talent for getting into scrapes.

The Gaynor daughters had inherited streaks of independence
from their father. They would grow into strong-willed, strong-
minded, argumentative, domineering women, without, however, Gaynor's intellectual bent. They would become beauties and acquire a
reputation for being "very cussed." Their beaux found the going
rough at Eighth Avenue. Should one venture to pay a call, promptly

at curfew time, generally early, a shout would come down from the second floor, "Get that goddam puppy out of here!" Small wonder that several of the girls would make runaway matches, or that the judge's sons-in-law would stand in awe of him as a "terrible cuss."

The girls managed to outwit their father on the edict of early-to-bed-early-to-rise whenever a party or a dance beckoned. Packed off to bed, they would slip up to the attic, clamber through the roof scuttle, then down by the scuttle of the Mirabeau Towns house next door, where the butler was their ally, and so away. The return trip was over the same route. Gaynor was a long time finding out, and when he did he had the scuttle nailed shut.

The judge's eccentricities were shown on surprising occasions; they baffled his friends. William Ziegler died in 1905, and at the funeral, held in the Ziegler home at Noroton, Connecticut, throughout the service Gaynor sat on the porch outside reading a book. His affection for Ziegler was deep-seated, and the confidence Ziegler had in their friendship was shown by his naming Gaynor a trustee and executor of his $30,000,000 estate.

On another occasion, at the wedding of Theodore Roosevelt, Jr., Gaynor found the pew assigned to him already occupied, and was so incensed he refused to stay for the reception.

Politics occupied the judge in a reflected way all during these years. In 1898, 1901, and 1904 he was boomed for governor of the state, but showed little interest. The 1898 election was interesting because the *World*, which was strongly attracted to the sharp-speaking jurist, urged Gaynor's nomination by the Democrats to oppose the Republicans' Theodore Roosevelt, just home from Cuba and wearing his Rough Rider laurels cockily. Said the *World* of Gaynor:

"He is as brave as Roosevelt and his superior as a stump speaker. No boss could control him. He has shown himself to be a reformer who reforms evils."

The editors of the *World* would never cease to believe that had Gaynor run in 1898 he would have won in a landslide, and the spectacular career of the egocentric Roosevelt might have been nipped right there.

The 1897 mayoral election in New York City had marked the inauguration of an epoch because it was the first to be held in the consolidated city. Brooklyn and the outer dependencies of Manhattan—Queens county, the Bronx, and Staten Island—had been absorbed into the greater city as boroughs, each with a large degree of autonomy, and the contest was spirited to become the first mayor of Greater New York. Tammany Boss Richard Croker, who had retired to his estate in Ireland and a winter home at Palm Beach, came back to manage this campaign. The candidate he put up for the Democrats was Robert Van Wyck, member of an old family, who possessed manners but no mind of his own.

The reform element, marshaled by the Citizens Union, advanced as their candidate Seth Low. The Republicans nominated Benjamin F. Tracy, and there was another formidable contender, Henry George, the single-taxer and exponent of a better deal for the common man. George, immensely earnest and earnestly honest, had won the loyalty of a host of people by his fight for wider social justice; to tens of thousands of New Yorkers he symbolized their hope of deliverance from the rule of predatory politicians and self-seeking rich. Under the banner of the Jeffersonian Democracy, George was contributing more confusion to an already confused contest. There was a fifth candidate of sorts, the Mayor Gleason of Long Island City whom Justice Gaynor had flagellated for his attempted water-supply steal.

Because of his prominence, Judge Gaynor's endorsement was eagerly sought, and at one point it was rumored that Croker had proposed to substitute Gaynor for Van Wyck—a tale that made Gaynor laugh. He was believed to be inclining toward George, for whose ideas he had respect; but as the fight warmed up, with Croker offering two to one that his man would sweep the board, the judge remained noncommittal. During a vacation stay at Great Barrington, in Massachusetts, he did remark that the apparent rule for political candidates throughout the country was "to say nothing and do nothing; I might almost add, to know nothing. That seems to make them eligible." No candidate, however, wished to appropriate that observation to his own case.

The newspapers tried every ruse to wrest a statement of preference from the judge, and their frustration was entertainingly told by a *Herald* reporter. This persistent chap pursued Gaynor for a week, and finally told his city editor that "only a thorough knowledge of the inner workings of telepathy" could penetrate Judge Gaynor's thoughts. But although this reporter got no opinion on the candidates, he did glean much of interest regarding Gaynor.

"I began the wearisome task of endeavoring to extract from Mr. Gaynor an opinion on the present political situation on Sunday," this reporter stated. "When I called he had just finished tea, and was somewhat less perturbed about the unhappy condition of the human race than is customary with him."

" 'You don't want an interview?' said he.

"That was precisely what I desired and I told him so. . . .

" 'See me tomorrow or Tuesday,' he said, 'and I shall see what I can do for you.'

"It may be mentioned here that . . . when he desires to take the people into his confidence Mr. Gaynor writes out his own interview. . . .

"In accordance with his desire, I called at his house on Eighth Avenue [on Tuesday]. He was finishing the lead of a lecture on 'Cervantes' for the Brooklyn Literary Society. . . .

" 'I am holding court here now,' Judge Gaynor said, referring to his daily work, 'and I don't think I ought to say anything about politics. How is the political situation, anyway?'

"I managed to say that the situation was still complicated. This safe assertion he agreed with by inclining his head.

" 'There are four tickets in the field,' he mused, looking up from a page of *Don Quixote*.

" 'And a fifth, if you include Mr. Gleason,' I said boldly.

" 'That's so,' and he laughed pleasantly. 'I shall see you tomorrow some time and prepare something for you in the meantime.'

"I saw the judge in the courthouse on Wednesday. The dignity and the restraint that convention imposes on judges of the Supreme Court struggled hard with the desire to be the Messiah of a misled and perplexed people, and the result was a draw. He asked again if there was any change in the situation. I told him of the big Henry George meeting of the night before, but he was not impressed by big meetings.

" 'That much in a newspaper is better,' he said with much force and dignity. The amount he indicated between his thumb and forefinger was almost four inches. 'That is,' he qualified the remark, 'if it is properly said.'

"I took new heart at this and went boldly for just that much, but he shook his head.

" 'I haven't the time today to prepare anything,' he said with gravity, as if he had been indiscreetly led into unwise speech. 'But I shall have something ready for you tomorrow.'

"My last visit to Mr. Gaynor was made yesterday. He was in the office adjoining the court and came to the door to meet me.

With the directness and simplicity of all great characters he said:
"'I haven't prepared anything for you.'"

All of which was brighter and in some ways more informative
(though not on the subject of the candidates' merits) than a routine
"Memo to City Desk: Chased Gaynor all week but he won't talk."

Which also illustrates why Justice Gaynor was popular with
bright newspapermen: he gave them something to write about. And
on his side, while the sight of reporters apparently filled him with
repugnance, he knew their uses, and he used them.

In the course of this campaign Judge Gaynor issued a ruling
that set forth his concern for the essential safeguards of elections.
An attempt was made to keep the name of the independent candidate, Seth Low, off the ballot on the grounds of waste of the taxpayers' money. Ruled Gaynor:

"It is a part of the history of the state that, at the time our
present election statute was first enacted, municipal government had
generally fallen and settled into the control of dishonest and criminal
persons, who were mere politicians by trade, and without any lawful occupations, and who had no interest in government or in politics
except to obtain opportunity to enrich and aggrandize themselves
by looting the public treasury. They obtained and held such control
by means of their control of the party organizations and of a
system of voting which exposed the voter to the oversight and strong
influence of such party organizations at the polls.

"In this way they were enabled to nominate and elect to high
offices not themselves, but individuals of better name and fame,
willing, however, to be their mere tools when elected. . . . The government of many of our cities had in this way become so low, base, and
corrupt, that no account of the like could be found in past history,
except in the case of governments and nations which were fast
tottering to their fall, either from the general debasement or the
general despair of their citizens.

"It was with the avowed purpose of helping the electors to lift
the government out of this condition that our election statute was
passed. Its object was to make independent nominations and independent voting not only possible but easy; to enable everyone to
vote freely, according to his manhood conscience. Such object was
expressed in its title, which designated it as 'an act to promote
independence of voters at public elections.'

"The foregoing conditions have been called to mind only to put
in contrast . . . the contention in this case, very ably presented, that

the provisions of that statute . . . should be technically and strictly construed with the paramount view of preventing the cost to the public of printing too many nominations upon the ballot. . . . To put such questions of expense above the great purpose of the act . . . would be a grave misconception. To print nominations like these is a matter of small expense. To reject them would be to prevent many conveniently voting as they wish to, and might sometimes destroy a great movement struggling to prevent government from becoming a mere subject of individuals' spoils."

In a letter that same year Gaynor expressed his belief that the traditional political parties were in a transition stage, which would be completed when "the present awakening of economic and political thought among us has run its course."

In another letter he advised that "this theory of opposing everything the other party or the government favors for the mere sake of being in opposition does not deserve the name of politics, much less of statesmanship." He preached constantly that "ideas in politics are far more potent than patronage."

Little wonder that machine politicians could not fathom a reasoning so cross-grained, from their point of view; they could only put it down to culpable indifference to the party's weal. Even the press was cast into repeated astonishment upon discovering that Judge Gaynor's name appeared on no list of registered Democrats; his party seemed to be himself.

In the 1897 mayoral election, on the eve of the vote Henry George died and received the spontaneous tribute of more than fifty thousand New Yorkers, many of whom knelt in the street and wept as his coffin passed by. Van Wyck carried the election, and four years of plundering ensued. During this spate of venality and graft, Gaynor's popularity as a candidate-in-prospect for a higher office remained unbroken. In 1900, and again in 1904 and 1908, Gaynor supported William Jennings Bryan, to the scandal of Tammany Hall and New York conservatives who held Bryan's "free silver" heresy in abhorrence. Gaynor did not advocate a single monetary standard, but a dual one, of gold and silver; but though he tried valiantly this was one distinction he never succeeded in making clear. But then, neither did anyone else make bimetallism comprehensible.

From time to time he favored the Democratic National Committee with disinterested counsel. The war with Spain he treated lightly, referring to "these times of war and destruction, which still seem to be the most delightful state of man." After the war he tried to keep Bryan from making anti-imperialism the crucial campaign issue.

"You can only lose by it," he warned. "A few people are making a noise disproportionate to their numbers about [the Philippines]. . . . Our conquests are facts accomplished and will be sustained by an overwhelming majority."

In a second letter he cautioned the Democrats against turning the war over to the Republicans—the fatal error of the Democrats after the Civil War. He wrote to the secretary of the Anti-Imperialist League:

"I only know that we have the Philippines, and that we must educate the people there to prepare them for self-government, which will take a couple of generations, I assume. To throw them on their own resources now would be a crime."

In 1908 Gaynor was Bryan's choice for the Vice-Presidential nomination; but his divorce and alienation from Catholicism were raised against him. Gaynor had expected to be nominated, and it was said had prepared an acceptance speech, even though he was not enthusiastic about taking the second place. But at word of his rejection he only said:

"I asked for nothing, expected nothing, and therefore I am not disappointed. That is all. I have nothing more to say."

He could find solace in the honors that had already come to him. In 1905 he had finally accepted an appointment to the Appellate Division of the Supreme Court, after having declined a similar appointment four years earlier. Still, he confided to a friend:

"I am reluctant to leave the trial bench, which is of far more importance to the community than all of our appeal courts. Indeed, our present judicial system is top-heavy with appeal courts, the exaltation of which has steadily tended to lower, if not degrade, the trial courts. Only about 10 to 20 percent of a trial judge's work ever goes up on appeal. It is the trial bench which should be made as strong as possible."

In this new capacity, Gaynor displayed the same dispatch and zest for work that he had shown as a trial judge. He did not muzzle his pen, but dealt as unsparingly with the laxity of lawyers and the lawlessness of the police as ever. In reversing the sentence imposed on a boy arrested for playing craps on the sidewalk, he pointed out that the game of craps was not criminal, nor was it illegal to bet.

In 1907 Gaynor received the highest possible professional

commendation when all parties joined in nominating him for a second term as judge. The *Brooklyn Eagle*, proud for its city of the rare event, recalled that fourteen years before, Gaynor had been nominated by the Republicans reluctantly, "without either much hope or much desire for his election. His unanimous re-election will be the greatest tribute of his life, so far, and as great as any ever offered in the life of any jurist by the people here whom Judge Gaynor serves and leads."

An inevitable result, the *Eagle* foresaw, would be the uniting "of many New York Democrats upon him as an eligible and a formidable force, around whom could rally all the Democratic sentiment of this state for the Presidency of the United States, at the next Democratic convention."

The boom to make Gaynor President was on, and would build up intermittently in the years ahead.

Meanwhile, the judge remained his querulous, cantankerous, highhanded, sententious, upright, and unpredictable self.

Two persons who never laughed at the judge's peculiar ways were the Kohlers, father and son. In 1901 James P. Kohler and Gaynor parted company, after Kohler had published an open letter to the mayor of New York, warning that unless a resolution in favor of increasing the pay of county judges was rescinded, he would bring a taxpayer's suit to withhold the salaries. Did not the state constitution say that "the compensation of any county judge shall not be increased or diminished during his term of office"?

"In my opinion," this epistle to the city fathers wound up in Gaynoresque style, "about $250,000 is taken each year from the pockets of the taxpayers and handed over to public officials who . . . have no right to it whatever, by just such resolutions. . . . It is high time that this sort of robbery of the taxpayers . . . be stopped, and that our public officials either do the work which they are elected to do, or that they must step down and out and allow those who are willing to abide by their contracts and their oath of office to have a chance."

The joke was that politicians saw Gaynor's hand in every line, either as having written the letter or at least having inspired it. In reality Gaynor had been quietly lobbying for the increases, which did not affect him. But he saw nothing amusing in the publicity that ensued, and fired Kohler.

A short while later Philip Kohler took on the job that his

father had found impossible, and made a similar discovery for
himself. One of Gaynor's rules was that no typewriter could remain
at Eighth Avenue overnight. Since Kohler did much work there, in
the second-floor library, he was obliged to carry his typewriter in
and out. When summoned to St. James, which during the summer
was frequently, Kohler had to lug the typewriter along on the train,
and carry it (for no means of transportation was provided by the
judge) upwards of a mile to Deepwells. During the later years of
his tenancy, Kohler used a machine manufactured to his specifica-
tions, with an aluminum frame, to reduce weight.

When things went wrong, Kohler got the blame. If lawyers
called to find out why their papers were not signed, the judge would
summon Kohler and berate him for neglect; and if Gaynor had
just downed a glass of "Old Senator" from the bottle he kept in his
desk, books were apt to fly.

The Kings County Law Library had a balcony running around
it, reached by two stairs. One day Gaynor entered, followed by
Kohler holding his overcoat to help him on with it. Gaynor walked
up the stairs to the gallery, around it, and down on the other side,
with Kohler close behind. At the foot of the stairs the judge glanced
back and snapped:

"What do you mean by following me about? Stop it!"

Gaynor's personal court attendant in the Appellate Division
was Frederick W. Brink, a man well read, whom the judge liked and
often visited at home. But he liked to bully him. Gaynor was fond of
oysters, and sometimes sent Brink to fetch a plateful into chambers.
One day the judge was just starting on a dozen when important
visitors arrived. The oysters were whisked to a window sill where it
was hoped they might not be noticed; but they were; whereupon
Gaynor, affecting great surprise, rang for Brink and upbraided him
harshly for "bringing your oysters in here. Get them out of here and
don't ever do such a thing again!"

Another time Gaynor sent Brink to fetch something, and thinking he was taking too long, when the door opened heaved a book at
it blindly—and caught another court attendant, a man of learning
for whom Gaynor had much respect, full in the face.

Small wonder that James P. Kohler described his period of
service with the inflammable jurist as "nine years of hell," or that
some of Philip Kohler's reminiscences of the judge would prove
more catty than kind. Yet despite Gaynor's churlish and sometimes
childish aberrations, the men around the law courts developed an

intense admiration of him. The flaws in his character were not over-looked, but they were counterbalanced by his humanity and inflexi-ble dedication to the furtherance of justice.

Themes that Gaynor never ceased to emphasize during his years on the bench were the defense of personal liberty, and opposition to the ill-advised attempts of meddlesome reformers to remold social concepts and correct long-standing abuses by restrictive legislation and force. Again and again he preached:

"The law knows of no greater folly than the notion that the police are the custodians or conservers of the private morals of the community, or could be made such with any safety whatever, or with any possibility of uplifting morals instead of debasing them. The moral growth of a community depends on its churches, schools, and teachers, and the influence of a healthy and comfortable home life, and not on the police."

Nothing good or lasting can be accomplished in a hurry, he counseled over and over. In a speech before the New York Agricul-tural Society he would embody the fullest statement of his belief on this basic point:

"Some things that exist in the body politic which are wrong can not be abolished offhand; we have to move slowly, so that all we can do under such conditions which society has created is to lessen them by degrees, little by little, here a little and there a little, until we gradually climb down to the level we want to reach, and do no injury to anybody. Everything is of slow growth, my friends, in this world, that is good. . . . In all things, material, moral, political, economical, the rule is slow growth. We must do the best we can, and if we find a thing wrong we must wait a long period of time to fix it."

This truth, of course, was unpalatable to those who were calling for social realignments and reforms *now*, and a main target of Gay-nor's exasperation with reformers-by-statute became Dr. Charles H. Parkhurst, the Presbyterian minister who had stirred up the city to a housecleaning in 1892.

Parkhurst, a native New Englander, as a country boy had en-visioned New York City as "a kind of Jerusalem." He changed his opinion after serving a while as pastor of the Madison Avenue Church, at Twenty-fourth Street, on Madison Square. Outraged by the evidences of police collusion with the criminal element to promote and prey on the vice that honeycombed the city, Parkhurst preached a sermon on February 14, 1892, denouncing "the polluted harpies that, under the pretense of governing this city, are feeding night and day on its quivering vitals . . . a lying, perjured, rum-soaked, libidinous lot." Publication of this sermon brought denials and demands for proof. Parkhurst had none that would meet a test, and realizing that he must "put up or shut up," he pluckily toured the purlieus of vice, watched the system in operation, and a month later preached a second sermon using a stack of affidavits as texts. So damning were his charges, a legislative investigation (the Lexow committee) followed, and in revulsion from the subsequent shocking disclosures the people elected a reform administration headed by the nonpartisan mayor, William L. Strong.

Having once drunk the wine of popular acclaim, Dr. Parkhurst, as president of the Society for the Suppression of Vice, continued to agitate for the elimination of gambling and prostitution by rigid enforcement of the laws. He felt fully justified in his attitude by his basic creed, namely, that "the world is put in charge of the Church, and that what is bad in the world is there for the reason that the Church has not yet encompassed all the ground that by divine right belongs to it."

Talk about "divine right" always upset Gaynor. At first he had been in virtual accord with Parkhurst, for their objectives were similar; but as the stridulous woe-wailer of Madison Square grew more and more demanding, Gaynor set him down as a meddler and a busybody. By 1896 Gaynor was criticizing Dr. Parkhurst's "violent utterances, "and writing to the *New York Times:*

"I have so much sympathy with Dr. Parkhurst in some things he has done that I should regret to have it become the case that it would be enough to put the word 'scold' on him to let people know where he lives."

From that genteel dissent, Gaynor would progress to the point where he would refer to Parkhurst as thinking he was pious, "when he is only bilious."

While Parkhurst and his ilk were agitating for more and lustier vice raids, and demanding that gamblers, cardsharps, pimps, and prostitutes be driven from their dens and sent to prison or otherwise dispersed, Justice Gaynor vigilantly resisted such affronts to human liberty and human dignity. That his setting aside of vice arrests made without warrants might and did help outcasts of society did not trouble him. In respect of "wayward women," he was compassionate rather than punitive. "They are what men made them," he would say, and he refused to penalize them more than the strictest letter of the law required.

"We have more to fear from the growth of arbitrary power in officials than from all other vices and crimes combined," he repeated. "It might be well if the police authorities should break into and smash the interior of one of our leading clubs, with mob violence; for then every one would perceive the enormity of their offense, although it would be no greater than their lawless trespass against the houses and persons of the weak and uninfluential."

L'AFFAIRE DUFFY

The words of the wise are as goads.

—ECCLESIASTES

WHILE WILLIAM J. GAYNOR had been treading judicial paths, the City of New York had been passing through successive crises of corruption and reform. In 1894 Mayor Strong's election had been the reaction of the public to the Lexow disclosures; but that administration had been torn apart by the jealousies of its divergent elements—Republican, Democratic, and independent factions squabbling over patronage and policy—and as a result Tammany had rolled back into power with Van Wyck in 1897. But the seaminess of Van Wyck's administration led to another revulsion, and in 1901 Seth Low was elected mayor with nonpartisan, reform backing.

The same fate befell the Low administration that had befallen Strong's, and the mutual jealousies of the ill-assorted elements composing it proved fatal to Low's reelection. His popular appeal was slight, for though able and progressive, he lacked the common touch. In the words of a brilliant young Supreme Court justice and spokesman for the reform group, Samuel Seabury, Low and his crowd "believed in government by the good, they being the good." The fusionists went down to defeat in 1903, and Tammany surged back, electing as mayor George Brinton McClellan, Jr., the eminently respectable son of the Civil War general.

McClellan's election had been engineered by the rising star of Tammany Hall, Charles Francis Murphy. Upon Croker's reretirement in 1901, a triumvirate, of whom Murphy was one, ruled the Hall briefly, with Murphy emerging as the real leader. His story was a New York saga of rags to renown. Born of poor Irish immigrants in the old Eighteenth (Gashouse) Assembly District on the far East Side of Manhattan, he had quit school to go to work as a boy, and had been a ship caulker and a horsecar driver before becoming a saloonkeeper and political recruit of Tammany. He made his saloon the political gathering place of the neighborhood, and in 1892 was elected leader of his district. Tall, jowled, rotund, ruddy, and reticent, Murphy possessed great personal dignity and an inexhaustible fund of silence; he seldom spoke, never made speeches or gave press interviews, and almost never wrote a letter. Even a telegram from him was a rarity. Under his long reign Tammany Hall would attain the apogee of its power.

Mayor McClellan appointed Murphy Dock Commissioner, the only public office he would ever hold, though at the Hall he would be addressed as "Commissioner" for the rest of his life. There was one jarring note, though a minor one, in the perfection of his plebeian virtues: that was his daily custom of betaking himself from Tammany Hall, on East Fourteenth Street, north to Fifth Avenue and Forty-fourth Street, to lunch at Delmonico's. An upstairs private dining room was reserved for his use, the table supported by carved tigers, the symbol of Tammany's power.

After the disaster of the Van Wyck regime, the term of office of New York's mayor had been cut by the legislature to two years. Low had served two years, and so did McClellan when elected in 1903. Thereafter the term was restored to four years, and in 1905 Murphy set out to reelect McClellan. This brought roaring into the foreground another figure who would bulk large on the political scene of New York, millionaire newspaper publisher William Randolph Hearst.

Born the only child of a California mining multimillionaire, Hearst had startled his native San Francisco at an early age by revitalizing a moribund newspaper there, the *Examiner*. Then with a jingle of cash and a ruffle of sensationalism he invaded the East, bent on displacing the most successful publisher and newspaper in New York, Joseph Pulitzer and his *World*. For several years the two fought each other, between them earning the title and stigma of "yellow journalist," and materially fomenting the 1898 war with Spain. Hearst finally became one up on Pulitzer when he was credited with having inspired the assassination of President McKinley.

Meanwhile, by vigorously championing progressive causes,

Hearst had rendered some public services, though by means often so unscrupulous and discreditable that they drew the reproach of other publishers and journals. In the view of the conservative *Century* magazine, when such "tainted journalists" undertook to work for the public benefit, it was "only donning the livery of heaven to serve the devil in."

Having launched a chain of newspapers capable of carrying his views to millions of readers daily, Hearst directed his gaze toward the White House. At his request Tammany Hall sent him to Congress for two terms. He encountered bad luck when a Madison Square fireworks display celebrating his election exploded, killing twelve persons outright. Six more died later, and perhaps one hundred were injured. Damage suits resulting from this disaster Hearst would still be fighting in his old age; at one time they were said to amount to $3,000,000. He disclaimed responsibility, contending that the city had been negligent in enforcing safety regulations.

In 1904 Hearst attempted to capture the Democratic nomination for President, and at the national convention in St. Louis he got two hundred and thirty-six votes on one ballot. The prospect of having this blatant self-advertiser in the White House sent shivers through conservatives of all parties.

In 1905 Hearst decided to carry his reform platform into the New York mayoral election, pitting himself against the might of Tammany Hall—the Hall that had elected him to Congress, and which he now denounced as a foul blot on the face of Manhattan. He organized his own party, the William Randolph Hearst Municipal Ownership League, and looked for a candidate to run for mayor. His choice fell on Justice Gaynor, who was both progressive and popular; and Arthur Brisbane, Hearst's chief editorial writer, was sent to persuade the judge to accept League endorsement. Brisbane tried hard, but although Gaynor approved of some of Hearst's achievements, he was not to be enticed. Hearst then nominated himself.

The Republicans put up William M. Ivins, a pert and clever lawyer who had started in Brooklyn at the same time as Gaynor, and Murphy sent in McClellan for a second round. Hearst concentrated his fire on Murphy, picturing him as an archcriminal. Murphy retaliated by blaming Hearst for McKinley's assassination. Ivins chirped and sniped at both from the sidelines.

Although the enrolled membership of the Municipal Ownership League numbered barely nine hundred—mainly Hearst em-

ployees, printers, mailers, truck drivers, reporters, and their friends
—when the campaign ended, after tons of fireworks had lit up the
Hearst rallies and innumerable brass bands had blown themselves
breathless, the returns showed that Hearst had come within 3,500
votes of winning, polling 224,925 votes against 228,395 for McClellan. Ivins was nowhere. In Tammany-dominated New York City
this was a stupendous feat, and Hearst charged that the election
had been stolen. This was probably true, but a recount failed to alter
the result; the frauds lay further back, in doctored registration
lists and destroyed ballots. In the hassle Hearst allowed one of his
newspapers, the *Journal*, to publish a cartoon of Murphy in prison
stripes, underneath the legend:

"Look out, Murphy! It's only a short lockstep from Delmonico's to Sing Sing."

This Murphy never forgave, and he had his revenge a year
later. Since it was clear that neither the Democrats nor the Hearst
party could win against the united Republicans in the coming state
election, a truce was patched up between Tammany and the Municipal Ownership League (rechristened the Independence League),
and in 1906 Murphy forced the state convention to give Hearst the
party's nomination for governor. State Senator Thomas F. Grady,
Murphy's floor manager, carried out the order by ejecting sixty
anti-Hearst delegates properly accredited, and seating a rump
Hearst delegation in their stead. After ramming the deal through
the sullen convention, Grady frankly confessed:

"Boys, I've just done the dirtiest day's work of my life."

Brooklyn's new Democratic boss, sharp-featured State Senator
Patrick Henry McCarran, who had succeeded McLaughlin, was
competing with Murphy for control of the entire New York City
Democracy, and on election day he instructed his forces to scratch
their tickets, with the result that every Democratic candidate was
elected except William Randolph Hearst—the Republican Charles
Evans Hughes becoming governor, with Lewis Stuyvesant Chanler,
Democrat, his lieutenant governor. Murphy was understood to be
not displeased.

Hearst now decided that instead of king he would be a kingmaker, and in 1907 made a deal with the Republican state boss,
Benjamin Odell, in an attempt to elect a sheriff of New York county.
The attempt failed, and Hearst began looking toward the 1909
mayoral election. The detestation in which by this time he was held
by other publishers and newspapers was expressed in contrasting

ways by the courtly *New York Evening Post*, on the one hand, and the racy Frank I. Cobb, editor of Pulitzer's *World*, on the other. Commented the *Post*:

"It is not simply that we revolt at Hearst's huge vulgarity; at his front of bronze; at his shrieking unfitness mentally for the office he sets out to buy. . . . It is not a question of politics but of character. An agitator we can endure; an honest radical we can respect; a fanatic we can tolerate; but a low voluptuary trying to sting his jaded senses to a fresh thrill by turning from private to public corruption is a new horror in American politics."

Cobb, writing about the abominable Hearst to his own publisher—blind, shrewdly perceptive, irritable Joseph Pulitzer—said he would consider it "a precious privilege if you will lift the lid and give me permission to scatter his intestines from the Battery to the Bronx."

Such was the feeling as the 1909 mayoral contest drew near.

During his second term, Mayor McClellan quarreled with Murphy and attempted to wrest the Democratic leadership from the Tammany chief. In this test of ability, however, he was overmatched; gentlemanly and charming, he was honest but ineffectual. Cobb thought McClellan suffered from an hereditary failing, saying:

"He is the son of his father. Just as he starts to do something it rains, and he has to go back into camp again."

Early in 1909 the customary fusion sentiment that cropped out regularly in election years began appearing. This year the fusionists were cocky and confident, while the Democrats were glum. On the basis of evidence of gross irregularities turned up by McClellan's energetic young Commissioner of Accounts, John Purroy Mitchel, Governor Hughes had removed John F. Ahearn, a Tammany district leader, as borough president of Manhattan. When the Tammany-controlled Board of Aldermen reelected Ahearn, Mayor McClellan refused to recognize the action.

Hughes then removed the borough president of the Bronx, Louis Haffen, a Tammany man, for profiteering in city real estate transactions. Charges also were brought against the borough president of Brooklyn, though these were not pressed to a conclusion before he resigned. Everywhere the cry was going up to get rid of Tammany, and not for years had the chances seemed so good.

The Democrats themselves were split into three hostile factions headed by Murphy, McCarran, and McClellan. Murphy's need of a victory was great, if he was to control the city organization. Intellectually superior to the run of machine bosses, Charles F. Murphy understood the expediency of bending before an adverse wind and waiting for calmer weather. He also comprehended that a political machine, to survive, must not only respond to popular needs; it must to some extent anticipate them. When reform was the watchword, it was sound politics to join the reformers. It was, therefore, early rumored that Murphy was considering offering the Democratic nomination for mayor to Justice Gaynor.

This placed the Republicans and other anti-Tammany elements in a quandary. They could hit upon no candidate who held even a fraction of Gaynor's appeal for the voters; but there was a marked lack of enthusiasm among the leaders for taking the judge. His independence of party control was held against him. Still, as summer approached it began to appear that no other course lay open, except to nominate him, if they earnestly wished to beat Tammany.

Hearst, the turncoat of many colors, held the key to the Pandora's box that contained both parties' hopes, for his Independence League following probably would control the outcome of the election. Hearst had spoken kindly of Judge Gaynor in his newspapers; but for the time being he refrained from making a commitment and concentrated upon noisily promoting his pet issue, municipal ownership of public utilities, especially new subway lines.

At this juncture, through two actions fortuitously timely, Gaynor projected himself into the forefront of the political picture so prominently that all rivals for the mayoral nomination faded into the distance.

In the May, 1909, issue of the widely read *Pearson's Magazine*, there appeared an article, imposingly signed by "Hon. William J. Gaynor, Justice of the Supreme Court of New York, Appellate Division," and titled, "The Looting of New York." An editorial foreword called attention to its importance in these words:

"If it be true that our great national peril lies in the indifference to corruption bred in our large cities, what American can read the following description of the monstrous traction conspiracy in the metropolis of America without a thrill of shame and indignation? . . . It is one of the most shocking scandals in the history of the American people."

The facts contained in Judge Gaynor's article had been revealed before; but nowhere had they been brought together, digested, and retold in a way that made the financial double-dealing which had brought ruin to thousands of investors in street railway securities understandable to the nontechnical reader. And the exposé carried the prestige of Gaynor's name.

Step by step, he traced the haphazard development of the whole system of public transportation in New York City. Manhattan Island, he pointed out, held the "most valuable street railroad routes in the whole world. You need only to look at the map and consider the population to see it." And yet, for two years the system of surface and elevated lines had been in bankruptcy, operated by court-appointed receivers, although the revenues of the lines at all times had been "ample to pay interest and just and generous dividends, several times over, on all the capital invested in these corporations, including generous profits and bonuses to the promoters and builders."

Why did this anomaly exist? In explanation, the judge took his readers through a labyrinth of amalgamations, leases, and purchases, each accompanied by a watering of stock, which over a long period of time had brought all the surface lines into the control of a holding company that "scarcely owned a steel rail or a stick of wood in the world, and was practically without assets or resources." This company had sold millions of dollars' worth of stock to the gullible public, under the promise of a guaranteed dividend of seven percent for nine hundred and ninety-nine years—a period "which lawyers appear to regard as one day short of forever, but which every one else is willing to admit is forever and a day."

The public's mistake was in not looking into the value to be attached to such a fantastic guarantee; and because it was essentially worthless, the stock, boomed to $250 a share, when the crash came plummeted to $16 a share, leading to the "ruin of honest people, and their anguish and distress."

As a result of the successive mergers and continuous watering of stock, the total of all the securities—stocks and bonds—of the companies involved in the smashup came to $701,135,911. This, Gaynor estimated, was at least ten times the sum that could have been legitimately invested in the construction and operation of the lines. To earn profits on so enormous an overcapitalization was obviously impossible, and the result had been inevitable—inadequate service, rickety equipment, pinch-penny wages, harsh working conditions, and more crippling and fatal accidents caused by under-serviced operation.

"The city is being bled at every pore," was the conclusion, and Gaynor's anger really flared at the thought of the multitude of claims "for redress in damages for all the persons killed and maimed for five years on the street surface railroads of Manhattan and the Bronx," which had been abandoned after the bankruptcy, being considered not worth continuing.

Yet, said he, "the 'financiers' and exploiters who did this thing are not to be blamed too much for it. Some of them are men of good heart—tiptop fellows, who pray in church, give to charity, and with whom you could live and get along first rate. They are 'the soul of honor,' as some do say. They are to be judged, to some extent, by the general moral tone of the community in which they live and scheme.

"The community, and its low, base, vulgar, and corrupt government, are primarily to blame. No voice of public authority in the city—of mayor or lesser officials—was raised against what they were doing. Instead, those in chief rulership over the city, and the bosses whose mere despicable, harlot-like tools and puppets they were, were in it up to the armpits, and several of them are now living the lives of millionaires—very vulgar little pitiful millionaires—some of them abroad, and some of them here, as a result. And now that it is all over, there are many people among us to whom no misgiving of their own honesty and respectability has ever occurred, who look upon it rather with a lenient shrug of the shoulder than as degrading to an educated and intelligent community."

No other public figure had spoken so tellingly against the mulcting of the people by traction magnates. Gaynor brought out that Thomas Fortune Ryan, one of the principal promoters of the gigantic swindle, had sold his own holdings just before the crash, unloading them on investors hypnotized by that seven percent dividend guaranteed "forever and a day." It was also noted that Croker was living as a country squire in England, and Van Wyck enjoyed luxurious living in Paris.

Gaynor's article made an impression all over the nation, where other cities were having traction scandals, and in New York it was sensational. Especially were Gaynor's words on the vexed question of building new subways, imperatively needed to relieve the inhuman congestion on the city's sole existing line, welcomed by advocates of municipal ownership. On this point he said:

"If the city is to build the subways, it should own them absolutely, the day they are completed and opened, without anyone having any strings on them whatever, and then be free to lease them out at public competition for the highest rent obtainable for a reasonable term of years."

In his view, the city could easily afford to construct the lines required, and "in eight or ten years the work would be fairly complete."

It was on a different front and a different issue, however, that Gaynor threw New York into a fever of excitement and made himself without question the leading candidate for the mayoralty that autumn.

On June 2, 1909, a letter reached the desk of Mayor McClellan and appeared simultaneously in the newspapers. Under date of May 29, it began:

"I had written a letter to the governor of the state to get redress for the scoundrelism hereinafter mentioned, through the power of removal of city officials which he possesses, but on second thought I concluded to withhold it and first ask such redress from you."

The circumstantial report that followed brought to light a quarrel that had arisen between Gaynor and McClellan's commissioner of police, Theodore A. Bingham.

A retired army general, Bingham had stirred up much controversy during his tenure as commissioner by his authoritarian handling of the police force. Determined to treat it as a "quasi-military" organization, he demanded ramrod discipline, bellowed at the men, was strict on saluting, and highhanded generally; but he had kept favor hunters and politicians at bay. Tammany Hall hated him. Bingham had been military aide to President Theodore Roosevelt, and Gaynor had met him first, in all his toggery of uniform and medals, when Mrs. Gaynor and he were White House guests of the Roosevelts. Privately Gaynor called Bingham a "strutabout." Now he was ready to call him something worse publicly, and to back up his statements with facts.

The letter he sent to McClellan concerned George B. Duffy, a nineteen-year-old Brooklyn youth, whose photograph was in the police "rogues gallery," although he had never been convicted of any crime. Gaynor had asked that it be removed, and Bingham had refused. The judge's letter to McClellan recited the facts:

Duffy, then seventeen, had been arrested on June 16, 1907, near his home in Brooklyn, by a police officer, without a warrant, and had been locked up overnight. "No charge of any criminal offense was made against him, but only that he was 'a suspicious person.' He had never been arrested before. He had lived in the neighborhood all his life, and could be found or identified at any hour.

"The next morning he was taken to police headquarters, or central office, and subjected to the routine and indignities of a felon. He was stripped, measured, and photographed, and his picture was hung up in the 'rogues gallery,' and his name entered in the index of felons. The next day he was taken before a magistrate and discharged. No complaint of any kind was made against him."

This, according to Gaynor, started a steady police harassment of Duffy. On November 26 of the same year he was again arrested and locked up overnight "with filthy persons. When taken before the magistrate the next day no criminal charge could be made against him. He was therefore charged by the police with violating an ordinance by obstructing the street, and discharged with a suspended sentence.

"He did not obstruct the street except by being on it," the judge bristled. "The charge is a stock one, used for lack of a truthful one. But it is neither a felony nor a misdemeanor, but one of those small things not included among crimes at all, which magistrates are allowed to summarily dispose of, and the boy felt it was useless to contest it. After being locked up all night he was glad to get away without any dispute.

"Just think of the boys of our city being locked up and brought into court with the felons on such a charge, and trumped up at that! What effect must such an experience have on the future of the average boy?"

Nearly a year went by, and then on September 22, 1908, Duffy was "again arrested in the street and locked up overnight on the terrible charge by the police of assault and highway robbery. His parents were shocked. Two days later he was brought before a magistrate. The man who claimed to have been assaulted and robbed was brought there to identify him, but immediately said on seeing him that he was not the culprit; that he was robbed by a man, not a boy; and he was discharged."

Meanwhile, Duffy's father had tried to have his son's photograph taken out of the police files, without success. Duffy's mother was distracted, because the fact was the scandal of the neighborhood; and when finally a small child taunted her in the street with "your boy's picture is in the 'rogues gallery,' " she could bear it no longer, and begged her husband to apply to Judge Gaynor for help.

The judge investigated, found corroboration of young Duffy's story, and wrote to Bingham explaining the situation and pointing out that it was a violation of the law to keep Duffy's photograph and name in the police files.

Bingham had replied pompously, maintaining that the police were justified in keeping the picture, first because the law forbidding its retention had been passed several weeks after the photograph was posted, and was not retroactive; and second, because the record showed that Duffy had been "convicted" and given a suspended sentence. However, the commissioner professed his willingness to comply with the judge's request if he would ask it as a personal favor.

That was the wrong way to approach Justice Gaynor, who neither asked nor granted official favors, and Bingham was quickly made aware of his mistake.

First, Gaynor replied in a tone disarmingly mild; in him this was usually a harbinger of wrath to come.

"Dear General Bingham," the letter fairly purred. "I have carefully examined into the case of George B. Duffy. The case before [Magistrate] Tighe was not for any crime, whether misdemeanor or felony. . . . The other arrests seem to have been founded on no evidence whatever. . . . The boy is at work in a responsible place, but of course he can never get along with his picture in the 'rogues gallery.' You are very kind, dear general, in saying you will take down the picture if I ask it, but I am averse to asking it outright, for I should prefer that if it be done you should get the credit for it yourself. No law is in the way that I can see, and I hope you will do it. It may save this young chap. He has good parents and a good home and is not so bad himself. He is, like many boys brought up in the city, subject to many bad influences."

This was signed "Sincerely yours," but the obstinate commissioner failed to read it aright. In a stiff response, he repeated his former stand, and added that "the police reports are that [Duffy] is a very disorderly person and has a bad character." Furthermore, Bingham said he had twice sent for Duffy to come in and talk the matter over, but the youth had refused and had "even consulted an eminent lawyer who advised him against it. Under the circumstances, my dear judge, my duty is clear to take no further steps in this matter."

That reference to consultation with "an eminent lawyer" Gay-

nor could construe only as a sneer at himself, and back came a
reply of a very different nature from the "dear general" letter.
This one began:

"Dear Sir: Yours in the case of young Duffy is at hand. I have
done all I can to see this poor boy righted. Nothing seems to be left
for him but to submit to absolute ruin for life at your hands, or else
proceed to teach you in ample ways open to him that autocrats are
not suffered under our system of government. Let me say to you
that your repeated statement that this boy has been convicted of a
crime is known to you to be untruthful and is a libel. . . . You speak
about some law, but there is no law permitting you to hang this
boy's picture among murderers and thieves, and it is a scoundrelly
thing to do. I may as well speak plainly, for such lawless treatment
of people needs plain speech. Nor do I believe that you ever sent for
him to come and see you. I would have brought him to you myself if
you asked. I am fully assured that he never received a word of any
kind purporting to be from you."

This letter was signed, "Yours, etc." The war was on, and Gaynor's fury became uncontrollable when he learned that his attempts
to help the Duffy lad were hurting him instead. As he now related
to Mayor McClellan, on the previous Sunday Duffy had been
arrested "at 8 o'clock in the evening, on the street, in the sight of
many, by a headquarters detective in plain clothes, who told him his
picture was in the 'rogues gallery,' and took him to the police station
and locked him up overnight. The false and malicious charge of
vagrancy was entered on the station blotter against this boy who
works every day of his life and has a refined and good home with his
parents.

"Monday morning he was taken to police headquarters, or
central office. A squad of about fifteen detectives, with their faces
masked, were called in to look at him. They yelled at him and shoved
him about. The officer at the desk told them his name, and that he
was a well-known thief, and added with a sneer that he thought he
had pull enough to get his picture out of the 'rogues gallery,' and
turning to the boy, told him that he might as well get that idea out
of his head at once. This had reference to my poor efforts with the
police commissioner.

"I am fully conscious of my lack of power to put a stop to the
outrageous violations of our laws and system of free government,
which occur unchecked in this city daily, and are fast debasing us.
Such occurrences often make me wish that I had the power even for

a month or two. In that time the official lawlessness could be stopped. . . .

"Need I say that this boy must get redress from this criminal official wrongdoing and oppression or be ruined for life? He has a position in which he earns $18 a week, and he and his parents have lived in daily dread of the day when his employer would learn that his picture is in the 'rogues gallery' and discharge him."

In reference to Commissioner Bingham, Gaynor reminded the mayor of the decision in a case of similar import, recently brought against Bingham and decided against him, and how "the next day after the decision he made public announcement that he would not obey it, and he has continued to this hour to disobey it, without reprimand or check, much less removal."

Publication of this letter brought Bingham scurrying to his office at night, and he immediately handed out copies of all the correspondence in the Duffy case. He was not worried, he indicated, assuring reporters:

"I have two hundred and sixteen more days to serve as police commissioner and I am going to serve them."

As for Judge Gaynor's assertion that Duffy had never been adjudged guilty of any criminal offense, the general retorted with military logic:

"He was convicted, wasn't he? If he was convicted he was guilty, and if he wasn't guilty of a crime I'd like to know what he was guilty of."

Judge Gaynor promptly told him: guilty of nothing.

"The whole matter is of record and plain to anyone," the judge commented to reporters. "Not only has this boy never been convicted of any crime, which is a prerequisite by law to his being put in the 'rogues gallery,' but they were unable to even make a charge against him in police court. . . . This is a government of laws and not of men. Mayors and police commissioners are no more above the law than anyone else. It is a sad thing to see a great and intelligent city in the rulership of persons who think they have us all by the back of the neck."

That, it began to appear, was exactly where the judge had Bingham. Mayor McClellan opened a personal investigation of the case, called police witnesses whom he examined himself, and brought in Duffy, his parents, and a dozen character witnesses, lay and clerical, all of whom testified that they had known Duffy since his birth and that he bore an honest reputation. During these researches the mayor received periodic communications from Judge Gaynor, one of which philosophized:

"The laws have not authorized any official or authority, however high, to put the pictures of our boys in the 'rogues gallery,' even though the police commissioner may think they are 'wild' or 'bad.' There are many 'bad boys' who turn out not to be so bad after all. A good many of us could serve as examples in proof of this. My understanding is that the police commissioner's duty is to guard and protect our children, not oppress and wrong them. Their temptations and annoyances in this great city are many, and we have to do the best we can for them to save them. I am myself the father of eight children and know what they contend with, and especially is it one of the first duties of government to protect the weak and uninfluential in the community, old and young. The influential and powerful are generally able to take their own part."

While McClellan was questioning witnesses in the case, a man with a battered face walked into City Hall and told the mayor that he had been assaulted in his store by several policemen for no reason, had been arrested, taken to jail, advised there to hire bail, and when he did so, was released without charge. He had been in the hospital with his injuries, and his pregnant wife, who had been kicked during the fracas, was in a dangerous condition.

Gaynor himself was deluged with letters circumstantially recounting unprovoked police assaults. One man came from Philadelphia to tell personally how, when he was running a store in Brooklyn, he had been arrested by policemen who put leg irons on him, photographed and beat him, insisting that he owed money for a consignment of goods of which he had never heard, and promising to release him if he paid the bill. He had refused, and finally he was freed without any charge being entered against him; but in fear of further assaults he had left the city to live elsewhere.

After a month-long study, Mayor McClellan issued a sixty-page report, denouncing certain police methods, especially the system of promoting and demoting detectives according to the number of arrests they made—the more arrests, the higher the rank and pay they were graded into. The mayor rebuked Bingham; ordered him to return Duffy's photograph to him; and to discipline or fire several high departmental officials, including a deputy commissioner and Bingham's own secretary.

The general carried out some of the mayor's orders, refused to execute others, and praised the men he had been told to dismiss. Whereupon McClellan removed him, and Bingham brought suit for slander against Justice Gaynor, asking $100,000 damages. An expert on the law of libel, the judge gave no sign that he was perturbed.

This episode, which kept the city stirred up for a month, further boomed Gaynor's popularity. Almost every newspaper had sided with him against Bingham, although the *Sun* did regret that the judge had "allowed his temper to run away with his judgment." Nevertheless, said the *Sun*, Gaynor had served the public well "by insisting so eloquently upon the immunities of an unconvicted citizen."

Political leaders were equally impressed. A Tammany man believed that "if the election were to be held next week, Judge Gaynor would be elected by an overwhelming majority." A Republican put the case on their side as forcefully:

"It is becoming clearer every day that we haven't got the right man for the job. All this talk of electing some bank president or some other unknown businessman is buncombe. We have no man available who will make the appeal to the people that will be necessary to defeat Tammany. Gaynor can do it, and he will be elected if we nominate him. I know positively that he will accept a nomination from fusion, if it is given with anything like unanimity. He will then have the support of the Hearstites and the other radicals and reformers, and everybody who runs on the ticket with him will be elected. Q.E.D."

Hearst did not wait for others to move. Under no necessity to consult committees, he invited Gaynor, through a subordinate, to his residence—the top five floors of a Riverside Drive apartment house. There he asked the judge pointblank whether he would run for mayor in the fall. Gaynor parried by asking Hearst why he didn't run himself, saying that in that event he would not stand in the way. Hearst protested that he would never be a candidate for public office again, and had said so. This was true, and Gaynor thereupon asked what ticket he might be expected to head. Hearst's answer was:

"I don't care what ticket you run on; I'll support you on any ticket."

All this was seen, heard, and recorded by the intermediary, who at this point threw in a remark about the rumor that Tammany

might nominate the judge. To this Hearst rejoined, again according
to the intermediary:

"I'm not opposed to Tammany but to Tammany methods, and
when it does right it is entitled to credit."

Gaynor thanked the publisher for his interest and said he would
consider the matter. Hearst, who was about to leave for Europe,
offered the free run of the *Journal* and *American* should the judge
have something to communicate to the public.

Then Hearst sailed, and the rumor flew that Justice Gaynor
had been picked as the mayoral candidate of the Independence
League. This incensed some of Hearst's true-blue supporters, who
hoped the publisher himself would get into the race.

Gaynor said nothing. The day Bingham was dismissed reporters
found him at St. James, out in the fields pitching hay. His comment was:

"This matter has nothing to do with politics. It has now been
established that there is no place under our system of government
for an autocrat. No official, however high, is above the law."

The mayoral situation? Well, on that subject he had absolutely
nothing to say. Tossing a forkful of hay to the man on the wagon,
he did suggest, however:

"If I ever run for mayor it will be because the good people of
the community make a demand for it, and I believe you know that
I have not the vanity to think that this will ever happen. And let
me say, I hope it never will."

This last was spoken without a smile.

A few days afterward the judge himself departed on his annual
holiday trip abroad, leaving the political pot to simmer during his
absence.

"THE WORST CANDIDATE"

———◦◯◦———

> *They don't go in for literary business*
> *much downtown, but these men are all real*
> *gents, and that's what the people want.*
> —GEORGE WASHINGTON PLUNKITT,
> OF TAMMANY HALL

WHEN JUSTICE GAYNOR RETURNED from Europe on August 29 he found the air filled with reports of political trafficking. The anti-Tammany forces were locked in rivalry for dominance of their temporary alliance, the Republicans and the independents each claiming the lion's share of nominations and honors. The dispute was disheartening to many well-wishers.

Individual reform groups by the dozen, more than fifty all told, had gone on record endorsing Gaynor for mayor, and petitions to enter him independently of either the Democrats or the fusionists had gathered fifteen thousand signatures already. Even Dr. Parkhurst had had a good word to say for the judge. The only question seemed to be which of the major parties would offer him a nomination, and would he accept? Especially, would he accept Tammany Hall as his sponsor?

The experts were sending up trial balloons, but they got no satisfaction from the judge.

"The sparring of these political organizations for points does not interest me at all," he said at the end of a long walk at St. James. "I have nothing whatever to say, except that you can't pull the wool over the eyes of intelligent people."

153

Some might think this a debatable proposition, and a suspicion gained currency to the effect that Gaynor himself was engaged in doing just that. He was said to have reached a secret agreement with Murphy that he would accept the Democratic nomination, but meanwhile no statement would be made until as many independent endorsements as possible had been obtained.

The two main forces in the fusion aggregate were the Republican Party and the Committee of 100, a citizens' group originally formed for the purpose of screening the candidates to determine their fitness. The Republicans, who had the active machine, insisted on naming the ticket; the committee rejected this demand; and for a while negotiations bogged down. No candidates had been announced by the middle of September, when a "harmony meeting" was called by the committee. But this quickly degenerated into what one disgusted participant described as "like nothing so much as the crew in a ship debating which is port side and which starboard."

Gaynor had decided tentatively to respond to the surge of independent support. He was relying on Hearst's pledge of backing and was hopeful of being selected by one or the other major party, and perhaps by both. On Labor Day he took his first overt step and formally entrusted his interests to a Committee of 9, nearly all his personal friends. This group was got up at Gaynor's request by Charles M. Hyde, and it included Abraham Abraham, perhaps Gaynor's closest adviser in Brooklyn. The committee's announced purpose was to circulate petitions for an independent nomination. In accepting its good offices Gaynor stipulated that it was with the reservation that "I shall not take the nomination from any organization to which is annexed any pledge, promise, or condition whatever, other than to be mayor in fact and do my duty if elected."

This attitude did not sit well with either the patronage-hungry Republicans or the necessitous Democrats, nor did it please certain leaders of the Committee of 100. These last were obsessed by fear of Tammany infiltration; and to link their cause with a candidate who refused in advance to repudiate Tammany they felt would be disastrous. Their sentiment was, "We can't fight Tammany with a Tammany candidate"; and to make sure that they would not be somehow euchred out of a victory they demanded Gaynor's pledge that he would not accept an endorsement by Tammany or the Democrats.

So partisan a demand, after all the talk about fusion's nonpartisan aspect, angered Gaynor, and he struck back in a scandalized "Address to the Public" in which he denounced the "insolent pretense" being played before New York's voters "under the delusion that they are a pack of fools. . . . But they will not be deceived.

"These so-called leaders, who should be called misleaders, are only deceiving themselves. Like the ostrich, they stick their heads in the sand and think they have concealed themselves, when the broadest part of their bodies is still big with exposure. . . . It is said somewhere in Holy Writ, 'Surely the net is spread in vain in sight of the bird.'

"I do not ask to be nominated, and I hope I shall not be, but surely someone ought to get up and expose this sham and fraud. . . . Engaged in it I see men who between elections are absolutely nonpartisan in working with the scoundrels of all parties in the buying and selling of laws, the grabbing of public franchises, the levying of tribute and even blackmail on corporations and honest enterprises, and in spoliating the public treasury in a hundred ways. Out with them all!

"These so-called nonpartisans are now gathered around a table trying to divide up the offices of the city and boroughs among their followers, it being proposed when they cannot agree to cast lots! . . . And they are the ones now shouting 'Stop thief!' the loudest of all!"

Privately he was no less bitter.

"The pledge exacted of me by the Republican machine was an outrage," he wrote to a friend. And to another: "The resolution . . . that I could not be nominated unless I gave a pledge not to accept nomination or ratification by the Democratic city convention I could not regard otherwise than as a gross insult. Men must be lacking in moral perception to make such a proposition. If I gave such a pledge I would have insulted every honest Democrat, and would have immediately put myself in a minority. . . . The Republicans can not elect anybody without the help of Democratic votes, and yet they pretend to ask me to insult every Democrat by such a pledge."

Reporters pursuing the judge to his St. James farm were taken out to the pig barn, where Gaynor kept thirty-nine fat porkers.

"Don't you think it would be a good thing to bring the politicians down here to look at the pigs?" he asked. "It would teach them how to be honest and straight, and they wouldn't be exacting pledges from people."

He told one newsman who pressed him for comment on the plethora of political statements being put out:

"I have a little book in my library on *The Power of Silence.* Did you ever read it? It would make good reading for some people just now, who consider that their importance grows in the ratio of their words."

Watching from Europe, canny Joseph Pulitzer cabled the *World* to get behind Gaynor.

"Urge vigorously Gaynor's nomination by the Democrats," came the order from Aix-les-Bains. "Admitting his defects he is an able man; nobody's pocket judge."

Hearst was the enigma; he remained ambiguous and aloof. Refusing to be drawn out, he said cautiously:

"When the Independence Party knows for what Judge Gaynor stands, and with whom he stands, it will know whether or not it can support him for mayor."

Personally he liked the judge very much, Hearst conceded, but it was "unfortunate" that Gaynor had not "come out more strongly for municipal ownership of the transit lines."

To Gaynor this seemed "like asking St. Paul if he were a Christian. I was teaching municipal ownership when it was obloquy to espouse that cause—long before Mr. Hearst hove into sight from California."

Some of Gaynor's supporters suspected that Hearst had already consented, or was on the point of agreeing, with the fusion leaders to boycott Gaynor unless he repudiated Tammany. Seabury raked the publisher over the coals at a Gaynor rally in Cooper Union, saying:

"Mr. Hearst through his newspapers has repeatedly praised Justice Gaynor and pointed out that he would make an ideal candidate for mayor. He is now unwilling that Justice Gaynor should succeed where he himself has failed. In union with the Republican bosslets . . . he will support Justice Gaynor only if the justice will attempt to insure his own defeat. . . . It is rumored that Murphy looks with favor upon the nomination of Justice Gaynor and that Tammany will nominate him. I shall be glad if it is so."

Hearst still hedged, and the fusionists were unable any longer to postpone the announcement of their slate. In a final huddle, they argued all day and into the night, then adjourned to an all-night restaurant, Jack's, and argued until four o'clock in the morning. The result was a ticket, and a strong one.

The election was not only for mayor, but for comptroller, president of the Board of Aldermen, the five borough presidents, and numerous county and borough officers. The mayor, comptroller, president of the Board of Aldermen, and borough presidents comprised the Board of Estimate and Apportionment, which was the city's real ruling power, controlling the purse. Therefore control of the Board of Estimate was crucial, and the fusionists chose their nominees with this in mind.

Their selection for mayor was Otto T. Bannard, a bank president and generous contributor to Republican funds, but little known to the public. The candidate for comptroller was William A. Prendergast, a businessman long interested in municipal problems. John Purroy Mitchel, aggressive, sharp-tongued grandson of a celebrated Irish nationalist, was named for president of the Board of Aldermen. George McAneny, a veteran of civil-service reform and president of the influential City Club, was nominated for Manhattan borough president, and Cyrus W. Miller, Alfred E. Steers, Laurence Gresser, and George Cromwell, respectively, for presidents of the Bronx, Brooklyn, Queens, and Richmond. For district attorney of New York county, another key spot, the fusionists selected Charles S. Whitman, a former judge and effective prosecutor.

Confronted by such a challenge, Murphy summoned his district leaders and laid the facts before them. Their only chance of winning—and it was a slim chance at best—lay in their nominating Judge Gaynor, he said. Most of the leaders demurred, and McCarran warned bluntly that if they elected Gaynor, they would rue it. But Murphy's logic could not be faulted: Gaynor was a Democrat, he was popular, and he certainly had the bulk of the reform element behind him. Reluctantly, acquiescence in his choice was given.

On September 30 the Democratic city convention met in Carnegie Hall. Edward M. Shepard (who himself had run for mayor on the Tammany ticket against Seth Low and had been soundly defeated) placed Gaynor's name in nomination. The delegates listened apathetically while Shepard paid Gaynor dubious compliments, saying:

"There is not, I fancy, a man who has taken an active part in public affairs in this city whom he has not offended. Of this I can speak, for I am one of those who have been thus offended, again and again." However, the judge's "intellectual ability, his powerful will, his long and extraordinary public services, his very face and figure, his voice and peculiarities of speech, his prejudices and his faults— for I understand that he is human and not a demigod—are as well known in the shops of tradesmen and merchants, by laborers and mechanics, by the masses of poor and rich, and most of all by the great mass of citizenship, in remotest Queens or Richmond as they are on Fulton Street in Brooklyn. . . . He has held, and has not concealed, strong and sometimes peculiar opinions. . . . But I feel assured that . . . this man is large enough and his mind is open enough to make the permanent welfare of the city his first care."

The newspapers remarked on the feeble response that this tempered eulogy aroused. The cheering at introduction of Gaynor's name lasted less than a minute, though by contrast every mention of Murphy, or McCarran, or Daniel F. Cohalan, Murphy's subleader, produced thunderous cheers. In a listless way the vote was taken and Judge Gaynor was nominated. Named to run with him (and also lustily cheered) were John F. Galvin, a manufacturer, to oppose Mitchel for president of the Board of Aldermen, and Robert R. Moore, another bank president, to oppose Prendergast for comptroller.

Gaynor was informed of the convention's action at the Knickerbocker Hotel, Broadway and Forty-second Street, where he was dining. He said he was relieved to get the nomination, because of the expense of running independently.

"I had thought to pass my life in my present exalted position," he told reporters, "but man proposes and God disposes. I have not asked for the nomination, and it comes to me without even the suggestion of a pledge, understanding, or condition whatever. I know the people of New York and they know me. They know the hour has struck. They know that in the slow ripening of time . . . we have reached the end of an old and the beginning of a new era in the government of this great city.

"And now," he concluded with punctilious courtesy, "I enter upon the canvass, first extending my esteem and good will to my distinguished opponent."

Nothing could be more chivalrous than this dipping of his lance in knightly salute to his antagonist before the jousting began; it augured well for a campaign conducted on a high level of propriety.

CERTAINLY DID SWALLOW HIM.

Courtesy of the New York Historical Society, New York City

New York Herald, October 9, 1909

But the reaction of the metropolitan press to this startling alliance between the town's foremost "boss-buster" and the town's foremost boss was neither chivalrous nor prophetic of an orderly contest. Some of the comments were sorrowful, many were bitter, and the consensus was that the Tammany tiger, of loathsome stripes, had swallowed the upright judge.

The *Tribune*, which despite its sturdy Republicanism had often discerned virtue in Gaynor as a judge, was wrathful:

"Well, it is done. Murphy has Justice Gaynor on his ticket, and Justice Gaynor has Murphy on his back. Murphy has all the better of it. He won't have to make any explanations. The association is creditable to Murphy. It is discreditable to Gaynor. It will call for a lot of explaining from him, and some of it will never be explained away. . . . He will have to tell the public how he, who has always fought political corruption and fought bosses and machines, could lend himself to the most corrupt machine and one of the worst of bosses. . . . The people have believed in him, we ourselves have supported him, just because he did not do such things or raise such doubts as he has now done and raised."

The *Sun* was contemptuous. In a leading editorial of fewer than a dozen lines it said:

"Tammany completed last night its somewhat protracted and complex agreement with Judge Gaynor and made him its candidate for mayor.

"We congratulate the Brooklyn jurist, and we felicitate the eminent Mr. Murphy. A worse man than Judge Gaynor might have been chosen, but it would have entailed a good deal of trouble to find him."

The next day the *Sun* apologized for this "hasty appraisal."

"A more mature consideration convinces us that we have been unjust to Judge Gaynor," it said. "We shall not again so egregiously err as to assert that a worse man than he might have been chosen."

The *Times* was sure that thousands of property owners would view with dread the possibility of Gaynor's becoming mayor.

The popular magazine of opinion, *Outlook*, dismissed Gaynor as "an erratic reformer with radical tendencies, and a judge without judgment."

Even the *World*, whose candidate Gaynor now was, while contending that Tammany had been forced to take a candidate "nominated by public opinion," still served notice that it was aware of the nominee's "serious faults, for which we have criticized him in the past and for which we shall probably have to criticize him in the future."

William Travers Jerome, the district attorney of New York who had come under Justice Gaynor's castigation more than once for his highhanded and highly publicized vice raids, termed the Tammany nominee "a man aptly described as a combination of a demagogue and a fanatic . . . a political charlatan, shown in the past to be utterly destitute of political courage, and whose erratic ability is tinged with a morbidness akin to mental unsoundness."

At Tammany Hall the braves were blue. Nobody knew anything about the judge's plans, or whether he would continue to tear into Tammany during the campaign. Many believed he would.

A letter from the Civil Service Reform Association addressed to Judge Gaynor at Tammany Hall was returned marked, "Not found."

A cold fog of bewilderment settled upon the Wigwam.

"THE ELECTION OF
AN UNDESIRABLE CITIZEN"

Sentence first—verdict afterwards.

—ALICE'S ADVENTURES
IN WONDERLAND

I N THE HISTORY of politics, few men have been so unsuited to engage in the rough-and-tumble of political competition as was William J. Gaynor in 1909.

Though he was sixty-one (and admitting to fifty-eight), it was not age that told against him. His hair and beard were gray, but his step was light, his movements agile, his perceptions quick and clear. It was by temperament, training, and experience that he was ill equipped to withstand the stresses produced by political strife.

Name almost any quality generally believed needful to success in politics, and Gaynor lacked it.

A politician must have the hide of a pachyderm or a pig to shed criticism without a quiver of sensitivity. Judge Gaynor was abnormally thin-skinned.

A politician works within a party, supporting and supported by it. Gaynor had no party; he stood alone.

A politician functions by means of compromises. Gaynor's conclusions were abrupt, forthright, and final.

A politician's private life is open to public scrutiny. Gaynor defended his private concerns from intrusion of any sort fanatically.

And so on down the list. Greatest anomaly of all—Gaynor in

many respects represented political trends and ideals that were already somewhat anachronistic; men with his concepts of public morality and public responsibility were going out of fashion.

But since Gaynor was Gaynor, despite all these deficiencies and contrarinesses that told against him, he was not daunted for a minute.

The day after his nomination reporters found him working on a backlog of cases pending before the Appellate Division, preparatory to resigning from the bench and giving up the handsome salary assured for years to come.

"We have nearly three hundred cases undecided, and the court meets next week to agree upon the opinions," he explained briskly, "and of course I will not do the bar the injustice of resigning until every case is disposed of, so that no reargument will be necessary."

He was asked who would be his campaign manager.

"I don't think I will appoint any political manager," was the matter-of-fact response. "I scarcely know what that means. I have made no plans for the campaign, and in fact would hardly know how to go about it anyway. The truth is, I am absolutely a novice in all matters pertaining to the routine work of a political campaign."

This startling intelligence was duly published and provoked explosions of ribaldry and skepticism. So did the judge's further announcement that his campaign headquarters would be in his home at 20 Eighth Avenue, Brooklyn. The notion of a candidate for mayor of *New York* making his bid from *Brooklyn* seemed to Manhattaners to be grotesque in itself; but when Gaynor began returning campaign contributions, press and public were dumbfounded by this Mad Hatter's tea-party excursion into politics.

The first two checks sent back, with warmest thanks, were one for $1,000 from Gaynor's friend Abraham, and the other a voluntary gift of $500 from Schuyler Parsons, president of the Coney Island Jockey Club. In covering letters Gaynor explained that "lying and misrepresentation" were already at work to defeat him, and he had decided not to spend a dollar to be elected. An astounded reporter asked whether he realized that money played a big part in political campaigns, and Gaynor answered:

"If that's so, I'm a goner in this election. Money is required to hire halls, of course, but is not necessary otherwise. The old boast of rulers that one-half of the people could be hired to shoot down the other half doesn't obtain in this day, to my way of thinking."

A week after the city convention, the nominee was formally notified of his selection by a delegation of Democratic leaders from all five boroughs. The judge kept them waiting in the parlor downstairs while he wrote out his acceptance speech in the library upstairs; then descending, he stood for an hour with bowed head under a drenching of oratory, after which he read his acceptance in a crisp, dry tone, without emphasis. It was a repetition of his nomination-night remarks, with classical allusions added and assurances to the people of the city that if elected, he and his associates, Galvin and Moore, would be steadfastly independent.

"No one will stand back of our chairs and nudge us how to vote," he promised, then repeated that he was prepared to "devote the next four years of my life to the service of the people of New York, if they want me, and if they do not, I am content."

Reporters tried to get something more colorful from him, but he repelled them with:

"I don't care to be interviewed. That is unseemly. I have made news enough for one day."

He did divulge, however, that he intended to make very few speeches, maybe six or eight, and that one would be in Tammany Hall.

The weather that day was nipping, but it seemed bland to the politicians and newsmen trooping away from this frigid send-off of a campaign. The *New York Tribune* was editorially disgusted:

"The judge's egotistic dithyrambs proclaiming that 'the hour has struck,' and 'in the slow ripening of time' . . . how silly they sound now! . . . Gaynor, the man for whom time has been waiting! . . . What is the use of the lessons that 'for now these many years, even with the persistency of Cato calling for the destruction of Carthage, have I taught,' if the teacher himself has learned no better than for the sake of regularity to herd with the low, vicious, and degraded elements in municipal politics!"

But Hearst supplied the headline many had been waiting for when he at length made clear that he had no intention of supporting the Democratic nominee.

As recently as five days after Gaynor's nomination he had indicated that he was still on the fence, telling the *World:*

"I believe Judge Gaynor is a good man and would make a good mayor, but I am sincerely sorry that Tammany is to be allowed to use his good name for another raid on this pillaged city. . . . I think the independents should do their best to elect Judge Gaynor and defeat Tammany."

Then several things happened that changed the picture totally. The Independence League's primary election was held, and behold, most of the delegates chosen to the city convention pledged themselves to nominate Judge Gaynor. Hearst immediately, at the top of his editorial voice, charged that Boss Murphy had stolen his party by infiltrating its ranks, and forbade the party secretary to call the convention.

Then, on the day of Gaynor's official notification, Hearst told the *New York Times* that he was appalled by the slate Tammany had picked to run with Gaynor, although he did not come out flatly against the judge himself. Hearst's exact words were, as quoted by the *Times:*

"The main objection, and perhaps the only objection, to Judge Gaynor is that he is allied with the most atrocious array of soiled and damaged political rags and remnants that have ever been exposed for sale on the bargain counters of Tammany Hall."

The day after that, in a boisterous rally at Cooper Union, complete with red fire and bands, Hearst was beseeched to accept an independent nomination for mayor, and he accepted.

This defection came as a shock to Gaynor, who had been banking on Independence League support, and he issued a bitter blast to the press. This included a letter written to Gaynor by Rudolph Block (identified as "a member of Mr. Hearst's distinguished editorial staff, at a large salary"), revealing that Block was the intermediary who had arranged Gaynor's meetings with Hearst, and telling of Hearst's positive assurances that he would support Gaynor for mayor on "any ticket whatever." Gaynor now recounted that this voluntary pledge had been renewed since Hearst's and his own return from Europe, in September.

"He [Hearst] came out into the hall to the elevator as I was leaving and took me by the hand and told me to come out with a statement that I would run and he would support me," the judge added specifically. "He repeated this several times. . . . Then after the primaries Mr. Hearst began to cry fraud, as usual, and that his ballot boxes had been stuffed. . . . There were not enough ballots cast at any poll to stuff a teacup, let alone a ballot box. . . .

"I never had a moment's jealousy of Mr. Hearst, and hate to see his heart so blinded with jealousy and hate of me. I am fully conscious that his great estate of from $50,000,000 to $60,000,000 gives him a huge advantage over me in one respect, but I am ready to meet him before the people of New York. . . . It may be that with all his money and his newspapers and power the people of New York may not let him run over me so easily as he thinks."

Hearst's reply to this was a satirical denial:

"If Judge Gaynor has stated that I promised to support him under any and all circumstances, and upon any and all tickets, he states what is positively untrue. . . . Judge Gaynor is not a lifelong friend or a deeply loved brother, to whom a blind devotion is due. . . . It is not true that I ever asked Judge Gaynor to come to my house in order to urge him to accept a nomination. He came humbly up to my house, once, twice, thrice, hat in hand, of his own accord and in his own interest. And I have no doubt that he had previously visited Mr. Murphy's house in the same abject attitude.

"It is not true that I told Rudolph Block or Judge Gaynor himself or anyone that I would support Judge Gaynor under any and all conditions.

"As for Mr. Block, the 'distinguished editorial associate' to whom Judge Gaynor so respectfully and ludicrously refers, he is the editor of the comic section of my Sunday newspaper, the sponsor for Happy Hooligan, the Katzenjammer Kids, and Judge Gaynor. His interest evidenced so peculiarly in Judge Gaynor's candidacy merely goes further to prove that he has a sense of humor, if not a sense of honor."

Gaynor had only one reply to this:

"The fact is exactly as I have stated it."

It thereupon became a matter of how much credence could be placed in each man's word. But stung by the charge that he had somehow defiled himself by association with Tammany's "rags and remnants," the judge issued a general challenge to his critics, charging in turn:

"All this bellowing against me because of some local nominations in Manhattan, Richmond, or Queens is purely dishonest. Under the charter each borough has its own local government and party organization, and if any unfit person be nominated, it is for the voters to defeat him."

He certainly had no intention of substituting himself for the electorate, any more than he would do the work of lazy lawyers.

"I am not a borough candidate," he insisted. "Everyone knows this who knows his knee from his elbow. I am not responsible for the nominations made in the boroughs. Some of the newspapers over in Manhattan seem to think that the borough of Manhattan is the City of New York. When they bellow to us over here about Tammany we don't understand them. If they have any grievances with Tammany, let them have it out at the polls. I was glad to get the nomination of the Democratic convention. It relieved me of great embarrassment over the cost of running alone. And if I am by my past life fit to be mayor, what difference does it make who nominates me? . . . No organization made me, and by the Eternal, none will ever pull me down—nor do I expect any will ever try it."

Privately, to Abraham Abraham, the judge confessed that he was "going through an experience of breach of faith and plighted word that I did not deem possible in this world. . . . If the people of New York do not want to elect me on my life record and my life work for good government and to destroy low and corrupt government, and those engaged in it, I assure you . . . I shall be content. . . . Do you know I feel like the pitcher in the saying of the Talmud: 'If the stone fall on the pitcher, woe unto the pitcher; if the pitcher fall on the stone, woe unto the pitcher; alas, whatever befall the pitcher, woe unto the pitcher.' Poor pitcher! But we shall wait for the count."

The stones had begun falling on the pitcher of Gaynor's good intentions even before Hearst's switchback. William M. Ivins, certainly one of the cleverest lawyers in New York, had opened an attack, as a Bannard supporter, on Judge Gaynor's fitness for office. Immediately after Hearst's independent nomination, Ivins proposed that the independents endorse the fusion ticket, except for Bannard, and in this way in effect leave only the race for mayor open. The proposal was distasteful to some of the fusion candidates, notably Prendergast and Mitchel, but it was adopted; whereupon Ivins, as Hearst's mouthpiece, became personal in his denunciations of Gaynor as a "paranoiac." The judge's personal liberty decisions, Ivins sneered, had been the fruits of a criminal collusion with lawbreakers.

When pressed to answer this accusation, Gaynor handed newsmen this typed statement:

"I would not contradict any lie of that man. I do not need to. . . . Please do not come here to ask me to contradict any hireling, no matter what he says. I leave all such things to my neighbors and those who know me, and what I have been and tried to do all my life."

Prodded to be fuller, he said:

"Yes, I see that Ivins said I was a paranoiac, a lunatic, an upholder of gamblers, and so on. I would not deny it for the world, even though it was said by anyone having a shred of veracity. Those who know me and my life answer it. I shall not abuse anyone nor answer abuse. No one ever got a dividend out of his abuse. As Epictetus says, 'That which another saith of thee more concerneth him who saith it than it concerneth thee.' "

Epictetus? The reporters were stumped by this name, heretofore unheard in New York politics. Scurrying to their encyclopedias they learned that Epictetus was a Stoic philosopher who flourished around A.D. 100, and though he had been a slave, there was no indication that he was ever active in politics. Within twenty-four hours Epictetus entered upon a resurrection of renown along Broadway, and "as Epictetus says" became a catchword attachable to further nuggets of wisdom and erudition let fall by the ever surprising Democratic candidate.

From this point the canvass rapidly lost all resemblance to the debate based on principles that Gaynor had envisioned. When Ivins ran out of conventional epithets of opprobrium to hurl at the judge, he invented new ones. He called Gaynor "a symbol for everything that is indecent and disgusting"—"a poor, I will go further and say a bad judge"—"a hypocrite"—"a learned fraud"—"a pseudo-paranoiac"—"a man afflicted with moral strabismus"— "mentally cross-eyed"—"beset by Messianic mania"—"incapable of telling the truth"—"an intellectual freak"—"intellectual prig." He accused Gaynor of gross misconduct on the bench, asserting that a racetrack decision had been agreed upon in advance in conferences with gamblers. This would have been an impeachable offense, and would have brought instant action had there been the slightest corroborative evidence, but there was none.

Gaynor struggled to hold himself in check, quoting the proverb, "The shallows murmur, the deeps are dumb," and adding with a decided ripple of anger: "We leave all the blackguards and abusers to go their way, and the mudslingers. We have got important things to talk about. Even though they bespatter me, I shall not turn to answer."

And Ivins kept at it. The *Sun* described this gadfly as "brisk and lively as a cricket in a neat suit of brown, brown spats, brown Ascot and topaz, with a brown Derby by his chair—intangible as air and as active as a Jersey mosquito"—blithely swinging a loaded shillelagh. But when Ivins raked up Gaynor's divorce and his Christian Brothers connection in a slurring way, the *Sun*, though unfriendly to Gaynor, obtained and published a letter from Brother Joseph, provincial of the order, stating categorically that Gaynor had taken no vows and had left the Christian Brothers "without a stain on his character."

But ecclesiastical crossfires were coming from other sources. Rabbi Stephen S. Wise—a pulpit orator who at times fancied that he spoke for the Jewish community at large, when he did not—mourned in a sermon that Judge Gaynor had proved "unequal to the great refusal," and by accepting a nomination "from polluted and polluting hands" had "brought low a great jurist of learning, probity, and distinction. . . . He is sinning against the light."

And Dr. Parkhurst revised his good opinion of the judge in view of the Tammany alliance. Estimating Gaynor's capacity for resistance to evil by his own, Parkhurst regretted:

"I haven't sufficient confidence in my own integrity to say what sort of a mayor I would be by the time I had completed four years of municipal administration under Tammany auspices."

Under goadings like these, Gaynor's friends wondered how long his temper could be smothered. Especially irritating was Ivins' repeated taunt that the judge had not resigned from the bench ("which he treats more like a perch"), although Gaynor was still laboring to clear up the Appellate docket, as a service to the bar. He still had not become free to resign when he opened his campaign on the home grounds, before a capacity audience at Brooklyn's historic Academy of Music.

Interest in this performance, with the redoubtable judge cast in a new role, was intense, and it was reported in great detail.

The press noted the light applause when Gaynor walked onto the stage. He looked tired, and he told the audience that he was in no condition to speak; but sensing the undecided mood of the crowd, he set to work to arouse their sympathy, with the result that (in the words of the possibly prejudiced *Brooklyn Eagle* representative) "before he had been talking fifteen minutes every person in the vast auditorium was hanging on his words."

The *New York Times* drew a pen picture of Judge Gaynor

"standing primly before the crowd, with hands clasped behind him
and eyes burning, shooting out a dispassionate, deliberate stream of
slangy, idiomatic, sometimes almost coarse language. His voice is
not powerful but has a resonant . . . twang that enables people in
large halls to hear him easily. The crowd enjoyed his dry, sardonic
humor; but when he said things that provoked roars of laughter he
did not laugh, he did not even smile."

Gaynor's fighting trim was shown in the sarcasm he poured on
Bannard's nocturnal nomination in Jack's restaurant:

"After a night amid the cigar butts and the empty champagne
bottles, there was produced a ticket bearing the names of Bannard,
Prendergast, and Mitchel. Had Charlie Murphy and other leaders
of Tammany Hall gone to such a place and under such conditions
produced a ticket, it would have been laughed out of town. If I had
been nominated by a conference of leaders in some chophouse in
Brooklyn, I would have been characterized immediately as the
'saloon candidate.' And had I been placed on a ticket conceived amid
such surroundings, I would have had nothing to do with it. And yet
it is these men, who took part in that early morning conference,
who fear I will be swallowed up by the Tammany tiger! If there is
any swallowing to be done after I get into office, you may rest
assured that I will be on the outside after the swallowing process is
over."

Gaynor spoke for two hours and ten minutes, and never was
at a loss. Whenever he quoted the Bible he asked a clergyman sitting
in the front row to correct him if wrong; and when he described
the ways by which dishonest officeholders robbed the taxpayer
struggling to pay for his home, a hush came over the audience. A
few moments later cheers and shouts greeted his dramatic declaration that if he were elected mayor, these robbers of the taxpayers
would be "crushed into the earth."

He had given no pledges, he repeated, and would give only one,
namely, that if elected mayor he would not use the office as a step-
pingstone to the governorship, but would remain the full four years
in the city's service. Speaking with the frankness of a friend to
friends, he said:

"I have received a stack of demands that high [indicating with
his hand] for pledges of all kinds, from woman suffrage to how to
build a subway; but I have given no pledge and don't intend to
give any. If the life of a candidate is not a pledge of his future conduct, then what is the use to ask of him a pledge?"

To Hearst he paid elaborate attention, and his thrusts cut deep. He told of his meetings with Hearst, and said:

"He gave this promise, and I thought I was big, that I had something, in view of the great cost of running for mayor by petition. Why, a man with $65,000,000 at his back can run for mayor on a petition and the expense is nothing to him. He can put down a million as easy as I can put down five dollars. But I had the promise. Huh, I had something! He says I had it, but it wasn't unconditional.

"Oh, that tiger! He was afraid of that. And yet he told me two years ago that he was walking hand in hand with the tiger, and running for office with the tiger, after having put some of them in stripes; and though they were in the chain gang he came out as jaunty and as sleek and as nice, and was right in the procession with them inside of six months! And that man says he is a man of principle! 'Tainted with Tammany!' That's what he says of me. Ho, ho, ho! 'Tammany! Tainted with Tammany!' Just think of it!

"He reminds me of a passage of Cicero when he spoke of a young man of vast wealth with an aspect 'combining the face of the sheep with the eyes of the hog.' . . . You know the yellow will come out in a man if it's in him!"

The crowd cheered and stamped in agreement. Then, speaking quietly and distinctly, while the audience listened carefully, Gaynor went on:

"Now, I must say just this in conclusion about Mr. Hearst. He came into politics not many years ago. His father, a very rich man with great mines throughout the West and in Mexico, died, leaving a princely estate, one of the largest in America. Not as large as Rockefeller's, to be sure, but as estates go, very large, with this young man sole heir. And what was the first thing you heard of him? The first thing you heard of him was that he should be President of the United States, and that immediately. . . . With a straw hat with a blue ribbon around it, and so jaunty, so sleek, and so feathery, with no experience, never held a public office, unknown, amid Greek fire and bombs and Roman candles and rockets, right over the heads of all the statesmen and venerable men and good men in the country, right into the flower bed in front of the White House, first jump! . . .

"Well, then he came down a peg and asked Mr. Croker to make him mayor, and Croker only looked at him and probably smiled. Though I hate to talk about smiling, because they say I never smile, but a thing like that certainly would make a horse smile. And he went to Congress, and the roll call shows five times, I think, when he was there. He may have been behind the door somewhere, but he didn't answer.

"And then he ran for mayor, and such expenditure of money in this city was never seen before or since, and I trust for the sake of decency and the institutions of my country will never be seen again. That is what moved me this year to send back checks, and say I wouldn't spend a dollar. . . .

"Then he had a notion that he wanted to be governor . . . and the first thing we knew, as jaunty, and as sleek, blue ribbon, white hat, and all, there he was with the Tammany tiger, and with Murphy and all of them, cheek by jowl, and he was going to be governor. Did he feel that he was tainted by Tammany? Oh, how solicitous he is now that we are tainted by Tammany! But enough of that."

These blows hurt, and the skeptics who had been inclined to laugh at the judge's quaint notions about the way to conduct a political campaign were less so after this demonstration of blunt speaking. And they would become less and less inclined to levity as time wore on.

Ivins rushed to Hearst's defense, asserting that Gaynor "talked incoherently" and was "wandering in his mind." Let everybody just read the judge's "wild speeches," Ivins exclaimed, and see from them how unfit Gaynor was for public office. There were six thousand lawyers in New York who knew Gaynor, Ivins said, and every man Jack of them would vote to make him mayor just to get him off the bench!

Hearst took the stump with his usual noisy entourage of rocket shooters and brass bands, and in his high-pitched treble called Gaynor "my aged friend," who would "rather be right than honest." He warned of dire consequences if Gaynor were elected:

"In Manhattan and the Bronx behind Gaynor stand the hungry hordes of Tammany. Murphy leads the charge against the eight hundred million dollars to be spent in the next four years. They cry 'No quarter!' because they do not want a quarter—they want it all!"

Gaynor, Hearst told street rallies between thumps of the drum, "is something less than the ordinary man. Rather ill-natured he is, and ill-informed, addicted to vituperation and without sincerity."

He tried to explain his turnabout allegiances—first blasting Tammany as unspeakably vile, then clinging to it, then rounding on it again as a thing of loathsomeness. What he could not explain was why Murphy and Tammany Hall should have been fit to associate with in 1907, and unfit directly before and directly afterward. Cynical reporters watching the performance guessed that Hearst was rattled.

The judge, however, had only started. Trying though it was to muzzle his temper, he succeeded moderately well until he made his first campaign appearance in Manhattan, at a Carnegie Hall rally got up by independent groups. A few hours before this meeting he had filed with the secretary of state his resignation as Supreme Court justice, effective immediately, and he now felt at liberty to follow his bent in speaking.

The auditorium was crammed and a crowd was turned away. Gaynor started mildly:

"I have received all kinds of advice as to how to answer attacks upon me. I shall answer those who attack me simply by my past life. My life has been a beeline on a certain course. I have followed a resolution that I would devote some of my time and energy and education to the interest of good government. So that is all I am. If that record does not commend me to the citizens of New York for their votes, now that I am unwillingly brought before them as a candidate, then I have nothing else to offer, not a thing, and you will have to vote against me."

This was in the high Stoic tradition. Then Gaynor repeated his tiger-swallowing prediction, already being quoted all over town, while Boss Murphy, sitting in a box, listened impassively:

"If any man says I am a man likely to be swallowed up by a boss or a tiger, I can only say that I have never been swallowed up yet."

He then turned his attention to Bingham, the ousted police commissioner. Bingham had been canvassing for Bannard, telling crowds that Judge Gaynor was a "humbug" who had simply roped in Tammany to foot the bill for his campaign—"out of your money." Gaynor returned these sneers by calling Bingham a "buffoon" and a "White House butler."

The senseless arresting of people for trivial causes did not originate with the policemen, Gaynor said; they were compelled to to make such arrests by the "buffoons and foreigners" who had been placed in command of the force.

"We elected a mayor four years ago," he went on, "and what

is done? The first thing we men of New York know the head butler of the White House is brought here. He thought he was at the head of a military force, and said so, and was not rebuked for it either."

Adverting to the Duffy case, he drew the moral:

"Law and order we must have, but first of all in a free government we must have law and order among those who rule."

Then turning to another familiar theme—a liberal Sunday, and the graft that was extracted under cover of Sunday closing laws— he told the crowd, alternating between humor and indignation, how the system worked:

"A great many years ago I made a move on a notorious criminal, John Y. McKane. I finally did destroy him, and in my innocence I thought graft at Coney Island was at an end. Little did I know that there were other men who would collect money as well as McKane. Things went on all right for two years, and then about two weeks before the time for the opening, the chief of police said he was going to close up everything for the season. Has a familiar sound to you?"

The crowd laughed in recognition.

"That has been going on for fourteen years. And a 'defense fund' would be raised, though there was never any defense put up because there were never any arrests."

Drawing a bead on Bingham, the judge continued with obvious relish:

"This year I particularly noticed that three weeks before the opening at Coney Island and Rockaway the police commissioner said—and he said the mayor sided with him—that this year everything at Coney Island and Rockaway was to be closed tight on Sunday. The reporters came to me, and I said I had been hearing the same thing for fourteen years and I hadn't seen anyone closed up yet, and meanwhile I had seen a committee go around and collect money.

"I am free to say that this year I took the trouble to advise people not to pay a cent. On the first day we learned that no arrests had been made, but written notices were sent to the proprietors of the swings and merry-go-rounds that the next Sunday the arrests would be made.

"I believe myself in the observance of the Sabbath. I was brought up that way and couldn't get over thinking that way if I tried; but if we go to church Sunday morning, or do something good, can't we go to Coney Island or Rockaway? Can't our children go on a merry-go-round there without being hounded by a police commissioner or a mayor? This thing is all wrong, this meddlesomeness, and it is this meddlesomeness through the city and at these places out of which millions of dollars have been collected, and collected by coercion and extortion.

"If I should become mayor, and my police commissioner conducted himself as some commissioners have done in recent years, his head would come off so quick he wouldn't be able to pronounce his name! In place of filling his pocket with graft, he would walk home without a head, if he could walk at all, and I would try to be police commissioner myself for a few weeks."

The applause was deafening. With grim earnestness Gaynor went on to say that it was not the business of the police to enforce moral standards. Especially in cosmopolitan New York, "the government should be as lenient with the people as possible, should not interfere with the social inclinations of the people beyond a certain trend."

He took solid shots at other abuses, including the practice of acquiring property by condemnation at excessive valuations, a process by which the taxpayers were mulcted of millions annually. He diverged a moment to praise ex-President Roosevelt, his Long Island neighbor and friend, saying:

"There was a man, I tell you, there was a man, who did what he thought was right, in spite of all the bosses and the politicians; even though he was sometimes wrong and had great defects; because I tell you a great man does not exist unless he has; the defects show what a great man he is."

Detractors of the city, clergymen and others, came in for special roasting. New York, Gaynor declared, was "the greatest and cleanest city in the universe"; yet fusion speakers were raising a howl about the alleged lax enforcement of the public health laws, and were claiming that the city was so sunk in debt it would never be able to find the money to build new subways. Against these "slanderers" Gaynor inveighed with the righteous wrath of an Old Testament prophet:

"There is one thing I want to say a word about," he prefaced, "and that is that the slanderers of the city shut up. They have defamed us around the world, and certain ragbag newspapers have picked up their slander and carried it around the world, until over in Europe they think that New York is putrid with vice. Why, I undertake to say this is the most decorous city on the face of the earth.

"These same slanderers and mudslingers—shame on them!— have lied about the health of the city—trying to give the impression that the officers of the city are letting disease run riot. Why are they doing it? Why, in the name of a little partisan advantage. Shame on them!

"What else have they defamed us in? Why, gentlemen, in our credit. How irksome it is to say that public officials of this city for the last four years have declared month after month, almost week after week, that the ten percent debt limit was exhausted and we were bankrupt. Public officials—do not urge me to say the first fiscal officer of the city [the comptroller]—over and over again declared that we have no money to build subways. Over and over; and then cool as a cucumber thirty million dollars of bonds may be flung on the market right on the heels of this statement. What can we expect from such business—that bonds will go up?

"Oh, ye hypocrites!" he shouted. "Stand out, all of you, and be counted this year! Ye Committees of Fifty and One Hundred, who every year for the past twenty years have uttered loud protestations for reform only to block every movement for reform—stand up, all of you, with William-Run-for-Everything Hearst—William Rule-or-Ruin Hearst—stand up, with him at your head, because the honest people of New York, Republicans and Democrats, are going out to meet you!"

It was a challenge that found an echo all over the city, and "Willie Run-for-Everything" and "Willie Rule-or-Ruin" became standard taunts used by hecklers at Hearst meetings.

In calmer mood, Gaynor stated in a few plain words his conception of the relationship between the mayor and the citizens:

"My purpose if elected is that the humblest man in this city can have a hearing at the seat of government. He will not have to come to me with any boss or any influence."

Again he pledged himself to serve a full term if elected, and repeated that no boss had made him and no boss could pull him down. At all times he held the audience in complete control, even when a well-known suffragette, whose ploy was to create disturbances at political meetings, broke in to demand that Gaynor state how he stood on the suffrage issue. There were cries of "Throw her out!" but Gaynor rebuked the audience, reminded them that a lady was speaking, and then turning to her, appealed:

"My dear lady, my dear lady—if you will allow me, my dear lady—you are a nice, amiable lady, but the question you ask is not pertinent in this campaign. But I will ask you, so as to keep out of all trouble, to go first and consult my wife."

This brought a burst of laughter, and when the heckler proved unsquelchable, police escorted her out of the hall.

From this stage of liveliness and plain speaking the campaign dipped to levels of personal abuse that caused the press figuratively to hang their heads in shame. The Committee of 100 opened a side-show in Union Square—the "Tammany Chamber of Horrors"—complete with Coney Island barker to pull in the crowds with his shout: "It costs you nothing to see it; it costs you millions to pay for it!" A papier-mâché "municipal cow," quivering under the never-ending pulsations of a milking machine, was placarded, "4,500,000 People Help Feed This Cow," and a tenement basement room was reconstructed, with charts and photographs pointing out the absence of every necessary health and sanitary provision.

Two doors away the Democrats opened a rival peepshow, also with a barker in a checkerboard suit. It featured a live elephant named "Herbena Hearst" that munched hay all day—symbolic of "what the Republicans hope to make." Reporters found the attractions doing about equal business.

Speaking in the hall housing the Tammany show, Gaynor contributed a fresh attack on Hearst, who "thinks everybody to be a fool to be deceived by fury and noise. The surroundings and the habiliments and the methods of the demagogue are with him wherever he goes. He is filled up to the weasand, yes, into the goozle, with promises!"

The reporters' dictionary thumbs grew sore from trying to keep up with the judge's recondite vocabulary, and at Tammany Hall the braves despaired. "Epictetus" and "Cicero" and "weasand" and "goozle"—was that the way to talk to voters? Right or wrong, good or bad, that was the way Gaynor talked. Speaking to three hundred traveling salesmen in a Wall Street noon-hour rally, the judge cried in his prophetic vein:

"Oh, ye people, I almost said woe to ye people, ye scatterbrain people, who would rather follow the scatterbrain talk of demagogues than read a closely written article of facts! These scoundrels profess to say that they are horrified that I, after a life of integrity . . . should accept the nomination of the Democratic convention of the

City of New York. Out with them! Out with them all! Hypocrites, scoundrels, defamers! Shut up or get out!"

Yet after such an outburst, in the meditative atmosphere of his library the judge could say with calm earnestness:

"I am not answering every little whelp that wants to bark at me. I have got something more important to do than that. I have got to lift this canvass up, if I can, and make it educational and respectable before the people of New York—and the whole of them may bark and whine, while I am doing it, all they see fit."

Although they tried their best to outdo Gaynor in vituperation, his opponents lacked his virtuosity. Bannard was lackluster on the platform. Hearst's fireworks and bands produced more excitement than he did. Mitchel, with barbed tongue, "talked right back" to the judge in a way that seemed impertinent rather than effective. And both Mitchel and Prendergast were handicapped by their refusal

A CAMPAIGN OF EDUCATION!

New York World, October 15, 1909

to junk Bannard and support Hearst for mayor, although they were running on the Hearst ticket also. Hearst was furious at their obduracy, and his anger, and that of more compliant fusionists, was vented the more harshly on Gaynor.

The judge was accused of being delinquent for years in paying his personal-property tax; but so was practically everybody else in New York, in regard to that particularly detested tax. Bannard leaflets distributed by the bale charged that tenements owned by Gaynor reeked with violations of the health laws. Gaynor made no bones about owning several tenements, but denied that he was being prosecuted for violations, as the fusionists asserted, and the press could find no ground for the fusion accusations.

The mudslinging brought constant exclamations of reproach from the press. Said the *Sun*, strongly Republican: "We doubt if even Gaynor himself ever realized, until lately, how bad a man he could be once he let himself go," and listed the qualities which made up this "ideal candidate for mayor." The list began:

"He should be violent and coarse in speech, Thersites with the benefit of a year's study of Billingsgate, to show his 'sympathy with the people' and that he is not 'stuck up.' "

The *Tribune* believed that Judge Gaynor had come to regard himself as a "sort of Statue of Purity—he frowns on 'slander' and undertakes for Tammany the championship of the city's fair name. He means to earn his keep, too, by shouting that Tammany's town is a good old town, well governed, where everything is lovely." *

Of the city's major newspapers—the *Herald, World, Tribune, Times, Globe, Mail, Post, Telegram, Eagle, Press, Journal, American*, and half a dozen others in several languages—only the *World* and the *Press* supported Gaynor. The *Press*, Republican in politics, carried little weight, but the *World* had the largest circulation in New York and spoke with the greatest authority. Yet midway through the campaign the *World* published that Gaynor was admittedly "irascible, suspicious, and vituperative," prone to believe that "everyone who opposes him is a heretic with a wicked and depraved heart."

Yet the *World* saw more than ordinary hostility provoking

* There were others singing this song, one being a young law student and song writer making his first bid for election to the city assembly. His name was James J. Walker, and he announced his platform boldly. It consisted of a single plank, namely: "I am making my campaign on the issue that Tammany Hall is a grand old organization, and it is near to the people and is their friend."

Gaynor's worst outbreaks. "Even Tammany has been treated with a consideration not accorded to a man who for sixteen years had been regarded generally as an able, fearless judge, and whose integrity during that time had been publicly questioned by nobody." Speculating on the possible source of the virulence displayed against the Democratic candidate, the *World* saw a clue in the fact that Gaynor's battles had "always been on the side of the masses and against privilege. One thing is evident: the desire in certain quarters is very much stronger to beat Gaynor than to beat Tammany. Much of the pretended opposition to Tammany is little more than a mask to cover the fight to beat Gaynor." Apparently the forces arrayed against him were powerful and not all of them political.

Despite every attack, Gaynor refused to dissociate himself from his slate or from Tammany. Again and again he told crowds it was just as necessary to elect his running mates, Moore and Galvin, as to elect himself, in order to secure control of the all-powerful Board of Estimate. He was not prepared to "fret my life away" contending with a hostile board, he said, and in Brooklyn he exclaimed:

"I have no hesitation in saying that if my associates on the ticket can not be elected, then I do not want to be elected. I want no barren scepter put in my hand."

The hostility of the press he defied. Striking back with disclosures that shocked politicians, he informed the public how much money the newspapers skimmed from the municipal gravy train in the form of payments for official advertisements that nobody ever saw. He told a crowd in Queens:

"The people who own the *New York Times* don't want me. You bet they don't! The people who own the *New York Sun* don't want me. You can bet your life they don't! They would like to cut my throat sooner than see me mayor."

The reason why the newspapers were against him was because they feared for their particular graft—payment for advertising "you never know anything about and is put in some vault in the basement and never goes out of the basement at all except in one or two or three copies so they can make affidavit that it was published. Well, listen to this. The *New York Times*, during the last three years and six months of the present administration, has received from the city for advertising $232,994.23.

"Do you think I will allow them to get that? Why, they are trembling in their boots!

"The *Globe*—oh, how it loves me!—$191,250.22. The *Mail*—

$204,720.90. The *Sun*, that says it 'shines for all,' though it don't shine for me—it knows a good thing when it sees it—the *Sun*— $168,932.63. If I had a lead pencil I would total it up." A pencil was handed to him and he figured on the table. "How much do you think? $796,897.98—enough to build five schoolhouses."

The rashness of this exposure appalled Gaynor's friends and, indeed, all right-thinking campaigners. Gasped Colonel Alexander S. Bacon—he who had led the assault on McKane's citadel years before and had landed in the Coney Island jail privy:

"Great Caesar's ghost! This is suicide! Attacking the newspapers' graft!"

The *Herald* acidly advised the judge that "as a politician and a candidate, he needs the newspapers, but they can get on without him; and whereas he can attack them on one day, they can attack him three hundred and sixty-five days in the year—and in every year."

If Gaynor's tactics really were suicidal—and according to all the rules they were—he remained cheerful about it. And there was more than one way to view his startlingly unorthodox behavior. Here and there in New York were a few who saw underneath the surface eccentricity. Even the disapproving *Herald* suggested that his abusive "lack of tact" and apparent disregard for consequences might make Gaynor more efficient as a mayor, should he by chance be elected. And a writer for the *New York Times* noted that the crowds who turned out for the judge were different from those usually seen at political meetings. "Queer," this observer called them— the mute multitude—the "common people," impressive only by their numbers—voiceless for the most part, but gifted with an instinct that enabled them to distinguish between a politician and a friend. Only one other man in New York's recent history had been able to drag this class of people to a political rally, the writer pointed out— Henry George. And the feeling of these curious crowds toward George, as it was toward Gaynor, had been one of trust: even when they laughed, they trusted him.

This same writer saw another quality in Gaynor, and that was his consistent underlying political philosophy. Everything Gaynor had done on the bench, and everything he had said for years, this writer maintained, could be traced to one thing—"a fanatical devotion to a certain epigram. Wide apart as his decisions and speeches may seem to be, they can all be traced to that, and it is the epigram, 'That government is best which governs least.' "

Joined to this basic article of faith was an unwavering sense of the interrelation between elected officials and the people who by their votes entrust them with temporary power—the concept that the prime duty of authority is to protect and indemnify, as far as possible, from the injustices and deficiencies of the social order, the unimportant, uninfluential, poor, and feeble.

Gaynor caught the ear of this multitude by the knack that lay in him, a knack personal to himself. With a single sentence he was able to make complex political and legal questions clear even to the uneducated. His speech was homely and graphic. To a workingmen's audience at Cooper Union he said:

"You don't need a mayor who carries bridge and subway contracts in his pockets. You don't need a mayor whose arms are steeped up to the shoulders in political jobbery. This is a government of laws, not men."

To the same group he said that if he were elected he would watch out for the interests of every citizen, regardless of social standing; nobody would be excluded from City Hall:

"There will be no guard to keep you out. The poorest man will be as welcome as the greatest financier of Wall Street, contractor, or traction looter in the city."

The most important thing, he maintained, was to protect the right of the individual citizens "to live and enjoy themselves according to their consciences."

Gaynor could startle an audience of Staten Islanders by hailing them as "ye Huguenots and ye descendants of the English," ignoring the many Irish in the crowd, and go on to convince them of his sincerity by tossing in:

"You can't teach an old dog new tricks, and I am too old now to begin to reverse my life and go backward."

His mail became enormous, and for the first time he allowed his secretary to keep a typewriter at Eighth Avenue overnight.

Every day produced a fresh surprise. Gaynor toured the Jewish East Side, where kosher butchers had been ordered to close their shops on Sunday, even though they closed on Saturday, and noncompliers had been harassed and arrested by the police. He showed up with a copy of the Penal Code under his arm, and speaking before an enthusiastic crowd on Canal Street he said:

"I've been here before, though not in circumstances like these.

On Sunday afternoons I often stroll through the streets, observe your men and women and children, and see how you live. I fear there are many mayors who have never seen you and don't know how you live. And there have been police commissioners, and I know of one big buffoon of that name, who came here only to annoy and persecute you.

"There are persons running for mayor this year who have never read the city charter in their lives. I do not need to tell you that I have been a student of government for forty years. . . . They ask me how I stand in this campaign, and I tell them I stand on my head! I need no boss to tell me what to do."

Quoting the Talmud regarding Sabbath observance, he pointed out that people of different faiths set aside different days in the week for their holy days. Then reading from the Penal Code, he demonstrated that the law recognized this condition, and allowed a man to work or run his business on Sunday if he observed some other rest day in the week.

"Why have not your mayor and police commissioners come here and read this law to you, instead of arresting you for petty violations?" he asked. "How many people here have been in Essex Market prison?"

A man in the front row retorted with a laugh: "I refuse to answer!"

An automobile tour of the district followed, with two more lively meetings. At one a listener called out, "You can bet the Jews will stick by you!" and Gaynor shouted back, referring to the Manhattan Bridge, just completed:

"And you can come to Brooklyn to see me after I am elected before I go to City Hall. Do you know how to get there? The new bridge, you know, is called the Jewish passover."

The leprechaun twinkle appeared in his eyes, though he hardly smiled.

A means of striking at Gaynor through the one important newspaper that supported him—the *World*—was devised by Brisbane on behalf of Hearst. Brisbane sold Pulitzer on the idea of carrying in the *Evening World* a daily article written by Brisbane "giving Hearst's side." It was a fine promotion stunt, and day after day Brisbane chopped Gaynor to bits with a malice totally unscrupulous. He asked the *World* readers—in capital letters:

"WHAT DO YOU KNOW INDIVIDUALLY ABOUT

GAYNOR THAT JUSTIFIES YOUR VOTING FOR HIM? ... Has he done anything more than take a salary from the people and do a little talking calculated to promote himself politically?"

He sneered that Gaynor made "a fine living out of a boy—not his own—as executor of the Ziegler estate. He draws at least ONE HUNDRED THOUSAND DOLLARS a year from the estate, yet he goes down to the East Side whining about his eight children and how much it costs to feed them."

These attacks drove Gaynor to fury, and ten days before the election he capped all his eccentricities by suing the *World* for slander for publishing Brisbane's articles, demanding $100,000 damages. After recovering from shock, the *World* took the action in good part and offered it as final proof that as mayor Gaynor would be controlled by no influence or interest on earth—even self-interest.

The *Tribune* agreed that Gaynor was immune to control—even self-control—but found that no recommendation for holding public office.

"The Katzenjammer Kids are all over this campaign," groaned the *Tribune*.

Nor could the *Tribune* and other frustrated onlookers be blamed for feeling they had been cast utterly adrift from all mooring lines of reason when they reported Judge Gaynor's first appearance at Tammany Hall. The auditorium was jammed, and an array of sachems sat on the platform, although Murphy remained at his desk on the floor below. With him remained most of the district leaders.

Gaynor arrived late, and upon being introduced stood a moment looking around with evident curiosity. Then he said:

"So this is Tammany Hall. This is the first time I was ever here. In fact, strange as it may seem to you, for you no doubt feel it is very important here in Manhattan, I did not even know where it was. I had to inquire by telephone before leaving my house as to how to get here."

A snicker seeped tentatively through the balcony and spilled a little to the main floor.

"So this is Tammany Hall," Gaynor repeated. "But if this is really Tammany Hall, where is the tiger? That tiger which they say is going to swallow me up, but as to which I said at Carnegie Hall and have no hesitation in saying here, that if there happens to be any swallowing, it is not at all unlikely that I may be on the outside of the tiger."

Again there was a ripple of what might have been a timid attempt at laughter (though one reporter called it a "collective gulp"), and the dignitaries on the platform shifted uneasily in their seats. But the judge's next remark eased the tension. Said he cheerfully:

"You look very much like the audiences I have addressed in the virtuous borough of Brooklyn and other parts of the city."

That brought a real laugh, and when Gaynor lit into Hearst and denounced the Brisbane articles the applause became frenzied.

"Why," he cried, "Hearst even hires the columns of other newspapers at enormous rates and hires writers to puff him up for pay. We had an expression when I was a boy, and it is a good one yet, 'It is enough to make one puke just to look at it.' The indecency of it!"

If anybody in the crowd still retained doubt of Gaynor's absolute independence, it should have been dispelled by his next words— a plain warning:

"I want to reiterate here tonight that I did not ask any man or organization to nominate me; that no approach, overture, or suggestion of any kind or shape was made to me as to what course I should take as mayor. I am an absolutely free man, and if there is anyone here or elsewhere who thinks or hopes that I shall as mayor abandon my life record . . . that I shall abandon the unbroken hostility of my life among you against bad government, against meddlesomeness, oppression, wrong, and corruption in government, let him go to the polls and vote against me."

On the subject of subways, he vowed that the speculators who had ruined the surface lines of the city should have no part in the program:

"By the Eternal, if Mr. Moore and Mr. Galvin and myself are elected to office . . . and we have a majority in the Board of Estimate, if that happens, by the Eternal, they will never get their clutches on the building of the subways!"

The cheering at this point grew so vociferous that Gaynor requested it be toned down; but his concluding remarks brought another storm of applause:

"In all this conflict I have had with corrupt government . . . I never answered any man except as I stood naked before the world in my public capacity and as he stood in the same way, and never struck except at the point of the chin, and these things I say are all public matters, open to legitimate discussion—a discussion that should not be shirked."

Throughout the final week of the campaign the city resounded with oratory and confusion. More than two thousand speeches were made that week, by a hundred orators, in several languages. Ten thousand men marched for Bannard. Hearst added what the *Sun* called "music, Hearst, and holler." But Judge Gaynor grew relatively calmer, and several times he lifted the edge of the secretive curtain that shrouded his inmost thoughts and hopes. In one unguarded moment he confessed, "For thirty-five years I have been thinking and building up what I could do as mayor," and he often spoke of his view of the office he had set his heart upon obtaining. The Bannard campaign was based on the contention that he could give the city what it needed—a "business administration." This was a fallacy, in Gaynor's opinion.

"The government of this great city is a complex legal and political machine," he said. "To say that you can call a man from a belting factory or a dry-goods store to run it without training is the greatest folly on earth. He's doomed to failure from the start. It's something more than a business. You have to know how to do it."

In winding up the canvass in Brooklyn, he described what he thought a mayor should be and do:

"It seems to me that in this great city the mayor should be somewhat closer to the people of the city than he has been. . . . The mayor ought to be the vision of the community. He should see everything, hear everything, and what he doesn't see or hear he ought to be able to smell. He ought to have the sense of 'mental smell'; to know everything, and to know every pin that falls—to look out for the community. As the Scripture says of rulers, 'When there is no vision the people perish.' The ruler should have a vision for the people and lead the people and be with them."

People was the issue he came back to constantly; not monetary figures or political abstractions, but people—all the people.

Nor did he lose sight of the sort of corruptionist he was determined to combat. He told a reporter for the *Chicago Evening Post:*

"The man I am down on is the respectable fellow who gets away with a million of the city's money, and then hires some committee to discover that five dollars too much was paid for a ton of straw and make a big noise about it."

And Hearst exacerbated him to the very end. In his last Academy of Music speech Gaynor struck once more at this antagonist who, he said, "advertises himself as though he were a patent medicine or a nostrum. . . . What would you think of me if I were to ... hire a man at the rate of $50,000 a year to slobber over me, just as though I were a pain-killer of some kind, or a fool-killer? Why, we used to say—and it was not offensive to the ladies, and is not now—when I was a boy, 'It makes me puke.' We could not describe our disgust in any other way."

Nemesis, he predicted, would overtake these slanderers after the election:

"It is time that libelers be taught a lasting lesson in this great and intelligent city through the criminal law, and I intend to take care of the ringleaders as I did of McKane. He laughed when I warned him; let them laugh now."

The final days of the hectic struggle brought open appeals to bigotry by the judge's opponents, and a crowning example of spleen on his part.

Three days before the voting, several newspapers reproduced on their front pages photographic facsimiles of Gaynor's reply to a letter sent to him at Eighth Avenue by A. B. Kerr, chairman of a Bannard campaign committee. The letter maliciously inquired whether Gaynor had protected gamblers and prostitutes on the bench; whether he had "told the truth" when he said he didn't know his way to the Tenderloin, and so forth. The facsimiles showed that on the typed reply Gaynor had drawn a line through "Kerr" in the address, and had written above it "Cur." It was a childish thing to do, but Gaynor defended it, saying that Kerr knew that his letter, sent to the family home, might readily come to the knowledge of Mrs. Gaynor and the daughters. There was no attempt at extenuation; Gaynor said simply:

"This man Kerr asked me whether I was telling the truth about not knowing my way to the Tenderloin. I told him I was telling the truth. I have no reason to go there. I spend my time in Brooklyn, and evenings I make calls or receive them. I know most of the clergymen of Brooklyn, and they call on me and we discuss theology to beat the band. Lots of Brooklyn people live like me and don't know anything about the Tenderloin."

The next day, Sunday, the Rev. William J. Dougherty, pastor of St. Athanasius Roman Catholic Church in the Bronx, denounced Gaynor from the pulpit as a divorcee, a renegade from the Christian Brothers, and an atheist, and urged his parishioners to "cut off the head" of the Democratic ticket. The priest asserted that Archbishop John M. Farley had tried in vain to prevent Gaynor's nomination as offensive to Catholics, and went on:

"This man has denied his God. He has turned traitor. His wife divorced him on the most serious of charges. Such a violation is one for which the Irish will not stand. . . . I am a Democrat, and on Tuesday I will vote the Democratic ticket, but I will cut off the head of that ticket."

Charles F. Murphy swiftly issued one of his infrequent public statements denying as an "absolute falsehood" that the archbishop had made any representations whatever regarding the nomination. No other Catholic pulpit echoed Father Dougherty's attack.

Almost simultaneously, however, the city was flooded with viciously anti-Gaynor circulars, one of a sudden series mailed from Midwestern cities. This one quoted an article from a St. Louis religious weekly, the *Western Watchman*, signed by the Rev. D. S. Phelan, calling on Catholics to reject Gaynor at the polls. Not only had Gaynor renounced his church, the article said, but his children were being reared as Episcopalians, and "there is not a Catholic in the world who would not prefer to see his mother or sister dead than turned Protestant."

The effect of this last-minute attempt to inflame religious hatred was hard to gauge, but among many Irish voters it backfired. Said John J. Connor, president of the Irish-American Union, the day before the election:

"I received one of the circulars, and I met fifty men in the Union who got them. They are all of one mind now—to vote for Gaynor."

The newspapers deplored the outrage. The *Sun*, firmly opposed to Gaynor, repudiated the attack and charged it had emanated from "the managers of Bannard, even if it was suggested by the managers of Hearst."

The religious issue was present, of course. In several Protestant churches prayers were offered for the defeat of Tammany, and Rabbi Wise took to task thirteen Jewish rabbis who were working for Gaynor and the Tammany ticket on the East Side.

Gaynor's reaction to the St. Louis attack, coming after the circulation of similar broadsides mailed from Chicago, was one of sadness. He made no reply to the charges, but told a windup audience at Durland's Riding Academy:

"Just think of it! That sort of thing being done today, after two thousand years of Christianity!"

He had ascertained, he said, that the postage alone on the whole series of libelous leaflets must have cost $75,000, which was evidence that the attack was not the work of a single person, but was financed and carried out by some well-organized group.

"It is very regretful," he concluded, "but I am content, because I find that the bigotry of one man is generally offset by the fairness and decency of many others."

The outcome of the election he awaited with confidence, whatever it might be, and he repeated, "I am content." As for Hearst—"Let him stew in his own juice."

These words were spoken on the eve of the election, and on election day the newspapers carried their own judgments of the campaign.

The *Tribune* said flatly that never had a political contest been fought on such low terms, and it guessed that had Gaynor not already been well known to the public, people "would believe his mind to be unhinged. . . . With all his ruffianly vocabulary . . . he

FATHER KNICKERBOCKER: "PLEASE TURN THE HOSE ON ME."

Courtesy of the New York Historical Society, New York City

New York World, November 2, 1909

has reduced himself from a respectable figure to the most despicable one that was ever presented for high office in this city."

Bourke Cockran, a veteran of thirty years of New York politics, inside and outside Tammany, already had branded the campaign "one of slime—no politics in it—not even a campaign of personal virtue, but one of personal depravity."

The *Sun* called the canvass "malodorous" and spoke of "a contest of despumation" and "besmirch." Its measured judgment, and its fervent hope, was that never again would the people of New York "submit to such degradation and humiliation as it has brought upon them."

The *World*, also, doubted "if ever a campaign was fought on a lower intellectual and moral level"—a mere frenzy of "mudslinging, of calumny, of slander, of vituperation, of abuse, and of ignorance."

Privately editor Cobb wrote to Pulitzer:

"Our friend, the 'Christian jurist,' will probably be elected. He has done what he reasonably could do to defeat himself, but the time was too short. . . . If he is really sane, I doubt if anyone was ever crazy; yet there is much to be said in favor of having a lively lunatic at the head of the city government for four years. Nothing has been gained by a safe and sane administration; so it is possible that an energetic crazy man could do some good."

The betting odds stood at two to one that Gaynor would be elected. In the last few hours $100,000 in wagers was said to have been registered in Wall Street.

Election day dawned blustery. Judge Gaynor spent the forenoon at home, and after luncheon went for a walk, alone. At four o'clock he visited the polling place, in a tailor shop near his house, and cast his ballot; then, correct in frock coat and top hat, and carrying an umbrella, he set off briskly again through Prospect Park. He was seen there several times chatting with the gardeners.

By dinnertime the returns showed that the judge was running well ahead, and newspaper reporters gathered in the parlor at 20 Eighth Avenue. About eight o'clock Gaynor strode in.

"Well, what do you want?" he asked brusquely.

The group—all but one or two of them representing newspapers that had pilloried him for weeks—stood up, and the boldest of them hazarded:

"Judge—I think you can be called Mr. Mayor now that you have been elected—won't you say something on the result of the election?"

"Have I been elected?" was the imperturbable response.

"Yes, the returns indicate that you have been elected easily."

"Well, if you want to wait around a little while perhaps I may have something to say, but I've walked twelve miles today and I'm hungry. I want my supper. But sit down till I get through my supper."

He strode up the stairs and the newsmen settled down to wait.

Shortly the Rev. James F. O'Donohoe, pastor of the Catholic church of St. Thomas Aquinas, walked in and disappeared upstairs to sit with the judge while he dined.

Then the Rev. Dr. William Morrison, pastor of St. John's Episcopal Church, dropped in, and he, too, joined the confab upstairs.

The newsmen waited.

After a while refreshments for them arrived—a pitcher of ice water and one glass.

At 9:45 the judge's secretary descended with a slip of paper on which was written the mayor-elect's victory message:

"I have nothing to say, except to present my compliments to the newspaper proprietors and editors."

The attention of the reporters was particularly called to the punctuation, which they were requested to follow—"there is a comma after 'say.' "

For the most part, the newspapers were neither terse nor elliptical in their election results comments. But the *Tribune* yielded gracefully:

"Judge Gaynor's favorite deliverance, 'I know the people of New York and they know me,' seems to have been authoritative. It is clear now that the people made up their minds to vote for him, probably even before he was nominated. . . . We wish to record our profound conviction that if he had chosen to stand in Madison Square Garden not on his metaphorical but on his physical head, maintaining his prophetic gravity, the people would still have voted for him with unabated unction."

The *Sun* was bitter:

"Judge Gaynor, certainly the most unfit candidate ever offered for the mayoralty in the history of this community, has been elected by an impressive plurality. The fact is full of bitter significance."

This homage to perversity triumphant was headed:

"The Election of an Undesirable Citizen."

A TIME OF WAITING

—————————|o◯o|—————————

> *"What is it in reality,"* said Sancho,
> *"that your worship means to do in such
> an out-of-the-way place as this?"*
> —DON QUIXOTE

THE ANOMALY was that Gaynor had been elected, but the entire rest of the Tammany ticket had gone down in defeat.

Prendergast was elected comptroller, Mitchel would head the Board of Aldermen, George McAneny was elected Manhattan borough president, Steers president of Brooklyn, Miller president of the Bronx, and Cromwell, of Richmond. Even Laurence Gresser, elected president of Queens borough, although a Democrat, had run independently and was not a Tammany man. Charles S. Whitman in the contest for district attorney of New York county had snowed under his Tammany opponent, George Gordon Battle.

In the final count, Gaynor received 250,678 votes, or 43% of the total cast; Bannard got 177,662, or 30%; and Hearst ran third with 153,843, or 27%. Both Bannard and Hearst said they were satisfied with the result, since Gaynor would be faced by a hostile majority on the Board of Estimate. The "barren scepter" which he had said he did not want had been thrust into his hand.

Mitchel almost tripped over himself in his haste to capitalize on the outcome. Before the votes were fully tallied, he called on Gaynor to carry out his promise to refuse to serve. In such event, Mitchel would legally succeed.

"Mr. Gaynor has stated publicly and repeatedly," Mitchel taunted, "that in case Mr. Murphy's Board of Estimate was not elected to office with him he would resign. We expect so eminent and pious a jurist to keep his word. In that event it would be my duty to assume the office of mayor under the law. I am determined to do so since Mr. Gaynor is determined to thrust the honor upon me."

Privately he wrote to a friend:

"No chance that the pious jurist will keep his promises. When did you ever know him to do so?"

Gaynor thrust nothing upon the cheeky young man except a letter invoking harmony for the good of the city. And some canny observers suddenly recalled that in the heat of the campaign Gaynor had never attacked Mitchel, Prendergast, or McAneny as he had Bannard and Hearst.

The outlook, however, was not indicative of smooth sailing. In the Board of Estimate and Apportionment, the mayor, comptroller, and president of the Board of Aldermen each had three votes; the presidents of Manhattan and Brooklyn, the most populous boroughs, had two votes each; and the presidents of Queens, the Bronx, and Richmond, one vote each. Except for Gaynor, the only non-fusionist elected to the incoming board was Gresser of Queens, and in a straight party division his would be the only vote to be cast with Gaynor's. Thus their combined four votes would be nullified by the twelve the fusionists would control.

This prospect in no way seemed to depress Gaynor. He was cheerful about it, and told a newsman why:

"The powers of the mayor are very great. Some newspapers that don't know their knee from their elbow are now discussing what I can do with a Board of Estimate elected on the opposing ticket. But what they don't know about the government of this city would fill a book, and more, too."

The mayor's strength, Gaynor comprehended, lay in his jurisdiction over every city department except two—the fiscal department, which was under the comptroller, and the Board of Education. The commissioners, or heads, of all the departments except these two he appointed and could dismiss at his pleasure; and even the members of the Board of Education the mayor appointed, though he could not remove them during their five-year terms. This placed in his hands absolute control of the city's administrative machinery, and of this fact Gaynor was perfectly aware.

The day after his election the mayor-designate encountered a bevy of reporters in his parlor when he returned from a morning walk. He seemed in excellent spirits. He parried their questions good-naturedly, saying that "now that the election is over nobody has any immediate reason for lying," but he gave out no indication whatever of his plans. In the midst of the banter his manner suddenly changed. Noticing a magazine artist sketching him, he exclaimed in a gust of anger:

"What are you doing there? Leave this house immediately! This is damnable! It's an outrage!"

That made copy for the day, and so did his refusal to drop his slander suit against the *World*. He had thanked the paper for its editorial support during the campaign, sending a one-line telegram; but weeks would elapse before mutual friends would succeed in persuading him to abandon the action. Belatedly and wonderingly the *World* comprehended that it had been no campaign gesture; Gaynor had meant it. This *was* something new in political annals.

Shortly after the election Gaynor sent to Bannard and Hearst the numerous scandal letters about them that he had received. And he filed with the secretary of state his sworn statement of his campaign expenditures. It was brief and clear-cut, to wit:

"I did not contribute or expend any moneys in aid of my election, either directly myself, or through any other persons."

Throughout the rest of November and into December Gaynor secluded himself at St. James. He refused to discuss appointments, and though from time to time prominent politicians alighted from the train at the St. James station, the silence at Deepwells was not broken. The single exception was the appointment by Gaynor, early in December, of his City Hall secretary. His choice fell on Robert Adamson, a *World* reporter who had covered City Hall for eleven years. Adamson was from Georgia, and his appointment gave no satisfaction to Tammany; as a *World* alumnus he was automatically antimachine.

Shortly after announcing this appointment, Gaynor undertook a number of public addresses which, while revealing nothing about his future plans, did make clear his broad intentions in office.

Before the Press Club on December 10 he begged the newspapers to tell the people of New York that he intended "to serve my four years as mayor and to do my duty to the people who elected me." He had said the same thing in the campaign. Was it possible that he meant it?

"I hope to work in harmony with the press," he told the newsmen, "for I am not of a quarrelsome nature. But I will do the right thing by the public, and if the papers don't agree, they can shout as much as they like."

A few days later at New Rochelle he paid his respects to the press again, although adding that "the less said about some of the newspapers the better for the community. Mental deterioration is the only way to characterize the people who read those papers. . . . If such newspapers wish to contine to invent lies about me they are at liberty to do so."

Hearst's treachery obviously was not going to be forgotten.

In the same speech Gaynor repeated his promise to be accessible to everyone, high or low, saying:

"I am glad to have people come to me. They have a right to do this, and I am willing that they should come, because sometimes I learn something—I learn what to avoid."

His attitude toward different types of reformers—the self-seeking and the self-effacing—he stated pungently:

"There are thousands of good men, ministers and priests and others, who are working day and night to ameliorate conditions. We do not hear so much from them as from the sensation mongers. With these workers I am going to work. With the sensation mongers I am not going to work. There are only a few of them, but, dear me, how stridulous they are!"

Mindful of his obligations to the Democratic organization, the mayor-elect appeared at a "victory banquet" of three hundred party workers at Shanley's, and gave them a pep talk that rather threw a wet blanket on the celebration. There was quiet as the braves heard the man they had helped to elect exhort:

"I am going to ask all you people to be patient, to summon up your best virtues, and to give me the best assistance that you can for four years, and don't be disappointed if things are not as you expect them. Don't be disappointed or disagreeable."

The well-heeled members of the Montauk Club got a lecture from Gaynor on the same subject. These men of wealth and position were told:

"Of course we have to look out for our private interests and family welfare; but something is due from everyone, and much from some, to the general welfare."

He cited his own example in giving up an assured income considerably larger than the salary paid to the mayor of New York.

In the middle of December, a couple of weeks before Gaynor

was to take office, Hearst through his newspapers set up a fresh cry
of "scandal." Hearst was determined to link Gaynor with the
plunderbund at Tammany in some way or other. After the election,
Murphy had gone to Mount Clemens, in Michigan, for a rest cure.
While there he had been kept posted on events at the Hall by trusted
lieutenants. Suddenly Hearst's *American* began publishing certain
letters that the boss had received at Mount Clemens during November.

How these highly confidential communications had come into
Hearst's possession soon became known: a chambermaid in Murphy's
hotel had been bribed to smuggle out the contents of his wastebasket daily. Murphy had a habit of tearing up letters after he
read them and dropping them into the wastebasket. The handymen
at the *American* had painstakingly patched and glued the scraps
together, and some of the letters were reproduced in the *American*
photographically.

From the jumbled assortment the *American* deduced that
Murphy and Gaynor were laying plans to strip the city's treasury.
What some of the letters did show was that Charles M. Hyde, Gaynor's close personal friend and relative by marriage, was in touch
with Tammany in reference to appointments. Two correspondents
on whom Murphy seemed to lean heavily—lawyer Daniel F. Cohalan
and Joseph D. Carroll, a contractor—had written about the prospects of jobs, and Carroll had reported:

"All applications that the Judge receives at St. James, he
forwards all of them to Hyde, to file, so when the time comes, as I
suppose from Hyde's remarks, on your return to the city, they will
be taken up. Charlie is very friendly. . . . Applications for positions
are coming in by the thousands. Hyde told me he did not think that
out of the whole bunch received there are ten fit for the jobs they
were seeking. . . . Hyde says there has not a thing been decided in
reference to any office whatever. He says for you not to worry. . . .
One strange thing he said was that Judge Gaynor would go very
slowly. . . ."

In the midst of these advices to the "Chief" (or to "Dear
Commissioner," as most of the superscriptions read) appeared a
letter from Murphy himself, written to Judge Gaynor during November, although the date was missing. It referred to a call Murphy
had paid at the judge's home before leaving New York. Because of
its rarity (it is one of the exceedingly few letters, other than social
acknowledgments, written by Murphy, the text of which is known to

survive), and because of its bland ambiguity, it merits attention:

"My dear Judge: Your very kind letter was forwarded to me here, and I am indeed pleased to hear from you. It is certainly very gratifying to know there was such a hearty welcome for me at your most hospitable home.

"Of course I should have telephoned your house, but I anticipated getting there early in the day, and would have, but for an unexpected blowout, requiring a new shoe and inner tube, and a delay of forty-five minutes. I am taking the baths here and thoroughly enjoying the much welcome rest. I take long walks every morning and afternoon, and am feeling good. I may be in condition to compete with the long walks you take at St. James, and would indeed very much like to cover that part of the country with you some day. I will be in New York about December 1.

"Before leaving town, and since my arrival here, I have had numerous applicants desirous of serving under your administration in some capacity or other. I advised, in each case, that they make application to you direct, stating 'positions' they feel qualified to fill, and references, and then when I was consulted I would gladly state what I knew concerning them.

"I hope you are well, also keeping up your exercise, and with best wishes, I am, sincerely, C.F.M."

There were other letters showing disgruntlement at Tammany Hall, where some braves were sarcastically alluding to the aloof judge as "His Royal Highness," and because of his silence on jobs, "The Veiled Mahatma."

Striving to establish a line of guilt, the *American* called on Gaynor to dispel "the most alarming impression created . . . that you, the mayor-elect, are in such close and regular association with Boss Murphy and Tammany Hall. . . . If you are going to be a Tammany mayor we want to know it quick. If you are going to be an honest people's mayor, we would like for you to emerge quickly from the shadow of suspicion."

Having no respect for the source of this challenge Gaynor disdained it; but he was reported to be wroth with Murphy for being careless with his mail. At a conference of high-level Tammany officials at Delmonico's, Gaynor's indignation was said to have been conveyed in stinging terms by Justice Martin J. Keogh, a personal friend, who had just come from Deepwells. The session was described as "very solemn."

As the time of his taking office drew near, Gaynor made appearances before two groups that held special appeal for him. The first was at the dedication of an addition to the Hebrew Orphan Asylum in Brooklyn. In his speech the mayor-elect repeated his admiration for the Jewish people and their civic-mindedness. He recalled a bit of local history that probably was new to most of his audience:

"When the first Jews arrived in New York harbor they were not allowed to come ashore until they had promised to care for their poor. That was by order of Peter Stuyvesant. That was Christian charity then. . . . Since you landed, you have always provided for your poor and orphans. . . ."

Coming away from the ceremony, Gaynor bristled at the sight of twenty-five uniformed policemen supposedly "maintaining order." Three would have been enough, he exclaimed to his host, Simon L. Rothschild:

"Does the captain of this precinct think there is any danger of you people quarreling? There may be a change in this kind of performance after January first. This is tommyrot. It's rank foolishness. What is the sense of having a lot of policemen at these orderly, quiet meetings?"

The next day Gaynor was honored by the bar of the four counties of New York City (the Bronx was not yet a separate county) at a banquet at the Waldorf-Astoria. A thousand lawyers and judges were present, and Gaynor was moved. He was severing his connection with the profession he had served for a quarter of a century and to which he had given the best in him. With unaffected humility he asked the help of all in the task that lay ahead.

"I have always been content to work, and I claim nothing more," he said. "I have been a drudge all my life, and am now about to change from one form of drudgery to another. I do not say that I am taking leave of you or of my past life tonight. I could not do that if I would. My very flesh and bone are of my past. My character, such as it is, with all of its deficiencies; my views of government; my hatred of official corruption (I can not state it in milder terms), and my habits of work and thought are irrevocably formed by my life and work among you."

When he suggested that "the courts would do well to enforce the laws of libel more strictly," his listeners, mindful of the recent campaign, shouted with laughter. But when he lit into "sneak

thieves of journalism" he drew hearty applause. His closing words
were spoken with revealing candor:

"I hope I may say with propriety that the hard work I did at
the bar . . . constitutes the rudder of what remains of my life. . . .
Would that I were fully prepared! Without the support of intelligent and unselfish men I can do little indeed. I shall no doubt make
mistakes; but judge me justly, and help me."

On the last day of 1909, Mayor McClellan performed his final
official act by leading a parade of automobiles and carriages across
the Manhattan Bridge, opening it to traffic. At midnight he would
cease to be the mayor of New York.

At about the time McClellan was making this valedictory
gesture a copy of a letter reached the city desks of New York's
newspapers. It was written by Gaynor, and was the forerunner of
tens of thousands that would pour from the City Hall in the years
to come—a mountain of self-expression without an equivalent in
the career of any other public figure. This letter, which arrived so
modestly on the eve of Gaynor's assumption of office, was reproduced
textually in the morning newspapers of New Year's Day. It was
addressed to Thomas J. Higgins, a member of the Board of Education, living in the Bronx. It read:

"Dear Mr. Higgins: I propose to appoint you commissioner of
parks for the Bronx tomorrow, and I trust you will accept, for a
thorough reform in that office is needed. Among other things, I find
that every one appointed to work in the park there, in whatever
capacity, is required to join a political club of the present commissioner and pay it dues and assessments periodically levied, to be
used in primary contests and for other purposes. Let all of that be
stopped immediately. No political interference or influence whatsoever will hereafter be suffered in any department of the government
of New York City.

> "Sincerely yours,
> "W. J. GAYNOR."

And so dawned the new day.

A DOZEN NEW BROOMS

Nine-tenths of all Republicans want honest government; nine-tenths of all Democrats want honest government; the dickens is to take care of the other tenth.

—GAYNOR

THE SIGNIFICANCE of Gaynor's initial letter, should it indeed prove to be the harbinger of a firm policy, was only too apparent, and at Tammany Hall New Year's Day was passed in determined but wan hope. There were other straws in the wind which indicated that a change was coming. Fifteen minutes after midnight on New Year's Eve, a policeman in Brooklyn had arrested a tipsy youth outside a restaurant, complaint having been made that he was pinching the women entering and leaving the place. The prisoner was belligerent, and on the way to the station house threatened to have the policeman "broke." The desk sergeant asked his name, and when he said, "George B. Duffy," like the figurative hot potato he was dropped and the arrest expunged.

On January 1 Gaynor left his home shortly before eleven o'clock, accompanied by his official secretary, Adamson, and headed on foot for New York's City Hall, three and one-half miles away. The wind whistled as the pair crossed Brooklyn Bridge, but it failed to bother Gaynor. A little before noon he bounded up the steps of City Hall, cheeks ruddy and looking the image of health. Adamson looked tuckered.

The new mayor was spic and span, dressed in black coat, gray trousers, wing collar, dark tie, and top hat. Hundreds of well-wishers were on hand, and policemen had difficulty in clearing a lane to let Gaynor reach the room where McClellan was waiting. The two men chatted a few moments, and Gaynor remarked that this was his first time in City Hall; the building impressed him as "very old but very handsome."

On the stroke of twelve they entered the reception room, where Gaynor was sworn into office. During the ceremony his family— wife, five daughters, and two sons—stood strung out along his right; McClellan stood at his left. The outgoing mayor then bade his successor Godspeed on a "very difficult journey," and Gaynor replied with a statement of his intention to do "the best I can for the City of New York. That will have to suffice; I can do no more." Then McClellan left by a rear door and the handshaking began.

During the next forty-five minutes Gaynor shook some twelve hundred hands, by police count. Many of those in line he knew well, others he was familiar with by sight. The new president of the Board of Aldermen, thirty-year-old John Purroy Mitchel, tall and lank, was given a quick handshake and a genial:

"So you are Mitchel. Well, you are a young chap. I saw you once before, not long ago, when you were a mere boy. I'm always glad to see young men get along."

"Young Torquemada," as Mitchel was dubbed at Tammany Hall, was uncertain how to take the greeting; he was defensively self-conscious about his age, and he looked embarrassed.

Behind Mitchel came a man, Colonel C. H. Smith, whose name was figuring in the news because of his dismissal from his city position on the last day of the outgoing administration under circumstances that seemed peculiar. Gaynor greeted him cordially:

"You are the man they put out of office on the last day after you had served thirty years. Well, we will have to look into that, I guess."

When Thomas J. Higgins stepped up, Gaynor failed to recognize him.

"Are you the man I appointed?" he asked in surprise. "I didn't know you all dressed up."

And so it went. A woman schoolteacher was told, "You may be mayor yourself, if you live long enough." Tammany was represented by four leaders, including John F. Curry, the deputy register, but Murphy did not appear. A numerous delegation of Brooklyn Democrats was led by the new party leader in that borough, John H. McCooey, who had succeeded when McCarran died during the election campaign. Gaynor knew many in this group and welcomed them cheerfully.

A few minutes before one o'clock the mayor called quits and retired to his office. There he greeted several bigwigs and carried out his first official chore by swearing in a number of appointees to minor borough offices. Then he signed financial documents submitted by the outgoing city chamberlain, and paid a call of ceremony on District Attorney Whitman in the Criminal Courts Building. Coming back to City Hall he posed with his family for an official photograph, and at three went out to lunch; but finding no restaurant open, he called it a day and set off across the bridge for home.

That was the first day. The next day, Sunday, he did not go to his office, but from his home announced seven major appointments. The intently watching politicians at Tammany Hall suffered a shock: not one of the seven appointees was a politician, some were anti-Tammany Democrats, and others were suspected of being Republicans or some nameless breed of mugwump. Political activity had played a significant part in the careers of none of them.

The mayor's friend and confidant, Hyde, was named city chamberlain. This was not only the best-paying position, at a salary of $12,000 a year, but at that time was an office of much responsibility and influence. The chamberlain had charge of banking the city's funds.

For corporation counsel, to head the administration's legal department, Gaynor chose Archibald R. Watson, editor and publisher of *Bench and Bar*, a law journal. Watson was studious, diligent, and alert, but in no way active in politics.

As commissioner of docks and ferries (the post once held by Boss Murphy) Gaynor appointed Calvin Tomkins, president of the Reform Club.

Kingsley Martin, an engineer who had helped to construct the Manhattan Bridge and was reputed to know every bolt and nut in the East River spans, was named commissioner of bridges. He was a stranger to politics.

Michael J. Drummond, named commissioner of charities, was a retired iron manufacturer. While an enrolled member of Tammany Hall, he was described significantly as "not the Tammany type."

Henry S. Thompson, wealthy builder, was Gaynor's choice for

commissioner of water supply, and he, too, was politically almost unknown.

For fire commissioner Gaynor named Rhinelander Waldo, member of one of the city's oldest and wealthiest families. Waldo had had some minor links with Tammany and had been serving efficiently as a deputy police commissioner.

After releasing this list of major appointments, that Sunday, Gaynor went for a long walk alone. Reporters found him that afternoon in his library, immersed in a collection of the pithy sayings of Benjamin Franklin compiled by John J. Murphy, a former secretary of the Citizens Union. He was asked whether any political leaders had been consulted in making his appointments. Laying down the little book, the mayor answered benignly:

"I feel there is one great act of justice which I should do. I was nominated without even a suggestion being made as to what I should do as mayor. Since election Mr. Charles F. Murphy has called on me three times, each time asking me to appoint the best men to be found. His suggestions were few, he urged nothing, and kept saying to me that the responsibility was solely with me. I can not say the same of everyone else.

"I fear there are a good many people in this town who do not know Charles F. Murphy. Some of them seem to think he has horns and hoofs. I can only say of him what I have seen. He fully realizes that a political organization can not survive and grow broader on patronage alone, without political ideas and virtue, but must shrivel up and die of worse than dry rot. I would advise some good women and clergymen who are writing to me about Charles F. Murphy . . . to go and see him and say a kind word to him. They may be surprised. 'Thou shalt not bear false witness' is also one of the Commandments. There are more vices than one."

Leaving the newsmen to explicate that pronouncement as they might, the mayor returned to Benjamin Franklin.

On Monday, January 3, the mayor's first full working day, he arrived at City Hall about nine o'clock, after covering the distance from his house in fifty minutes. He said he expected to walk to work in all weathers, as storms seldom bothered him.

In the corridors of City Hall he lost his way and wound up in the Marriage License Bureau. A policeman stationed there had to direct him how to reach his own office. When this was reported in the newspapers, it was suggested that the novelty of having a mayor so unfamiliar with the labyrinth of politics that he lost his way in City Hall would not be resented by the citizens; it might be refreshing.

The press already was expressing gratified amazement at the high quality of the mayor's first appointments. The *World* repeated that "it looks as if Mr. Gaynor means exactly what he says," and the somewhat dazed *Tribune* admitted "an agreeable impression" had been created by Gaynor's first exercise of power. The *Evening Post*, palladium of culture, caution, and conservatism, said merely that in view of the mayor's "strange praise of Murphy—strange if it was not sarcastic"—his friends would be wondering whether he had measured the difficulties facing him.

If he had, he gave no indication that he believed them to be insuperable. All day he dispatched routine business, and still found time to transmit to the Board of Aldermen his regret that he had been unable to send them a statement of the city's financial position "as of the close of business December 31, 1909," inasmuch as the comptroller's office had not yet furnished it, but promised "to have it in my hands sometime this evening." The aldermen had never felt the importance of a day or two of delay in such matters.

Gaynor also passed along to reporters the declination of Herman Ridder, influential publisher of the German-language daily *Staats-Zeitung* and spokesman for the city's powerful German element, of appointment as commissioner of parks "on account of his being a newspaper proprietor and president of the Newspaper Publishers Association. I regret to lose him," the mayor commented, "but recognize the propriety and delicacy of his position. There is one thing in all this business that has struck me forcibly, and that is that although those of German blood represent the largest percentage of our population here, namely about thirty-two percent, almost no Germans apply for office."

This was construed as a backhanded swipe at the Irish, whose avidity for attaching themselves to the public payroll was proverbial. The mayor's position with Boss Murphy's crowd was not improved by a jocularity he let fall in reply to a question put by an earnest mutual friend, who asked, "What can we do for Mr. Murphy?"

Gaynor pondered, then suggested gravely, "Suppose we give him a few kind words."

"A few kind words for Murphy" was flashed through New York's political underground almost instantaneously, and the next day the round, beatific, rubicund features of Charles Francis Murphy appeared at City Hall. He was ushered at once into the mayor's office, remained for three-quarters of an hour, and emerged smiling.

Gaynor said that the Tammany leader, just back from a stay in Atlantic City, had merely dropped by to pay his respects, and that the meeting had not been arranged. The press was skeptical, but the mayor was in no way ruffled. At 5:30 he knocked off work and despite an angry sky set off for home, bundled in a wool muffler and mittens, wearing overshoes, and with the collar of his greatcoat turned up around his ears. Firmly clamped on his head was his high hat.

The day after Murphy's "courtesy call," Gaynor announced four more major appointments, and not one of the four men chosen had any connection with Tammany Hall. Three of the appointees— John C. Maguire, Richard Welling, and Alexander Keogh—were named to the municipal civil service commission; all three were ardent advocates of strict civil service administration. The fourth appointee, John J. Walsh, a former city magistrate, was named to be third deputy police commissioner, in charge of the departmental trials of policemen accused of infractions of the rules or more serious offenses.

Before making this appointment, Gaynor had called in the acting police commissioner, William F. Baker, and had impressed upon him the importance of having accused members of the force tried by a competent person. This, he said, had not always been the case in the past. Walsh, he pointed out, had distinguished himself as "one of the best police magistrates the city ever had," and was thoroughly qualified to handle the men "properly and strictly."

Then, upon swearing Walsh in as a deputy commissioner, the mayor delivered this homily, a copy of which was sent to the newspapers:

"And now, Mr. Trial Deputy, you are experienced in the trial of persons, and there is no reason why you should not try the policemen fairly and strictly. Be reasonable and lenient in the case of things that happen rather through misfortune and are not very serious, but in the case of serious things which show a man unfit for the force do not hesitate to dismiss him. We want all bad men off the force. For instance, it is a most serious thing for a policeman to leave his post and sleep in a hall or elsewhere, or pass the time with his friends when he ought to be on guard. Let such men be dismissed. We do not want such men on the force. There are plenty of good men on it, and plenty of good men waiting to get on it. And do not allow any persons whatever to get your ear or influence you in any way in the trial of men. Do not let any clergyman, or any politician, or any man high or low approach you on that subject. If you conduct yourself in this way the police force will very soon find it out and half of the evils of the force will disappear."

The same day the mayor notified J. M. Kennedy, holdover parks commissioner for Brooklyn, that he would be retained, and shared the reason why with the public by sending a copy of his letter to the press.

"I have concluded to continue you as parks commissioner for Brooklyn and Queens," the letter read. "This I do on your past record in that office. . . . It may be that some of the building by you has been rather too fine and extravagant, but you never had 84 foremen to 119 men, or any padded payrolls."

This was an allusion to Higgins' report that in the Bronx he had found foremen who bossed two to four men each, and one foreman who had no working force whatever. The letter to Kennedy continued:

"These things must come to an end in the City of New York. Although you had reason to believe you were to be superseded, you have remained in your office to courteously receive and help your successor, in contrast to what has been done elsewhere."

Then more appointments were made, and neither Murphy nor McCooey got a thing worth mentioning with which to appease their faithful. Even the manner in which some of the appointees were selected seemed willfully malicious to the famished henchmen. William H. Edwards, McClellan's street cleaning commissioner, was a mountain of a man, a former Princeton football star, who was universally known as "Big Bill." Soon after taking office Gaynor began to receive letters complaining that the men in the street cleaning department were being pressured to contribute toward the cost of a farewell dinner to their commissioner, inasmuch as he expected to be replaced. Gaynor sent a bundle of these complaints to Edwards. Back came a note:

"Dear Judge: The dinner is off. W. H. Edwards."

A man who took that attitude and could state it so tersely suited Gaynor down to the ground, and "Big Bill" stayed on as commissioner.

Charles B. Stover was a settlement house worker, wrapped up in humanitarian idealism. He had studied for the Episcopal ministry, but became interested in bettering the condition of the slum dwellers of New York's East Side, and for years had been fighting to obtain more playgrounds and parks, and improved housing and schools, in that congested area. He had no political connections. Dreaming of what he could do if he were in charge of the city's parks department, he solicited an interview with Gaynor. The mayor listened to Stover's ideas, and then for a couple of hours they congenially discussed the Bible and Shakespeare. Gaynor checked with trustworthy acquaintances of Stover, and the latter's appointment as the city's chief parks commissioner followed.

Such methods of handing out political plums seemed, to men who had passed their lives in political jobbery, insane, if not wicked. Gaynor was not perturbed, and the day after Stover took office he sent him his first letter of instructions:

"Please let steps be taken for the immediate resumption of the running of the stages on Riverside Drive from 72nd Street to the viaduct, unless there is sufficient reason to report to the contrary. That fine drive was made by the city for all and not for a few."

The stages were those double-decked buses beloved by generations of New Yorkers and tourists. The previous commissioner, at the instigation of wealthy residents whose mansions lined the drive, had barred the buses, alleging that the top-deck passengers stripped leaves and branches from overhanging trees.

Gaynor's next letter to Stover was written to right a wrong. It read:

"Please take measures to reinstate Clinton H. Smith in his office of secretary unless there is something that should be reported to me to the contrary, and his case can, later on, be calmly dealt with. That done in heat or haste is as a rule ill done. We must not only deal with people with justice, but also with the appearance of justice, the latter sometimes being as essential as the former."

And so the Tammany tiger grew leaner and leaner as the days went by. John J. Murphy, compiler of the apothegms of Franklin and prominent member of the Citizens Union, an organization dedicated to the downfall of Tammany, was named tenements commissioner; while Dr. Ernest J. Lederle, an unabashed Republican, was appointed commissioner of health. Dr. Lederle had given good service in that department for fourteen years and had been its commissioner under Mayor Low; at Gaynor's suggestion he severed his connection with the Lederle Laboratories, a drug firm with which the city did business, for the duration.

Herman Robinson, an organizer for the American Federation of Labor and associate of Samuel Gompers, was put in charge of the bureau of licenses. Raymond B. Fosdick, twenty-six-year-old lawyer who had been serving as assistant commissioner of accounts, was made commissioner.

Boss Murphy paid a second call at City Hall and talked with the mayor privately for half an hour. Again he left smiling, and a rumor spread that "something good" was coming Tammany's way. What came turned out to be something very different. It was a policy letter from Gaynor to his new fire commissioner, Rhinelander Waldo.

For years the fire department had been notoriously graft-ridden and shot through with political favoritism. Appointments to the force, and promotion through its ranks, had been openly bought and sold, in contemptuous defiance of civil service provisions. Now the mayor wrote to his commissioner:

A SOCIAL CALL   *Jan. 6, 1910*

NEW BOOK FOR AN OLD BOSS
"For the common benefits of air and light, for useful fire and delicious water—
Good God, I thank Thee!"—From the Wisdom of Benjamin Franklin,
edited by John J. Murphy.

Jan. 11, 1910

"I have selected you to head the fire department after careful consideration and in full confidence that you will be able to carry out my intention of banishing all political and outside influence and favoritism from that department immediately and once for all. Let appointments and promotions hereafter be made without such influences. The present method enables those who stand low on the eligible list to be appointed over the heads of those who stand higher. As soon as a list is published, clergymen, businessmen, political leaders, and all sorts of persons claiming to have influence, come in or advocate the selection of their friends thereon. Worse yet, some of such influence is sold and paid for. Let there be an end of all this, and see that every one on the list be treated on his ascertained merits.

. . And let not such influence be tolerated in the trial of charges against members of the force. . . . On the first sign of any such importunity or influence being permitted by the trial deputy let him be removed."

This *was* a precedent, and the newspapers by text and cartoon gleefully pointed up the disparity between Murphy's bland smile and the brickbat that overtook him on his stately departure from the new seat of municipal authority, the City Hall, whither it had been successfully transferred from that other Hall situated farther uptown on East Fourteenth Street.

But Charles Francis Murphy was a persistent man. A third time he presented his poker face at City Hall and was closeted with the mayor. This time it was observed that he departed without a smile. Badgered by reporters to express an opinion of the appointments made so far, he murmured in his soft-speaking way:

PROFITABLE READING
Suggested for these long winter evenings.   *Jan.* 17, 1910

"I know nothing about appointments. The new officials are all good men, I suppose."

Gaynor declined to divulge whether the Boss had conveyed Tammany's displeasure. But a few days later a flicker of optimism brightened East Fourteenth Street when three men with Tammany backgrounds were assigned to important positions. One was the Wigwam's corresponding secretary, Patrick A. Whitney, a privileged inmate of the tiger's den; he was named commissioner of correction—in charge of jails and prisons.

The next day the flicker was doused when the mayor disclosed that when he selected his latest appointees he had no inkling of their political affiliations. Nor would it have made any difference if he had, he added; what he looked for was competence and honesty, and a man could "have Tammany written all over him," but if he was competent, honest, and independent, he would be eligible for consideration. Anybody, in or out of politics, he said, was free to make recommendations, and they all would be considered, "but I can not entertain the proposition of giving offices to men to stimulate their political activity."

To Whitney the mayor addressed the now ritual allocution, this time, in view of Whitney's background, with special emphasis:

"I desire to say to you, in the most emphatic words, that no political influence whatever can be permitted in the Department of Correction. I place great trust in you to exclude all outside influence, and put the department on the very best footing."

The *Evening Post* foresaw rough going for a mayor who was so insensitive to the needs of necessitous politicians. In polished prose the *Post* ventured to surmise that "the run of Tammany braves will not soon admit that, while kind hearts are more than coronets, kind words are a full equivalent for missing offices."

Characteristically, Hearst's newspapers listed prominently Gaynor's Tammany-connected appointments, ignoring or slighting the others. Readers of those papers in consequence bombarded the mayor's office with indignant reproaches. A ministerial critic, who wrote from his home in Jersey City, across the Hudson River, deplored Gaynor's drift into "apparent entanglements," and received a reply from City Hall disabusing him of any such notion in the mayor's best phrasing:

"Dear Sir: I thank you very much for your kind letter, but I must say I do not know what you mean by my 'apparent entanglements.' I never was entangled with anybody in my life, and if you lived here you must have known that to be true. No politician or political organization have had any influence or control over me whatever, and I do not believe there is anyone who has lived here for twenty-five years who does not know that perfectly. More than that, it was and is generally known throughout the state, and to some extent throughout the country. So you see I do not know what you mean when you talk about my 'entanglements.' "

More than once Gaynor expressed surprise that people should think it odd that he was doing just what he had said he would do— be mayor in fact, without regard to politics. He had not been in office a month before he was writing to a well-wisher in Brooklyn:

"I thank you very much for your kind and encouraging letter. I had been so long engaged in work for good government without falter that it was a surprise to me that any one, especially over in Brooklyn, ever had any doubt about what I would do if I became mayor. I feel humiliated about it."

Surprised itself, the *New York Times* registered its full approval of the mayor's course in an editorial carrying the title: *"Politics To Live By, Not On."*

"The taxpayers are bewildered, and are wondering if the day of the common man, the man in the street, the man who pays the taxes, has come at last," the *Times* ruminated.

The man in the street, unused to such consideration, wondered, too, and was cheered by the reports he read daily of reforms instituted. The costly panoply of luxury-indulgent officeholders had long been a cause of popular resentment. Fire Commissioner Waldo found in the department stables the following equipages, reserved for the personal use of his predecessor: a surrey, a brougham, a top wagon, and a sleigh, all complete with horses, harness, and drivers. There was in addition an electric automobile. Waldo got rid of the lot. He had all official automobiles painted "N.Y.F.D." in letters a foot high so that anyone using them for private purposes could be easily spotted. He slashed the number of fire-line passes, which had been distributed so plentifully that holders often outnumbered the firemen at a blaze. He ended the practice of handing out horseshoeing contracts to political favorites. He transferred men from "soft snap" assignments to active duty. He installed an accounting system and presided personally at departmental trials. The results soon showed in improved service at reduced cost, and after six weeks in office he was able to inform the mayor that the payment of money for promotion, or promotion through any payment whatever, was a thing of the past.

Scandalous mismanagement meanwhile was being uncovered by Commissioner Thompson in the water-supply department. Industrial plants had been getting city water free. Many houses were not even entered on the water register. Tugboats filled their tanks from city hydrants without cost. There had been no house-to-house inspection of meters since 1901. An eight-inch bypass was found in a sugar refinery in Queens of which the department had no record. One man employed as a meter reader was seventy-five years old and blind. The politically appointed water register, a protégé of powerful Tammany interests, Thompson recommended be fired for "incompetence, lack of discipline, use of bad language, insubordination, and absolute disregard of the responsibilities attached to his office." He was often absent, had removed meters illegally, had given all meter-repair work to a single plumber and a monopoly of installing meters to two firms who never bid against each other. For his personal use he had purchased an automobile with city funds; it cost $995 and the bills for repairs and maintenance in nine months totalled $4,185.85. For some abstruse reason, considering that all his work was done sitting at a desk in his office, he had also bought an "official" yacht.

Gaynor shared Thompson's reports with the public through the newspapers. When, swamped with work, the commissioner requested permission to extend the working hours of his staff from 4 to 5 P.M. the mayor not only assented, but put into effect a full eight-hour working day for all municipal employees, and installed a time-card system for use by everyone, from top to bottom. Loud was the outcry from the city's twenty thousand employees, but the millions of taxpayers felt like raising a cheer.

So thoroughly did the water commissioner carry out his house cleaning, three months after taking charge he notified the Board of Estimate that $937,504 allocated to the department would not be required, thanks to economies effected.

The Croton Aqueduct Commission, created by the legislature in 1883 to provide New York City with better water, had been a sinecure for years, its usefulness long since exhausted. In order to keep themselves on the payroll the four members had boondoggled outrageously, but nobody seemed to know how to get rid of the incubus. Gaynor solved the problem. He dismissed the incumbent commissioners and named four others to replace them under instructions to wind up the records and voluntarily put themselves out of business.

He gave them three months to do it. The ousted four appealed to the courts, but Gaynor was upheld. From first to last, the salaries paid to that board of futilities had cost the city more than $8,000,000.

The Catskill Water Commission, a separate entity having charge of the city's new source of water supply drawn from the Catskills, a hundred miles north of Manhattan, had become a prolific breeder of "soft snaps" and padded payrolls. A swarm of appraisers brought in from all over the state had been employed to assess the value of lands taken over within the watershed; these appraisers had been paid as high as $50 a day, and some had been paid or had due to them as much as $20,000 in fees.

After a careful study, Gaynor instructed Corporation Counsel Watson ("subject to your advice and further consideration") to see that "all clerks to condemnation commissioners, and all appraisers of land values save two for each condemnation commission, be discharged. Each commission has a stenographer, who is actually its clerk. If any more clerking be necessary let one of the commissioners do it. . . . It is regrettable to have to discharge so many people, but on the other hand it is a criminal offense to pad city payrolls, or employ unnecessary persons. A large number of those to be discharged, if not all of them, were not employed for the good of the city, but apparently for reasons of state politics. They include men from all over the state. Men from a remote part of the state appraising land in the Catskills has long been the subject of ridicule. It is too bad to have to deal with things like this. Of course you understand that I am in no way reflecting on your predecessor. It was not he who did it.

"Also let the advertisements hereafter be cut down to the number of newspapers permissible under the statute. The waste of money in such advertising of condemnation proceedings is useless, even ridiculous. Notices of the beginning of condemnation proceedings are served on resident land owners by being advertised in newspapers, when they could be simply handed to such owners, except for this foolish statute. Also stop the printing of the stenographers' minutes of testimony. No reason exists for this except the wasteful expenditure of the city's money. Also dispense with the services of special counsel, except where absolutely necessary. The amounts paid in that way seem to exceed all reasonable bounds. Let a staff with an alert head be organized to do the work, and let all commis-

sioners sit full days. If they refuse, please move the court to super-
sede them."

This interoffice memo, like many others, Gaynor shared with
the public by means of the daily press, and it was published widely
throughout the state. It put the seal of proof upon the mayor's
readiness to shoulder responsibility for decisive action, as well as his
grasp of the complex problems he was tackling—his determination,
again, to be mayor in fact, of which he had given notification in the
campaign. It illustrated, too, the only sense in which he was willing
to be called a "radical." The word, he repeatedly pointed out, meant
one who went to the root of a matter, and it should be a term of
honor, rather than of opprobrium. In that sense he was cheerfully
radical.

ANOTHER OUTRAGE
Veteran employe of the city let go, without even a word of commendation.
Jan. 7, 1910

SH! THE MAYOR IS BUSY!

When the corporation counsel reported back that he had trimmed the Catskill payroll to the extent of seventy-nine appraisers and clerks who were purely supernumerary, Gaynor complimented him but pointed out that "if we had a thoroughly alert and healthy public sentiment here," such instances of runaway politics and favoritism could not happen. "The spoliation of the city in this matter alone has been over $1,000,000 a year. Such looting of the city must come to an end."

When the Catskill board, maundering along in time-worn grooves, thoughtlessly increased the salaries of seven engineers at a time when Gaynor was cutting expenses everywhere, the mayor spotted the action and called the board members to order sharply:

"This action of yours, at a time when a united effort is being made by the heads of the city departments to lessen city expenses and purge padded payrolls, has excited unfavorable comment and made a disagreeable impression. It is due to you that I say thus early that if you entertain a notion that you are independent of the city government, or of this [the mayor's] office, in the expenditure of the city's money, I can not join you therein. The just interpretation of the act which governs you, and under which the mayor appoints you, is, in my opinion, that you are not independent of other authority, but subject to the warning and advice of the mayor, to say the least. I trust I shall always be just to you or your successors, but I shall not look on in silence while expenditures are being made by you of the city's money without any deference to the source of your department or strict regard to prudence and economy."

No department of the government escaped Gaynor's scrutiny. Day by day he directed his assistants in terse, pointed notes. He drove them hard, while maintaining his grip on the reins of authority with apparently no effort.

Among the appointments that the mayor was empowered to make were those of police court magistrates and judges of General Sessions. To no subject did Gaynor give more earnest and thoughtful attention than this. For years the magistrates had been largely political hacks, the positions being considered among the perquisites of political hangers-on; yet these courts touched the poor and humble directly, and by them the whole tone of the government was set. Magistrates were appointed for ten-year terms, and they were not removable by the mayor; hence Gaynor exercised the greatest care in making his selections, and he was constantly reminding his appointees of their obligations and limitations.

SLIPPERY DAYS   *Jan. 7*, 1910

WHAT! NO OLD FASHIONED COURTESY LEFT IN NEW YORK CITY?

March 2, 1910

For chief magistrate in Manhattan and the Bronx he chose William McAdoo, a former police commissioner, commending to him the necessity of keeping the closest watch over the courts in his jurisdiction. For chief magistrate in Brooklyn and Queens, Gaynor named Otto Kempner, who had been a fierce opponent of Tammany's Boss Croker. In making this appointment Gaynor told Kempner, simultaneously publishing the letter:

"I trust you will . . . let the magistrates know that you are at the head of them, and that they must obey rules or be reported either to the mayor, or to the Appellate Division, or the Bar Association. You have some hard things to deal with."

In notifying Moses J. Harris of his appointment as a magistrate, the mayor admonished him, and shared the admonishment with the public through the press:

"Let the case of no one, however humble or unfortunate, go by you without careful consideration. Be not elated with your powers, which are very great, and apt to turn one's head, but humble and patient. Do not convict anyone unheard. Since I have been mayor my attention has been called to cases of offhand and ostentatious convictions of humble persons by magistrates which are gross wrongs. I sent a secretary to copy the record in two of the cases and found no evidence whatever was taken. See to it on the other hand that arrested persons are not discharged when they should be held. . . . I write this for more than you, for I believe it is high time that the appointing power take note of the conduct of some of our magistrates."

To another appointee to the magistrates' bench the mayor wrote:

"I hope and trust that the morning of the day you assume this powerful office you will feel more like bowing your head for assistance and strength than strutting about. Be a good man, and you will be a great magistrate."

In naming Professor Isaac Franklin Russell to be chief justice of the Court of Special Sessions, Gaynor advised:

"I desire to call your attention to the arrears of business and other conditions in that court. I appoint you to see that they are done away with. . . . I receive constant complaints of the said delays and conditions. It is coming to pass that businessmen prefer to let criminal offenses against them go than prosecute them. They have to go before a magistrate, often several times, and then several months later that is repeated in the Special Sessions. The annoyance is more than should be borne. The administration of justice in these courts should be prompt. Nor should gross offenders be induced to plead guilty with a promise of being dealt too lightly with. Trials are troublesome, but should not be avoided in that way."

Gaynor had been unaware of Russell's political persuasion, and the newspapers were just as uncertain about identifying him as a Republican or a Democrat. This Gaynor found amusing. Privately he wrote to Russell:

"My secretary calls my attention to the fact that one newspaper says this morning that you are a Republican, and another that you are a Democrat. We have worked together all these years for certain principles and ideals in government without it ever occurring to me which you were. If you really are a Republican, I am more convinced than ever that between a good Democrat and a bad Republican there is very little difference after all."

Sometimes the zeal of his appointees exceeded the bounds that the mayor thought necessary. Kingsley Martin, the bridges commissioner, fired drones in his department so enthusiastically that Gaynor had to caution him:

"Be careful about dropping people to ascertain just who they are and what injury it will inflict on them, for in the winter months especially, we have to be as charitable in these things as possible, without, however, doing any injustice to the city."

Stover and the borough park commissioners were urged to work out a system of rotation whereby the extensive layoffs of outdoor workers during the winter months could be curtailed.

The street cleaning department—one of great importance in that era, with thousands of horses on the streets—was given a vigorous shaking-up by Commissioner Edwards, and Gaynor backed him. The first move was to dismiss the chief deputy commissioner, Owen J. Murphy, for incompetence. In a long report to the mayor, Edwards elaborated on the indictment against Murphy, namely, that he had "devoted more time to carrying out his political interests than he has to the interests of the department." He related how Murphy's friends fared wondrously well when they happened to be brought up for departmental trials; how the time books had been falsified; how extra men were carried on the time sheets as drivers of sprinkler carts when snow lay on the ground; how a particular pal of Murphy had been detailed to the "snow office" summer and winter, drawing the same pay in July that he did in January. To cap all, the obliging deputy had been in the habit of sending several loads of manure daily from the department's stables to Calvary cemetery as a "favor," using city carts, city teams, and city drivers for this benevolent donation.

In mid-January one of the heaviest snowfalls since 1888 dumped nearly fifteen inches of snow on the city, and Edwards' Herculean exertions in clearing the streets won Gaynor's praise. The event also occasioned one of his best quoted letters. It was written immediately after he had arrived at City Hall, covered with snow like a snowman, with icicles on his beard, after completing the long walk from home. It read:

"Sir: As I walked down Flatbush Avenue, Brooklyn, on my way over this morning, I noticed that all of the drivers of a long line of snow wagons which were being filled by the shovelers were standing about doing nothing or sitting on their wagons. I called one of them to me and asked him if the drivers did not help to load the wagons. He answered: 'No, not when the city removes the snow, but when contractors remove it, then we do.' How about this, please? Should they not take a shovel and help? They may freeze to death."

Shortly after this Gaynor found a new forum for preaching civic responsibility—the street cleaning department's big stable at Kent and Flushing avenues, Brooklyn. While several hundred horses stamped on the floor above, five hundred and fifty uniformed "white wings" lined up at attention in response to a bugle blast announcing the mayor's arrival. Facing the men, Gaynor complimented them on their appearance and good record, and then continued:

"I suppose some people who don't think will regard it as odd that I come here to speak. There is nothing odd in it, for we are both engaged in the service of the city, and it is fitting that I should express the wish to you that the streets of New York be cleaned as efficiently and as economically as those of any city in the world. Every reasonable man will admit that good work was done in clearing away the snow, but there are some pious persons, or I might say bilious persons, who are always ready to criticize you and me."

Emphasizing that he wanted every man in the department to have confidence in his leaders, he said:

"If they are not worthy, without regard to politics or any political organization whatever, they will have to 'git.' "

In the department of docks and ferries, Commissioner Tomkins attacked the long-entrenched corruption among the dockmasters. Some of these had been pocketing the wharfage fees, instead of turning them over to the city. Warrants were issued for the arrest of six of these offenders, all protected, supposedly, by top-level Tammany influence. Three of the six immediately fled to Canada. The mayor, exercising a prerogative of his office that had been dormant for a century, himself issued the warrant to arrest one dockmaster, who was not only a relative of Boss Murphy, but the brother-in-law of one of Gaynor's own appointees. Though the most strenuous pleas were made to bury the whole affair, Gaynor, sitting as a magistrate, held the man for the grand jury.

Tomkins organized a ferry-repair service to supplant the wasteful system of farming out the repair work to favored companies. In three months he lopped two hundred and twenty superfluous employees off the department payroll.

Gaynor was aware of everything that was going on. In mid-February Tomkins received the following letter, which showed how closely the mayor was watching:

"I beg to enclose you a letter of Mr. Campbell. I have received many like it. Will you be so good as to let me know whether you have raised the salaries of any employees in the dock department, and if so give me the list with the amount of raise in each case. It wears a bad look, it seems to me, for us to discharge poor people and raise the salaries of other people. . . . Please regard this as a personal letter and not a faultfinding one. These things all fall on my shoulders, and I assure you that I want to be entirely just to everybody and discriminate against nobody. Of all things I do not want to be laid open to a charge of ingratitude. I am coming down to see you before long as I want to talk with you and see your department. I hear good things of you from many quarters."

He had said that not a pin should fall in the city without the mayor knowing it, and the "old graybeard" seemed to possess that faculty.

An accomplishment which Gaynor took particularly to heart was his infusion of new life into the cobwebbed Bureau of Weights and Measures. This concerned everybody, and the poor above all. The city was full of dishonest scales and measuring devices, and no effective enforcement of honest weight regulations had been attempted for years. Gaynor's investigators found the widest variations. Of seventy one-pound boxes of candy bought at random in a chain of shops, sixty-nine were underweight. Two-thirds of all the gasoline pumps in the city were inaccurate. By "shaving" tricks the buying public was being cheated out of millions of dollars annually, and most of this gouge came out of the pockets of the poor.

Gaynor had the position of bureau chief transferred out of civil service jurisdiction in order to let him pick the right man to carry out a reformation. He chose Thomas J. Driscoll, a belligerent, flamboyant Irishman, and told him:

"The department of weights and measures has given me much trouble and anxiety. Short weights exist all over the city, especially in stores that sell to poor people. There is no place in the city government where more good can be done. It will be necessary for you to reorganize the department. The demoralization there is complete."

Driscoll set to work ruthlessly. False-measure vegetable baskets were confiscated by the thousands and burned, crooked scales were smashed, and within a few months the hoary swindling tricks of tradesmen—the "butcher's thumb," the lead sinker in the chicken's craw, the waterlogged ham—became merely bad memories. Driscoll gave main credit to the little man in City Hall. He reported:

"The records of this office show . . . that at no time during the administration of the previous mayor was there anything that even resembled the support given the bureau [by Gaynor]."

The Bureau of Municipal Research, an independently endowed organization engaged in studies of municipal administration, said of the transformation worked in this field:

"No more striking or thrilling demonstration of reform in method was ever witnessed."

In another direction Gaynor ordered the corporation counsel to take steps to end the scandal of the system of condemnation of property for city use. The difficulty was that the commissioners of appraisal and award were named by the Supreme Court justices. Gaynor told Watson that these commissioners "invariably take months and years to do what could well be done in hours, days, or weeks. In that way they run up expensive bills for their own fees and expenses, which the land owners have to pay, and also postpone necessary improvements. I have cases before me where from four to ten years were taken in proceedings to open short streets, or a few blocks. In addition to this, grossly excessive awards are made . . . from two to six times the fair value." Directing Watson to petition the courts for the removal of dilatory commissioners, he concluded: "I look to you to make a complete reform in these matters. Millions in money will thereby be saved annually to the city. Remember always that yours is a great administrative department, and not one of mere litigation, technicalities, and delays."

On reading this letter Edward M. Shepard wired the mayor that it was "one of the best things done by any of the men of your generation."

The "heavy gravy" to the newspapers which Gaynor had assailed during the campaign was cut off abruptly. The mayor limited advertisements of the opening of new tax books to one newspaper in each borough, as prescribed by law. Under the previous administration seventy daily and weekly newspapers had shared in this handout.

Gaynor fired the executive secretary he had inherited from McClellan when he caught him grafting in connection with the city advertising. The man had been editing the lists of newspapers designated to receive advertising, striking out some names and substituting others—and "receiving from the proprietors of the newspapers so unlawfully substituted . . . a percentage of the money paid to them by the city for such advertisements."

William Jay Schieffelin, president of the Citizens Union, a very upper-crust reform leader, commended this action in the warmest manner and tipped the mayor off that the ousted man had been promptly hired by Hearst. "He is the kind of man the *American* would be expected to employ," Gaynor replied, announcing that the papers in the case were available for public inspection at any time, and adding, regarding the secretary's falsifications, "I think there were 299 such forgeries."

In a related action the mayor totally reformed the *City Record*, under the direction of a new supervisor. Thousands of dollars had been squandered in publishing public notices of dreary prolixity; Gaynor demanded brevity, and got it. One department that had filled 892 pages with its 1908 report cut the roundup of its 1909 activities to an even hundred pages. And this was only a start. Search of the records revealed that during the six years of the McClellan regime the city had spent $4,855,798.57 for advertising in 362 newspapers and magazines, including newspapers in St. Louis, Chicago, Boston, Washington, and other remote cities—and even 22 newspapers in Great Britain. The total outlay in 1909 was $842,829.91; in 1910 Gaynor planned to hold it to $100,000. Many of the laws regulating city advertising, he found, had been deliberately worded so as to encourage the most reckless extravagance.

The irregularities disclosed in this branch of activity for some reason shocked even the blasé who considered themselves shockproof, and during his first few weeks in office Gaynor was said to have given more attention to eradicating this abuse than to any other.

The new board of tax assessors, a most important group, all men of standing in the community, Gaynor inducted into office with a lecture on their duties of unmistakable meaning. He told them:

"I have selected you to make valuations of real estate uniform throughout the entire city. The law requires a fair sale value to be adopted. Establish a standard and then make it uniform. Favor no one, and see that your deputies favor no one for political influence, love, or money. If political leaders come asking for favors in valuations tell them to go away; that that day has gone by. Politics must be banished from your department. Let every deputy who sets down a manifestly wrong valuation be dismissed at once. . . . Try to find out some owner trying to corrupt a deputy and we will have him indicted. No meaner person exists than one capable of trying to get rid of some part of his taxes by throwing it on his neighbors. No jury would spare him. . . . I have appointed you . . . to give all of your time to this business, and have it accomplished in one year. The deputies must no longer be left to do as they like. The charter says they shall act under your direction. . . . Go out and direct them. You can not do this work by sitting in your office."

So multifarious was the mayor, the newspapers were driven to print daily "box scores" of the activities at City Hall. On February 24 the *Herald*'s "scoreboard" was headed, *"So This Is City Hall, or What Happened Yesterday,"* and the list included, "Total salaries cut in all departments since January 1—$2,355,000."

There was more, much more, to come. Gaynor was never satisfied with progress registered. But despite pressure from all sides to undertake this or that reform instantly, he refused to be diverted from his first goal—to restore honesty and economy in the government. After several months at breakneck pace he advised a friend: "I still have things on my desk that I expected to dispose of during my first week in office." And though there were evils which he ardently hoped to abate or eliminate, he said, "a thousand times more do I wish to make the government of the city honest and intelligent." Other improvements would follow, once that foundation was securely laid.

The press was unable to restrain its enthusiasm. Within three months after taking over the City Hall, the mayor was being praised as vociferously as he had been denigrated and scorned at the time of his election—and by the same newspapers and periodicals. Said the friendly *World*, "Almost every day has brought forth something that amazed and annoyed the politicians used to a different order of things." Other editorial comments went further. The *Nation* called the administration, young as it was, "a landmark in the history of

New York City," and the formerly pro-Hearst *Harper's Weekly* took back all the belittlement it had published during the campaign.

The *Outlook*, having recovered from an initial shock of mortification at the excellence of Gaynor's appointments, now said flatly:

"We doubt whether ever in American history a public official has, in so short a time, so effectively changed political critics into political admirers, and the atmosphere of suspicion into one of confidence and affection."

Only the Hearst press remained obdurate. "William Rule-or-Ruin" kept probing for some weakness in the mayor's armor, and as early as March, Gaynor was warned that a Hearst reporter and cartoonist were dogging his steps. Gaynor dismissed the warning with a "Humph."

The impression made on the city generally by Gaynor's first fourteen weeks in office was reflected at a dinner of the Bronx bar, when Magistrate James J. Breen said amid applause:

"And how is it with our city? Mayor Gaynor only three months at the helm—and students of municipal government see the solution of problems heretofore regarded by many as unsolvable. The saving of the taxpayers' money is the least part. The change in the moral aspect is the surprise. The public conscience has got a new tonic. For the first time, public officials, high and low, are on their good behavior. Idlers and sinecurists in the public service no longer see the protecting hand of the politician. The petty boss is stalled. His political pull is retired to private life, and, like Othello, his occupation's gone."

An even plainer demonstration of the mayor's popularity occurred a week later at the opening of the baseball season at the Polo Grounds. As Gaynor walked across the field while the band played "Hail to the Chief," twenty-five thousand fans stood up and cheered continuously. Again and again Gaynor raised his top hat in response, and throughout the afternoon, as the *Herald* put it, "the mayor and the Giants broke even" as main attractions. There was no keener fan on hand than Gaynor. He threw out the first ball, and then watched the game with intense excitement, munching peanuts all the while. At some fast play he would jump up and yell "Fine!" and he announced himself as entirely happy when, after George Wiltsie of the Giants had forced the Boston Doves to "eat out of his left hand all the way," the Giants won, 4 to 0. The leprechaun twinkle was discernible in Gaynor's eyes that afternoon.

THE MAILBAG

*"By the life of my father," said Sancho, when
he heard Don Quixote's letter, "it is the
loftiest thing I ever heard. Body of me! . . .
I declare your worship is the very devil,
and there is nothing you don't know."*

*"Everything is needed for the calling I fol-
low," said Don Quixote.*

—DON QUIXOTE

ON FEBRUARY 7, 1910, Mayor Gaynor wrote to a student at Berea
College, in Kentucky, in answer to a request for his view of the
desirability of the commission form of government for municipalities,
at that time a lively topic:

"I would prefer the negative of your question. Government by
more or less secret commissions is contrary to our system of government, and dangerous to the last degree, in my opinion. Everything
in this country could be done in the open. The tendency in Europe
is to do the business of municipalities by large councils. The London
County Council consists of three hundred members, and the membership of all the councils of Europe is very large. The tendency in
this country has been in exactly the opposite direction. The subject
is a large one, and I hope your debate will bring out all the pros
and cons."

The policy of running the city in plain sight of its citizens was
Gaynor's from the start. His means of communicating with the mass
of the people were two: the daily newspapers and the United States
mails. In the City Hall the mayor's office occupied the northwest

corner of the first floor, with windows overlooking Broadway, Chambers Street, and the county courthouse, Tweed's monument to graft. Figuratively they overlooked the entire metropolis, and beyond.

Attached to Gaynor's suite was a corridor and waiting room, presided over by Police Lieutenant William Kennell. Since 1895 it had been Kennell's job to shunt aside the cranks and intruders who are drawn to public figures. This he was supposed to accomplish diplomatically if possible, but by brawn if necessary. Kennell was capable of doing this; during the Low administration he had thrown John L. Sullivan out of City Hall bodily. The only pass that could get an unknown by the lieutenant was a letter from the mayor himself, and since he spoke five languages as well as several Yiddish dialects, Kennell was seldom at a loss for the right word of refusal.

Gaynor had retained Philip Kohler as his personal secretary, continuing to pay him out of his own pocket. There was also an executive secretary, appointed under civil service, and there were three full-time stenographers to take care of the mayor's correspondence. Adamson was the official secretary and generally in charge.

From the start Gaynor's mail bag bulged, but once it became known that every letter sent to him was read and acknowledged, the intake became enormous. It was Gaynor's custom to deal with this mass of correspondence at odd moments during lulls in other business. There was always a basket heaped with letters on his desk, and when a break came, he would buzz for a stenographer, and leaning back in his chair, would take the basket on his lap and dictate. Adamson had already gone through the batch and weeded out the letters he believed the mayor need not see. Of those in his basket, the mayor read every one, unless it was too long or the handwriting was too crabbed; such letters he ordered to be digested in a page or less. He was not annoyed by frivolous letters, if they were brief, amusing, or clever. As he finished dictating each reply he would slide the letter across the desk and go on with the next. He read rapidly and dictated swiftly, using no superfluous words, going directly to the point, and keeping an eye out for anything that might be of interest to the public. When such occurred he would say, "Flimsy it," which meant make twenty-four copies for distribution to the press.

The rule Gaynor enforced as nearly as he could was that every letter must be answered promptly, typed, signed, and mailed the same day. He signed every letter individually, sometimes adding interlineations in his bold, legible handwriting.

During his first three months in office, Mayor Gaynor was publicly credited with writing fifteen thousand letters, and his secretaries answered probably as many more on his behalf.* This pace was maintained with fair regularity throughout his term, and at times was even accelerated. The motive for this incredible labor (even though thousands of his letters consisted of a single sentence or two) Gaynor once told a reporter:

"Sometimes I can do something. More often I can only send a little comfort or encouragement or advice. Do you know, it is wonderful how often the friendless and poor need a little advice more than anything else, how ready they are to accept it, and what good it does them. Cranks? Well, some of my correspondents are in prisons and asylums. That doesn't make any difference; they are entitled to anything I can do for them. I never talk of cranks. I call them 'alert people.' "

Of the brief messages, hundreds streamed from City Hall day after day.

"Dear Sir: I have received your letter but fail to see why I should be troubled with a question of the tariff at this time." (Dated January 8, 1910, one week after Gaynor had taken on the job of mayor of New York.)

"In answer to your favor of April 17th, I would say that I do not recall that I know anybody by the name of J. D. Warner, of Cincinnati, Ohio." (This in reply to a query from Los Angeles.)

"Dear Sir: I thank you very much for your kind letter. It may be that I have not the power to make the ordinance which you suggest, but I will see if the matter can not be done through the Street Cleaning Department."

"I thank you very much for your kind and encouraging letter of March 31st." (This, with the salutation and signature, was the complete letter.)

"I have referred your letter to the Civil Service Commission and it will be attended to."

---

* This estimate seems almost certainly excessive, although there is no way to prove this since the files are incomplete. But even if divided by two, the figure is fantastically high.

"I thank you very much for sending me the Kipling poem. I shall put it in my scrap-book."

"Dear Miss Albrecht: Your letter is at hand, and I hope the railroad will employ you, for you are very deserving and very intelligent."

"I thank you for sending me the *Diary of Philip Hone*, and I shall take it home and read it."

"Dear Sir: I never made any promise to appoint you to office. I never sent Mr. Towns to see you. I regret that there are so few offices and so many applicants that I have not been able to assign a place to you."

"Your favor of April 6th is at hand. If any mistake was made about the date of your birth take this letter to Mr. McGuire of the Civil Service Commission and he will have it corrected."

"Dear Madam: The matter you write me about is one which I have no right to interfere in. It has to be disposed of by the courts."

"In answer to your favor of March 26th I would say that I fear the speech of Alderman Dowling is not available, no matter how interesting it might be."

"Dear Madam: Your favor of May 13th is at hand, and I shall do what I can to find your boy."

"Dear Sir: All that I can gather from your letter is that you came to City Hall and someone directed you to the County Court House. I do not see any implication of graft in that."

"Dear Sir: I often walk through the neighborhood you mention and I have always found it a most peaceful one."

"Dear Sir: I care nothing for common rumor, and I guess you made up the rumor in this case yourself."

"Yes, your letter should have been promptly answered. Men are put in office to receive complaints and investigate and answer them."

"Dear Sir: Your statement that a snow shoveler has to pay $25 to the foreman is a falsehood. Very truly yours."

"Dear Sir: Your favor is at hand and I have read enough of it to see that you are a mere scamp. Nevertheless I sometimes derive profit from the sayings and doings of scamps."

"Sir: I have a letter purporting to be from you of date May 14th, but as it is signed in typewriting I do not credit it."

"Dear Sir: I am trying, as you must know, to do away with this pesteration about the personal property tax."

"My dear Mrs. Stewart: I thank you very much for your letter. It seems strange that people so far away as Colorado should be knowing all about the little things we do here in New York."

"Dear Sir: Inasmuch as the Magistrate passed upon your case that is the end of it."

"It is not at all likely that I shall reinstate you to the police department. When a policeman is so much out of joint with things as to get dismissed he had better stay dismissed."

"Dear Miss Thompson: Since your dog bites I fear there is nothing that can be done for you."

"As a rule, I would prefer to have police stay away from funerals. I never saw any violence at a funeral."

"Dear Madam: It seems from the statement you make that your lawyer would be able to obtain a divorce for you."

"Reverend and Dear Sir: Your favor of April 8th is at hand, and will be duly considered. It may be that you do not understand that it is a pretty hard job to make men better than they are. You can not judge all men by your own standard."

"Dear Sir: In answer to your letter of April 22nd, I regret to say that your picture is legally in the Rogues Gallery."

"Dear Sir: Your favor of March 3rd is at hand, but as you do not give the name of the attorney, or any of the principal facts, I assume that you do not care much about the matter, and you will please trouble me no more about it."

"Dear Professor Woodbridge: I thank you for your letter calling my attention to immodest lettering which you saw on the sidewalk, and I shall have the matter called to the attention of the police commissioner to see if he can not lessen such indecency."

"Dear Sir: If you have any facts you can vouch for please write them to me and I will attend to the matter. Nor do you need to quote the Constitution of the United States. I think I am quite familiar with it. Just come down to the facts as briefly as possible."

"Dear Mr. Zimmerman: I thank you exceedingly for your kind note and for the melons."

"Dear Madam: Yes, I think they have a right to prevent your dog from swimming in the water."

"Dear Sir: I am sorry you lost your place. You should have been more careful."

"Dear General: I thank you very much for your kind note of June 27th. I am trying to do in office work which I was engaged in out of office for over twenty-five years. I have not changed."

"Dear Sir: Your suggestion seems to be good and next winter we ought to act upon it. You are not a bore at all. If some of us do not think of things everything goes by default."

"Dear Sir: No, I would prefer not to give an interview on the subject of the sewer."

Hundreds of answers went to people applying from all parts of the country to get on the New York City payroll. These replies varied little from the one-sentence form: "First you must pass a civil service examination and get on the eligible list; surely you must know that."

Many letters so obscurely written the mayor could not decipher them were acknowledged through the press, with Gaynor's suggestion that if the writers had anything worth saying, they should try again and write plainly.

All letters on arrival were stamped, "Received, Mayor's Office," with the date, and later "Answered" with the date. In most cases the dates coincided.

Anonymous letters received Gaynor's close attention, and some of these he answered through the press. He believed that frequently the writer of an unsigned letter would be telling the truth as he would not dare to tell it over his signature, for fear of reprisal; such fears he realized were often well grounded. One anonymous letter, released to the newspapers, "talked out of school" about a police inspector named McCafferty, who, "on the day after he saw you for the first time, remarked that he had jollied the 'old man' alright and was offering to bet 100 to 1 he would hold his position . . . saying that if 'the farmer' minded his own business and kept his hands off the police department things would be run as they always were . . . also that your order not to photograph prisoners 'would go *like hell*' with him, he didn't give a damn for 'the farmer.' "

Announcement of Inspector McCafferty's suspension, trial, and dismissal from the force followed with convincing rapidity.

The newspapers looked forward to receiving their daily quota of communications, piquant and instructive, from City Hall. The mood of the releases that came to the city desks might be furiously indignant, or sportive and airy, so unpredictable was Gaynor. And through this flow of correspondence he conveyed himself to the city at large, while the incoming mail enabled him to keep his finger on the pulse of popular feeling. When he received a letter of congratulations on the neat appearance of the streets in Brooklyn, where street sweepers had been seen "actually working, not loafing," Gaynor transmitted the letter to the press for general circulation, together with his ruminative response:

"We have got to get rid of all this petty graft and meanness in the government of the city if we can. How discouraging it is that many men who are honest enough as they go among us seem to feel that no such rule of honesty binds them when they get in the employ of the city. I am not applying this to any particular individual, but stating it as a thing which is general and to be deplored."

The press was also given Gaynor's reply to a letter interceding for a water department employee who had been dismissed for cause by Commissioner Thompson:

"Your letter . . . bespeaks the goodness of your heart. But the fact remains that Lynch is not able to add up a simple column of figures and that any clerk in his place could victimize him and swindle the city. I approve of Mr. Thompson's action."

During the election campaign Gaynor had invited the people to come to City Hall, after he became mayor, with their complaints and suggestions, and when the public realized that he meant it, the rush became overwhelming. So heavy was it, at the start of February he appealed through the City Hall press corps for a letup, saying:

"I should be glad if the newspaper men, who have treated me so well . . . since I have been here, would say that I now have to ask that those who want to see me personally will postpone their calls for a week or two, as there are some things which I must now do in discharge of my public duties. The impact on me has been very great, and I have tried to see everyone who called, but I must now have some intermission of that work or fail in some things which I should not postpone any longer."

The inescapable appeals for donations Gaynor dealt with brusquely. During the mayor's first month in office, Adamson wrote on the mayor's behalf to the Sisters of St. Catherine's Hospital in Brooklyn:

"The mayor directs me to return to you the enclosed tickets for a benefit concert . . . as he finds it impossible to subscribe for all the tickets which are sent to him at this office from various charitable enterprises. His Honor has a list of charities to which he subscribes regularly, but this list is kept at his home, not at his office."

An approach from a source with which Gaynor was not in sympathy met with a rebuff from the mayor himself. The New York Anti-Saloon League was the offender, and its superintendent was told roundly:

"I beg to say in answer to your letter that I can not subscribe $10 for a box, and I think it very bad taste to ask me to do so. If I gave money in response to all the similar demands that are made on me I should be bankrupt in short order, and it is strange to me that there are so many people who do not know better than to ask me for money."

Privately he could write at the same time to the New York Taxicab Company:

"Will you be so good as to send me your bill for cab-hire up to date. The longer it runs the larger it grows, and I fear it will be so large at the end that it will frighten me unless I pay it by the month."

Officiousness, especially when exhibited by a numskull, was certain to catch the rough side of the mayor's tongue. To one such correspondent, who had advice to offer about new subways, Gaynor snapped in reply:

"I do not blame you for being a man of only one idea, but I can assure you there are more things than one for me to think of as mayor of this city, and perhaps I have thought more about subways, at that, than you have."

When a recipient of such a letter took umbrage, Gaynor would profess to be mystified. To Eugene V. Brewster, a well-known Brooklyn lawyer, went a plaintive protest:

"Your letter has just come to hand. I have read it over and over again, but I must say I do not know what you mean to refer to. You talk of some letter returned to you. I have no knowledge of any such thing. The best way is to write me right out about any matter of grievance or complaint which you have. Certainly a large man like you is not dissatisfied simply because you did not get appointed to some office?"

Sandwiched between letters on lighter topics came a stern instruction to Fire Commissioner Waldo, ordering him to investigate forthwith the case of a Brooklyn fireman who was getting an inordi-

nate amount of sick leave, which he apparently spent in running
two saloons.

Next might be Gaynor's relaying of the plea of a woman in
South Hanover, Massachusetts, for help in tracing her aunt, "Miss
Eliza Tanzy, a dressmaker by occupation, who some thirty years
ago lived in West 27th Street, and, as her niece puts it, was 'an old
maid' even then."

The same day the press was delighted to receive the mayor's
response to a complaint about a well-known, flashy East Side political boss glorying in the title, "The Duke of Essex Street," otherwise Joe Levy.

"The complaint is," the mayor wrote, "that he controls the
police, the municipal court, the magistrate's court, the theaters, the
saloons, and all the houses other than family houses in that part of
the city. The mayor promised that he would see if some of the powers
of the Duke of Essex Street could not be taken away from him, and
that if it could not be done in any other way, legislation from Albany would be applied for."

Such humorous touches lightened the flow of serious communications—statements on conferences with Comptroller Prendergast
on city bonds; instructions to Commissioner of Accounts Fosdick to
look into the cost of running the municipal ferries ("that such costs
are very excessive seems plain"); an order to check on the fees paid
by the city to appraisers of real estate (much amiss here); a report
on a call paid by the Chinese consul with a grievance and an inter-
preter; a conference with law-enforcement officers on the harsh
treatment of persons held in custody as witnesses, though charged
with no offense themselves; a comprehensive report clearing the
Policemen's Benevolent Association from a suspicion of racketeering;
reports on the dropping by of noteworthy visitors; invitations to
speak in a dozen states (Gaynor is too busy to accept); texts of
Gaynor's speeches (with a caution to the editors not to change a
comma); exposure of aldermen grafting on pushcart peddlers and
holders of licenses for sidewalk newsstands; talks on constructing
new subways; punitive action against policemen who assaulted citizens—the range of topics was prodigious, and the public was
entertained. Nor was surprise expressed when on March 1 the
mayor's hard-pressed secretary added his own communiqué to a
mayoral announcement, as follows:

"The usual immense mail for the mayor was swelled today by
letters from people applying to be put on the citizens' committee to

welcome ex-President Roosevelt on his return to this country [from Europe]. So much work passes over the mayor's desk that his staff of three stenographers has been found to be insufficient and two additional ones are being hired by the day from the outside. It is a question whether the staff will go on strike, or walk four miles morning and evening like the mayor himself."

A fundamental rule which the mayor dinned into every employee and representative of the city was unfailing courtesy. "It is my great wish that all complaining people be dealt with promptly and fairly," he told his commissioners. If a complaint seemed sufficiently important, the complainant would be invited to visit City Hall and discuss it. "I find that people are very much pleased when they are considered," he advised Bridges Commissioner Martin. And to Health Commissioner Lederle he wrote: "I find it very advisable that all [those] complaining be made to know that their complaints are being examined into, and that generally satisfies them." To Commissioner Edwards the mayor confided after one month in office: "The policy of the city seems to be to annoy people whom it owes and I want to put an end to that if I can."

The mayor was constantly in touch with his commissioners, directing them along broad lines of policy. He wrote to precedent-setting Fire Commissioner Waldo (who already was inaugurating the change-over from horse-drawn to motorized equipment) reminding him to think twice before making his changes, saying:

"In government we have to make precedents on the assumption that dishonest and improper men will come into office. A good man in office should never make a bad precedent for a bad man who might come after him."

Gaynor took a dim view of granting time off with pay on religious holidays, which became quite a problem in multireligioned New York. When Bronx Borough President Miller abolished the practice there, Gaynor commended him, commenting that "it is very easy to be religious or patriotic at the public expense."

Manhattan Borough President McAneny soon charmed the mayor by his tact, sincerity, and ability. Pert and hirsute like Gaynor, McAneny was often in the mayor's office and early was assured by the mayor that "certainly you may have anything or anybody I have to help you."

District Attorney Whitman also received the mayor's commendation. At first Gaynor had been suspicious, but Whitman had taken hold energetically, enlarged his staff, weeded out the deadweights, and begun a vigorous prosecution of reckless automobile drivers, who were beginning to terrorize the streets. Wrote Gaynor to Whitman:

"I am glad to hear some one every day speaking well of the able, systematic, and orderly manner in which you are conducting your great office. We waited for it a long time."

Comptroller Prendergast, a fighter of the kind Gaynor respected, worked cooperatively in revitalizing his office, and within a few weeks was writing the mayor about the "very fine spirit of harmony that has so far pervaded this administration and which I am sure will be the dominant note to the end."

Only with Mitchel did Gaynor's relations remain equivocal. Mitchel was fretful—trapped, he sensed, in a political dead-end as the presiding officer of the antiquated Board of Aldermen. He craved action, and his role was largely subordinate and, he felt, decorative. Hearst was partial to Mitchel, and this did not endear the latter to the mayor. The extreme difference in their ages, too, militated against compatibility; nevertheless, there was no open break between them.

Outside of his official family, in regard to the community, Gaynor sedulously cultivated understanding and mutual trust, and the public was delighted to discover that beneath the chilling judicial figure was a man of warm heart and simple tastes, devoted to beneficent ends. Gaynor yearned over his city, and when the talk about his being run for governor revived, he told a booster at Saranac Lake:

"I thank you very much for your kind and encouraging letter. Be assured that I have no desire whatever for any other office, but only to do fairly well in this one, and make government better here. The mention of me for any other office has no effect on me whatever."

Letters signed with that abomination, a rubber stamp, got short shrift. Roeser & Company, of Second Avenue, received a communication from City Hall of a sort they had not expected:

"Dear Sirs: Your favor of the 13th would be examined into except that you do not sign your name to it, and I must therefore deem it a mere irresponsible statement. Common courtesy should dictate to you to sign your name in place of using a typewriter when you address the mayor of this city."

Nor would the mayor turn snooper to please a Flushing busybody, female, to whom he replied:

"I regret to say that I can not come to your house and watch the saloon as you request. If it is violating the law so openly I do not see why you or some of your neighbors do not go before a magistrate and get a warrant."

Gaynor wanted no crocodile tears or belated congratulations from persons who had fought him during the campaign by means he considered reprehensible. The overtures of one such Brooklynite crashed into the following roadblock:

"Sir: Your letter is at hand, and I beg to say to you that until you make suitable explanation of the false circular about me which you signed during the campaign I can dispense with your congratulations or recommendations. Indeed until that time I do not even consider you an honest man."

Another letter which probably gave its recipient a turn read:

"You are evidently a dishonest scamp, but I acknowledge the receipt of all letters. I may, however, put your letter in the hands of the police as you ought to be locked up."

One by one the letters slid across the mayor's desk, pointed, provocative, just, and unaffectedly human. Commissioner Waldo asked for a directive on allowing to stand an order issued by his predecessor, banning the sale of fireworks in the city over the Fourth of July. Gaynor weighed the alternatives, then wrote officially:

"I have a strong feeling in favor of the boys having their firecrackers, etc., on July 4th, for it is a great comfort to them. In fact, I am as fond of fireworks now as when I was a boy, and I believe that is the case with nearly every man you meet. Nevertheless, if the damage to life, limb, and property from fireworks is so great as to outweigh the pleasure they give, I suppose the order should stand. Suppose you collect the statistics on the subject. . . . Also let us submit the matter to public opinion, for as a rule that ought to govern."

Eventually the order was allowed to stand, and Gaynor led the way in encouraging and organizing less dangerous activities to celebrate the Fourth in a fitting manner. But his heart was still with the boys, as he showed in his letter to Arthur Tag, of 135 West 127th Street:

"Dear Arthur: I suppose you can shoot your cap pistols on July 4th, but do not use any bullets and above all do not shoot the two nice dogs which are on your letterhead."

Any letter about dogs got a hearty response. Tossed in among official directives was a note prodding a neglectful dog owner in Richmond Hill:

"Dear Mr. Woodward: And what about the dog? I have a thousand things to think of besides your dog, but did they kill him or did you get him back? If the latter, do you not think you ought to let me know?"

The same brand of remissness brought this testy reminder to Miss May Lee Williams, of Richmond, Virginia, who had written to the mayor for assistance:

"Did you get your money back? Since you put me to the trouble of writing to them to send it back to you, do you not think it is possible that it might be pleasant to me to learn that they had sent it back to you?"

On the same day, however, he had the quiet fun of replying to an urgent invitation relayed by a Brooklyn correspondent:

"Dear Mr. Wilson: If Satan's Empire really has been overthrown, I should be very glad to attend the lecture of Pastor C. T. Russell and hear him describe how it has been done. I had not heard of so great an event being accomplished yet."

And a cry of distress from Galbraith Welch, of 1 Union Square, New York City, drew the answer:

"I agree with you that singing 'Always Remember Mother' through a megaphone daily in front of a man's house is a grievance of which he has a right to complain. I shall see what can be done about this matter."

Ball playing in the streets was another subject on which the mayor unburdened himself feelingly time and again. Neville Brooker, of 657 Second Avenue, was told:

"I am sorry that the woman throws water on you when you play ball. I would be willing to wager that she has no boys of her own. All of those who write to me complaining about the children in the streets are people who have no children. I wish they would walk through the East Side and the crowded districts of the city and then tell me where the children are to go if they can not be in the streets. Would they lock them up in the bedrooms?"

Master William Roach, of 1591 Lexington Avenue, got an even more incisive letter from the mayor, as follows:

"Dear Boys: If you show this letter to the policeman I think he will let you play with a soft rubber ball on 101st Street between Lexington and Park Avenues if you ask him and if you are careful not to hit other people."

Sunday observance was a topic of constant recurrence in the mayor's mail, and more than one citizen indignant at fancied lack of respect for the Sabbath got an answer less indulgent than his reply to Miss Lillian Freund, of 57 Mangin Street, New York. Gaynor merely corrected her in the proper use of terms:

"Dear Madam: I have just received your second letter to me about the Sabbath observance, by which you mean Sunday observance. I agree with you about observing the day of rest. But we must be fair and charitable to others. The Christians do not observe the Sabbath day, namely the seventh day, established by God according to the 4th Commandment, or the 3rd, as some number it. The Christians abandoned that day, and adopted Sunday, which is the first day of the week. It is all right for us to observe Sunday, but let us have no miserable little prejudice against the Jews because they stick to the Sabbath. Some Christian sects also adhere to the Sabbath, stoutly maintaining that no one had the right to change the day of rest ordained of God from the seventh to the first day of the week."

A letter that was quoted nationally went to the Rev. Thomas M. Chalmers, a street preacher, and president of the New York Evangelical Society, in response to his application for a permit to preach in a heavily congested Jewish quarter of the East Side. Such permits were issued by the mayor's office, and Gaynor wrote:

"Reverend and Dear Sir: It seems to me that this work of proselytizing from other religions and sects is very often carried too far. Do you not think the Jews have a good religion? Have not the Christians appropriated the entire Jewish sacred scriptures? Was not the New Testament also written entirely by Jews? Was not Jesus also born of the Jewish race, if I may speak of it with due reverence? Did not we Christians get much or the most of what we have from the Jews? Why should anyone work so hard to proselytize the Jew? His pure belief in the one true living God comes down to us even from the twilight of fable, and is the one great unbroken lineage and tradition of the world. I do not think I should give you a license to preach for the conversion of the Jews in the streets of the thickly settled Jewish neighborhoods which you designate. Would you not annoy them and do more harm than good? How many Jews have you converted so far?"

Jacob H. Schiff thanked the mayor for this courageous and tactful stand, and the Union of Orthodox Jewish Congregations of the United States and Canada formally conveyed its thanks for Gaynor's "noble expression."

Mayor Gaynor's fame was reaching far. Replying to a greeting from the Honorable T. McCants Stewart, of Monrovia, Liberia, he wrote:

"My dear Mr. Stewart: I am very glad to receive your letter from far-away Liberia. Give my best regards to Mrs. Stewart and the three daughters. I am glad that you are doing well. I am very busy here as a great many things press upon me constantly. In fact, I should be glad to get off to Liberia and see you and have a vacation."

But at home, a few sour notes persisted amid the general chorus of praise. The *Brooklyn Eagle*, for example, objected strongly to the administration's paring of payrolls in the sacred name of economy.

"Do they know," demanded the *Eagle*, "that it means poverty and idleness to hundreds of underpaid laborers and misery to their families? And this by a city . . . with boundless resources and boundless wealth. Reform! To hell with reform!"

The *New York Times* expressed fear that the mayor was mortally offending powerful interests which could and would exact revenge.

"Those who are forced from the trough are nursing their wrath sullenly," The *Times* gloomed, "and economical and efficient government will yet be on trial for its life. Those who like this sort of government should remark that they are getting it, and make note that they may lose it unless they hold up the hands of those who are giving it to them."

The *Tribune* deplored that the city's mayor should waste his talents in a mere display of versatility, sarcastically remarking that "nothing that does not concern him is too difficult for his brain." Yet the *Tribune*, like the rest of the press, was delighted to publish such exhibitions of the mayor's versatility as his greeting to a learned ratcatcher, Mr. Charles M. Frey, of 177 East 102nd Street. Mr. Frey, a graduate of the University of Zurich, had written to City Hall protesting that repeated calls to jury duty were interfering with his highly necessary profession. To him the mayor replied:

"Dear Mr. Frey: Your letter of March 15th is at hand, describing how your calling of ratcatcher is constantly being interrupted by your being summoned to serve as a juror. Sooner than have the city overrun with rats and everything eaten up by them I would have you relieved of jury duty. Do you not think we had better have a bill introduced in the legislature to exempt ratcatchers from jury duty? The difficulty is, however, that so many exemptions have already been passed by the legislature that there seem to be only the ratcatchers and a few other people to serve on juries. That might possibly impede the progress of your bill if sent to Albany. I will have to carefully consider the matter, and some day when you are down this way come in and we will talk it over, and also about rats. I see that you are a classical scholar, judging by the motto at the head of your letter. My experience is that learned men are to be found everywhere. As we read in *Don Quixote:* 'The mountains breed learned men and philosophers are found in the huts of shepherds.' "

The erudite ratcatcher did call at City Hall and had a long, companionable visit with the erudite mayor. They discussed Plutarch and Epictetus and how to eradicate rats, Mr. Frey expounding his scheme for doing it by electricity. Gaynor offered to send his guest a copy of Petrarch's *Letters to Cicero,* recently published, and the satirists and cartoonists had a happy time depicting the mayor as "something of a ratcatcher himself."

The fact was that Gaynor was interested in life in all its aspects, and he was perfectly natural in the way he showed it. Though he carried out the etiquette required of his official standing with aplomb and relish, he never posed, but spoke and acted as he felt. His staff often groaned, for he drove them unmercifully, kept long hours, and subjected those around him to fearful outbursts of temper. His lurid cursing at such moments could be heard in the park outside City Hall, and clerks and stenographers scurried out of sight. But his acts of kindness also were numerous and unpremeditated.*

Gaynor's observations on stray cats also were manna to the newspapers. He wrote to Mr. Cornelius S. Loder, of 30 Church Street, Manhattan:

"Your favor of the 31st is at hand. You ask me to tell you how to 'eliminate' stray cats in the neighborhood. You say they are a nuisance and disturb you, and also that they are a menace to good health. I rather like the sound of their voices. They are quite musical. I should think they would put you to sleep. The only objection I have to them is to see them going around in the summer neglected and poor, with nothing to eat or even to drink. I fear your only way is to exterminate them, as you suggest. . . . Or, if you prefer, you might catch them and send them all to the wife of the learned

---

* Mayor Fiorello LaGuardia's tantrums were to become a legend of City Hall, but men who saw them both in action said that compared with Gaynor's, LaGuardia's outbursts were "sissy."

NOTHING DOING   *Jan. 13, 1919*

Doctor William H. Hale of Brooklyn, who keeps a sort of stray cat
farm in her back yard, to the great disgust of her neighbors. They
complain about her to the Board of Health at least once a week, but
she goes right on in her work. Or, it may be, the Society for the
Prevention of Cruelty to Animals will lend you a hand in the matter.
If all other means fail, it may be that I would take it up again and
see what I could do if I went at it in earnest."

No criticism caused Gaynor to alter his style or modify the
contents of his letters a particle. A letter that came without signature, was fired back to the firm on whose letterhead it was written
with the comment:

"As the enclosed letter is written on your blank I return it to
you to see if we can ascertain who wrote it. I do not wonder that the
writer is ashamed to sign his name, for it is the most nonsensical
letter I have received this year. The writer is reading some trash in
the newspapers which he takes for gospel, in place of crediting
officials with care. The latter part about Croker and Tammany Hall
is enough to make one laugh. I suppose the writer thinks that Commissioner Waldo and myself are in with Tammany Hall. There

seem to be some very miserable people in the City of New York."

How little the mayor was "in" with Tammany Hall was reflected in the reports that Democratic district clubs were closing
because the members had stopped paying dues.

Onerous and time-consuming as were the burdens carried by the
mayor, Gaynor found time to appear as speaker before a wide
assortment of groups, representing every phase of city life. In his
speeches he never made any effort to play up to, or play down to,
his audiences, and he seldom "explained" his actions. Instead, he in
effect placed himself on exhibit, to be accepted or rejected as his
listeners would. He almost always spoke extemporaneously, but insisted on having his words taken down by a stenographer, and he
was prompt to challenge any misquotation.

The chairman of the Republican state committee, Ezra P.

**"OH THE LONG AND DREARY WINTER,
OH, THE COLD AND CRUEL WINTER."**

Jan. 11, 1910

THE MAYOR IS SOMETHING OF A RATCATCHER HIMSELF

April 15, 1910

Prentice, who offended the mayor by misquoting him, was "taken down" sharply.

"Dear Sir," Gaynor wrote without preamble, "It might be good for you to stop putting out false statements, even though you can not get your campaign speakers to do the like. . . . Suppose you pray every morning for a while to God to direct you to tell the truth, and see what fruits it will bring."

When Prentice angrily denied having the slightest intention to falsify, and corrected the misquotation, he was favored with this further from City Hall:

"I am glad to perceive from your letter, just received, that I have already so far cured you of your propensity to make false statements that you drop your forged quotation. . . . While the lamp holds out to burn the vilest sinner may return."

Speaking at the dinner of the Prospect Heights Citizens Association at the Montauk Club, Gaynor told the diners he had broken his rule of "not going out in the evening" only because the club was across the street from his home. Since he had spoken at numerous evening affairs elsewhere, the remark seemed gratuitous; but the mayor went on:

"Plutarch tells us that Pericles when mayor of Athens was never seen except going between the city hall and his home; I think I will emulate his example. If I mention Epictetus, Themistocles, or

Plato, it so astounds the journalistic world as to make subjects for caricatures for a month afterward. Epictetus ran two months, about the length of any popular show. Well, I'll take the risk on the rest of them."

Before the American Bankers Association he touched on the same subject and disclaimed any affinity with Epictetus:

"In the most harmless way I once quoted one sentence from Epictetus, and I have never heard the last of it up to this time. At first they seemed to think I had quoted from some bad book."

Then he went on to give the bankers—and attentive newspapermen—another dose of the classics. He quoted Cato the Elder, and noticing the reporters' blank stare, tossed curtly to them, "Cato, Cato, I said. Did you never hear of him before?" Resuming, he gave the bankers his translation of a passage by Cato indicating that in ancient Rome moneylenders were held lower than thieves.

"KIND WORDS CAN NEVER DIE"

Jan. 14, 1910

THE BIGGEST HIT IN TOWN *Feb.* 17, 1910

The Friendly Sons of St. Patrick invited the mayor to speak at their annual St. Patrick's Day dinner at Delmonico's, and he prefaced his brief remarks by congratulating his hosts on the antiquity of their organization, almost coeval with the republic, and then pejorated his Irish ancestry, saying that unlike most of them he could not claim unmixed Irish blood. Their first president, he reminded, "was a Presbyterian, and your present one may be, for aught any of you care." (From a far table came a priest's scandalized cry, "God forbid!") Gaynor then felicitated the sons of Erin on their broad-mindedness and freedom from bigotry, and sat down. The speech, released to the press, was short. It was also breathtaking.

To the Advertising Club the mayor breezily quoted Shakespeare as applied to their business:

" 'Oh what a goodly outside falsehood hath!' "

The Master Plumbers of New York State, dining at the Hotel

Astor in a blaze of diamonds, were advised by the mayor not to countenance the false rumor that New York City was a wicked place:

"Although you have read in the newspapers, you people of Syracuse, Buffalo, Rochester, and other places in the state, that New York is a bad city, I want to say to you that it is not as bad as Buffalo, Syracuse, or Rochester. Down on Long Island, in Suffolk County, the side door and kitchen door of saloons are open on Sunday and nobody says a word. But here in New York, oh, dear me! We have got people who make up societies and watch everything and we have to be better!"

The plumbers voted Gaynor an honorary member of their association.

The mayor husbanded his time and strength to the last minute. When he addressed the alumni of the Law School of New York University at a dinner in honor of the governor and bar of Connecticut

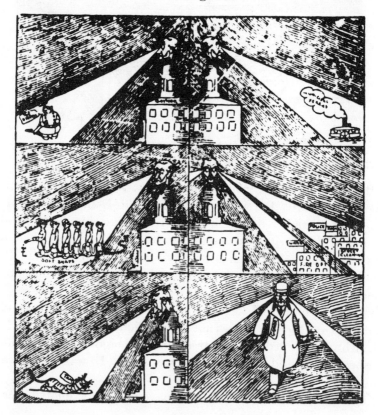

THE MUNICIPAL SEARCHLIGHT

March 3, 1910

at the Astor, he went directly from City Hall to the hotel, retired to
a suite and changed into evening dress. He then dined alone on
soup, duckling, and a pint of champagne; he disliked to arrive at a
banquet until the speeches were beginning. Resting from then until
a quarter to nine, the exact time he had promised to appear, he
entered the banquet room fresh and immaculate.

At that dinner so many Connecticut judges were present it was
said that a court order could not have been obtained in the state that
night. Being among professional colleagues, Gaynor humorously
read a passage from the Connecticut blue laws, with his comment:

" 'If any man shall after legal conviction have or worship any
other God but the Lord God he shall be put to death.'

"I wonder who determined who was the Lord God up there in
the Connecticut courts. Did the court take an adjournment to consider this question in the privacy of chambers?"

There was general laughter, but some of the Connecticut people
looked black; Gaynor's humor was often misunderstood. A few days
later the governor of Connecticut, George B. McLean, pointed out
that Connecticut's blue laws came from the Massachusetts code of
1641, which came from the Bible; so that Gaynor had been "making
fun of his own Bible." Furthermore, if he had compared the history
of Connecticut with that of New York and Tammany Hall, "it might
have occurred to him that blue laws are better than no law, the Old
Testament better than no testament, and the Lord God better than
no God."

A stickler for the deference due to his office, Gaynor upset members of the Suffolk County Association when, on arriving to address
their gathering at the Hotel Astor, he found no one on hand to
receive him, due to a misunderstanding. After waiting several
minutes outside the banquet hall, he left.

At a dinner for the Japanese ambassador he was all suavity,
and paid generous praise to the culture of the Orient, so much more
ancient than that of the West:

"Asia was walking in the halls of kings and standing in the
presence of princes when our ancestors were running naked in the
woods of Europe and literally burrowing in the ground. When Asia
came to Europe there were no damasks there, there was not a carpet
in Europe. . . . There was not a woman in Europe who was clothed
in more than a single garment, while the women of Asia had outer
and inner garments. Even the word 'chemise' is of Asiatic origin."

This curious learning was not the work of some compiler of

facts for the mayor's use, or some "ghost writer" of his speeches. Speaking extemporaneously, he simply poured out the oddments gathered in his lifetime of reading and exploration of history, languages, and philosophy, just as they occurred to him.

Early in March the mayor visited Public School No. 177, on the lower East Side, arriving there by subway as one of the early morning straphangers. He told the assembly of two hundred little girls that he had forgone his walk across the bridge in order to get there on time.

"The car was crowded when I entered," he said, "and I noticed women and working girls hanging to straps as I was. Just in front of me were five young men. They were comfortably dressed and in good spirits. One of them called the attention of the others to the mayor hanging to a strap. They also smiled at the young women standing but did not offer any of them a seat.

"I see before me a large number of bright, intelligent children. You are well dressed, and certainly you are not underfed or vicious, as some persons try to make us believe."

Relating how, when he was a boy, he went to a little schoolhouse in the country and wore mittens and ear muffs, he said to one little girl:

"You look very much like one of my little daughters. Tootsie, I call her. And when I go home I will cross-examine her and find out if she knows as much as you. If not I may send her to this school."

The pupils answered questions about affairs of government with a competence that surprised the mayor, especially when he learned that some of them had been in this country only a few months.

The Syracuse Chamber of Commerce, proud to honor the up-state mayor, was accorded a compliment in a loftier vein when Gaynor, in his speech, digressed to assure his hosts:

"I could in truth apply to you and your like, picked men of the community, that fine passage of Euripides: 'In every state are three classes: the greedy rich, indifferent to the public good, all their thoughts on more acquiring; those who, short of the means of life, struggle with want, and hence are rude, to envy much addicted, and prone to be led astray by the lying statements of selfish and deceitful leaders; and twixt these extremes, those who guard the state, conservers of order and the country's laws.' "

The modern Syracusans may have been vague about Euripides, but they warmed to the mayor under this praise.

At home the mayor was at times less laudatory—decidedly less in a formal communication to the district attorney of Queens county taking the grand jury of that county to task:

"I am in receipt of your letter of March 11th enclosing a resolution by the grand jury of Queens county directing where subways should be built and calling on the mayor and the Public Service Commission to furnish them with full and detailed information on all plans adopted or contemplated for the construction of subways. Be so good as to inform the grand jury that I shall do no such thing. It has become the custom of late for grand juries to set themselves up as having authority in all sorts of matters with which they have no authority whatever."

Appended, in Gaynor's firm handwriting, was:

"Their business is to inquire into crime."

The mayor himself did not always conform to precept. Interceding where strictly he had no authority, he obtained for the widow of a policeman a monthly payment out of the police relief fund when her claim to a city pension was disallowed on a technicality.

Gaynor was scrupulous in avoiding even the appearance of bringing improper influence to bear, however. Although he took a keen interest in the corporation counsel's work, when a case came before that office in which the plaintiff was represented by the law firm of the mayor's intimate friend, Mirabeau L. Towns, Gaynor wrote immediately to Watson, carefully marking the note *"Private"*:

"I am informed that when the injunction case came into your office yesterday it fell into the hands of one or more of your assistants, who remarked that as Towns & McCrossin were in it for the plaintiff I might be favorable to it. I hope there is no notion in your office that any such thing could possibly be true."

And when the Civil Service Commission notified him routinely of the scheduling of a hearing on reclassification of the position of executive secretary to the mayor, to allow him greater latitude in making a choice, Gaynor advised the commission:

"I never asked the board to take any such action, and I . . . particularly request that they act on their own judgment and not be influenced by any consideration of what would be pleasing to the mayor."

Yet when a Gargantuan aspirant to the police force appealed to the mayor for help in tackling the tests, Gaynor wrote to the chairman of the Civil Service Commission:

"This will introduce to you Mr. Joseph Hooker, who wants to be a policeman. He says he has undergone the physical examination, and passed, but fears your mental test. He is certainly a physical giant, 6 feet 5 inches tall, and I trust he is an intellectual giant also, because we are in need of the latter kind on the police force. He is too big for the detective force; he could not go anywhere without being seen. Is there no way to get a few little men, even hunchbacks and 'singed cats,' on the police force, so that we can make detectives of them? We do not need giants for detectives. We are more in need of little fellows who can go through keyholes and knotholes, and if they have eyes in the back of their heads also all the better."

The city marshals, brought together at City Hall, got a straight-from-the-shoulder talk from the mayor on how to conduct their often disagreeable business. Telling them that he regarded them as members of his staff, Gaynor said he had been looking into their records, and some of them would probably be dismissed for abusing their powers. Such iniquities as charging extortionate rates for hauling and storing the household goods of evicted families must stop, he warned, and in general he urged leniency and humanity in carrying out their work.

"I want to caution you to proceed like orderly men," he urged, "and above all to be gentle in the performance of your duty. Don't be rough and oppressive. Be careful, prudent, and good to people. You have to do many a hard thing, to be sure. I know it is a pretty hard thing to go into a house and take a man's goods away. When you have to do it, do it as silently and as gentlemanly as you can. Don't make levies where it is doubtful. Let the parties bond you. Where your own judgment tells you the man doesn't own the property, don't make a levy."

This note of compassion and concern for the welfare and dignity of the ordinary citizen recurred constantly in Gaynor's speeches, and he urged patience and forbearance, even when he could not exemplify his own preachments. A correspondent who chafed at the slow pace of progress was advised:

"Poor Human Nature can not be reformed all at once, but only by slow degrees and slow growth, by the operation of regular forces, and we must do the best we can in our day and generation."

And to a high school student at Matawan, New Jersey, the mayor disclosed the basis of his creed and the ideal toward which he strove, though, thanks to "poor Human Nature," constantly falling short of it:

"The subject of the discussion, you say, is, 'What is my worst temptation?' I hardly know what to say to you, as I do not know what your temptations are. I should think that pride is about the worst of the temptations. Pride excludes all charity. Proud people are never gentle and kind to others, and there is no charity without that, and charity is everything."

BLUE COATS AND BRASS BUTTONS

———————————————o◯o———————————————

Let the police learn . . .
———GAYNOR

NEXT TO RESTORING all the departments to a basis of impartial honesty, Gaynor's most cherished objective was a thorough reform of the police force. Before he had been in office two weeks he was personally acting to prevent arbitrary arrests, teach the policemen courtesy and respect for the law, and break up the demoralizing graft that honeycombed the ranks, from top to bottom. In the course of this undertaking he ran full tilt into opposition by moralists who strove to impose their notions of right conduct on the community through restrictive laws enforced by the policeman's club.

New York had ten thousand policemen, and the conditions under which they were employed sound incredible to a later generation. Although applicants were required to pass rigid civil-service tests, both physical and mental, one could get on the force only by paying money or using political influence. Men unable or unwilling to "shell out" might remain at the top of the eligible list for years and never be appointed. Promotions were sold in the same way. As a result, nearly every rookie started his career in debt, and remained in debt for years.

The pay was utterly inadequate, even by the low wage standards of the day. Salaries started at $800 a year and ranged up to $1,400—and $800 meant $66 a month. Out of this the men were obliged to pay for their uniforms, bedding, upkeep of their dormitories, bootblack's fee, and dues to the policemen's benefit association, and contribute to charity appeals whenever the precinct captain wished to make a "good showing" for some politician's preferred charity. Grafting was sometimes a literal necessity to make ends meet.

The station-house dormitories in which the men lived while on duty would have been outlawed by the board of health of any city twenty years later. One, quite typical, was a single room forty feet long, lighted and ventilated by two narrow windows at one end. The cots were lined up eighteen inches apart. Clothing, wet or dry, was hung on pegs along the wall. The men slept in their clothing, and one veteran described the stench as "atrocious." In winter the room was superheated by a potbelly stove, usually kept red-hot, forcing the men to pile out into freezing weather from a sweatbox. Deaths from pneumonia were commonplace.

Under the two-platoon system then in vogue a policeman was on duty, either on patrol or on reserve in the station house, for periods of thirty-six hours at a stretch, with no break except an hour for meals between tours. At the end of this interval he might go home for twelve to twenty-four hours. In addition, he had one night off every twenty days, at least in theory, for this was likely to be canceled by emergency calls.

Under such conditions it was surprising that the quality and morale of the force remained as high as it did, and in spite of all handicaps, the civil service requirements were gradually raising the general level. But there was still a preponderance of holdovers from less regenerate days, and these men because of their longer service filled many of the higher grades.

Gaynor's opening blows were struck against the abuse he had combated so vigorously while on the bench—the indiscriminate use of the club. Thirteen days after becoming mayor he sent to Commissioner Baker a furious letter, breathing anger in every line:

"Oscar E. Gregory called on me today to complain of Patrolman Devon who clubbed him in Broadway, Brooklyn, Monday night. The sight of this young man is shocking. It is impossible to look at him without rising indignation that any citizen should be subjected to such brutal treatment by a policeman. His face and eyes are so contused that he is scarcely recognizable, and his head and mouth cut. This young man was with his wife when the thing happened, and seems to have done nothing but remonstrate with the officer for assaulting another. . . .

"Let me say to you that these outrages have to cease. They

have been growing more common for years, and I regret to say have gone on with scarcely a rebuke. It is time that they be stopped, and that the police be fully informed that to commit a battery on a citizen, or to make a false or unnecessary arrest, or to unlawfully enter a house, is a far greater offense than to let a criminal escape. Please let Devon be brought to trial before your trial deputy in the shortest time possible and summarily dismissed if found guilty. Nothing short of dismissal will suffice in such cases."

When this letter was published, and the public realized that in this respect, too, Gaynor had meant exactly what he said when he had told McClellan, in the Duffy case, that he could stop police outrages in a month, victims of police brutality descended on City Hall in a procession, and every case received prompt attention. Men who had been beaten, arrested, and locked up without charges, only to be released by a magistrate in the morning—even children who had been clubbed by patrolmen for playing ball in the street—filed through the mayor's office, and the directives flowed from there to Commissioner Baker. Before January was out, Baker reported back to the mayor that the first three "clubber" policemen—including Patrolman Devon—had been tried, found guilty, and thrown off the force. Gaynor publicly commended the commissioner's energetic action, saying:

"Let all such men on the force be treated in the same way and as promptly as possible. You have a splendid force of men under you, and they should not be disgraced by the comparatively few men on the force who are not fit to be there."

Some of the police were slow to grasp that a new order had come to stay, and when, even after announcement of the first disciplinary actions, a bloodstained victim of a policeman's club staggered into City Hall, Gaynor exploded to Baker:

"I can not conceive any excuse whatever for a man being beaten in the cruel manner in which [this man's] wounds show he was beaten. His eyes and face are blackened, the bridge of his nose is fractured, and there is a great gash on the side of his head. Let the patrolman be suspended and put on trial forthwith."

But Gaynor was just, and he could be sympathetic, also. A mounted policeman who struck a driver and at first denied it, then changed his mind, came to the mayor and confessed that he had given the blow in the heat of anger and was sorry the next minute. Gaynor thereupon notified Baker:

"I think under the circumstances that leniency should be shown to this man, and that he should not be dismissed from the force. He appears to me to be an intelligent and good officer." But he at once added: "Let this leniency not serve as a precedent. I want [the men] to know that I have every confidence in them and desire only to do justice. On the other hand I expect them to be frank and truthful with the mayor and with you, and of all things never try to shield the men on the force who are doing wrong. For their own honor they should help us rid the force of such men."

By every means at his disposal Gaynor strove to instill pride in the policemen. To end the scandal of appointment and promotion through graft or favoritism he established the rule that vacancies on the force should be filled from the top of the civil service eligible list, in strict numerical order. He established the same rule for promotions, and constantly checked with Baker to make sure it was being observed. He turned up at a civil service examination being taken by lieutenants for the grade of captain, and after calling some of the questions silly, and doubting whether he could himself answer others, he assured the men that no influence, political or otherwise, would play any part in their grading and advancement.

On the practical side, the mayor set to work to remedy intolerable working conditions, and during his term the three-platoon system would be adopted, ending the oppressively long hours of sustained duty and giving the men a chance to see their families oftener than once every three days. At considerable pains he ran down and spiked rumors derogatory to the police, and was quick to take notice of and publicize meritorious action by the men in any form. Officer Walter C. Rosendale may have been startled to receive this personal letter from the mayor, and almost simultaneously to read it in the newspapers:

"My attention has been called to an act of bravery of yours on April 11th on Fifth Avenue in stopping a runaway team. I am very glad to be informed of it, and shall see that your superior officers take notice of it."

When Policeman Sheehan found two New Jersey boys lost in the city and without money, and gave them a dollar to get home, the mayor, on being notified by the boys' grateful family, wrote to Sheehan warmly:

"It was very kind of you indeed, and I am sure they will send back the dollar which you gave them. I have long known from personal observation that the patrolmen do many kind things, and I am in a position now to hear many of the good things they do, and I grow more proud of them every day. I shall always be glad to hear from you and also to do anything for you which I can legally and properly do."

But unworthy police behavior received retribution just as swiftly and emphatically. Two policemen who borrowed money from a saloonkeeper and neglected to pay it back were called to account. "Please see that they are tried forthwith," went the order to Baker. Several Bronx policemen who had pawned their winter uniforms, alleging that they had done it in order to have them mothproofed in camphor, so disgusted the mayor he called them "a good for nothing lot" and told Baker to "follow that matter up further." A Brooklyn patrolman who spent many of his duty hours in the back room of a saloon playing poker received no sympathy at his trial, especially when testimony was offered that he had called Gaynor and the police commissioner "a pair of grafters." And Patrolman Joyce ("No. 6473, 158th precinct") who owed "Pfeifer & McGinnis $9.67 for meat" and refused to pay it, was the subject of a curt directive:

"I find that not only is it not paid but that he is laughing about it. I trust that you will immediately see that it is no laughing matter and report to me. Let him be dismissed from the force if he does not pay it."

When the Chinese consul called at City Hall to seek relief for his nationals from long-continued police blackmail, he was requested by the mayor to pass the word around Chinatown that no one need pay any policeman for protection any more, and that any policeman found guilty of smashing into a Chinese home or store illegally, and wrecking the interior in order to extort money, would be thrown off the force. In a report of the visit sent by Secretary Adamson to the press, Gaynor's inspection of the scene of a police raid in Chinatown while he was a judge—doors ripped from their hinges, walls punched through, furniture smashed—was recounted with the comment that he had had no authority then to stop such outrages, "but now he has authority to stop it and he intends to stop it."

This communiqué wound up characteristically:

"The consul had two written statements of outrages on Chinamen in New York. The mayor tried to read them but the handwriting was so obscure that he asked the consul to take them away and have them typewritten and returned to him, and they are to be returned to him tomorrow."

No "buck passing" or evasion of responsibility by police officials was tolerated by the mayor. Hearing of an assault made by two policemen upon a woman in the back room of a barbershop on East 34th Street, Gaynor in rapid order told Baker to see that the accused policemen were "suspended and tried forthwith. We must get rid of all ruffians on the police force." Then he added:

"Let the captain of that precinct and also the inspector of that district come before me tomorrow. The whole disgraceful affair occurred so openly . . . that it is incredible that the captain and inspector should not have learned of it in the exercise of ordinary attention. It was certainly easier for them than for you and me to learn of it."

When Gaynor reached City Hall at 9:30 the next morning the captain and inspector were on hand, waiting. They were taken at once into the mayor's office and were informed by Gaynor (Adamson reported to the press) that he was "unable to see how such a thing could happen and be known to so many people without both of them knowing it. He also told them that two other policemen had come to the barbershop where the woman was and saw her and learned of the assault . . . and when they learned that two policemen were involved they did nothing nor did they report it to their station houses. The mayor stated to the inspector and the captain that he gave them the day to find the woman and find these two other policemen. The mayor informed them that if they did not produce them he had no doubt he would be able to find them himself.

"The result was that the inspector and the captain went to work, found the woman . . . also found the two officers . . . and found in addition a detective who had also come to the barbershop and learned the facts but made no report on them. These three officers were taken to police headquarters and suspended pending trial. . . . The mayor also called Deputy Commissioner Bugher [in charge of detectives] to his office before leaving for the day and told him to put the head of the detective bureau in charge of the case, and to say to him that the mayor would hold him responsible that none of the witnesses in the case got away before the policemen were tried."

All this action occurred within twenty-four hours.

The public responded delightedly to the new attitude toward the force. A catchword was, "Aw, go tell it to Gaynor!" And the way a policeman winced under the threat to report him to City Hall was balm to many a victim of brass-buttoned arrogance.

A demonstration of the popular feeling occurred on a rainy day in front of City Hall. An automobile pulled up in front of the

Hall, and somebody said it was the mayor's car. In a matter of minutes a crowd of fifteen hundred had gathered around it expectantly. When Gaynor appeared with the director of the Museum of Natural History, where he was to make a speech, he asked Lieutenant Kennell what it meant.

"They just want to see the mayor," the lieutenant replied.

And as the car rolled away, there was a call for "three cheers for Gaynor," and they were given. City Hall attachés could recall nothing like it for decades back.

Arbitrary and unwarranted arrests were the next target of the mayor's reform. Policemen must be compelled to issue a simple summons in lieu of making arrests for trivial offenses, Baker was instructed. In 1909 there had been 262,000 arrests in New York City, compared with 111,000 in London despite its larger population. Of the New York arrests, 60,000 had been plainly unjustified, inasmuch as the prisoners had been discharged the next morning for lack of a complaint.

Exclaimed the mayor, "This is scarcely civilization," and he visited the courts himself to collect instances of "stupid arrests" and obtain the names of offending policemen. No one could tell where or when he would materialize.

The order that no arrests be made without legal evidence was revolutionary. As Commissioner Baker euphemistically phrased it, the police previously "had not been so careful." The *Times* saw danger if the rule were enforced and believed many guilty would escape; but Gaynor stuck to his conviction that "the way of the law is a far better way than any way outside of the law and over the law."

He ordered protection for street orators and street marchers as long as they complied with the law. Under Commissioner Bingham, socialist meetings had been broken up; Gaynor forbade this so long as the meetings were orderly. When an attorney for the socialists submitted a brief defending their right to speak in the streets, Gaynor replied that he concurred:

"I agree with you that this is a free government and that the right of free speech here is held sacred. . . . While you have the right to speak on the public streets that right is subject to the rule that you can not create a tumult or unduly obstruct the streets, and if you interfere with that right you can be stopped by the police. You very intelligently admit this in your brief. . . . Please let me know when you want to speak next and I will have the police commissioner come here and get full instructions with regard to your rights."

During labor disputes and strikes, Gaynor ordered the police to preserve peace in the streets but to observe strict neutrality between the contending parties. Strikers and strikebreakers were to be treated alike if they broke the law, but otherwise were not to be interfered with. During 1910 immigrant working girls employed in the shirtwaist factories at wages of $3 to $9 for a sixty-hour week fought out a long, bitter strike, and Gaynor kept the police, who before had notoriously sided with the employers, out of the dispute. Five hundred arrests were made in suppressing street disorders, but there was no rioting, and many of the arrests the mayor reviewed personally to make certain that no one's rights were being violated.

When, early in his term, he heard of a renewed case like that of young Duffy—a man being arrested, held incommunicado overnight, then stripped, measured, and photographed for the "rogues gallery," only to be discharged without complaint—Gaynor flew into a rage and ordered Baker to destroy all photographs of unconvicted persons in the police files, put a stop to the practice, make sure that every person arrested was taken before a magistrate on the day of arrest, as the law required, and never, under any circumstances, be denied an opportunity to communicate with friends or family.

The mayor also forbade the arrest of boys for such things as playing in the streets, and to the many letters received complaining of the youngsters, he returned the same answer, over and over again:

"I brought up my children and they all played in the streets. There is no law against playing in the streets. What would you do with them? Lock them all up in bedrooms?"

But the real problem was that of drying up the saloon graft. This touched the whole police force, and had defied the efforts of other mayors to abolish or even control it.

The abuse stemmed from the Sunday closing law. This Puritan heritage was out of line with public sentiment in cosmopolitan New York City. In 1909, 78% of the population of the metropolis was either foreign-born or had at least one foreign-born parent. The customs and traditions of this overwhelming majority contained nothing resembling the Puritan Sabbath. Germans could not understand why anyone should forbid them to drink lager beer on Sunday; Italians had never heard of a "still Sabbath"; the Irish had never conformed to the Protestant ban on recreation after church time on Sunday. The city's saloons, responding to public demand, kept open in disregard of the law, and the result had been an invitation to the police to organize a system of blackmail. So thoroughly established was this graft, it flourished no matter who might be in the top command.

The way it worked was simple. A policeman, observing a saloon open and crowded on Sunday, would walk in and announce that his duty required him to arrest the bartender or owner, or both, for breaking the law. If the bartender slid a few dollars across the mahogany, the policeman would forget about his duty, accept a drink, and move along. But if the bartender balked, he was collared and marched to the station house to ruminate in a cell overnight. Then he would be put to the expense of engaging a lawyer and a bail bondsman (usually those recommended by the arresting officer) and suffer the ignominy and annoyance of trial on a trumped-up charge, and pay a fine. Meanwhile, his bar remained closed while his competitors were serving the customers he had lost.

The graft "take" under this system was estimated at millions of dollars annually. The dues collected by the liquor dealers' associations from their members were channeled largely to upper-echelon police officers, and these dues alone amounted to $2,000,000 a year. But that was only one portion of the graft; every grade of policeman shared in the rake-off. How to put an end to this many-tentacled evil was the problem Gaynor went at with customary determination. Ignoring the nagging of reformers who demanded that he shut down every saloon on Sunday forthwith, he carefully evolved a plan. With closing saloons he was not primarily concerned; his objective was to cut off the police graft at its source. When, late in March, he revealed his plan, it proved to be simplicity itself, consisting of nothing more than enforcement of the law by the means prescribed in the statute.

First Gaynor called in representatives of the saloon men and told them that the practice of paying to sell liquor on Sunday must stop, and that he knew how to stop it. The liquor men were gratified to hear that they should no longer submit to blackmail, but doubted that Gaynor could succeed where his predecessors had failed. A few days later Gaynor announced his method in a long, precise directive to Police Commissioner Baker.

First the mayor quoted the law, which required that all blinds, shades, or other obstructions on the doors and windows of saloons must be pulled up or removed on Sunday to provide a clear view of the interior from the sidewalk outside. Policemen on the beat were to watch to see whether business was being carried on inside; if it was, they were to do what the law said, namely, file an affidavit as to each violation with the district attorney, the prosecuting authority. Under no circumstances were the policemen to enter the saloon; they must make their observations from the sidewalk and make no arrests themselves. If the side or rear door of a saloon stood open and it was suspected that business was being carried on out of sight, plain-clothes men or regular detectives could enter and procure evidence, but they must not reveal their identity, under pain of dismissal. They would file their evidence with the district attorney, and only when the accused saloonkeeper was placed on trial would he learn who had denounced him. By preventing any contact between the policemen and the saloon keepers, Gaynor was confident that the graft would be cut off at its source, and by means strictly legal.

The Sunday the plan went into effect reporters roaming the city found the blinds up everywhere, and most barrooms empty; the back-room business, however, seemed as brisk as ever. Patrolmen filed hundreds of affidavits of noncompliance, swamping the district attorney's staff. But within two weeks violations had been reduced to a handful, and Gaynor was elated. Beyond a doubt he had given the system of saloon graft its death blow, simply by forbidding policemen to go into barrooms themselves, and the detectives who were assigned to spot back-room sales were shifted around from district to district to prevent their arriving at secret understandings. Beyond a certain point, the Sunday closing law was unenforceable in New York, Gaynor believed. As he once told the Lutheran Ministers Association:

"You may pass all the laws you please, but they will become a dead letter if they are not backed up by the will of the community. This has been true ever since the beginning of law and will continue to the end of the world. Against public sentiment no law, no matter how strictly enforced, will stand."

A chorus of praise greeted the mayor's deft solution of a problem that had seemed beyond human power to solve. Said the *Outlook* admiringly: "We do not remember who it was that cut the Gordian Knot, but his name might have been Gaynor." The president of the Board of City Magistrates called the action "a master stroke, if not the best thing Mayor Gaynor has done." Even the Hearst papers joined in the praise, conceding that "no mayor of New York has ever done anything so drastic."

But the moralists were not satisfied; they wanted Sunday drinking stopped. Dr. Parkhurst denied that the new regulations would cure the police of grafting. If a policeman could be bribed to let a saloon stay open, he argued scornfully, he could be bribed not to report a violation.

Gaynor defended his action against criticism with good spirit. A center of grumbling was the Clerical Conference of New York, an organization of Protestant clergymen, and at their invitation he spoke before three hundred of the members, and brought the issue home in a way that some of those present did not like. His opening was coolly candid:

"It was not easy for me to get away, and it would not be worth-while for me to come here and deliver a sermon. You all do that every Sunday—with what results you know."

Though here and there laughter greeted this, the gathering generally preserved stern silence.

"The difficulty is to be understood," Gaynor went on. "It is not always easy to get people to understand what is intended. Everything has to be done little by little; we have to feed some people with a spoon and many of them with a teaspoon."

Explaining the reasoning behind his order, he conceded that drinking was going on in the back rooms, and doubtless would continue to go on. There were nine thousand saloons and eighteen hundred hotels serving liquor in New York, and to station a policeman in front of each of these would require the entire force, leaving the city otherwise unprotected. And there was the human and social side to the problem. The workingman drinking in the back room of a saloon was only doing what the rich man did in his private club every Sunday without stirring up the least criticism.

"Why, these clubs up on Fifth Avenue, or Eighth Avenue where I live in Brooklyn, why, dear me, they sit in their common rooms and drink all day on Sunday, and I suppose that those people think they have as much right to do that as others; and they are absolutely right; they have as much right."

His listeners were shocked when he told of getting a drink himself at the side door of a London pub without difficulty, although the front door was locked tight. Of course, he said, there were some people who wanted drinking done away with completely; but that

THE NEW ROUNDSMAN

would require more than a law. Aiming a potshot at Dr. Parkhurst and his ilk he observed:

"There are a few clergymen who make more noise about reform than the rest of us put together, and do less of it than any other body of men that I know of. We haven't reached the millenium yet, and we are a good way from it. The 'inner room' business is hard to get at. We are doing the best we can with the Ten Commandments, and we haven't got them all observed yet."

Making clear that his main objective had been to break up the system of police graft that corrupted even the men who wanted to stay honest, he pleaded for charity in dealing with those who were tempted, adding:

"We are all just as God made us, and some of us are a good deal worse."

To make sure that he would not be misquoted, he had brought along a stenographer to take down his words, as was his custom.

The conference voted congratulations on "the executive efficiency which His Honor has already so signally displayed," although there was a noticeable reserve on the part of a few. Yet despite all criticism, there was no doubt that the mayor's reform was bearing fruit. Sunday selling of liquor fell to an irreducible minimum, and within a few weeks Gaynor was offering to bet anybody ten dollars that he could not find a barroom open and doing business anywhere in the City of New York on Sunday. The offer, renewed many times, was never taken up. And topers seeking a brass rail for a footrest and a bar to lean on, of a Sunday, mourned in a dirge published in the *Herald:*

> "Today the seeker for the solace that is prized
> Shall find above each fountain head the sad word
> 'GAYNORIZED.' "

In May the mayor reviewed the annual police parade from a stand in Madison Square, and the morale of the men seemed noticeably improved. Shoes were shined and buttons sparkled as five thousand bluecoats stepped smartly past, and there was no tobacco-

THE THIRD DEGREE

Feb. 15, 1910

chewing in the ranks. Gaynor made the men a speech, praised their alertness, and presented honor medals to five patrolmen cited for acts of heroism. The "system" seemed to be in for a withering away.

VENDETTA

———◦◯◦———

> *"Then by all that's good," said Don Quixote*
> *(now stirred to wrath), "Don son of a bitch,*
> *Don Ginesillo de Paropillo, or whatever*
> *your name is, you will have to go yourself*
> *alone, with your tail between your legs."*
>
> —DON QUIXOTE

THE FIRM GRASP with which Mayor Gaynor was conducting the city's government drew commendation from every quarter except one. Hearst was the holdout. In one way or another, the publisher of the *American* and *Journal* was still attempting to demonstrate that Gaynor's election had been the result of a corrupt bargain with Tammany Hall. But as the weeks passed and no convincing evidence could be found, and as Gaynor daily rose higher in public esteem, Hearst, ever the opportunist, bethought himself of the political axiom, "If you can't lick 'em, join 'em"; and before taking off on a trip to Mexico he authorized Colonel Bacon, Gaynor's one-time Brooklyn ally, to sound out the mayor on the possibility of a reconciliation, or at least a truce until after the coming state election. The Democrats would be facing a united opposition in the autumn vote for governor, and Hearst proposed that all "progressive Democrats" get together to work for the party's victory.

Gaynor was half receptive to the proposal, though still resentful of the campaign tactics employed by Hearst and his "hireling," Brisbane. Then Hearst made a false step.

During the McClellan administration, Daniel F. Cohalan, close friend and legal adviser of Boss Murphy, had done some work on franchise tax cases for the city, and had submitted a bill for $55,000 as his fee. The claim had been whittled down in the comptroller's office to $48,000, and at that figure it had been approved by the auditor on December 15, 1909. On December 31, the last day of McClellan's tenure, a warrant (i.e., a draft on the city treasury) for the $48,000 reached the mayor's office for final countersignature. Normally this was a formality taken care of by a clerk in the mayor's office; sometimes as many as a thousand such warrants were presented in one day.

For a reason never satisfactorily explained (though later it would be suspected to have been political spite or mischievousness, such was McClellan's rancor against Tammany), the mayor returned the warrant to the comptroller's office unsigned.

After Gaynor came in, the warrant, which already had become a legally binding obligation of the city, was sent through again, was signed by the clerk in charge, and was paid by the new city chamberlain, Hyde. This was a purely administrative action; according to legal advice, the mayor possessed no authority to refuse to approve a warrant that had been audited and accepted by the comptroller's office.

Hearst got wind of the payment to Cohalan and obtained a photograph of the warrant. On April 15 the *American* published, under lurid headlines, a facsimile of the warrant and a detailed account of its history, offering this as evidence of a secret "payoff" to Tammany by Mayor Gaynor.

The mayor did not see the article until a week later, when it was called to his attention. Instantly the chance of any reconciliation with Hearst vanished, once and for all, and a week later Gaynor struck back. He could not have done so with greater éclat. The forum he selected was the convention dinner of the American Newspaper Publishers Association and the Associated Press, in the Waldorf-Astoria Hotel. Present were more than seven hundred owners or representatives of every newspaper of importance in the United States. The mayor, the most newsworthy person in New York, had been invited to be principal speaker. (A secondary speaker was Woodrow Wilson, president of Princeton University.) His text was, "The Press in Its Relation to Public Officials," and he had been urged to speak freely.

The fact that he arrived carrying a manuscript seemed unusual, because of his habit of speaking extempore, and throughout the dinner he was observed to be preoccupied and reserved. The scene was brilliant: the cream of the newspaper world seated at small tables distributed through the grand ballroom, while in the surrounding boxes were women guests. At the speakers' table Herman Ridder presided, as president of the publishers association, with Adolph S. Ochs, of the *New York Times*, and Frank B. Noyes and Melville E. Stone of the Associated Press. George Ade, the humorist, was among the celebrities on hand, but Hearst was absent. However, there were representatives of his newspapers present.

In introducing Mayor Gaynor, Ridder referred to him as "probably the next President of the United States," and the applause was hearty. Gaynor sat impassive. When he arose to speak his face was set and stern. He glanced at his manuscript and then began in a quiet, unemotional, precise tone. His voice did not fill the great room, and those seated at a distance caught only snatches of his words; but those close at hand quickly realized that something more than the perfunctory pleasantries expected on such occasions was coming.

"You have given me the subject, 'The Press in Its Relation to Public Officials,' and told me to speak plainly and freely; that that is what you want; that your object in associating together is to improve the press," the mayor led off.

"Those having power should exercise it justly, kindly, and moderately. That makes their acts all the more effective. I measure my words in saying your power for good is immense; your power for evil is not as great as some may think. That is especially so when any of you try to do evil by falsehood or mere scandal. . . .

"The public official who tries his best to do right, and who knows how to do right (for both of these essential things do not always exist in the same public official), can not be hurt by you. Some may abuse him, even lie and forge about him, but they are powerless to hurt him. You can neither make nor unmake an honest and competent official."

This was certainly not flattery of his hosts, and the mayor allowed his words to sink in. Then he went on unemotionally:

"The press as a whole is just to public officials. When the election is over, its wholesome wish is to see that the one who is elected gives good government and to help him to do so. This is true of all honest and unselfish publishers and editors. But if a publisher or editor be himself a perennial officeseeker, he may desire to assassinate everyone whom he thinks in his way, and then, alas, what a disgrace he brings upon journalism. It is painful to mention such exceptions and to speak of their acts, but we should not shrink from doing it in a kindly spirit and for the sake of good."

In just that "kindly spirit" the mayor then got down to brass tacks, while tense silence gripped the room.

"You expect me to be plain and not abate a jot or a tittle. A newspaper proprietor or editor who is simply bent on cutting throats is an awful spectacle. In no nook or corner of his head or heart is there the slightest sense of truth or justice. We may pity him, but can not in the interest of public morality and decency remain silent about him.

"Let me illustrate by mentioning one thing out of many. As late as the 15th of this month W. R. Hearst printed in his principal newspaper here the facsimile of a draft on the treasury of this city for $48,000, with headlines and an article attributing such draft and the expenditure to the present mayor. The headlines and the article assert that I fixed the award and amount, and paid it, and the draft on the treasury is printed to prove it. But when you look at the draft as given in the article (but how few people scrutinized it that closely) you perceive that the date of it is left blank. I have brought it here as printed in this newspaper to show it to you, and here it is."

He held up the page from the *American* showing the facsimile. Then beside the facsimile he held up the original warrant, saying:

"When you look at the original draft, which I have also brought here for you to see, you see the date of it at the top in large letters and figures is 'December 31, 1909,' which is before the present city administration came in. When you examine the said original further you see that it also bears plainly the date when the audited voucher, which established the claim as a legal liability of the city, was recorded in the city comptroller's office, namely, December 29, 1909.

"In plain words, two state prison felonies, namely, forgery and falsification of a public document, were committed in the eagerness of this publisher and editor to wrong the mayor of the city of New York.

"A day or two afterward," Gaynor continued while his listeners held their breath, "when he heard rumors that the members of the grand jury were taking notice of the matter, he published as an excuse that the dates were so faint in the original draft that the photograph did not reproduce them. Now just look at this original draft again. The date at the top as you see is in larger and more pronounced letters and figures than any other part of the draft. I had the draft photographed as a test that the date would take like all the rest, and here is the photograph." He held it up. "You see it shows the dates as plainly, to say the least, as any other part of the draft.

"But if it were true that Mr. Hearst's photographic apparatus would not reproduce the dates, why should he print the draft without the dates? Why did he not put them in, in some way? The truth is, I am assured, that the dates were actually cut out of the plate with a routing machine."

The audience sat in stunned fascination; there was simply no answering the evidence he was presenting. Gaynor continued:

"Now, I do not call your attention to this low crime because it annoyed or embittered me in any way. A public official has to be patient. The newspapers of this man had done as bad or worse to me and others, but it was borne in silence, except that I spoke of the criminal aspect of such things before the bench and bar at the dinner they gave me in December last, because I thought it due that some-one should do so for the sake of society and of the decent and honest newspapers.

"I need not say to you that the indebtedness for which this draft was drawn was incurred several years before the present members of the city government were elected, and that it was audited and made a fixed and legal obligation of the city before we took office, instead of any of us 'fixing the award,' as the article says.

"Probably I never would have seen the publication of this draft had not an official brought it to me last Friday and pointed out the crime to me. I mention the matter to you because right here is where it should be mentioned. And let me add that it concerns you, the publishers and editors of the decent newspapers, far more than it concerns me. If you can stand such things in your great profession the rest of us can stand it, until the hour arrives when we shall make up our minds to utterly destroy it, and take effective measures to that end.

"It is high time that these forgers and libelers were in state's prison, and the time is not far distant when some of them will be there. And just think of a man who is capable of doing things like this being possessed of the notion that he is fit to hold any public office from mayor to President of the United States! Morally speaking, his mind must be a howling wilderness. Never will the voters anywhere put such a man in office.

"I might say," he concluded, "that some of us think that journalism has gone astray in recent years in some fundamental respects. ... Of some looseness and exaggeration that has grown up in recent years, following a pernicious example, no one needs to speak. ... I feel certain that a return to a lean statement of facts in the news columns, without adjectives or statements of conclusions, would be gratifying to all intelligent readers."

For a long moment after Gaynor sat down, unsmiling, the stillness held. Then applause broke out, so thunderous it shook the hall. Amid this, Thomas T. Williams, business manager of Hearst's New York papers, pushed his way to the speakers' table, his face livid, shouting:

"Mr. Hearst is not here, but I am a member of this association and I claim the right to say a few words!"

From all sides came cries of "Throw him out!" "Let him put it in his newspaper!" Other diners left their seats and converged around the speakers' table, while women in the boxes stared in amazement at the shoving, milling, fist-brandishing throng. Somebody yelled, "Three cheers for our honest mayor!" Williams, leaning across the table and shaking his fist in Gaynor's face, bellowed: "You're a brave man, aren't you! Vilifying a man who is not here! Are you afraid?"

Gaynor sat as cold as ice, calmly looking Williams in the eye, unmoved by the uproar. Ochs stood up on his chair and tried to gain attention for Williams, but was howled down.

After twenty minutes of din and confusion, the resourceful maître d'hôtel, Oscar, summoned house detectives and Williams was induced to leave. Calm being restored, after a fashion, the other speakers (Woodrow Wilson balanced by George Ade) were given a somewhat distracted hearing.

This broadside, fired with devastating aim before the assembled press of the nation, threw Hearst off balance. He was sensitive to the opinion of his fellow publishers, and knew that his reputation was unsavory among many members of his craft. To be disliked privately a man of Hearst's limitless complacency could bear; but to be held up to contempt before the very men whose approval he craved, even though he would do little to earn it, was galling. This assault Hearst would never either forgive or forget. And that suited Gaynor: he would never forget or forgive William Randolph Hearst.

GAYNOR STANDS BY HYDE

I am not surprised that you feel hurt at the way you have been treated by some newspapers. But let us not be affected by that. I know of no way to prevent it, and if I did I do not know that I would take the trouble to prevent it. I rely on the good sense of intelligent people.— From a letter written by the Mayor to his Chamberlain.

March 7, 1911

An instant rejoinder was published in the *American,* and the intensity of Hearst's fury was betrayed by the absence of that air of mock innocence which he was wont to assume when he was called to account. The involved wording of the reply also betrayed Hearst's confusion, for ordinarily he wrote clearly and crisply, being in this respect a worthy antagonist of the crisp, clear mayor. Denouncing Gaynor's statements as "falsehoods," Hearst said the mayor had merely "indulged in two thousand words of his usual blackguardly language. And in two thousand words of his usual evasion. And with all these two thousand words he has not answered the question why his administration allowed the money to be paid. . . . Why did he not prevent Cohalan from receiving the money? Don't waste time in evasion or mendacity, but tell exactly why he got it and why you gave it to him."

The next day Hearst let loose a second installment of invective. This began:

"To your blatherskite abuse I am indifferent, for in all such matters I consider the source and the natural irritation that a public official feels in being exposed."

He tore into Gaynor for harping on the failure of the date on

"I TALK TOO D——D MUCH"

May 8, 1910

the warrant to appear in the facsimile, although it had been carried in the fine type of the accompanying article.

"What a petty quibble for an important man—or rather, what a quibble for a petty man who holds an important position! . . . The January fourth signature was affixed by the assistant chamberlain in the office of Chamberlain Hyde, Mr. Gaynor's law partner . . . popularly known as 'Gaynor's Thick Hyde.' . . . The two constitute the Dr. Jekyll and Mr. Hyde of law and politics. . . . I know perfectly well what is going to happen to you, Mr. Gaynor. The people are going eventually to find you out and repudiate you and tan both you and your thick Hyde. And even those newspapers that are now truckling and lickspittling to you in the hope of securing the city advertising will in the end sacrifice these lucrative contracts for the priceless privilege of telling the truth about you."

Presumably among the newspapers "truckling and lickspittling" was the dignified, conscientious *Evening Post*, which welcomed Gaynor's speech as "a great public service."

Losing all self-control, Hearst entered libel suits against the *New York Times, Brooklyn Eagle, Louisville Courier*, Associated Press, and papers in Boston and San Francisco which had carried the mayor's words. Since the Hearst press, too, had carried the speech, these actions evoked more derision than alarm. Commented the *Eagle:*

"When Mr. Hearst can bring and sustain a libel suit against himself, the *Eagle* will be in danger. Until then we can not help being amused."

Temporarily Gaynor withheld further fire. His only reply to Hearst's infuriated blasts was a succinct "Let him stew in his own juice." Then the mayor left the city for St. James, while Hearst summoned his political hatchetman, who had managed some of the publisher's futile bids for political power, and giving him a staff ordered him to maintain a drumfire of disparagement, ridicule, and belittling against the mayor every day of the week, every week in the year.

CREST OF THE WAVE

*Woe unto you, when all men speak well of you;
for so did their fathers to the false prophets.*
                                    —ST. LUKE *6:26*

THAT SPRING OF 1910 passed and summer came with no letdown
in Mayor Gaynor's easy mastery of the municipal machinery. At
sixty-two he had flowered; all his previous life now appeared to have
been a schooling for this culmination, and the possibilities for the
future seemed boundless. On the national political scene Gaynor was
the rising star. In his own party, William Jennings Bryan had gone
down to defeat three times as the Presidential candidate, and there
was no other Democrat besides Gaynor who commanded nationwide
attention. He was that rare phenomenon—a New Yorker whom the
rest of the country could cotton to and understand.

In Texas was a man who had nominated himself to be the kingmaker of the Democratic Party, Colonel E. M. House. Looking over
the field, he decided that the party's brightest hope lay in New
York's City Hall, and that William J. Gaynor, with House's help,
might become the Democrats' winning candidate for President in
1912. To check on his impression, House set out for New York,
where, through James Creelman, a publicist close to Gaynor, a private dinner for the three men was arranged at the Lotus Club.
Gaynor was a brilliant conversationalist when he chose to be, and
at the dinner he exceeded the Texan's expectations. As House said
later, rarely had he encountered Gaynor's equal for "depth of learning in political and governmental problems." And also in charm.
Then and there, across the dinner table, Colonel House assured

Mayor Gaynor that if he would run for governor of New York state that fall of 1910, and be elected, he would be what racetrack people term (though the slightly pompous, humorless Colonel House did not) a "shoo-in" for the Presidential nomination two years later.

But Gaynor balked at the prospect of relinquishing the mayoralty, arguing that the mayor of New York held a position of greater power, complexity, and responsibility than the governor of any state. House replied with equal insistence that there was not a single instance of a man passing directly from mayor of a city to President of the United States. Still impressed, but doubtful of Gaynor's tractability, the would-be kingmaker departed for Texas.

House was only one of many politicians whose eyes were turned toward New York's City Hall. The headlines day by day told their interest. "Mayor Too Busy to Go West," the New York papers announced on March 8 in reporting Gaynor's breezy response to an invitation extended by a delegation of Democrats from Springfield, Missouri, to address their Jefferson Day dinner there. The mayor had accepted tentatively, he told his visitors, because he had understood they meant Springfield, Ohio.

"As I have a brother living there I thought I might run out and see him at the same time," he explained with offhand affability. "But when I found it was Springfield, Missouri, that was another matter. So you see I love my brother more than I love national politics. I would like to go to Missouri, but it would take more time away from my work than I have any right to give."

On March 14 the *Herald* headlined a report: "Democrats of Many States Turning to Gaynor." The roundup started, however, that "to inquiries coming from many parts of the country as to his accepting the Democratic nomination for President in 1912, the mayor replies 'Humph!' "

At the dinner of the Peace League on March 26 Mayor Gaynor shared honors with President Taft, and laughed heartily when Taft uttered his celebrated witticism that "God takes care of children, drunkards, and the United States."

"Texan Sees Gaynor 1912 Candidate," read a headline on April 7. United States Senator Joseph W. Bailey was quoted as saying, during a stopover in New York:

"If the Democrats of New York state nominate and elect Mayor Gaynor governor to succeed Hughes, he will at once become the logical candidate for President in 1912."

On April 19 Bryan, leader of the Democrats, returned from a

South American tour, and the first call he made was on Mayor Gaynor.

In London, Seth Low, Republican leader and former mayor of New York City, was bombarded with questions about Gaynor, and told reporters:

"I must admit that Judge Gaynor is making a very good mayor. He appears to be popular with both parties."

Invitations to speak in cities as far west as Denver rained into the mayor's office. He declined them all on the ground of his pressing duties at home.

Upon ex-President Roosevelt's return from Europe, Gaynor led the civic welcome. Landing at the Battery, Roosevelt was greeted by the mayor in a short allocution notable for including a reminder to the ebullient Teddy that "this is a government of laws, and not of men." Then the two rode up Fifth Avenue together to the cheers of immense crowds.

Still the busy mayor found time for the sort of activities that endeared him to plain folks. As the guest of the pupils of De Witt Clinton high school he inspected their vegetable gardens at the foot of West Forty-second Street. Each student had a garden plot eight feet by two, and Gaynor complimented them on their crops. Under a shelter erected against the sun, he was served a luncheon of vegetables grown by the boys and cooked by the girls. Noticing one boy so small he had difficulty in managing his hoe, the mayor asked his name. "Raphael Angelo Hogan," he was told.

"My! You have a heavy load to carry!" was Gaynor's amused exclamation.

As the guest of the Old Guard at its banquet at Delmonico's, Gaynor heard his administration praised as "the best New York has ever known," and in his speech he stood up sturdily against the detractors of the city, such as the sensational Hearst press.

In addressing a committee formed to organize an exposition in 1913 to commemorate the three-hundredth anniversary of the settlement of Manhattan, the mayor called the *Journal* and *American* "libelers of New York" and said:

"These two newspapers seem bent on doing everything they can do and saying everything they can say to degrade the city. Every vice, every low thing, every mean thing, they attribute to us. . . . The meanest of vices and of crimes, of everything evil, is saddled on New York, and that reputation for the city is spread over the country and the earth in an attempt to give us the status of the meanest city in the world. But New York is not the city of its libelers. It is the most moral and most wholesome, the most decent of any of the great cities of the world."

The mayor encouraged every activity looking to the betterment of the city, whether organized on an impressive scale or not. He adjourned a Board of Estimate hearing on the city's budget in order to receive a delegation of seventy-five Brooklyn boys who had come to report on their work as helpers of the street cleaning department. Looking over the group, Gaynor spotted a very small boy wearing a very large badge, Will Wertheimer by name, and told him:

"You won't be twenty-one for a long time, Willie, but remember, if I am mayor then I will make you street cleaning commissioner. Be sure to remember that. If I am here when you are twenty-one years old, come here and remind me of it."

The mayor helped the office boys of Wall Street by securing for them a ball ground at Battery Park, where they could play catch during their lunch hour. Businessmen had complained that the boys were trampling the grass of Bowling Green.

A delegation of automobile owners coming to protest the designation of a stretch of Ocean Parkway as a speedway for trotting horses was advised by the mayor to "be generous. You seem to think automobiles own the earth, but you can't have everything."

On the twelfth anniversary of the influential People's Institute at Cooper Union, the distinguished founder, Professor Charles Sprague Smith, praised Gaynor as "the cleanest and most popular mayor in the city's history." He cited as particularly commendable the mayor's recent signing of a bill creating a Board of Inebriates, the first official attempt in the city to treat alcoholics intelligently, instead of "mixing them up in the poorhouses and hospitals with other people," as the mayor put it. Gaynor's personal belief was that excessive drinking was on the decline. As one who remembered a previous generation of hard drinkers he remarked that "there used to be five topers for one that you see now."

The mayor attended the opening of bids for a $50,000,000 city bond issue, the first under his administration, and was delighted when it was oversubscribed nearly four times. He had written many letters to stimulate interest among small bidders especially, maintaining that there was no safer investment in the world than the bonds of the city of New York. (His own surplus capital, however, he kept invested in guaranteed mortgages; he was always in the market for this sort of security.)

How the city's Jewish people felt about Mayor Gaynor was manifested at a celebration of the fiftieth anniversary of the New York Hebrew Orphan Association, held in the Hippodrome Theater. Gaynor, seated in a box with Louis Stern, president of the association, watched with intense interest seven hundred orphans perform an intricate drill on the stage and then sing "America." He made no attempt to conceal his pleasure at the spectacle, and when he himself stepped on the stage he was given a standing ovation that continued for minute after minute, even after, by a slight wave of the hand, he had indicated his embarrassment. He then told the crowd:

"This extraordinary demonstration sent through my mind . . . the work of fifty years of unceasing toil by you men and women that such a performance might be. . . . We hear a great deal from time to time about Christian charity. According to my way of thinking, the word 'charity' should have no prefix. . . . In the time of my predecessor, Peter Stuyvesant, the Jew was looked upon with suspicion, if not with actual disfavor. . . . I thank God that in New York today there are few if any bigots. . . . Today, so long as a man is a man, decent in his business and decent in his home life and his duties as a citizen, nobody cares very much what his name, religion, or place of nativity may be."

A few weeks later the mayor welcomed the convention of the Independent Order of B'rith Abraham to the city, and took occasion to compliment the Jews in America upon not having "gone together clannishly in any one political party, as some races have done, but have spread out according to their individual notions and have become affiliated with all parties." He called over an honor roll of Jews to whom the whole world was indebted, starting with Jesus ("born a Jew, bred a Jew, and died a Jew") and taking in Heine, Mendelssohn, Spinoza, Montefiore, de Hirsch, Ricardo, Disraeli, and many more.

Gaynor took an interest in the theater and deplored the cheapening of the stage which he believed he saw. In a letter to Mayor Fitzgerald of Boston he was sharply critical of the "indecent plays" on Broadway, and received a prompt retort from a friend of years' standing, Marie Dressler. At once the headline bloomed: "Ah, Ha! Mayor Writes to an Actress," and the typewritten reply Gaynor sent to Marie was reproduced in facsimile:

"Dear Miss Dressler: I thank you very much for your letter. It makes me feel just like an old dolt. You convince me that I am an old fogy. I must go up and hear your play, 'Tillie's Nightmare,' as you call it, and get cured. I am certain that you never gave anybody the nightmare. I am willing to admit that when I wrote the letter to the mayor of Boston about the unwholesome plays of today I left you out mentally. You have amused many people, including myself, and added to their joys, and I am willing to admit it. . . . All the same, there are a whole lot of plays on the stage that I would like to sweep off with a broom." *

That same feeling that the stage had fallen upon evil days the mayor confided to a Connecticut correspondent:

"When I first came to New York I used to go to hear the Shakespearean plays, and once I heard Booth, Davenport, and Bangs all together in 'Julius Caesar.' Since then the stage here has been constantly going down, until finally it has become almost vile. I quit going to the theater about fifteen years ago. I can not sit out an ordinary play. I hope that there is about to be a revival and that the stage is to become what it once was. It depends on the public morals and tone."

But Gaynor refused absolutely to sponsor a general censorship of the stage. Let every playgoer be his own censor, he urged, and if a sufficient number of people should complain about any given production, he would look into the case and if the facts warranted would revoke the theater's license; but everything must be done within the law. Mere talk about doing things annoyed him, and at a dinner honoring Glenn H. Curtiss for his sensational airplane flight from Albany to New York, Gaynor said frankly:

"We are present at a great fact. I suppose we are here to talk about it, but talk in this world amounts to very little without the fact, and here is the fact."

Comparing rural life and city life, he asked:

"How does it happen that a young man away up in Hammondsport in the state of New York did this great thing? No man in the four million down here did it. The reason is that these people up there have time to think. They not only have time to think, but they are willing to think. . . . But down here our young men, with all the advantages of education we give them . . . failed to do this thing for the simple reason that they scarcely have time to think."

* In *Tillie's Nightmare,* her greatest stage hit, Marie Dressler, in the role of a boardinghouse drudge, sang the classic ballad, "Heaven Will Protect the Working Girl."

In the midst of incidental activities (like posing for a photograph on the City Hall steps with twenty-five girls from Kentucky and Tennessee and telling them he would like to take them on a hay ride), the mayor struck hard, again and again, at the exploitation of the poor and ignorant, especially recent immigrants. As strangers in a strange land these people were often the prey of extortionists. A racket that had long scandalized those in the know was the regular traffic carried on in pushcart licenses. In a minutely documented release Gaynor confronted an alderman with proofs of his having obtained peddlers' licenses fraudulently, which he sold or rented out for sums ranging from $6 to $19. The alderman contended that he was the victim of certain malicious pushcart men who were out to ruin him, but the evidence was irrefutable.

Another racket that Gaynor exposed was the systematic preying upon aliens seeking naturalization papers. When he received complaints that applicants were kept waiting in line for days, unless they paid money to be moved to the head of the line, he sent detectives who collected evidence. This Gaynor turned over to United States Attorney General Wickersham for prosecution, observing:

"When men can not get naturalized without having to pay corruption money for it they can't be expected to feel otherwise than that the government is corrupt throughout."

Holders of licenses for sidewalk newspaper and fruit stands complained to the mayor that they were held up by politicians whenever they tried to take out or renew licenses. The law empowered the mayor to issue such licenses, but in each case the written assent of the alderman of the district had to be obtained. Gaynor took affidavits swearing to the extortion, and then addressed a special message to "The Honorable, the Board of Aldermen of the City of New York," inviting them to put a stop to the racket being worked by some of their own members. The message, shot through with subtle irony, quoted the wording of the city ordinances regulating the issuing of licenses, and then said:

"Shortly after I became mayor a woman who had a licensed newsstand came to me and complained and made oath that she could not get the license renewed except by paying $250 to the political district captain of the district in which the stand was. I investigated the matter and found her statement to be true. As I refused to grant the license to another person, who was brought forward for it, she is in possession of the stand yet and is likely to remain there. Shortly after many complaints began to come to me of the same extortion by district political leaders, both Democratic and Republican. Later on began to come complaints that the said district leaders would not permit the applicant to get a license until he first joined the political club of the district, Republican or Democrat, according to which party the alderman of the district belonged. I investigated this matter and found it to be apparently true. . . . I want to be understood as not even intimating that the members of your honorable body are implicated in this general extortion. It would seem that some of you are being imposed upon. The fact remains, however, that . . . the members of your board, and the mayor's Bureau of Licenses, which really means the mayor himself, are being 'delivered,' as the phrase is, in the granting of these licenses for sums ranging from $5 to $500 in each case. . . . It is too infamous a thing to be permitted to continue, and I ask the privilege of uniting with the honorable members of your board in putting an end to it."

SHOWING MISSOURI

March 9, 1910

A GREAT AMERICAN SCHOOLMASTER
July 11, 1910

Upon the reading of this invitation to reform themselves, the aldermen were thrown into uproar. Twenty demanded to be heard at once, and after much incoherency a motion was adopted stigmatizing the mayor's allegations as "too ridiculous to investigate."

To reassure the newsstand people, Gaynor sent an open letter to the president of the Newsdealers Protective and Benevolent Association promising that "if you will all cease to pay outsiders in order to get your licenses, I will, as mayor, protect you all and see that you get your licenses without paying anything but the license fees."

The city's bootblacks, caught in the same squeeze, thereupon carried their complaints and evidence to City Hall and received the same unequivocal public promise that they would be protected if they would simply cease to pay the blackmail.

Shortly after this Gaynor sent to the acting district attorney the following eloquent memorandum:

"I beg to enclose to you three affidavits of money being paid to aldermen and others to get licenses. It seems to me that it will be most wholesome to indict and convict some of these people."

Meanwhile the mayor kept in touch with his family, writing to his brother Tom about Civil War matters, and advising him, when he was thinking of running for sheriff, not to spend a dollar to get elected; and gently taking sister Mary at Utica to task for her carelessness. ("My dear Mary: I must again request that you mark your letters to me 'Personal' on the outside. Affectionately . . .")

The safe and sane Fourth of July celebration organized by a citizens committee, at Gaynor's prompting, proved successful, although some members of the National Guard grumbled about having to give up their holiday and march in the heat. Gaynor wrote to one such grumbler in disgust:

"I hope that all people of your mind will be excused from being in the Independence Day celebration. I should hate to see you there. I shall be glad to join publicly in a request that you and all like you be prevented from joining in the celebration."

But to make sure that the grumbling did not take effect, he telegraphed to Governor Hughes not to yield to the protests, reminding the governor also:

"I served term on National Guard. Stands nearly up and everything nearly complete. Trust you will not interfere."

The Guard paraded.

A really serious crisis developed on that Fourth of July. On that day the widely heralded Jim Jeffries-Jack Johnson heavyweight championship fight took place in Reno, Nevada, and an intensively organized campaign was pressed among clergymen and other public moralists to prevent the showing of the motion pictures of the fight in New York. Agitation against the bout had been going on for two months, whipped up by the Rev. John Wesley Hill, of the Methodist Metropolitan Temple. The mayor had been deluged with demands that he forbid the screening of the films in the city's theaters, despite the fact that he saw no legal way in which the films could be banned, and that, as his friend Dr. Morrison assured him, nine-tenths of the people of New York wanted to see them.

Gaynor's position was plain. He had no personal interest in the matter, and had never seen a prize fight; but he could find no provision in the law that gave him the right to interfere. Prize-fight pictures had been exhibited in the city before without raising serious objection. His patience, therefore, was strained to the breaking point —and sometimes beyond—by the demands that he prohibit the films. Hearst contributed to the popular clamor by throwing the weight of his editorials against the films, terming the refusal of the mayor to act "the shame of New York." This although Hearst's own papers printed every photograph of the match they could lay hands on.

Again and again, in reply to the remonstrances, Gaynor repeated that he had no power to act. He told the Rev. C. R. Miller, who had denounced the films as the head of the Reform League of New York State:

"If it lay within my power to say whether the pictures should be exhibited or not it would not take me long to decide it. . . . But will you be so good as to remember that ours is a government of laws and not of men? Will you please get that well into your head? I am not able to do as I like as mayor. I must take the law just as it is, and you may be absolutely certain that I will not take the law into my own hands. You say that you are glad to see that the mayors of many cities have 'ordered' that those pictures should not be exhibited. Indeed? Who set them up as autocrats? If there be some valid law giving any mayor such power, then he can exercise it; otherwise, not."

A reader of the New York Herald urged that this letter be displayed in every American home. The Herald did not go that far, saying merely:

"If it becomes part of the furniture of the offices of those in high places it will be quite enough. In reminding his clerical correspondent that this is a government of laws and not of men, that persons holding high executive office are the servitors and not the masters of the people, Mr. Gaynor served a well-merited and clean-cut rebuke to those whose mad desire to have their way causes them to forget the law and their sworn obligations."

Gaynor refused to accept the word of overwrought clergymen that the fight pictures "outraged public decency." (Actually the films were very tame.) He detected a different motive behind the outcry, as he told a friendly cleric, the Rev. D. J. Hickey, of St. Francis Xavier Church in Brooklyn. Some people, he remarked, begrudged any amusement to people less well off than themselves. "They are willing to see any number of high-priced theaters with loose morals, but they hate to see a moving picture show, or any healthy show, to which people in general go."

In the same vein he told a businessman:

"The moving picture shows, apart from some pictures which might be omitted, are a great solace to poor people, and give them a great deal of enjoyment. Why people should be opposed to them I do not know. They are far better than some of our high-priced theaters uptown. I would very quickly stop [the fight films] if it were in my power, but I am very sure that an intelligent man like you would not advise me to do a thing for which I have no legal authority. Some day I might issue an order interfering with your business, once I began to do as I liked regardless of law. . . . Did you ever think of that?"

Hearst cartooned the mayor in the flashy garb of a Coney Island barker, drawing people in to see the slaughter. Gaynor retorted that Hearst was "an habitual liar" and a "mere scamp willing to invent and retail any lie."

At the height of the agitation, an evangelist, Alexander A. Lowlande, took to City Hall a protest against showing the fight films. He said the protest was on behalf of Christian Endeavor, an interdenominational organization of young people. Lowlande was kept waiting in the mayor's outer office three hours while others were interviewed, and when he finally faced the mayor, Gaynor was both tired and running out of patience at hearing the same irresponsible demand.

"How can I prohibit these pictures from being exhibited?" he asked. "Now, can you tell me any way by which I can prohibit them?"

Lowlande referred airily to several laws which he said would apply, and Gaynor snapped in disgust: "You are a fool and sent by fools." (Gaynor later denied that he had used those words, although he did use them on other occasions when goaded beyond endurance.) Lowlande hurried to the *American* with this rebuff, and the paper played it up sensationally as a fresh "disgrace to New York."

It was the season of the dog days, and in spite of the clamor Gaynor strove, with more or less success, to control his temper. How he managed it he imparted to an interviewer in words which even the reporter did not take literally:

"I forgive everybody for everything every night. 'Let not the sun go down upon thy wrath.' "

Feeling the need of a respite from harassment and of rest, the mayor laid plans to sail for a vacation in Europe. In seven months he had accomplished much, and his place in the affections of New Yorkers had been made secure by his quaint sayings and actions, as well as his sweeping reforms. Top-hatted and severe, he was reported stepping up to an astonished ditchdigger in City Hall Park and growling, "What's this? Chewing tobacco? Let's have some." Then striding to his office he could dictate a note of punctilious apology to Mrs. Joseph E. Choate, wife of New York's most eminent counselor at law, explaining how it had happened that she had inadvertently been seated, at the dinner for a visiting Chinese prince, at a table not in keeping with her social position or strict protocol.

In June St. John's University, at Annapolis, Maryland, conferred an honorary doctorate of laws on the learned Gaynor, and he made sure beforehand that his speech of acceptance would be distributed to the New York press and nationally by the Associated Press. At the same time the newspapers found material for columns of fascinating information about the mayor's activities as country squire, at St. James. Every morning he went for a walk of five to ten miles, escorted by his dogs. In the afternoons he might pitch hay, inspect crops, or lend a neighbor a hand in the fields.

In the city, the mayor was just as spontaneous and various. He entertained occasionally, though always at a hotel, never in his home, and he did not hesitate to correct the menus submitted by the hotels' master chefs. For a private dinner of twenty-five at the Knickerbocker, the mayor struck out the word "salad" and substituted "hearts of lettuce," and replaced the indefinite phrase "fish course" with the specific "oysters."

For all his Quixotic inconsistencies, his uncertain temper, and his impatience with the woolly-witted and stupid, the mayor's genuine accomplishments and the multiplicity of his good deeds in a brief space of time by August of 1910 had converted his worst critics (Hearst excepted) into friendly admirers. Even William Travers Jerome, who once had called Gaynor "a political charlatan" and "a most abhorrent product," by midsummer was won over. Interviewed at a resort in Massachusetts where he was vacationing, Jerome conceded that he had changed his opinion.

"I confess," he said, "that I have been most agreeably surprised in Mr. Gaynor. He has made a good mayor, in fact, one of the best the city ever had. He is a peculiar man, but he is a big man, and he is doing things."

This generous amendment by a former antagonist who was noted for the asperity of his tongue was made on August 8, 1910.

The next day Mayor Gaynor was shot.

A TIME FOR PHILOSOPHY

*Let death and exile, and all other things that
seem terrible, be daily before your eyes, but
death chiefly, and then you will never entertain an abject thought, and will never desire
anything beyond measure.*

—EPICTETUS

When Mayor Gaynor came up the gangplank of the North German Lloyd liner *Kaiser Wilhelm der Grosse* at Hoboken on August 9,
the ship was dressed with flags, and members of his official family were
waiting to bid him Godspeed. Rufus Gaynor was with his father; he
was going along as a companion. The two were immediately surrounded by the greeting party, among whom were Commissioners
Lederle, Edwards, and Thompson, with Corporation Counsel Watson, Secretary Adamson, and friends. Reporters were on hand, and
the mayor spoke a few words for them and posed with Rufus for the
news cameras. The President of Chile, Pedro Montt, and his wife
passed along the deck during this chatter and the mayor was introduced to them. Finally, as the newsmen left, Gaynor appealed to
Lederle quietly on behalf of a health department employee who had
been discharged for cause. Give the chap another chance, Gaynor
urged, not for his own sake but for that of his family. Lederle was
disinclined to be lenient, and Gaynor jokingly accused him of having
no heart. Reaching out, he touched the commissioner's left side, then
his right side, and nodded, "No heart at all. On which side is your
heart?"

At that moment an unkempt stranger darted out of the circle

of spectators, and shouting, "You have taken my bread and butter away from me!" thrust a pistol at the back of Gaynor's neck and fired.

It happened that William Warneke, an *Evening World* photographer, had arrived late and was close by. By reflex, he snapped his camera and obtained one of the most celebrated of all action photographs, showing the mayor an instant after he was shot.

Almost at the same instant, "Big Bill" Edwards hurled his three hundred pounds at the assailant in a football tackle that brought him crashing to the deck. The man kept firing wildly, and one bullet grazed Edwards' arm; but the gunman was quickly disarmed, handcuffed, and turned over to the Hoboken police.

The mayor, meanwhile, had been caught by bystanders. He was bleeding profusely and breathing with difficulty, but after a few moments he managed to signify that he wished to get away, and he was led to his stateroom. There the ship's doctor examined the wound, which was just below the right ear, and bandaged it pending the arrival of an ambulance. When it came Gaynor was carried off the ship on a stretcher and taken to St. Mary's Hospital nearby.

Word of the tragedy was flashed around the world. At first it was stated that the mayor of New York had been killed. Later information indicated that he might recover. Eminent physicians summoned from New York City made clinical tests, and their prognosis was favorable; the mayor's organs of speech, it was intimated, might be partially paralyzed, but he would survive.

The assassin, it was learned, was James J. Gallagher, a laborer formerly employed by the docks department. He had been dismissed several weeks previously for failure to report for work on time and insolence to his foremen. Since then he had been several times at City Hall, demanding to see some official or other, usually the mayor, and complaining that he had been deprived of his "bread and butter."

Herbert Bayard Swope, of the *World*, rushed to interview Gallagher in jail. A reporter for the *American* was already there. Swope asked Gallagher what newspaper he read, expecting he would say the *American* or *Journal*. Instead, he said the *Times*, at which both reporters burst into uncontrollable laughter. (Later a policeman said he did find a *Journal* editorial abusing Gaynor in Gallagher's pocket.)

During the next two weeks the public was kept informed of the mayor's fight to live by bulletins from St. Mary's. Messages of condolence and sympathy flowed into the hospital from around the world—thousands of them almost instantaneously. Gaynor was not permitted to see them. Adamson and volunteer helpers struggled with the torrent, conscientiously acknowledging every one, as they knew the mayor would have ordered. The General Committee of Tammany Hall—Theodore Roosevelt—the governors of B'rith Abraham—the White Rats of America, an actors' group—Mr. and Mrs. Jacob Schiff—the boys of the Alert Athletic Club in Brooklyn—Jacob Riis, from Denmark—Cornelius Vanderbilt, from France—the United Colored Democracy of Queens County—the Slavonian Benevolent Society—the United Citizens Peddlers Association of Greater New York—the United States Volunteer Life-Saving Corps—Bricklayers Union No. 37—the Pittsburgh Association of Credit Men—the Rivington Street Citizens Association—Champ Clark—the Harlem Peddlers Association—the trustees of Sailors Snug Harbor—the Sheriffs Association of Texas —Bishop Raphael and the clergy of the Syrian Orthodox churches —the Belmont Avenue Peddlers Association of Brooklyn—"an admirer from away down here in Greensboro, Alabama"—bankers, clubs, clergymen of every faith—from these and thousands more, messages of hope and encouragement poured into City Hall and St. Mary's.

Most of the messages came from strangers, though a few were poignantly personal. One, from St. Louis, was a telegram: "Thank God you are getting better," signed "Brother Justin," Gaynor's preceptor in the Christian Brothers.

Prayers for the mayor's recovery were offered in churches of every sect and denomination. Bishop Joseph H. Mooney of the Roman Catholic chancery, in calling for prayers, stressed that Gaynor's loss "at this time would be nothing less than a calamity." The Bowery Mission and men in the Tombs and prisons added their prayers. A round-robin message signed by all the justices of the New York Supreme Court conveyed their prayers that Gaynor might recover. Homely advice came from many a well-wisher, such as the one who wrote: "Put your own spit on the wound as often as you can and that will draw out the poison." The horror and grief felt by the mass of people everywhere was epitomized in a letter from a humble dweller in the Bronx, one Oscar Müller, who wrote four days after the shooting:

"When I left work at twelve noon last Tuesday to go for dinner, the first man I ran against was a news-man calling out 'Mayor

Gaynor shot.' I could hardly believe it, till I bought a paper. When I arrived home for dinner, I said to my wife there are extras out. 'What is it about?' she asked, and when I said Mayor Gaynor is shot, she allmost jumped up from her chair pale and terror in her face. I am sure that his Honor the Mayor will appreciate the good wishes for a speedy recovery from a humble worker like myself just as high as the good wishes from people high in life. It is stated in one of the newspapers that his Honor said he will save up all the letters pouring in on him, and read them some day when he feels blue. I doubt the Mayor after his recovery will ever find time enough to read all the letters sent him to the Hospital, but if he should, I wish he will run against my few lines also and hope that they will make him feel happy."

The press, meanwhile, was outdoing itself in eulogizing the stricken mayor. The *Sun*, which once had called Gaynor "an undesirable citizen," went on record: "Those who like us doubted the wisdom of his election bear hearty testimony to the wisdom of the people and to his fine qualities." Said the *Times*: "Mayor Gaynor is the last one who should have been made the victim of insensate anger, of blind and mad hatred, especially at the hands of a member of the class to which his would-be assassin belongs. His heart has been as pitiful as a woman's for the hardships that relative poverty brings and no one would more unwillingly increase them."

The *Times* then paid Gaynor the highest compliment of which it was capable professionally by thanking him for having lightened the editorial load, saying:

"His vigorous and original personality, the peculiar angle under which he sees life and its happening, the native wit and stored learning at his instant command, the delightful tangents from the usual orbits in which he indulges, his impatience with fools, and the strain of kindliness that shows in incalculable ways . . . made the chronicling of his daily life an exceedingly pleasant relief from the routine of newspaper work."

Across the nation the shock of indignation was the same. The editor of the Danville, Illinois, *Daily Press-Democrat* sent an editorial appreciation under the heading, "Gaynor Trotted Square"— just "to show you what we think of you out here." The *Toronto Globe* saw in the assassination attempt "an event of more than civic or even national importance. Judge Gaynor . . . has in a few months . . . drawn to himself the sympathetic attention of the whole civilized world." And the *Utica Press*, in Gaynor's home city, summed up that city's and the world's feeling perhaps most accurately of all when it commented on "the depth and extent of interest taken in his welfare since the shooting. . . . If he were the President of the United States the fact would have been self-explanatory; but it would not have been believed that so much interest all over the country would have been taken in the condition of any mayor, even of the metropolis. It would be difficult to exaggerate the amount of anxiety felt for that patient in St. Mary's Hospital.

"A Utican who was in New York on the day of the attempted assassination and for a day or two thereafter said that everybody spoke of it, that it was the chief theme of conversation, and that the regret felt was deep and sincere. Particularly noticeable was the fact that each man spoke of it as he would have had the mayor been his close personal friend or relative. Everywhere there seemed to be the sense of personal loss. . . . If he has time during his convalescence to read a tenth part of what the newspapers of this country have been saying, he will learn . . . that when a public official fearlessly and faithfully does his duty he reaches the hearts of the people."

Only the Hearst press remained stubbornly outside the circle. The *Journal* and *American* reported the shooting, but printed no word of regret or condolence—no editorial comment at all.

Mrs. Gaynor had hurried from St. James at word of the shooting, and she moved into St. Mary's Hospital to give constant care. Brother Tom came on from Ohio and took charge of the farm temporarily. The children called daily at the hospital, and the public was kept informed of the patient's progress by the medical bulletins. It was learned that his speech was much affected, and that in fact he could speak at all only with difficulty. Some of his first inquiries had been about affairs at Deepwells, and particularly about a dog belonging to Mel Smith, that had been hit by an automobile. When told that the dog was getting well, he whispered:

"Poor pup! His wound is behind the ear, too, where he can't lick it. I'm better off; I have attention."

Beyond saying that he did not know his assailant or his motive, the mayor refused to discuss the shooting. Nor would he prosecute Gallagher, who temporarily had been charged with assault upon Edwards.

On the sixth day the crisis was reached and passed successfully. The bullet had lodged in the vault of the larynx, and surgical advice was against an attempt to remove it, since it seemed to be sealing itself off rapidly. Ten days after entering the hospital Gaynor was able to sit up and read for two hours. The books he chose were Macaulay's *Essays* and two entitled *Physics and Politics* and *The Morals of Jesus*. He grumbled when the books were taken away, insisting that he was not tired.

Dr. John H. Finley, president of the College of the City of New York, sent to the hospital a large-type edition of the *Meditations* of Marcus Aurelius, with the suggestion to Mrs. Gaynor that it could be propped up at the foot of the mayor's bed, so he could read it without strain. Gaynor did reread the entire work, thoughtfully, and drew strength from its Stoicism.

On the eleventh day, the patient was allowed to take a few steps around the room, and to sit by the window for an hour reading Benjamin Franklin. And on August 28 Gaynor finally left St. Mary's for St. James. A dozen luxurious summer houses in the mountains and by the seashore had been offered for his use, but he insisted on going to Deepwells. A police launch took him from Hoboken to Long Island City, where he was to board the train. Saying he wanted to go ashore unassisted, he groped his way uncertainly down the gangplank from the launch and managed to reach the taxicab waiting to convey him to the railroad station. But as he attempted to get into the taxi his strength failed, he fell to his knees, and had to be helped. The train ride was made in silence, but when he saw a little crowd of villagers at the St. James station he smiled. His own automobile took him to the farm, and there again he insisted on walking from the car to the house without help. On the steps of the porch he stumbled and fell, but waved back those who sprang to assist, and with an effort succeeded in climbing the steps and seating himself in a rocking chair.

Two neighbors sat with him for a while, giving him news of the town, and to them, speaking in a faint voice, the mayor made the only direct comment on his reaction to Gallagher's attack, saying:

"I am content. My great hope is that the event will help to make me a better man and more patient and just."

At last consenting to be led to bed, he slept well, and in the morning ate a good breakfast.

HOW IT FEELS TO BE ASSASSINATED

———————————— o◯o ————————————

> *Finding that my wound was not immediately*
> *mortal, I had determined to make a fight*
> *for it. . . .*
>
> —GAYNOR

WILLIAM J. GAYNOR emerged from St. Mary's Hospital in some respects a different man from the one who had been carried into it, and the weeks of his convalescence would mark a watershed in his career. The alteration, not immediately noticeable, consisted in an aggravation and intensifying of certain flaws of character by the shock of his wound and his emotional turbulence. Always inclined toward introspection (Gaynor once said he would have liked best to be a librarian and scholar), the mayor had been forced to spend days in silent self-communion. In one part of his divided nature, in which the impulse to act strove against the cool restraints of contemplation, Gaynor had been brought closer to his ideal of philosophic detachment; in another part of his nature he had been stirred to accomplish what he could while there still was time, since no man could foretell the moment of his death. Impelled on the one hand more strongly toward practical action, on the other hand, by a spiritual revitalization he had been rendered less fit to endure the jolts, jars, and contradictions that are incident to the agony of life. His intransigence, his suspiciousness, his disdain of other strong-willed natures, his intolerance of opposition when embarked on a course that he believed to be necessary and just, his impatience with the dull, the obstructive, and the malicious—these were intensified by the impact of Gallagher's bullet upon his spirit as well as his

296

body. His physical wound and the psychic shock exacerbated each other. The loftier his contemplation, the less sure would be his grasp on contrary realities. His days would become a history of more intense aspiring and more fiercely resented falling short of his objectives. He told a friend:

"I often repeat to myself the words of the philosophical emperor, Marcus Aurelius: 'There is but one thing of real value, namely, to cultivate truth and justice in the midst of lying and unjust men.' "

But on the practical level, "lying and unjust men" could drive a naturally combative person to furious and often illogical measures.

During the pleasant autumn weather, the mayor was content to rest, to loaf in Monaghan's blacksmith shop swapping gossip, and to tramp the roads in sunshine and rain with half a dozen dogs for company. He was gratified when told how the pushcart peddlers of the East Side had staged a parade to City Hall, where they deposited resolutions of sympathy and encouragement, and how the bootblacks and newsstand dealers of New York were proclaiming that Mayor Gaynor had done more for them "than any other mayor even attempted."

Politics and the shooting were subjects he avoided, though he thought much about them. In a letter to his sister, Mary Gaynor, laboriously dictated after a week at Deepwells, he set down some of his thoughts, for the first and only time telling his sensations when he was shot, and of his feeling since. This "Epistle in Courage" was like a window opened on Gaynor's inner self. It was dated Sept. 3, 1910, from St. James, L.I., and read:

"My dear Sister: Your letter encouraged me very much. I was so glad to get it, for I was feeling depressed, although coming home from the hospital had braced me up for the time being. I felt shaky and doubtful of myself until Tuesday, the first day I walked out, but now my strength is returning fast. The barking neuralgia in all the side of my head and my ear has subsided. The wound healed without trouble. You remember how quickly the two bad cuts I got when a boy healed, one from an axe and the other from a scythe. The doctors looked at the scars in the hospital.

"I still find it difficult to talk, but my voice comes back a little every day. But I shall not inflict my aches and ills on you. I am sorry for the worry I have caused you all. You remember my dog 'Spot,' when we were children. He got hurt once and crawled under a pile of logs and lay there for more than a week before he came out. Well, when any trouble happens to me, I feel just like poor 'Spot'—I would like to crawl under the log pile and stay there.

"I have not read any newspaper since I was hurt, nor have I been told how the thing happened, except that Commissioner Thompson told me on the deck that I had been shot by a former employee of the Dock Department. I do not remember the name he gave. It is my intention never to read a line of what has been published in the newspapers about the matter or me since I was hurt. It might warp my mind about myself. What I am I am, with all my shortcomings, and I am content with that.

"My own knowledge of the occurrence is of course very limited and may be inaccurate. I think I shall tell it to you now, so that there may be some family record of it, and in a year or two I wish you to turn this letter over to Rufus to keep. I was taking him with me for company. As you know, he and I have traveled much together. He was on the other side of the ship and did not see me shot.

"I was standing on the deck talking with Commissioners Thompson, Lederle, Edwards, Corporation Counsel Watson, my secretary, Mr. Adamson, and several friends who had come aboard to see me off. Mr. Montt, President of Chile, and Mrs. Montt had just passed by, and I had spoken a few words with them. Mr. Adamson pointed out that the ship was dressed with flags for me, but I said I did not think it could be for me. My next consciousness was of a terrible roar in my head. It filled my head, which seemed as though it would burst open. It swelled to the highest pitch, and then fell, and then rose again, and so alternated until it subsided into a continuous buzz. It was sickening, but my stomach did not give way. I was meanwhile entirely sightless.

"I do not think I fell, for when I became conscious I was on my feet. I suppose they saved me from falling, and they were supporting me. My sight gradually returned, so that after a while I could see the deck and the outlines of the crowd around me. I became conscious that I was choking. Blood was coming from my mouth and nose and I tried all I could to swallow it so those around me would not see it. But I found I could not swallow and then knew my throat was hurt. It seemed as though it were dislocated. I struggled to breathe through my mouth, but could not, and thought I was dying of strangulation. I kept thinking all the time the best thing to do. I was not a bit afraid to die if that was God's will of me. I said to myself just as well now as a few years from now. No one who contemplates the immensity of Almighty God, and of His universe and His works, and realizes what an atom he is in it all, can fear to die in this flesh, yea, even though it be true that he is to be dissolved forever into the infinity of matter and mind from which he came.

"In some way I happened to close my mouth tight and found I could breathe perfectly through my nose. I then believed I could keep from smothering. But I kept choking and my mouth kept opening to cast out the blood. But much of it went down into my stomach. That night in the hospital I had five hard chills in succession, and got deathly sick and vomited up this blood all over the bed. The poor sister who was watching me called the doctors, but they said it was a good thing. I felt much better after that, but grew very weak. The trouble was to get nourishment as I could not swallow.

"But I shall not speak of the hospital but only of my recollection (or impressions) of things on the ship. They wanted me to lie down on the deck, but I said no, I would walk to my stateroom. I could now see faces, and I wanted to get away from the crowd. I could not bear to have them looking at me in the plight I was in, especially the crowd of newspapermen, and especially those with cameras. Two of them rushed up from the line where they all stood and put their cameras right in my face and snapped them. I finally put my hand up and I think I said 'don't.' I hope those pictures were not published. The other newspapermen acted decently as they always do.

"We were on the opposite side of the ship, and I was supported through the gangway down a few steps, and then up the same number, and my stateroom was there. As we were crossing I said to Commissioner Thompson on my right hand to send for two of the best surgeons of the city, and be sure and tell them not to discourage me. Finding that my wound was not immediately mortal, I had determined to make a fight for it, and did not want anyone to come near me who would discourage me. I had difficulty to make him understand me, but he finally did. Nothing annoys me more than to have persons come about and express doubts when I have set my mind upon doing a thing.

"They lifted me into bed, but had to prop me up on account of the choking. I told the poor captain who bent over me that I was sorry for the trouble and delay I was causing. The ship's doctor and the ambulance doctor who soon arrived washed my face and beard and bandaged the wound. They carried me on a litter and put me in the ambulance. As it started I was filled with joy to see my dear Rufe spring up on the rear seat. I knew then that I was not to be alone. How relative happiness is in this world. He had been encouraging me by words all along and kept on doing so, but broke down completely in the hospital when mamma arrived, as I afterwards learned.

"The excitement being over, I began to grow weak, and was quite weak when I was wheeled into the operating room. I forgot to tell you that as I stood or was supported on the deck I heard some one crying out, 'Kill him,' and others saying, 'No, do not kill him.' They had seized the assassin. I heard no struggle, nor did I hear any shots fired, but I concluded that I had been shot in the head by an assassin. I did not hear or feel the shot that hit me. There was an interval at the first when I seem to have been unconscious.

"Though the thing had not entered my head that morning, I was not surprised when I realized that I had been shot. I had had a feeling for some weeks that I might be assaulted on account of the anonymous threats I was getting by mail. I had not received so many since I was opposing the ring corruptions and the McKane conditions in Brooklyn and Gravesend when I was a young man. I had ceased walking over the Brooklyn Bridge.

"The matter of the pictures of the Reno prize-fight had come up. I had no way as mayor to stop the theaters from showing them. By the city charter their licenses were revokable by the judges of the Supreme Court, not by the mayor, and the district attorney and corporation counsel decided that there was no law forbidding such pictures. They had been shown for years without objection. But the Hearst newspapers kept on denouncing me for not stopping them. I suppose you know the way they had belied me ever since I became mayor. Finally, one day they printed in large type that an officer of the Christian Endeavor Society named Lowlande had called on me at the mayor's office and asked on behalf of that society to stop the pictures, and that I told him he 'was a fool and was sent by fools.'

"I had never said such a thing, as you may well know. It was made up. I learned that Lowlande was a process server for lawyers. The officers of the Christian Endeavor Society put forth a statement of their own motion that it was untrue that they had sent Lowlande or anyone else to me, and that he did not represent them. But it made no difference. These newspapers went on repeating the falsehood, and even tried to get up a public meeting to denounce me.

"Meanwhile, people of wicked or disordered minds, of whom there are a large number in New York, would cut these articles out and send them to me with abuse and threats written on the margin, or else with anonymous letters threatening me. Some of them said I would be killed. Probably they cared nothing about the pictures, but the particular disorder of their minds was inflamed by reading how bad a man I was. Finally they printed that terrible cartoon of me entitled 'The Barker.' I was dressed up as a ruffian and standing outside of a prize-fight ring twirling a cane and barking for people to go in and see the sport. Two men slugging each other, one of them down and bleeding, were exposed in the ring.

"Think of one who has been more of a library student than anything else all his life, and who never saw a boxing match, being pictured like that. But the ignorant and disordered minds believed it, and I suppose many others who read no other newspaper did, and were naturally inflamed against such a ruffian being mayor. That was the object these newspapers had in view, although they printed all the pictures of the fight in the most revolting form, as they had been doing for years with all such fights. Even some sensational ministers wrote to me as though they believed it. It was during this time that it first entered my head that I might be in danger, especially in walking over the bridge, although earlier in the year I had received a few similar threats when these same newspapers published that we were discharging small employees and taking on expensive ones.

"Such journalism is, of course, in absolute defiance of the criminal law, and it did enter my mind to publicly call on the grand juries and the district attorney to protect me from it, but I was weak and feared people would say I was thin-skinned. But the time is at hand when these journalistic scoundrels have got to stop or get out, and I am ready now to do my share to that end. They are absolutely without souls. If decent people would refuse to look at such newspapers the thing would right itself at once. The journalism of New York City has been dragged to the lowest levels of degradation. The grossest railleries and libels, instead of honest statements and fair discussion, have gone on unchecked. One can not help sympathizing with the decent newspapers.

"But I will weary you with all this. Tom saw me at the hospital twice, and I must write to him. He started immediately on hearing that I was hurt. What a good heart he always has. Give my love to all. I long to see you, and to go out to the old farm, and walk the old roads. I am certain it would do me good, but I fear I can not go this year. I wish I could go back to work. It would take my mind out of my throat."

This letter remained private only until September 20, when the *New York Evening Post* obtained a copy and printed it, maintaining it belonged to history. In the interim, Gaynor had begun to pick up the threads of his correspondence, in spite of his hoarse whisper of a voice. He dictated several letters, the first being to Judge Dickey, a justice with whom Gaynor had feuded furiously while on the bench:

"My dear Judge Dickey: I was exceedingly glad to receive your kind letter of August 29. It did me much good, as at that time I was somewhat despondent. I am glad to say that I have recovered my normal strength, and also my voice sufficiently to dictate answers to some letters. I am not able to write much with my own hand owing to the lameness of my collarbone and shoulder by reason of the injury to some cord or muscle in my neck."

To Elbert Hubbard, publicist and lecturer, went a similar letter the same day:

"Dear Mr. Hubbard: I thank you very much for your kind letter of August 31st, and also the article which you enclosed. I do not deem myself lucky in having been shot, and I should be sorry to see the same thing happen to you. I would give a great deal if it had not happened to me. It happened in a crisis of my life, and at a time when I was very anxious to do certain work which I have long thought of in my own way, and sometimes spoke or wrote about, although it was difficult in this vast community to get anyone to listen or pay any attention to me. . . . I have now recovered nearly my normal strength. I walked eight miles yesterday."

Some of the things that he wanted to do were indicated in an article he had written for the *Century* magazine, and which appeared almost simultaneously with the shooting. That article he had concluded with the words:

"There is much to be done, and I am fully aware of how little I am doing, and of how little, at best, I shall have done when my time is up. Corrections and improvements in government, as in all things, may not be done all at once, but only patiently and gradually, and, I say, charitably, explaining and teaching as you go, even as Isaiah says, 'Precept upon precept, line upon line; here a little and there a little.' "

In another article, written for the magazine *Good Housekeeping* and published at the same time, Gaynor had pleaded the cause of children, saying:

"The American child may have too much candy, too much finery, too much freedom of speech within the family circle, and too much theoretical education, but it has never had too much attention from the government, national, state, or municipal. Take, for instance, the problem of the child on the street. We receive stacks of complaints. And I ask, who has the greater right to the streets of New York, a child or an automobile? Within reason a child has a right to play in the street. . . . Most of the complaints . . . come from childless men and women. They have grown to hate themselves and everybody else, but even these ill-natured complaints must not be lightly dealt with. They are signboards pointing to the need of more room for children to grow up in."

Alluding in the same article to the agitation over the prize-fight pictures, the mayor had added:

"I have never seen a prize-fight, but I have no quarrel with the man who wants to see one. If pictures of a prize-fight will teach a boy how to defend himself when called upon to do so, then I say let him see the fight pictures. . . . I feel the same way on the subject of dancing. . . . Young people want to dance. It is a perfectly wholesome, natural desire. I wanted to dance when I was young. I did it and it never hurt me."

But dictating letters brought on fits of coughing, and Gaynor was able to answer his mail only sparingly. One letter he did attend to was from a convict in Dannemora prison. The mayor replied:

"Dear Mr. Hoyt (No. 7494, Clinton prison): I thank you exceedingly for your kind letter and am glad to receive the good will of yourself and all your companions in the prison. I am well aware that many of you are not really bad men, but unfortunate men, and that God so sees you. There are many of us who would be the same as you are if we had had the same trouble and obstacles in our lives. So do not be discouraged. I shall not speak of my trouble in view of the greater trouble of all of you. Let us all be patient and content."

Soon after sending this letter the mayor suffered a relapse and could dictate no more for a while. During this interval letters continued to pour into Deepwells, among them a note from his crony, "Captain" DeMott. The "captain" was doing time in the Riverhead jail for (of all things) stealing Gaynor's prize turkey and selling it to a poultry dealer for the wretched sum of fifteen cents. Even

A NEW STATUE ON THE OLD PEDESTAL

March 21, 1911

though incensed by this insult to the pride of his barnyard, Gaynor
at the time of the theft had tried to intercede for his friend; but the
justice of the peace had become tired of seeing the "captain"
brought before him, and this time gave him the limit. Now DeMott
wrote jauntily from the jail congratulating Gaynor on his recovery
and announcing that he would soon be at liberty and would be
pleased to dine with the mayor. Gaynor looked forward to the event,
too.

Then, on September 20, the *Post* published Gaynor's letter to
his sister, and other newspapers saw in it political implications, in

view of the coming state election. Hearst was in Europe. The *Times* and the *World* cabled the gist of the letter to him and asked whether he cared to comment on the mayor's implicit charge that the vituperation of the Hearst press had prompted Gallagher's action. This touched Hearst in a sensitive spot, for he had been accused, justly or unjustly, of having contributed to the assassination of President McKinley, and to other successful or unsuccessful attempts upon the lives of public men. Back from Enghien-les-Bains came the publisher's answer:

"I am exceedingly sorry that Mayor Gaynor was shot, and if Mayor Gaynor has said what you tell me I can only add that I am exceedingly sorry that his injuries have affected his mind. After his apparent recovery Mayor Gaynor expressed the hope that his illness would make a better man of him. Many others entertained the same hope, but unfortunately his experience did not abate his evil temper or his lying tongue."

On the day this rejoinder was published in New York, Hearst's *American* gave the lie direct to everything the Gaynor administration had accomplished, carrying headlines of which these were a few:

"City's Extravagance . . . Claims of Economy Disproved . . . Expenses for First Six Months Increase $1,307,043 Over 1909 . . . Reign of Vice . . . Crime Prevalence Confirmed by City Officials . . . Gambling Wide Open . . ."

Conspicuously exempted from the blistering condemnation of Gaynor and his subordinates was one name—that of the president of the Board of Aldermen, John Purroy Mitchel.

MITCHEL'S MISSTEP

Everything has two handles, one by which you can carry it, the other by which you can not.

—EPICTETUS

POLITICS—AND MITCHEL—were very much to the fore during the weeks while Gaynor was struggling back to comparative health at St. James. Late in September the Democratic state convention met at Rochester, and the expectation everywhere was that it would nominate Mayor Gaynor for governor. The attempt on his life had projected him even more strongly into national prominence, and already the political seers were spotlighting him as the Democrats' most brilliant hope for the Presidency in 1912. Calling Gaynor "a man of destiny," "Marse Henry" Watterson, editor of the *Louisville Courier-Journal* and elder statesman of the party, sent word that the shooting had brought the mayor "to the knowledge of thousands of people who have heretofore considered him as the shadow of a name."

Watterson personally thought Gaynor would be stronger if he stuck to the mayoralty, instead of accepting the nomination for governor. Other party chiefs thought differently, and Boss Murphy journeyed to St. James to suggest that the route through the governorship would be preferable. After the visit Gaynor was willing to say only:

"Charlie Murphy is a fine fellow. He is a very good-natured man. I like him. He inquired for me every day while I was in the hospital."

The mayor was reluctant to consider changing offices, but again pressure was brought to bear, and he wrestled with the problem. Never one to discount the importance of organized support, he had no wish to rebuff the party that had nominated him for mayor. Nevertheless he shrank from relinquishing the mayoralty for numerous reasons. His basic attitude toward the alternatives he had stated plainly as far back as the previous April, in a letter to the clerk of the Court of General Sessions. Talk of his nomination for governor was rife then, and he had written:

"To tell the truth, my great desire is not to have my name mentioned in connection with politics at all. The one thing in my mind is to try to get time to fulfill the duties of this office. As it is I am only doing things between constant interruptions. Except that I have been used to that sort of thing for twenty-five years I would not last a month."

Faced in September with the necessity of making a decision, Gaynor confided to a Brooklyn associate:

"I note all the things you say, but the question whether I should leave the mayoralty is one which I should have to consider gravely. . . . In deciding it I shall have to leave all questions of my own future or convenience out. It may come down to what is a mere matter of what is right and best for others. . . ."

That he had a moral right to move on from the mayoralty he did not doubt. While still undecided, he wrote to a friend on the staff of the *New York Press:*

"I should very much like to see you, as much pressure has been brought to bear on me of late, and I think you could advise me properly. Their persistence has worried me a great deal, and I only want to do the right thing, without regard to myself at all or what they call my future. I have no future, but only the present."

All this went on while he was passing sometimes active, sometimes listless, depleted days at Deepwells. Finally, on September 28, he gave to James Creelman, who had become a trusted consultant, a letter to take to Rochester and show to the convention leaders there. In words almost identical with those he had used once before, he stated:

"I could not abandon to their fate the splendid men whom I have appointed to office, and who are working so hard for good government; nor could I abandon the people of the city of New York after so short service. . . . Every honest man will understand me."

Upon receiving this definite declination, the convention proceeded to nominate John A. Dix, an upstate lumberman, and went
on to elect him. The Hearst press sneered that Gaynor had been
compelled to refuse the nomination by an ultimatum from party
leaders that he honor his campaign pledge to serve a full term as
mayor. Anything Hearst said Gaynor was prepared to deny, and
he immediately (and in flat contradiction of the verifiable fact)
denied that he had ever given any such pledge or had been "compelled" to do anything. To a correspondent he wrote testily:

"Permit me to say that I never made any such pledge to serve
for four years as mayor. You are entirely mistaken in this. What I
did in declining the nomination for governor was entirely voluntary,
and not as the result of any pledge whatever. You must get the idea
of a pledge from reading the Hearst newspapers, which are invariably false about almost anything."

Meanwhile Mitchel, acting as mayor during Gaynor's absence,
had succeeded in stirring up a hornets' nest by his officiousness. He
accused Police Commissioner Baker of failing to suppress gambling
and prostitution, which Mitchel said were running wide open in the
city, especially at Coney Island. Sending out his own investigators,
the acting mayor collected a mass of evidence which he personally
presented to District Attorney Whitman. The list of alleged disorderly houses numbered more than three hundred, and Mitchel
charged that these were being protected by the police. Whitman
studied the data, but the upshot was the return of eleven indictments, four of them on evidence that had already been gathered by
Whitman's staff. Only five arrests were made.

Amid a flurry of belligerent statements, Mitchel stormed out
to Deepwells and demanded Baker's removal, but Gaynor said he
would take no action until he returned to City Hall. The mayor's
friends were indignant at Mitchel's antics, aware that not Baker
but Gaynor was the target at which the young man was aiming.
That Hearst continued to favor Mitchel was significant. Compiling
a twenty-nine-page report on Baker's "insubordination," Mitchel
placed this on Gaynor's desk for action on the latter's return. It was
there when Gaynor made his first appearance at City Hall since the
shooting. This occurred on Monday, October 3.

The day before, he had come into the city unobtrusively and
had spent Sunday night in his home. But Monday morning a news
cameraman was on hand to snap the mayor coming briskly down the

front steps, looking tanned and hale. Accompanied by Mrs. Gaynor he was driven in his own automobile across the bridge, reaching City Hall unannounced.

The first person to recognize the mayor as he stepped out of the car was a newsboy; he dropped his papers and clapped his hands. Then, even before the mayor could bound up the steps, people began to gather. The loungers in the corridors of City Hall were startled when Gaynor walked in, looking so fit and energetic. Only his voice provided a disagreeable shock; it was a rasping whisper, inaudible a few feet away.

Going directly to his office, the mayor immediately set to work on the official papers accumulated there, but was interrupted shortly. First to break in, breathlessly, were three school children from a school on Market Street, not far away. They brought a bouquet of flowers, and six-year-old Molly Prate, climbing on a chair, spoke the "piece" that she had been rehearsing for days, all in one breath and a loud, shrill voice:

"On the first day that you are back from the country we have come to bring you a beautiful bunch of flowers from an old-fashioned flower garden because we are glad you are back."

Then the members of the mayor's official family began appearing with congratulations, and Gaynor thanked them for their loyalty during his absence. Going next to the council chamber to preside over a scheduled hearing on the 1911 budget, he demonstrated that he had not lost touch with administrative details; one after another, the department heads were ordered to scale down their estimates of expenditure; they must make reductions, "and that is all there is to it. It is not for you to say you will not make the cuts."

During the session, Mitchel, sitting on Gaynor's right, maintained a frozen-faced composure, even when Commissioner Baker was rebuffed in his appeal for an increased budget.

A citizens' committee, which had been formed in expectation of the mayor's return, had assembled while the budget hearing was in progress, and was waiting to welcome Gaynor back with speeches and formalities. The group was headed by Dr. Finley and Jacob Schiff, and Gaynor replied to their felicitations:

"I find great difficulty in saying anything at all except . . . 'I thank you.' If the body of intelligent citizens, without regard to clamor and to senseless noise and vituperation, will continue to work with me in the three years which I have yet to serve . . . I think that in the four years you can accomplish something through me, as poor

an instrument as I am. I do not pretend—I have never pretended—
that I can accomplish anything alone. There are no short cuts to
results."

His voice was a faint croak. Only once during the day did he
make any allusion to the shooting. That was when Docks Commissioner Tomkins, in whose department Gallagher had been employed, bustled in, and Gaynor clasped his hand with a near grin,
whispering, "Here is the man who is responsible for all this."

At one o'clock, the Gaynors headed for home. Outside City Hall
a crowd of ten thousand stood waiting, and when Gaynor appeared a
cheer went up. Several times he raised his top hat in acknowledgment; then helping his wife into the car, he signaled the driver to
start. A policeman tried to clear a path, brandishing his night stick
and yelling, "Get back there!" Instantly Gaynor stopped the car,
and leaning out of the window rasped to the policeman:

"Don't speak like that. Speak to the people politely. They are
not in the way, and if they were they would get out of the way. You
policemen must learn to be polite to the public. You have no right
to speak like that."

The chastened cop drew back, the crowd opened up, and amid
more cheers the car rolled away. The mayor was back and in fine
fettle.

The next day Mitchel was made to grasp this fact. With the
fullest possible attendant publicity, Gaynor formally apologized to
Lt. Col. M. Gray Zalinski, Army Quartermaster Corps, for the insulting letter which Zalinski had received from Commissioner Baker,
charging that the building where he had his headquarters was a
gambling den. The letter had been written on the basis of the complaints submitted by Mitchel while acting mayor, on evidence
gathered by Mitchel's agents. Baker's letter had designated the
accused building as located on the southeast corner of Whitehall and
Pearl streets (Zalinski's quarters), whereas the one meant was on the
northwest corner.

Gaynor apologized officially for another mistake made by
Mitchel's aides, by which an army warehouse in Brooklyn had been
identified as a house of prostitution.

In view of these apologies, reporters wondered whether Gaynor
would take action on Mitchel's bulky report demanding Baker's
removal. Gaynor said he had not asked for the report and had not

had time to read it. What was he going to do about firing Baker, the reporters persisted. Gaynor's answer was curt:

"Nothing. Least said, soonest mended. Did you ever hear that? Let us hope that this city, as orderly a city as there is in the world, will never be held up by any persons or newspapers as a mere refuge and home of unfortunate women and gamblers."

He followed this double cut at Mitchel and Hearst by a letter to Chief Magistrate McAdoo, decrying "the periodical attempts of some persons to scandalize the city and give it a vile repute by declaring its wickedness from the housetops, although it is the most decent and orderly of cities." He also took occasion to commend McAdoo's progress in reducing the number of needless arrests by enforcing the use of summonses, "against the old barbarous method of grabbing everybody and locking them up in advance for a hearing."

The full extent of Gaynor's resentment of Mitchel's busyness while temporary mayor was made clear a couple of days later when he informed Baker that the list of alleged disorderly establishments submitted by Mitchel was "an old one, like or compiled from the list made up in a wholly untrustworthy newspaper office for scandal and sensation and sent to us last winter and found to be so trumped up and inaccurate that it could not be used as a basis for official action." As indication of its fraudulence, he pointed out that eleven of the places listed were buildings that had been razed five years before in clearing the site for the new Pennsylvania Station.

Baker was ordered to apologize to forty property owners whose premises had been falsely cited as used for disreputable purposes, and the commissioner himself was reprimanded for "having given credence to such a list."

At this indictment of his work Mitchel was furious. As he read the mayor's statement his face blanched, then flushed; it was fully a minute before he could speak. Then he exclaimed:

"It is a deliberate lie—lie—lie that any of the addresses which I sent to the police commissioner were not based on complaints received at my office through the mails! . . . I don't know whether they originated at St. James, at police headquarters, or in newspaper offices. . . . The way to control vice and eliminate gambling in New York is not to write letters to Sister Mary, Old Dog Spot, and James Creelman, but to investigate conditions as they are and then act!"

THE BUSY BEE

May 21, 1910

This outburst was ignored by Gaynor, but Creelman answered for him in the next day's *Times:*

"It is not surprising that Mr. Mitchel's weak head has been turned, first by his disappointment when Mayor Gaynor failed to do the city a distinct disservice by abandoning his office and turning the city government over to such a puerile and treacherous successor; and, second, by the mayor's dignified exposure of the sensational and faked-up charges against the good name of the city, through which Mr. Mitchel gained a little cheap advertising, while the mayor was lying wounded and helpless, and Mr. Mitchel was busy with ambition. . . ."

At the next session of the Board of Estimate Gaynor was all serenity. He praised Mitchel's good work in the budget committee. The latter did not respond, but sat stiffly, self-righteous and un-forgiving.

A few days afterward Baker resigned, in order, he said, to relieve the mayor of any embarrassment caused by the controversy. As his successor, Gaynor chose James C. Cropsey, a Gaynoresque

Brooklyn lawyer, who could attribute his appointment only to the mayor's having mistaken him for someone else. Astonished by his appointment, Cropsey said he had never even thought of such a thing and knew Gaynor only slightly. He was charged by the mayor with the task of carrying out a thorough reorganization of the police department along lines that Gaynor had in view, and he set about the job with vim.

A STOIC AT WORK

> *Consider which of the aims that you set*
> *before you at first you have achieved,*
> *and which you have not, and how some*
> *things give you pleasure to remember,*
> *and some give you pain.*
>
> —EPICTETUS

THE SECOND DAY of the mayor's return to work he walked from his home to City Hall, making the distance in good time. Now, however, he was closely accompanied by a detective, one of three who had been detailed to guard him around the clock, even during his sleeping hours. Wherever he went during the day and evening the mayor was also accompanied by Lieutenant Kennell, in uniform.

It quickly became evident, however, that the mayor's strength had been restored only fitfully. He would start the week energetically, but by Friday would be exhausted and more than usually irritable. In order to allow him a long weekend of rest, the Board of Estimate moved its regular meeting day from Friday to Thursday.

To those around him it was painfully clear that Gaynor was constantly fighting fatigue. The bullet in his throat brought on spasms of coughing that left him limp. During his convalescence this coughing had sometimes induced retching that brought up his food, and this had retarded his recovery. In a confidential letter to a friend he described this trouble:

"I kept throwing up my food in my coughing spells. I didn't get sick to my stomach—I simply bolted my food in paroxysms of

314

coughing. The result was that I found it very difficult to keep up my strength."

However, he did make progress, and by January, 1911, he reported to a doctor that he was improving, although still having difficulty with his voice and articulation. He wrote:

"The right side of my tongue does not seem to come right. I do not have the bad gagging or vomiting spells as much as I used to. They are gradually dying out, and I think on the whole I am improving."

To conserve his strength he ceased to go out in the evening, and declined all invitations to speak. Rather than alarm the public he based these refusals on the condition of his voice, which was apparent to everybody; but privately he made no secret of the struggle he was having to keep going. To Robert Underwood Johnson, editor of *Century* magazine, he confided:

"I have become conscious of the fact that the shock is still with me, and that it recurs with more or less intensity every few days, and reduces me in strength for the time being. I then catch up again, and in a few days the same condition recurs. The doctors did not advise me that this would be the case, and it surprised me, although my sister wrote to me telling me exactly what I am now finding to be true."

At the same time he confessed to the Rev. Norman N. Thomas, of Union Theological Seminary, in declining an invitation to speak there, that "my voice is in such wretched condition, owing to the severed cords and other wounds . . . some days I am not fit to go anywhere."

To go on at all was difficult, but he persevered, hope, pride, and a sense of duty animating him, and on occasion he could be whimsical about his plight. To a woman who wrote that he had "probably coughed the bullet up," he replied:

"I suppose you have read in Rabelais of the giant who after every battle combed cannon balls out of his hair; but I am sure that he would not have so very easily coughed a cannon ball out of his weasand."

And in reference to his silence during public appearances he joked:

"One of the ancient philosophers said that no fool could remain silent at a feast; but now I am obliged to whether I want to or not."

As late as the following spring, after a winter of intermittent agony, Gaynor was still occasionally discussing his illness with correspondents. To a physician, at that time, who had offered long-range advice from Los Angeles, the mayor sent as complete a clinical report of his injuries as he ever set down. Noting that the after-effects of the shooting were still with him, he wrote:

"The neuralgic pains are now setting in. The ball entered just behind my right ear, and seems to have followed at least three courses, and in some way went through my throat cutting cords which control my tongue, so that my tongue is still crooked and I am able to speak only with much difficulty. I also cough a good deal, sometimes most of the night. It has been nip and tuck for me to get over the winter, but I have stuck to it, and now that the spring

So glad you're having a good time, Charlie. Yes. Don't hurry back. Everything is going nicely here. Goodby.

Jan. 9, 1911

THE BLOT

weather is coming on I hope to improve. The month of April has always been a bad month with me. I never had a cough before I was hurt and seldom a cold. Up to about the end of January my cough was such that I threw up most of my food, in consequence of which I ran down considerably. But I trust I shall come out all right."

His Stoic philosophy was put to a test, and frequently he would repeat to those around him, with a fixed satisfaction, this from Epictetus:

"Ask not that events should happen as you wish, but wish them to happen as they do, and your life will be serene."

And he would add sententiously, "We must be content."

But philosophy was not always proof against the annoyances that cropped up to vex a particularly annoyable man. Writers of baseless complaints against the public services felt the edge of the mayor's exasperation in answers such as:

"Sir: Your letter is at hand. If you wish to write to me again please write shorter. I have had your assertions investigated and find them to be false. It is useless for you to quote trash from the Hearst newspapers. Your mind seems to be led astray by their falsehoods."

An indication of his increasing touchiness was the mayor's order to clear the Brooklyn Bridge of the panhandlers that infested it. After being braced once too often by these beggars, Gaynor told the police commissioner to round them up, and several were arrested. One was asked, in magistrate's court, "Did you solicit alms from the mayor?"

"If he's the little guy with the gray beard I probably did," was the response.

CHANGING HIS CHAUFFEUR

May 4, 1911

"Did you get anything?"

"Not a cent."

Still, the quantity of work the mayor got through, in spite of his weakened health and exacerbations, was enormous. On his "good days" he dictated a mass of correspondence, struggling against his rebellious tongue until he achieved tolerable clarity. The mayor's letters had become so much a part of his administration that the public would hardly have believed Gaynor was back at City Hall had not the flow been resumed, as copious as before and in many instances much sharper. As before, he was ready to discourse on any topic a correspondent advanced. A Brooklyn lawyer appealing for an aggrieved client, a gambler whose premises had been raided, was dealt with judicially:

"Dear Mr. Roy: Your letter explaining that Mr. Kauffman's place is held possession of by the police is at hand. A man's house is his castle, as you correctly say, but I have never yet heard it said that a man's gambling house is his castle."

The mayor's deft instruction to Parks Commissioner Stover took care of a bad situation without recourse to red tape:

"Complaint is made to me that Cobb, the contractor for furnishing the new Public Library, has violated the labor law by having things manufactured by a firm which does not comply with our highest rate of wages and eight-hour statutes. I hope you will let him know distinctly that if he persists in that he will find trouble in getting his bills paid."

Gaynor once plaintively remarked that if somebody spit on the Brooklyn Bridge he would be asked to do something about it, and he was, several times. A gentlemanly protest against such uncouth untidiness came from a member of the dignified Brookline Country Club, near Boston, and the mayor replied:

"I thank you for your letter calling my attention to the spitting habit in New York City, whereas in Boston, where you live, people have ceased to spit on the streets, as the ordinance against spitting there is strictly enforced. Yes, they do even worse than spit on the streets here. I walk over the Brooklyn Bridge every day, and a few not only spit on the bridge but blow their noses without handkerchiefs, to the disgust and danger of those behind them, especially in the wind. I shall have to take the matter up very soon. You know you can not do everything at once, but only gradually. I do not know how it is over in Boston, except by hearsay, but here in New

York we may not even observe the Ten Commandments yet more than fairly well."

The soft answer which, if it did not turn away the wrath of another letter writer (in this case a clergyman who complained of being accosted by streetwalkers), at least parried the protest, was embodied in the mayor's reasonable reply:

"Reverend Sir: Your favor of October 21st is at hand. I hope you will not find fault if I say that I think its tone is uncharitable and querulous. I am sorry to say that there are some clergymen who always write in that tone. Disposed as I am to work if necessary night and day to right whatever is wrong in the city, such letters are calculated to hurt my feelings, and would, were it not that I have long since schooled myself to receive everything in the spirit of charity. Moreover I am thoroughly aware that things are not as bad as you state. I regret to see you say that streetwalking here is worse than in London, Paris, or Berlin. Permit me to say that that statement is very inaccurate. You never saw a large city with less outward appearance of vice than this city. I note the following sentence in your letter:

" 'I do not assume that your Honor would propose to surrender these streets absolutely to this sort of business, but if they are to be given up to it I think that the fact should be thoroughly published.'

"Do you really think it is necessary for you to address such a remark as that to me? . . .

"I have taken pains to pick out of your long letter and its adjectives your real grievance, and shall have the police commissioner inspect the streets which you mention and preserve order in them. Now, I hope I have myself not said anything uncharitable, and again assure you that I shall always be glad to entertain any complaint from you."

But such cooperation did not satisfy some of the more strident crusaders against prostitution, nor were they edified by the mayor's pointing out that the world's oldest profession antedated them all, and would probably be flourishing long after he and his critics were dead. When Dr. Parkhurst called at City Hall to demand that the police display more vigor in suppressing brothels, he was bewildered by the mayor's treating him to a dissertation on the views of St. Augustine, Lecky, and other authorities on the subject of wayward women. Dr. Parkhurst wanted the police to break up all houses of ill fame and drive out their inmates; Gaynor foresaw no real solution of the problem so long as the moral standards of the community condoned the evil. And morals was the field of the churches and schools, not the police, he stressed. If the police drove the prostitutes and their pimps out of the houses, they would continue to ply their trade in the streets, and public decency would be shocked; and if the police drove them off the streets, they would congregate in houses; so the best to be hoped for the time being was to mitigate the evil and preserve outward order and decency, while the churches and schools worked to elevate the moral conscience of the community.

Such a procedure was utterly unacceptable to Dr. Parkhurst, who was becoming a hair shirt to the mayor; and when Hearst gave the crusader a daily column of his own (ornamented by his photograph) in which to air his strictures against the ungodly and Gaynor, the mayor lumped the clergyman with the publisher.

"Dr. Parkhurst does not want to help," he told a sympathizer. "He wants to quarrel. And yet, I have no ill feeling against him. I would give him a boost any day to help him to Heaven, if that is what he is after in abusing me. We must not let rancor or uncharity enter or influence our souls. We should be charitable to him and succor him and try to reform and lift him up. You say he has sold himself out to this sensational newspaper, and is hired to write against me as he does. Even so, we should not have any ill-will against him, but only charity and good-will. When a man hires himself out he must obey orders or quit. And he may be able, by some species of casuistry, to convince himself that he is doing right when everyone else sees that he is uncharitable, unkind, and doing wrong. Who knows, and who will be the first to cast a stone at him? 'Judge not lest ye be judged.' We must look upon him in charity and kindness. Yes, he puts a picture at the head of the daily column he writes. It is true that it is painful to see such a thing in a clergyman. But he evidently thinks he is a very handsome fellow, and prints his picture at the head of his column because he thinks we are all of his opinion about it, and go and feast our eyes upon it, the same as he does. He thinks he is giving us pleasure in exhibiting his picture for us to look at. So we must be kind and forbear with him in this also.

"It is true that we can not imagine Jesus doing such a thing if He were here. He would not hire Himself out to a sensational newspaper, and in addition put His picture at the head of His column. Much less would he write unkind and uncharitable things. His great heart would go out to all of us, and especially those of us who, like you and me, are sinners. Did you ever think of that? But still we must be kind and charitable to Dr. Parkhurst. No doubt he thinks

RESOLVED.
TO ASK THE
AID AND ADVICE
OF MR. HEARST
IN SHAPING THE
CITY ADMINIS-
TRATION. ALSO
TO TURN THE OTHER
CHEEK TO IVINS
THE MAYOR

Jan. 1, 1910

he is a good man, and that is an additional reason why we should be kind and charitable to him. To think one's self good, or better than others, is a mental trait which is hard to overcome by those who are afflicted with it. It is even reckoned a disease among physicians and has a name. That is an additional reason why we should forbear and overlook. And you know there are people who think they are pious when they are only bilious."

After this blast of sustained irony doubtless the mayor felt relieved. And that kaleidoscopic year he closed in mellow mood. To the editor of a newspaper in Des Moines he sent a Christmas message:

"By all means let us teach our children that there is a real Santa Claus. That belief has created more joy in little hearts than anything else that I know of. I still believe there is a Santa Claus every Christmas."

THE SARDINE CAN

Wise men change their minds; fools don't.
—GLADSTONE AND GAYNOR

TOWARD THE END OF 1910 two events focused attention again on the attempt on Gaynor's life. A public subscription had been launched to defray his medical expenses, but Gaynor put a stop to that, saying he would pay his own bills. The $15,000 which already had been raised then was sent as a Thanksgiving gift to the Sisters of the Poor of St. Francis at St. Mary's Hospital. Gaynor had contributed to the fund, and in reply to a letter of appreciation from the nuns wrote affectionately:

"Dear Sisters: I thank you very much for your kind letter. It would do me a world of good to call over there and see you. I am not yet in the best of health and would like to rest. I am glad that the fund was so large. If the time had been longer it would have been larger. A great many people did not know of it at all."

Shortly before this event James Gallagher had been indicted for assault on Commissioner Edwards; Gaynor's name did not appear in the indictment. Tried and convicted, Gallagher later was found to be suffering from paresis and was confined to the New Jersey Hospital for the Insane.

After the trial Gaynor gave a glimpse of the intensity of his feeling in a note to Edwards:

"Dear Mr. Edwards: I am glad to see that Gallagher was convicted for the assault he made upon you. I have never trusted myself to say anything to you about the occurrence, but I assure you that I have always realized that you saved my life by risking your own.

Without calculating the danger and consequences to yourself, you rushed in and prevented him shooting me a second time, or oftener. My brother could not have done more than that. Now that you have given your testimony in court and Gallagher has been convicted, I feel that I should put this testimonial in writing for you."

Toward the close of 1910 and in the early weeks of 1911 the relations between the mayor and the press became less cordial as a shadow fell upon the administration. The cause was the mayor's closest friend, Charles H. Hyde, the city chamberlain. In the autumn of 1910 a legislative committee looked into an alleged attempt to defeat an anti-racetrack bill at Albany by bribery, and the committee was told, by a witness of not unblemished credibility, that Hyde had been one of a group of men having an interest in racetracks, who, at a meeting in Delmonico's, had pledged a fund of $500,000 to defeat the measure in question. Reporters wondered whether the chamberlain would be called to testify. They were told by the committee's counsel that while he would like to ask Hyde a few questions, no subpoena would be issued. Shortly after this, Hyde absented himself from his office and his whereabouts became a mystery.

The *World*, which prided itself upon prying into dark corners, raised a hue and cry, which was taken up by other newspapers, the Hearst press outbraying them all. Gaynor refused to discuss his appointee's absence, beyond expressing absolute confidence in his integrity.

Hyde in fact was on leave of absence for reasons of health, and was on his way to Florida aboard a houseboat called the *Wait-a-While*. (The newspapers happily garbled the name as *Stop-a-While* and *Rest-a-While*.) Halfway down the coast, Hyde was overtaken by the *World*'s energetic Swope—a feat of detective work that was trumpeted with all the *World*'s and Swope's talents for vaunting their successes and ignoring their defeats. Hyde's refusal to be grilled by Swope or any other reporter indicated to the press that he had something to conceal, and the most was made of that suspicion.

Meanwhile, in January, with Hyde still absent, two New York banks failed, in both of which the city had large deposits. The city chamberlain banked the city's funds; he was responsible for their custody and selected the banks where they were deposited. The first bank to fold, the Northern Bank, had been made a depository at the suggestion of Comptroller Prendergast, it developed; but Hyde came under fire when the second bank, the Carnegie Trust Company (no connection with Andrew Carnegie), failed and it was revealed that just before the Northern's collapse, Hyde had pressured Carnegie Trust into extending a loan to Northern, under a threat to withdraw the $650,000 in city funds deposited in the Carnegie bank.

Hyde returned to New York and was assured of the mayor's perfect confidence. The chamberlain had simply done what the Secretary of the Treasury did with United States funds every time trouble loomed in Wall Street, the mayor contended; but the newspaper campaign kept up, and in May Hyde was indicted for various offenses. He immediately resigned, although Gaynor refused to credit his guilt. Tried and convicted, Hyde eventually won a reversal on appeal, and when that had finally disposed of the case, Gaynor let his wrath boil over publicly against what he called a plot on the part of certain political elements, spurred on by "newspaper clamor," to discredit his administration through an unwarranted attack on his friend.

"There wasn't a syllable of foundation for an indictment," he wrote. "The judges on appeal do what I never knew them to do before. They do not merely reverse the judgment and order a new trial, but dismiss the whole case on the ground that no offense is alleged in the indictment, and that no evidence of any offense appeared on the trial, and that the whole case is without a leg to stand on."

In the public mind, Hyde was not given so clean a bill of health, and the mayor's stubborn refusal to face the implications of his protégé's furtive behavior disclosed to Gaynor's supporters his growing propensity to blot out of sight inconvenient facts or circumstances that ran counter to certain prejudices or his own preconceptions. Yet he never lost touch with reality on all subjects except those to which he deliberately closed his mind. The Hyde episode hurt Gaynor. His own rectitude was never doubted by the public, but some of the city's cartoonists used the incident to portray the mayor in a new guise—one of sinister implications. The *New York Tribune*'s Boardman Robinson, a masterly satirist, was especially adept at giving the mayor's features an evil cast by a few strokes of the pen, and the *Tribune*, the most extremely Republican daily in the city, encouraged Robinson's deadly subtlety. The talented team of cartoonists for the Hearst newspapers, and those of the *World*, leaned more to ridiculing the mayor in their drawings; no matter how outrageous. the Hearst cartoons usually made a person laugh.

Coincident with the Hyde affair, the mayor came to grips with the all-important question of providing the city's subway riders with relief from the inhuman congestion. The long, tortuous evolution of New York's network of subways is a story of countless entanglements; perhaps no other public issue of the period, certainly not the tariff or free silver, bulked so large in New Yorkers' consciousness, or was debated with more heat and confusion, than subways. A political football in 1910, it would remain one for years after Mayor Gaynor came forward with a concrete proposal to end the muddle.

The first specific proposal for a system of underground tracks on which to transport people in trains of cars at high speed was projected by Mayor Abram S. Hewitt in 1888, but not until 1900 was anything done. In that year the city gave John B. McDonald, a successful railroad builder, a contract to construct the first line. The city provided the capital for the construction, and upon completion McDonald was to be given a fifty-year lease, renewable for another twenty-five years, to equip and operate the system. Eventually the city poured some $37,000,000 into the project, and on the day it was completed the city assumed title as sole owner of the plant.

To cooperate with the city in providing subways the state had created a Rapid Transit Commission, which was soon replaced by the Public Service Commission. McDonald's contract had been approved by the public authorities all along the line, but he found Wall Street capitalists chary of risking investment in so novel an undertaking. Finally August Belmont, an independent banker, agreed to back McDonald and take over his operating contract. For this purpose Belmont organized the Interborough Rapid Transit Company—the IRT.

The first subway line constructed comprised only a segment of the comprehensive system planned by the Rapid Transit Commission. This first line was intended to try out the feasibility of a subway; doubt of its success was widespread, and Belmont's secretary would recall the "gloom sessions" that were held periodically in the banker's office, with all hands wondering whether anybody would ever use the thing.

The first line was opened on October 27, 1904. Its instant popularity exceeded every expectation.

The first line—the only one existing in 1910—ran from City Hall along the East Side of Manhattan Island to Forty-second Street; turned west at that point as far as Times Square; and thence ran north along upper Broadway and eventually to Van Cortlandt

Park by one branch, and through Harlem by another branch to the Harlem River, without crossing into the Bronx. By 1910 the southern end had been extended to the Battery, to connect with the ferries to Staten Island; and by means of a tunnel under the East River it penetrated Brooklyn as far as Flatbush and Atlantic avenues, near the Long Island Rail Road station. The fare for a ride of any distance on this line was five cents, one nickel.

When superimposed on the map of long, narrow Manhattan Island, the outline of this subway's path resembled the crossbar and one-half of each leg of the capital letter "H." Extension of the legs had been envisioned in the original plan—one extension to reach north from Grand Central Terminal at Forty-second Street into the Bronx, and the other to extend south from Times Square through the lower East Side, and by a new tunnel to continue over to Brooklyn. Realization of this original plan had been talked about for years; it was popularly called "completing the 'H.' "

Because of its enormous success, the subway was overcrowded from the start. Designed to carry 400,000 passengers a day, the first year of its operation it carried a daily average of 800,000, and on one memorable day 1,200,000 riders were crushed, pushed, and pounded into its cars. The scenes enacted at the rush hours, morning and evening, appalled out-of-towners. Straphangers cursed the "human cattle trains" of the IRT, their outcries being the shriller because of the large profits the company was reaping, contrary to its dubious expectations.

The financing of the company had become complicated. While the subway was building, under a threat of competition by the surface and elevated lines controlled by Thomas Fortune Ryan, Belmont had bought the surface system, which already was teetering on the verge of bankruptcy. The IRT thus became saddled with the debts and bonded obligations of the decrepit surface systems, and the earnings from the subway had to be drawn upon to meet these, in part. Ryan then succeeded in displacing Belmont from control of the IRT and installed as president Theodore P. Shonts, a hardheaded practical railroad executive from the Midwest.

Meanwhile, strong sentiment had developed in favor of public ownership and operation of all transit facilities. State law stipulated that only the city could own subways, though private capital might be drawn upon to finance their construction. In the election campaign of 1909 all the candidates had come out flatly against granting any more long-term leases, like that held by the IRT, for operation

of the new lines. Some of the candidates declared themselves in favor
of public ownership and operation, without the least connection with
the existing company; Gaynor had said he wanted public ownership
of the new lines, "without any strings attached."

"Let me say to you," he had told audiences, "if the city is going
to build any more subways out of the money of the rent-payers and
taxpayers of this city, I want the city to own them absolutely, without a claim by anybody on earth."

All the appeals in that campaign had been directed toward the
public's distrust and hatred of the IRT, and had dealt more in emotion than in concrete programs.

Once in office, Gaynor lost no time in delving into the practical
aspects of the situation. He found more difficulties than he had
imagined.

The IRT was as eager as were the municipal authorities to
have more subways built, if it could operate them without competition; and before the end of January IRT president Shonts visited
City Hall and discussed the matter with the mayor for an hour.
Gaynor said that he found Shonts to be a man "of large and fair
views and a man with whom it would be easy to do business."

This sent a shiver of apprehension through the more determined advocates of a publicly operated system. During the campaign, Comptroller Prendergast had promised that "there will be
nobody in the next Board of Estimate who will take orders from
Brother Shonts," and he began to watch developments with jealous
suspicion. So did Aldermanic President Mitchel—and Mitchel and
Prendergast, with Gaynor as chairman, composed the transit committee named by the Board of Estimate to make subway recommendations.

Gaynor's first problem was to find the money needed to build
new lines. The city's borrowing capacity had been about used up,
and urgently as subways were needed, schools, street lighting, piers,
and other civic improvements were needed just as much. In order to
increase the city's borrowing limit, Gaynor ordered a uniform assessment of property throughout the five boroughs, and by this means
an additional $30,000,000 of borrowing capacity was picked up.
This, with a little more, he estimated, was all the city could sink
into subway construction during the next year, and the prospect for
the years after that looked even slimmer. Evidently money must be
found in other quarters.

Although many routes for new lines had been proposed, only

two were under serious consideration. One was completion of the
"H." This admittedly would be most serviceable to the public, because it would join all portions of the city in a single network, but
it would involve cooperating with the hated IRT. The very prospect
sent extreme advocates of public ownership into tantrums of opposition.

The alternative route being urged strongly was known as the
Triborough plan. It called for building a separate line with city
money exclusively, independent of the IRT—in competition with it,
in fact. The proposed route started at the Battery, proceeded up
lower Broadway to Fourteenth Street, where it veered over to Lexington Avenue, and continued through the upper East Side and into
the Bronx.

There were drawbacks to both plans, but two major objections
to the Triborough route were that it would fail to touch the West
Side below Forty-second Street, which had no subway service and
where the opening of the Pennsylvania Station that year was creating a heavy increase in traffic; and that, collecting its own fare, it
would force through passengers to pay two fares to reach their
destinations, instead of one. There was also the question of initial
cost: the Triborough, it was estimated, would require an outlay of
$120,000,000 to $130,000,000, and if built as a competitor of the
IRT no help in defraying part of the cost could be expected from
that company.

To Gaynor's mind, the chief requisites of any solution of the
subway enigma were speed in construction, to afford the long-
suffering public the quickest relief, and avoidance of a double fare.
He remembered times in his life when an extra nickel for carfare
had been a major consideration. He would not go as far as did some
critics of the Triborough plan who called it "a trip to the moon," but
the longer he studied it the less he liked it. Disdaining to pay attention to pressure from the press to "get going," he weighed the alternatives with scrupulous earnestness and impartiality, spending
hours on his knees poring over large-scale maps showing the proposed routes.

Shonts, on his side, was actively cultivating the mayor's interest. Mirabeau Towns, Gaynor's lawyer neighbor, was retained by the
IRT. Towns once described Gaynor as a man who would not take
advice, but would listen to suggestions; and in chats in Gaynor's
library Towns began to throw out suggestions regarding the desirability of utilizing the existing subway as the nucleus of a compre-

hensive, unified system that could be built quickly, and would reach into every section of the city, all under a single fare. Towns had to contend with Gaynor's deep-seated hostility to the transit companies, against which he had inveighed when on the bench; but gradually these prejudices were overcome and one day in April Gaynor startled his colleagues on the Board of Estimate by telling them that Mr. Shonts seemed to have "ideas for the public good as well as for the prosperity of his company, a combination which is always admirable."

Two weeks after that, on a weekend when Gaynor was at St. James, Shonts took steps to obtain a talk with the mayor "free and unencumbered." Shonts had never been to Deepwells, and he engaged Towns to drive him out; Towns hopefully brought along a bottle of champagne that he knew Gaynor liked. They found the mayor climbing over a fence. He did not invite them into the house, nor, to Towns's chagrin, did he uncork the champagne. For three hours Shonts and Gaynor tramped back and forth in the front yard, wearing a path in the snow that lay on the ground, while Towns shivered in the car. When finally Shonts rejoined him, the IRT president was in high spirits, and the extent of his satisfaction was indicated by the check for $5,000 which he sent Towns as his fee for that day's work. The next day Shonts gave a full report of his conversation to J. P. Morgan, Jr., who had entered the picture as a possible source of construction capital. The IRT directors voted Shonts a $10,000 bonus.

In evidence of good faith, Shonts had urged Mayor Gaynor, during their conversation, to send some qualified person to the IRT offices to examine the company's books and convince himself that nothing was being concealed or misrepresented. Accepting this invitation, Gaynor sent his commissioner of bridges, Kingsley Martin, with a consulting engineer, and they reported that the IRT estimates seemed just and fair. Through Martin, too, Gaynor worked out a concrete offer on the part of the IRT, under which, if the city would put $53,000,000 into "completing the 'H,'" the company would invest $75,000,000, the sum to be paid back out of revenues. The company agreed to equip and operate the entire system under a twenty-year lease, renewable for another twenty years. In addition, the IRT undertook to third-track some of the elevated lines to increase their capacity, operate a tunnel service into Queens, go deep into the Bronx, and by a new tunnel under the Narrows to tap

Staten Island—all under an agreement to share the profits with the city, and retain the five-cent fare.

Gaynor paved the way for announcing this startling proposal in a characteristically disingenuous letter to the Merchants Association, in response to their suggestion that a joint committee be set up to consider "the various routes, plans, and offers that have been made and may hereafter be submitted." He approved the suggestion, and added that "many are loudly demanding one route or another without any precise knowledge of any route . . . and with only a vague notion of the subject." Nor had such people any real comprehension of where the money was to come from. The city would have at the most only $57,000,000 to devote to new subways, but "if some company would put in all the capital needed over and above the $57,000,000 . . . the subway difficulty would be solved, and the work of construction could go on in all of the boroughs simultaneously, instead of piecemeal."

In longhand he appended to this letter:

"P.S. I add that no member of the Board of Estimate is pledged to any route, notwithstanding statements to the contrary, but all are open to a free consideration of this great matter."

This spilled the fat into the fire. Mitchel and Prendergast loudly protested that they certainly had pledged themselves to the construction of new subways with city money exclusively, to be owned and operated by the city, and positively not in conjunction with the IRT. But even they were taken aback temporarily when, a few days later, Gaynor announced the IRT's sweeping offer, with the suggestion that it be carefully and earnestly considered by both the public and the administration.

But tactically he had committed a blunder, for he had kept from his colleagues knowledge of his personal negotiations with Shonts; nor had he told the members of the Public Service Commission, which would have to pass on any final agreement. Furious when they learned how they, the majority of the Board of Estimate's transit committee, had been bypassed by the mayor, Mitchel and Prendergast drafted a thirty-three-page report riddling the IRT offer and recommending that it be rejected out of hand. The joker in the IRT program, they appreciated, was if it were adopted, all hope of subway construction by the city would be gone, inasmuch as all the city's available credit would have been pledged for years to come. So good-by for a generation to all thought of an independent line.

At the next meeting of the Estimate Board, Mitchel presented his and Prendergast's report as that of the majority of the transit committee; it required an hour and a quarter simply to read, and Mitchel then attempted to jam it through to adoption then and there. Gaynor, presiding, remarked acidly:

"My colleagues in the transit committee, with whom I find no fault, did not see fit to convene so that I might see a copy of this report. They evidently do not wish a minority report to be submitted."

When the mayor assumed his air of long-suffering under indignities, it usually boded ill for somebody.

McAneny refused to be stampeded into a decision of such magnitude; time was needed to study the report sensibly, he argued. Snapped Mitchel:

"I don't see how anyone who was elected on the same platform with me could refuse honorably to vote for a subway system controlled by the city."

LEST HE FORGET

Jan. 6, 1911

WHAT'S YOUR HURRY?

Stung by the imputation of bad faith, McAneny shot back:

"I have as sacred regard for that platform as anyone else, but I differ from some in interpreting it. This hasty action is not businesslike and I will not subscribe to it."

The other borough presidents also balked at being rushed, and the session grew so stormy that Gaynor several times had to restore order. He alone remained deceptively calm. Finally adjournment was taken without the report being acted upon.

Thereupon Prendergast and Mitchel took to the stump to denounce the mayor's "shameful sellout" to the transit interests, and the harmony that had prevailed in the administration was shattered. Several newspapers, including especially the *World* and the Hearst papers, took up the same theme. In vain Gaynor protested that he had never given any pledge except to do what seemed best for the city; the issue was "public ownership," and its devotees were fanatical. Taunted about doing an about-face, the mayor quoted Gladstone:

"Wise men change their minds; fools don't."

As the debate raged on, it became largely a dispute in semantics, arguments over the meaning of words spoken or written years before. On both sides (and the mayor had supporters) the arguments were shot through with prejudice and misconceptions, and in a few weeks the merits of the IRT's specific proposal had been so obscured as to be almost forgotten. Gaynor pointed out repeatedly that appeals to the principle of municipal ownership were beside the point, because by law nobody but the city could own subways; no matter who might build them, the city took title the minute they were com-

WELL, WHERE IS IT?

May 2, 1911

pleted. Under the law, too, the operation of the subways, as well as their equipment, must be allotted to the lowest bidder.

Meanwhile, the straphangers hung on and cursed everybody concerned. Their desire was to get relief, and quickly, and here and there some levelheaded observers understood that. A prominent member of the City Club told his fellow members that "the principal thing the New Yorker wants is to go—to go where he wants to go and when he wants to go. He cares little for the financial aspects of the matter, and I believe that we have been putting emphasis on the wrong thing."

Gaynor's opponents would have none of this, and paid no heed to advice such as that given by the *Herald*, which said that "the mayor's statement of cold facts" carried more weight with the great majority of New Yorkers than the "so-called arguments of persons in and out of public office who disagree with him." The mayor and the IRT offer continued to be pounded mercilessly by the public-ownership advocates, and by the Hearst press with positive glee. He refused to retreat, and in the confusion the IRT withdrew its offer.

Subway negotiations then entered upon two years of chaotic negotiations, of acrimony, recrimination, and bitterness. Throughout all, Gaynor, beset by a multitude of problems, was unable to continue in the lead; that role fell to McAneny, a man of tact and perseverance. Sometimes Gaynor helped, sometimes he held aloof, sometimes he stormily objected. Prominent in the opposition to whatever he might propose was "that whippersnapper," John Purroy Mitchel, and back of Mitchel was the vituperative Hearst. Meanwhile the disregarded straphangers clung grimly, cursing alike the delay and those causing it. Shrilled at by a section of the press more interested in upholding their theories regarding public ownership of municipal services than in bringing tangible relief to the subway victims, the people were invited to believe that Gaynor was the cause of it all.

REWARDS AND PUNISHMENTS

———⬛◦◯◦⬛———

There are some men who will not see good
when it is done, and even angels could
not make them see it.

———GAYNOR

ONE MAN WHO HAD BEEN WATCHING events from afar was that
determined President-maker in Texas, Colonel E. M. House. Gaynor's near escape from assassination, and his subsequent plucky
fight back to health, in House's words "shot Gaynor into national
renown." Soon after the mayor had returned to City Hall, House
went to New York, accompanied by two spokesmen for the Democrats of Texas, and formally invited Gaynor to address the Texas
State Fair at Dallas, and also the Texas Legislature. The objective
was to introduce the mayor to the Southwest, and thus to open the
way for invitations to speak in other parts of the country.

According to House, Gaynor accepted the invitation tentatively
and even enthusiastically. The colonel then returned home and on
January 23 wrote as follows to the mayor of New York:

"My dear Mayor Gaynor: I wish to remind you of the condi-
tional promise which you made to me this winter. The Legislature,
which is now in session, has already unanimously passed a resolution
inviting you to make an address and the people of Texas will be
greatly disappointed if you do not come. If you prefer to remain
with me quietly without troubling to speak I can arrange it that way.
In other words we would have your visit to us as free from care as
we can make it and your wishes will be our pleasure. The Legislature
will be in session until the middle of March and any time that will be

convenient to you would be agreeable to us. Mrs. House joins me in the hope that Mrs. Gaynor will accompany you."

The colonel might have saved his ink, for on that same day the editor of the Austin *Express* was telegraphing to the mayor of New York:

"Resolution passed inviting you address Texas Legislature on way to Mexico. Can you accept? Wire hundred words press rate collect."

And Gaynor was wiring back, finding fifty-three words enough:

"Your dispatch is the first news I have that I am going to Mexico. I suppose you have been relying on some of our New York newspapers which nobody here takes seriously. Please express my thanks to the Legislature. I should be most glad to meet them if I were going that way."

This display of indifference the humorless House construed as an affront to the state and people of Texas, and he thereupon "wiped Gaynor from my political slate, for I saw he was impossible." Later House would put down, with a certain smugness:

"It was one of the best illustrations I know of what instability can do to the fortunes of a really brilliant man. We elected Woodrow Wilson in 1912. There was no reason why, if he had been sensible, we could not have elected Gaynor. He was actually better known than Wilson."

What men like Colonel House could not conceive was that perhaps Gaynor had no serious wish to become President of the United States. The mayor certainly did not take House into his confidence regarding his motives, and there is no evidence whatever that Gaynor ever really thought earnestly about the possibility. Of course it was flattering to be spoken of as a potential candidate for the office, and it was pleasant now and then to toy with the idea of being elected; the temptation to daydream was real. But Gaynor had none of the intense ambition to sit in the White House that drove Theodore Roosevelt and Woodrow Wilson, for example. And there may have been in Gaynor's unresponsiveness a glimmer of his Puckish impulse to tease a man who took himself with enormous seriousness. Gaynor enjoyed deflating self-important, pompous people, and House, short in stature, had a trace of pomposity in his bearing. City Hall reporters, who saw Gaynor at close range day after day, were familiar with this occasional prankishness. Several of them took the mayor to lunch one day in a Park Row bar, and were amused when they detected Gaynor in the act of impishly filling up again with water the whisky bottle from which he had just poured himself a stiff drink.

But there were other considerations which outsiders like Colonel House could not take into account because they did not fall within their knowledge. James Creelman, who knew Gaynor's character well, always suspected that the mayor sent his telegram to spite Hearst, who had got wind of the possible Texas visit and had announced the trip as set. Then there was the fact that Gaynor knew he was not well; the lingering on of the aftereffects of the shooting made the prospect of undertaking major new duties unattractive. And finally, there was Gaynor's very real and fervid wish to remain mayor of New York; he either reasoned or sensed that there was his sphere, and there he wished to stay.

Mayor Gaynor started off 1911 by dictating a few bushels of letters. Right away, on January 3, he took up the case of a woman living on Lexington Avenue who was annoyed by the job of snow removal done in front of her house. Wrote the mayor:

"Dear Madam: Your letter is very long but I have tried to read it. Have you considered the large fall of snow which we had some weeks ago, and the length of time it remained on the ground, instead of thawing as usual? Are you aware that the city can not remove all of the snow, namely, from all of the streets? Are you a taxpayer, and do you know the cost of snow removal? Do you know that other cities do not remove the snow but leave the citizens to do the best they can with it? Do you consider that when the snow does not melt off soon, but remains for some time, melting gradually, it leaves dirt after it? In fact, have you considered the matter at all, or are you classed with those who merely find fault? Do you know 'Big Bill' Edwards? Do you know that he is very anxious to do right and would be glad to have your advice and assistance?"

On January 4 the mayor made public the correspondence he had had with two officials of the Central Labor Union of Brooklyn, about which they were expressing indignation. Otto Nichols, secretary, had forwarded his arbitrary views on the subway snarl without being asked for them, and in reply had received a reprimand from City Hall. The president of the union, Maurice De Young, came to the defense of his fellow official, and in return got his comeuppance, to wit:

"If you or your organization wish to discuss the question of subways I shall always be most happy to receive you, or to receive letters from you, but permit me to say that I know without consulting you that the workingmen of this city do not wish to be compelled to pay two fares to go about the city. It might be well for you to remember, also, that this matter of subways is a thing which I have studied for many years, and it is possible that I know something about it. It might be well also to remember that I sat sixteen years on the Supreme Court bench as a judge and had such matters to deal with. . . . These things might well have prevented you from addressing me in the insulting tone of your letter, attributing things to me which I never uttered and do not stand for. . . . Might I also suggest that if you write to the mayor again that you do not sign your name by a rubber stamp. Of course, I can not be certain that someone else has used the rubber stamp. I can hardly believe that the president of a labor union would so far forget himself as to sign a letter to the mayor with a rubber stamp."

The mayor then published the entire correspondence, including the insulting and abusive letter from De Young, signed with the detested rubber stamp.

At the same time Gaynor agreed with Cyrus Miller, Bronx borough president, that more action and less talk was needed on the subways, writing:

"Yes, we have been in office a year, and it is time for us all to redeem our promise to get to work at subway construction. We are under pledge to no particular scheme or system; it is for us to do the best for the city. One company is the same as another to me. . . . You say you hope I do not let newspaper clamor affect me too much. I can assure you that neither newspaper clamor nor any other clamor can affect me even a little bit. My own deliberate judgment outweighs everything else, and clamor is not worth considering."

January 13 was a trying day for Mayor Gaynor's staff, as was evidenced by a letter of apology sent to a congressman, regretting the delay in replying to the latter's letter. It should have been, Gaynor explained, "taken out of its order and presented to me, but I regret that the staff here is somewhat deficient."

On January 19 Gaynor attended the dinner of the Council of American Hebrew Congregations, representing the reformed congregations of the nation. Jacob Schiff presided and the thousand persons present heard Adamson read a brief speech prepared by the mayor, praising the adaptability of the Jewish people. Throughout their long history, Gaynor reflected, the Jews had not hesitated to modify or abandon "nonessential regulations and forms . . . in order to keep pace with the teachings of experience," but held fast to the fundamental tenets of their faith.

On January 23 (as this typical month unfolded), in a letter deploring the continued opposition shown by Mitchel to the pending IRT subway offer, the mayor pointed out that if his Democratic running mates had been elected with him to the Board of Estimate, "the subway matter would have been settled within ninety days better than I can settle it now with the discordant elements around me. But I do not complain. I must try to do the best I can. . . . But if the people of the city had good sense they would never elect a discordant government. For the best results you must have a united government."

Meanwhile, rumors were spreading of friction between the mayor and Police Commissioner Cropsey. Both men had minds of their own, and Cropsey was endeavoring to carry through some changes that ran counter to the rules Gaynor had laid down for the department, particularly the rule that appointments and promotions must be made in numerical order from the top of the civil-service list. Cropsey had other views, and serious trouble seemed likely.

In the midst of this incipient controversy—and also of the agitation over the Hyde affair and the subways—Gaynor attended a Broadway play entitled *The Boss* and cheerfully volunteered to pass judgment on its verisimilitude. He wrote to the producer, William A. Brady:

"Yes, I would be glad to attend and see 'The Boss' played. I shall be able to tell you whether the boss of your play is true to the boss in real life, for I have seen several. Sometimes we picture them a good deal worse than they are. My notion is that the man in office ought to be the boss, but always ready to listen to suggestions from other bosses and from everyone who has any sense."

A proposal to change the name of the Normal College to Hunter College ran against the mayor's disapproval. He told the Board of Education that he should prefer "New York Normal College, or something like that. To call it Hunter College would be to take out of the public mind that this is a college owned and maintained by the City of New York, and I do not think I can consent to that."

In February Gaynor attempted to enlighten the Board of Aldermen regarding that popularly regarded menace to good order and public decency, socialism and the socialists. Some of the aldermen had been uttering cries of alarm, and the mayor sent a quieting message instructing the alarmists about the right of socialist speakers to air their views in the streets, subject to the preservation of the peace, and explaining that the red flag had been adopted as the symbol of brotherhood, not of red riot and bloodshed, as some aldermen believed. For himself, the mayor made clear, he had no confidence in the capability of socialism to meet basic human needs.

When, as a consequence of this statement, the mayor was challenged to debate by a fiery socialist speaker, Gaynor declined, saying:

"The mere fact that you make the challenge is probably proof positive that you are not fit for such a debate. People who want to force things down the mental throats of others do their own cause more harm than good. . . . It is just possible that I have done more to make the people of New York understand the meaning of your flag and of socialism than all that you have ever said with stridulent voice. If you wish to be a teacher . . . just cool off a lot."

The same advice was passed along to belligerent advocates of the Henry George single-tax theory:

"In your speeches and writings in past years you have been a little too cocksure. Some of you have been acrimonious. Some of you say you think other people are very dense and ignorant because they do not think as you do. In other words, you try to ram your theories down the throats of people before they are ready to receive them, the same as they feed Strasbourg geese to make their livers swell. No one ever succeeded that way. Franklin treats of that in his *Autobiography*. He says the way to convince a man is to express a little doubt about it yourself. Just shake your head, or wag it a few times to this side and that, and maybe shrug one shoulder and then the other, and say, 'Well, it seems so to me, but I am not clear and may be wrong about it.' And then the other fellow will take it all in and turn around and try to convince you."

That was the method the mayor used in spurring Parks Commissioner Stover to find some legal way by which the heavy layoffs of outdoor workers in the parks during the winter months could be eliminated. "Surely there must be some legal way to do it," the mayor mused, in apparent doubt himself.

A letter of pure enjoyment went to a Brooklyn friend who shared the mayor's literary enthusiasms:

"I thank you exceedingly for Long's beautiful edition of Epictetus in two volumes which you sent me. The mechanical work is perfect, which always make a book attractive. I suppose if it were known that you read Epictetus the newspapers would be as much astounded as they were when they learned that I read him. Many years ago when I was a young fellow I read him through. Since that time I only take the book down from the shelf now and then."

On March 9 Governor Dix met with Gaynor in the city to seek ways of ending a deadlock in the legislature over the election of a United States senator. The candidate presented by Murphy was regarded as grossly unfit, and Gaynor's influence was invoked to help find a substitute. In this affair the mayor had dealings with Franklin Delano Roosevelt, a junior senator, and though they were on the same side and eventually won the fight, Gaynor was said to have dismissed the cocksure, arrogant young F.D.R. as "Mr. Know-It-All."

At the same time the mayor was endeavoring to get the legislature to approve a new charter for the city. This developed into a bruising fight during which Gaynor was denounced as a would-be dictator bent on taking all power into his hands, and opening the way for a return of Tammany control at some later date. Gaynor disclaimed responsibility for the main features of the charter, although he did believe that the mayor should be invested with the broadest powers; he once told a political associate that New York needed a "czar mayor."

The commotion stirred up by professional educators over the proposals to revamp the Board of Education annoyed Gaynor intensely.

"I have a notion that I have the good of the public schools as much at heart as any of them, for I went through them myself," he retorted, "beginning in the little clapboard district school and thence to the village school. . . . Is the teacher's craft so occult and inscrutable that the ordinary person can not see into it? Some persons may think so, but I do not see why."

But the uproar raised by many of the town's "leading citizens" was tremendous, and some of the newspapers—the *Tribune, World,* and Hearst papers especially—attributed the most ignoble motives to the mayor during this fight, with grossly unfair exaggeration.

Nevertheless, the news about Mayor Gaynor that appeared in the press day by day was not all sinister. For instance, on March 11 a headline announced, "Little Actress Gets Letter From Mayor," and it was reproduced. The actress was Juliet Shelby. She had

GOVERNMENT BY GAYNOR
The Mayor would reform the city administration by a new charter centring
much power in himself and largely subordinating independent officials.

April 24, 1911

visited City Hall a few days previously to ask the mayor for a permit
to appear in *The Littlest Rebel*. The child got the permit, and in
return sent Gaynor a pass for the show, which he acknowledged at
once:

"My Dear Little Friend: I should be most glad to go and see
your play but you know I have so many things to do that I can not
go anywhere. I am glad that you are as happy as you say. Everybody ought to be happy. It does no good to be any other way. When
anything discouraging or annoying happens just say to yourself,
'Well, it is all right. The next time something good will happen,'
and then you will feel bully. Sincerely yours, W. J. GAYNOR,
Mayor."

After thus reducing Epictetus to the mental range of a child,

Gaynor, in a letter to another juvenile actress, gave the back of his hand to moralists who deplored the exposure of children to the "contamination" of the stage:

"I am glad that you are pleased with your part on the stage. No matter what some good people may try to make themselves think, or some overzealous people, I am sure that you are not being overworked or hurt a bit. What little you do on the stage does you good."

Mixing into disputes was something the mayor could not resist, and that spring he became deeply involved in a major agitation. According to some newspapers, the city was suddenly deluged by a crime wave, and they blamed the mayor's "soft" policy toward arrests. The storm was first whistled up by a magistrate named Corrigan, who was smarting under the mayor's failure to appoint him chief magistrate. Corrigan charged that the police force had been "demoralized" by Gaynor's new rules, which so favored criminals that the police were actually intimidated from making arrests. As a result, lawless elements were flocking into the city, deeming it a sanctuary for their kind. Said Corrigan:

"We have had fifteen months of government by epistle, and this is the result."

Following Corrigan's blast, a judge of General Sessions charged that "it sometimes seems that we are not trying the crooks, but the policemen who appear against them. It is now nearly two years since I had a pickpocket before me for trial. . . . Apparently the police are afraid to do their duty."

Nine magistrates took sharp dissent from Corrigan's views, and Gaynor went after the magistrate hotly.

"This is now the third time, I think, that Magistrate Corrigan has uttered such seditious statements," the mayor stated. "They are intended to make the police force insubordinate or indifferent to their duty. . . . Magistrate Corrigan has just returned from a nine-week vacation in Florida, and feels so healthy he can not contain himself and must attack those of us who have been right here all the while working for the city. I wish I could have had such a vacation, or one-quarter of it, during the hard winter."

Hinting at instituting proceedings to have Corrigan removed, Gaynor pointed to the police record showing a sharp falling-off of arrests for trivial causes; he denied that there was any crime wave except in the imagination of faultfinders and sensational newspapers; and he maintained an acerbic correspondence with individuals and organizations which expressed fear that criminals were taking over the city. The grand jury took notice of the row, questioned both Cropsey and Gaynor, looked into the facts, and failed to discern any significant spurt in the crime rate. Nevertheless, the mayor continued to be pounded by his critics, and "Don't be a seditious!" was a catchword that spring.

Had the newspapers been fair in their strictures, the attacks would have been hard for an irritable man to bear, but they were not fair. Nevertheless, the mayor went ahead with his plans, and confined his chiding of critics to the mailbag.

"Dear Sir," he wrote to an ungenerous complainant: "Your

THE LID OFF
   This is the third time, I think, that Magistrate Corrigan has issued such
      seditious statements.—Mayor Gaynor.
                                                            March 24, 1911

ARE YOU A "SEDITIOUS"?

March 25, 1911

letter of March 7th is at hand. If you write a civil letter to Mr. Edwards you will be very certain of an answer. My rule is to answer even uncivil letters, like your present one, but I do not wish to impose such a rule on others."

And to a similar offender:

"Dear Sir: . . . I would suggest to you that you assume a more moderate tone in writing to city officials. I notice your threat to take the matter to the courts. I have no objection to your doing so."

In between such calls to order and common courtesy, the mayor reviewed the St. Patrick's Day parade from in front of the cathedral, only recently dedicated, and afterward was entertained at a reception by Archbishop Farley.

In late March the appalling Triangle shirtwaist factory fire, in which one hundred and forty-one lives were lost, shocked the city inexpressibly. Most of the victims were girls who jumped from the top floors of the ten-story, supposedly fireproof building. Gaynor started the relief fund for the families of the dead, and out of observations made on a personal inspection of the scene of the disaster would emerge the Fire Prevention Bureau. At the mass funeral held for several score of unidentified victims, a hundred thousand persons marched in silent protest. Fear of rioting had been expressed, but Gaynor forbade the police to interfere, and there was no violence.

SOMETHING THE MATTER WITH HIS EYES
"I can't see any of 'em."

April 12, 1911

ONE-SIDED VIEWS

April 5, 1911

Though the racking cough caused by the bullet in his throat continued to plague him, Gaynor was able to dictate letters almost without stint, and the correspondence brightened many a column in the daily press. A man in Oregon who wanted the mayor to find him a wife ("Ladies is scairs out here") was assured that his request would be published, and whatever response it might draw would be forwarded promptly. Another man, this one in Minneapolis, who also was wife hunting, received the sound advice:

"There are plenty of girls who would fill your description right out in Minneapolis where you live. Just pluck up courage enough to go right up to them and tell them that you want a wife. But maybe that would be too abrupt. I did not go about it that way, because I did not have pluck enough, and maybe you haven't. But get around to it the best way you can, and everything will come out all right."

The mayor expressed his views freely on the pending income-tax amendment (he favored it in principle), and on "some ministers of the Gospel who tax one's patience a good deal and seem to have no charity whatever." He denounced baseless denigration of the police force, contending that "most of the policemen are good, square men." Publicity seekers—Gutzon Borglum, the sculptor, among them—were "taken down a peg" with letters such as, "I think it would be just as well if you publish your letters without sending them to me." He lectured the grand jury on a "scandalous" disclosure of its secrets, and absolutely refused to associate himself in any way with the eminent Chauncey Depew, head of the New York Central Railroad and former United States senator. When the Montauk Club gave a birthday dinner to Depew, Gaynor informed his fellow members that "I can not join in honoring a lobbyist—one who

THE RECALL OF JUDGES IN NEW YORK
Messenger—Sire, a magistrate has expressed the opinion that your crown is worn too much on one side.
Mayor—Sedition! Sedition! Off with his head.
April 19, 1911

has been a lobbyist from his youth up, and nothing but a lobbyist."
He refused even to enter the clubhouse while Depew was there.

The quarrel with Magistrate Corrigan flared up sporadically,
and Gaynor traced it, to his satisfaction, to a whispering campaign
against both himself and Commissioner Cropsey which four demoted
inspectors had started, he said; and as for the newspapers' outcry,
well, that " 'wave of crime,' as they call it . . . recurs once a year
with the regularity that the marbles season recurs to boys. We heard
it last year and every year theretofore, and at this time next year we
shall hear it again." The number of arrests for frivolous reasons, or
no reason at all, had been cut by fifty thousand in a year, he pointed
out, and "the community is now being told . . . that this whole reduc-
tion . . . was in the case of burglars, pickpockets, and other felons,
who, it is said, the police are forbidden to arrest."

To reporters Gaynor scoffed:

"Don't persist in asking me about Corrigan. He is one of those
in this city whose heads are filled with vice and crime. How did their
heads get filled with vice and crime? You have only to follow them
around at night to find out."

Like everybody else, the country-loving mayor was susceptible
to spring fever. Strolling back from lunch one balmy day, he
stopped to chat with the policeman on duty in City Hall Park and
told him:

"I wish I had your job for a few days. I'd like to stay out here
in the sunshine. If I had your job for a while I think I might get rid
of this thing in my throat."

The patrolman sympathized, and the mayor moved along to
City Hall. Just outside, he encountered a small boy trying to whittle
with a broken knife.

"You can't whittle with a knife like that!" exclaimed Gaynor.
"Come with me and we'll get a good knife."

Together they went to a Park Row hardware store, where the
urchin picked out the biggest and shiniest pearl-handled knife in
the showcase. Complimenting him on his good judgment, the mayor
bought it for him, and the lad ran back to flash it in front of his
pals. By the time Gaynor got back to the Hall, a row of boys was
lined up on the steps, whittling away and doing their best to show
how dull their knives were.

The fight over the charter revision lasted into the summer, and
Gaynor fretted that his poor health kept him from more actively
participating. He told a friend:

"I have had nip and tuck to keep on my feet throughout the winter. . . . I am conscious of my shortcomings and how much I have tried the patience of everyone, but I have done the best I could to stick to my job."

The spread of criticism of his actions to the national magazines he considered uncalled for and in the main unjust, and in a spirited protest against the misrepresentations which he contended were being published irresponsibly in the *Outlook*, he told Dr. Lyman Abbott, the editor:

"Why not give me a fair show? Why mass every irresponsible falsehood to embarrass me, instead of helping me? I have stayed here all summer, principally to help in this charter matter. I want to do what is exactly right. That I know; do you know it also? Have you the least doubt about it? I did not start my charter. I found it in the legislature, about to pass, when I became mayor, and I had it held back for a year for examination and discussion, which is going on now. Why can not the facts be stated? . . . Away with all this petty political bigotry. I have hated it for a generation and hate it worse than ever today. I only want to have things honest and decent here."

While still harassed by this embroilment, Gaynor took off for a tour of the Catskill watershed region, to inspect the progress being made on the great aqueduct system that would carry to the city an abundant supply of pure mountain water. On his return, he made a vigorous speech before the Civil Service Reform Association in answer to their attack on some of his charter proposals, particularly those affecting civil service. Before this hostile audience the mayor pulled no punches.

"I have been tramping around on the watershed to see if we couldn't get some water headed down this way," he began. "I didn't know until I got a letter from James Creelman that I had been accused of trying to put through a charter that would give the mayor a power that would make the civil service board merely ornamental. I have discovered in the last few days that I have been the subject of a lot of uncomplimentary criticism. There is nothing particularly new in that. After reading the newspapers for the last sixty days I am glad to be alive. Let them go ahead. I am even willing to be shot if they will only come up to me in front, instead of behind.

"The first time I heard anything about civil service was as a young man, when I heard an address by Carl Schurz at Utica. It went in one ear and out the other, or perhaps it didn't go in one ear at all, for the subject was new and I didn't understand it. . . .

"For myself, I can say that in the departments and bureaus that come directly under my control not a single man has been discharged for political reasons. . . . Yet I find myself accused of trying to have adopted a charter that would give the mayor of the city a power that would put all civil service regulations out of business. . . .

"If I may be excused for making a rude pun, I have been more gasping than grasping during the last eight months. . . . Regardless of all the unfair criticism that has been heaped on me, I shall continue as I have been doing until the end of my term."

He then gave his listeners some of the wisdom he had garnered as an administrator:

"There is always a danger that societies such as yours, in their eagerness to do things well and thoroughly, overdo them by reason of their zeal. There are places in which it is impossible to apply the civil service laws and get results. Civil service is all right when it applies to a bookkeeper or a stenographer or a clerk, for these tasks are such as any number of persons can learn to do equally well; but when it comes to the selection of a man for a position which requires tact and judgment and discretion, the chances are a hundred to one that he could not be selected from any civil service list. It is impossible to determine by a specific examination whether a man is fitted for such a position."

As an instance of this he recounted the trouble he had had in getting the right man to head the Bureau of Weights and Measures, and why he had sought relief from the civil service rules in order to get the man he wanted:

"A lot of people were curious to know what I was so particular about in this position, but they didn't know that I had been studying up on the question of weights and measures, from the first record of these things in the Old Testament to the report of John Quincy Adams on the same subject to Congress in 1821. And let me tell you that was a classic in its line. Then, when I became mayor, I found myself with a problem of weights and measures on my hands. At that time there wasn't an honest weight or measure in New York City. I not only made every one of them honest, but as a result of my efforts the United States government revised what it called a 'customary' measurement on goods brought into this port. . . . I have tried to be patient and do good in the face of bitter criticism, but there are some men who will not see good when it is done, and even angels could not make them see it."

The *Herald* concluded that the belaboring of Gaynor over the charter, and the asserted crime wave, and the subways, and Hyde, was mostly " 'fuss and fury,' inspired by political animosity."

A new crisis arose, however, when the mayor's disagreements with Police Commissioner Cropsey came to a head and Cropsey was allowed to resign. Asked what the difference had been, Gaynor replied succinctly:

"I did not propose to be mayor and have someone else run the city. If it is run badly, here is the man that is responsible, right here; look at me."

This was a declaration, in effect, that henceforward he would run the police department himself, and he chose a willing collaborator to replace Cropsey—young Rhinelander Waldo, moving him over from the fire department. To succeed Waldo as fire commissioner the mayor named Joseph Johnson, who had been the first deputy commissioner.

On the day he made these shifts, Gaynor took part with President Taft, Governor Dix, and other worthies in opening the New York Public Library at Fifth Avenue and Forty-second Street. Of the many speeches made in honor of the event, Major Archie Butt, President Taft's aide, rated only Gaynor's as worth much. The mayor said he could not pass the building without taking off his hat, or feeling like kneeling on the sidewalk; and he never thought of the burning of the Alexandria library without a pang.

In direct touch with Waldo, Gaynor set about a realignment of the police force, starting with introduction of the three-platoon system. Waldo organized the first traffic squad on modern lines, and carried out other reforms and improvements. But the police commissioner was the most obvious target for public criticism; whatever went wrong, the police somehow were assumed to be to blame; and soon the new incumbent was providing the censorious with cause for carping.

In the hot weather, that year of 1911, the mayor's health appeared to droop, and this further frayed his temper. The nagging cough never left him entirely, and frequently he was overcome by weakness. Nevertheless, he managed to get through a heavy load of work, and his irritability could always yield before an opportunity to write a letter "just for fun." A man of Manhattan who was bothered by musical neighbors received an answer of this sort.

NEXT!

"Dear Sir," wrote the mayor sympathetically: "I am in receipt of your letter saying that all clubs should be closed at 10 o'clock, also all saloons, and also that piano playing and singing should not be allowed at any hour of the night, especially in summer, when people can not close their windows, so as to shut the noise out. I hereby authorize you to carry out all of these reforms. It may be that you will first have to get elected to the legislature, and pass laws therefore, for you know this is a government of laws, and not men, that is to say, those put in office may not do as they like, but may only carry out the laws as they are passed by the legislature. Did you never hear of this before?"

A short while after the date of this letter, Gaynor appeared noticeably gaunt and on edge when reviewing the street cleaners' parade. But in his office he seemed to rejuvenate, and there was no telling where he would turn up without advance notice. He visited the night courts, toured the city's institutions on Blackwell's and Randall's Island, and one day startled a great many people by invading the slaughterhouses on the far East Side.

The Bureau of Municipal Research had complained of serious

violations of the sanitary code by the meat packers, and Gaynor had come to inspect conditions. The superintendent of the first plant at which he stopped tried to steer him into the cold-storage rooms, but the mayor would have none of that, and when his guide insisted, lost patience and snapped:

"I have told you I did not come here to see your dressed beef; I have no doubt you keep that all right. I came to see the most offensive parts of your plant, and that is what I propose to see."

Equipped with a rubber coat and hip boots, he inspected the killing and rendering rooms, asking questions everywhere. Blood-spattered meat cutters sheathed their knives and clustered around the mayor in astonishment; he told them that he was surprised not to find the odors worse.

As he left, he noticed a wagonload of scraps standing at the curb and asked the driver what he was going to do with it. Render it to get fat for making oleomargarine, he was told. The mayor grimaced.

"That word 'oleomargarine' ought to be abolished," he said "Why don't you say 'butter substitute'? Then people would know what it was."

The result of this unorthodox inspection tour was a public reprimand to Henry Bruere and Dr. William L. Allen of the Municipal Research Bureau.

"I used to say a good word for them before I became mayor," Gaynor declared. "But when their chief aim is to make a sensation I can not work with them. Their report on the slaughterhouses was a great wrong to an industry that does $84,000,000 worth of business a year. . . . I found the report . . . to be grossly inaccurate and sensational. When I spoke to them they told me, to my surprise, that they had never been through any of the slaughterhouses but had sent an employee. I do not propose to have the industries of this city injured for the sake of sensationalism. I guarantee to the people of the city, however, that the slaughterhouses will be kept clean and obliged to observe the law."

Bruere retorted that the mayor did not go to the plants "immediately" but eight days later, and on a day when the wind was blowing the odors away, and if he had really seen everything he must have seen plenty of violations of the sanitary code.

The subways controversy boiled up afresh when Borough President McAneny laid before the public a plan by which the IRT and the Brooklyn Rapid Transit Company (BRT) would share with the city in building new lines. The offer did not seem as favorable as the one already rejected, and it included provisions to earmark some of the subway revenue to pay off the huge debts of the bankrupt Manhattan surface system. This outraged Gaynor, and he rained denunciations "in order to protect myself against deliberately fabricated falsehoods." The scheme, he maintained, was a swindle, and if adopted would lead to interminable lawsuits, which in turn would delay still longer any relief for the subway riders.

"I have too long written and spoken against such damnable rascalities to now turn about and ally myself, as mayor of this great and intelligent city, with them," he stormed. "I shall go out of office without putting that stain on my name."

Prendergast sided with McAneny in favor of the scheme, and in the midst of the turmoil Gaynor ladled out a special dose of anathema to Mitchel and Hearst when he signed an agreement with the New York Central Railroad for removing the railroad tracks from Eleventh and Twelfth avenues. For years this "Death Avenue" menace had been inveighed against by "certain politicians and newspaper proprietors . . . using the matter for political humbug," Gaynor charged. "It shows, I regret to say, how easy it is to gull honest people by deliberate lying."

Thus through the dog days the mayor stuck to his post and his duties, and the newspapers reported his every activity with interest, censure, or praise, and sometimes with sheer amazement. How the mayor occupied himself on one specimen day, July 25, the *Herald* amused itself by reporting as follows:

"After three days of rest, the mayor returned to City Hall and in a few moments was busy writing letters and making speeches on topics of popular interest. Before he left for home in the afternoon he had attacked editors of 'yellow' newspapers, ordered an investigation of a city magistrate's action in gambling cases, continued his public correspondence with President Lowell of Harvard, appointed a park commissioner for Queens, and expressed his views on 'ordinary men and women' and on 'genius'—all this besides attending to the daily routine of his office."

In signing a new eligible list for teachers, on this hot July day, Gaynor had remarked on its general mediocrity, but added:

"After all, the affairs of this life, in government and out, have to be done by ordinary persons, and perhaps it is all the better that that is so. The ordinary man and woman may be safer than a genius."

He vetoed one bill establishing a Bureau of Fire Prevention because it conflicted with a better bill he had drawn up; the vetoed measure, he said, had been "hurriedly put together by the agents of a certain newspaper proprietor in this city for the purpose of self-glorification and claptrap. . . . It is crude to the last degree."

In making public his latest letter to President Lowell, who had taken issue with the mayor on the question of a paid Board of Education, Gaynor said with peevish humor:

"It seems strange that when he writes to me and when I write to him, he straightway publishes his letter and suppresses mine. I had supposed that the college spirit was a very different spirit to that."

Such was the bare skeleton of his activities on one July day. At the close he left for a brief automobile trip through the Berkshires; but his car broke down, he refused to talk with reporters, and he snubbed welcoming committees along the way. The day he returned, July 31, there was a grand ceremony when the first spadeful of earth was turned on construction of an extension of the East Side subway line. Thousands struggled to get a glimpse of the doings at Lexington Avenue and 67th Street. The mayor was conspicuously absent; the affair was not really a start on serious subway construction, he sniffed, but merely some preliminary digging under a contract signed months before; the question of who was going to find the money to build the new lines, or who would operate them, on what conditions, was still undetermined.

On August 9, the anniversary of his shooting, there was an observance held in City Hall, against Gaynor's objections. He was ill and weary, and he had tried to put that episode out of his mind. When the preparations were started, he had written to Corporation Counsel Watson:

"I prefer that no such ceremony take place. The fact is I could not stand it. So please tell all who had united in the intention that the ceremony is not to take place."

His wish was overridden, although he tried again. On arriving at City Hall on August 8, he found a decorator festooning the pillars of the portico and angrily ordered him to desist. But City Hall was under the authority of Borough President McAneny, and *he* ordered the decorations to remain. The next day, as congratulatory messages poured in, Gaynor was presented with a silver loving cup, which he accepted tremulously.

"I am sorry to have to say anything," he responded in his wisp of a voice, "for the event is one I put behind me and have tried to forget. The year has been a long one—the longest of my life. . . . I was fully conscious of how much I was falling short of the duties of my office during the long fall and winter months, when I came here so often with an effort, and doubting I could hold out much longer. . . . To those who constantly tried to misrepresent me during that time and make my life as miserable as possible I have no resentment."

Then as an afterthought he added: "I suppose I should have resigned." But that would have meant turning the mayoralty over to Mitchel and Hearst, and to that Gaynor would not consent.

At the mayor's request, the flowers that filled the rotunda were sent to St. Mary's Hospital, and the next day was one of the busiest Gaynor ever spent in City Hall. Amidst everything else, he dictated a letter that became famous, one addressed to five boys. It was dated August 10, 1911, and read:

"Dear Boys: It is too bad that you can not play ball somewhere in peace. Of course the police can not always let you play on the

"THERE WAS AN OLD WOMAN WHO LIVED IN A SHOE, SHE HAD SO MANY CHILDREN SHE DIDN'T KNOW WHAT TO DO."

Aug. 4, 1912

street, but now and then they can wink so hard with both eyes as not to see you when you are doing no harm to passers-by and the street is not crowded. In the parks you may only play on the places assigned to baseball playing. The keepers will not chase you out unless you play where baseball is not permitted. I wish we had grounds for you all to play, but unfortunately we have not. So, boys, do the best you can, and I will help you a little now and then if you send me word.

"Masters LeGrande Sampson,

"William E. Westbrooke,

"Samuel C. Ward, Jr.,

"Joseph Carey, and

"Raymond Luetke."

After which—and after crossing swords with several critics and dispatching a mass of other business—in the company of his new police commissioner, the mayor of New York went by police launch to Coney Island. There he toured the amusement parks, and took Waldo for a ride on Luna Park's "Shoot-the-Chutes"—a toboggan slide down which flat-bottomed boats plunged at breakneck speed and shot out across a shallow lagoon in a shower of spray.

Asked how he liked the thrill, Gaynor replied:

"Fine! But I should have liked to go twice as far and twice as fast!"

LETTERS THEY READ
AND STORIES THEY TOLD

To The National Publicity Bureau:
> *You ask me to give an interview saying*
> *"What I would say to the readers of*
> *3,000 newspapers." I would say to*
> *them to be very careful about believing*
> *all they see in the newspapers.*

—W. J. GAYNOR

THE AUTUMN WEATHER did seem to renew Gaynor's vitality, and among other resumed activities he found himself able to make occasional speeches without undue difficulty. His voice was still indistinct except at close range, but by practice he had managed to subdue the distortion of his tongue. Nevertheless, he still had "bad days."

The state fair at Syracuse gave him a welcome respite from city cares, and he toured the exhibits with relish. The pigs won his admiration, and at a luncheon in the clubhouse he repeated his conviction that there was nothing like a farm to build perseverance in a man or woman.

Back in town, he attended the opening of New York's first theater for Yiddish drama, Kessler's, on Second Avenue. When he stepped on the stage he was cheered for five minutes, and in his response took a potshot at people who "think the East Side is some sort of slum. Oh, how they sympathize with you! And how much a year some of them are being paid for sympathizing with you! I wish they were all here tonight."

The title of the play, *God, Man, and Devil* ("I can't say it in Yiddish, but that is the way it is in English"), intrigued him as "pretty comprehensive"; he hazarded a guess that after a year and a half as mayor he might write a play on that subject himself. "The great trouble, though, very often is to distinguish the man from the devil; they look a good deal alike sometimes, and act a good deal alike, too."

The next day, rain discouraging people from calling at City Hall, the mayor had a chance to catch up on his correspondence at length. Some of the letters he dictated that day were published all over the country, with attendant chuckles. William W. Mummey, of Arkansas City, Kansas, one of the irrepressible wife hunters turning to the mayor for help, drew this response:

"Dear Sir: Your letter asking me to find a wife for you is at hand. How is this? Why do you send way up here to New York for a wife? Do you not know the proverb that he who goes far from home for a wife is apt to be fooled? And then again how could I recommend any good girl here to you? You may not be so attractive as you think you are. From my way of thinking most any woman a man happens to meet is altogether too good for him. But it seems that you are unable to find a wife among all the women of your locality. Do you not think that you are altogether too particular? I am very certain there are many there who would make good wives."

The next letter was to a little girl, Helen Roth, living at 89 West 105th Street:

"Dear Miss Roth: I have received your letter of September 11th, telling me that you and the little girls in your neighborhood have no place to play after school, and that wherever you go to play you are chased. I am very sorry about it, and I will see if I can do something for you. Some people think you ought to stay in the house all the time. But you must go out, and you must play somewhere, and we must let you play in the streets until there is some other place provided. Do you know I receive letters daily from men and women who hate to see the children play in the streets at all. But on inquiry I always find out that they are people who have no children of their own. You say you want to skate on roller skates. Maybe I can get the police up there to wink so hard with both eyes that they won't see you when you go by on your roller skates. But be careful not to run into anybody or bump into an automobile. But there are very few accidents of that kind. When one such accident happens a lot of people write to me as though it were the rule instead of the exception."

George C. Deaken, of Los Angeles, had written the mayor his contrition for a mean action he had done years before, and for him Gaynor had a stern answer:

"Your letter is at hand. You state that some years ago you were a witness before me when I was a judge, and a false witness, and deceived me, so that I decided the case wrongly, and that you make this confession to me because you have become a Christian and want forgiveness. Where anything is stolen or got unjustly it must be refunded before forgiveness can be expected, if the sinner is able to refund. That is the way I understand it. So you had better tell me what the case was so that I may look it up and see what loss the defeated party sustained; and then, you must restore his money to him or make good his loss. If this be not your view, I fear you are in error in supposing that you have got religion and are a Christian."

This rule in Gaynor's book was not applicable to strangers alone. He insisted on the same strict standard of justice in his own family, sometimes to the chagrin of his children. During his convalescence, he had attended a horse show at St. James, and had been highly pleased when his children won two cups and a ribbon. Marian, the beauty of the family, had captured the ribbon riding a Shetland pony, and Gaynor marched off the field proudly carrying the trophies. But learning that Marian's mount exceeded by a fraction the measurements for the pony class (her mount stood 14.3 hands, and the maximum for the pony class was 14.2 hands) he made her march back and return the ribbon.

In October Gaynor opened the city's budget exhibit on lower Broadway with a speech in which he said that the object of all free government is "to enlist the attention of all citizens who hammer the anvil and pay the bills. There is a good deal said about the taxpayers, and there is no fault to be found with that. But I began thirty years ago to say 'rent-payers and taxpayers.' There would be no taxpayers if there were no rent-payers. So that those who pay the taxes haven't all the say by a long shot. Those who pay rent have as much to say."

Most people, he went on, expected the city's annual expenditures to decrease, "but I am not going to humbug you. The budget will be increased right along. . . . Some persons point to what we spent twenty-five years ago as compared with what is now spent by the city. A comparison indeed! We are growing. It costs more for your family as it grows. I have found that out, and it will keep costing me more until I get them all married off. Criticize as much as you want to, but . . . first find out something about the city government and the facts."

Noticing a chart with a legend saying there was no merit in saving money "squeezed from the bodies of men and women," Gaynor told Charities Commissioner Drummond, who was responsible for the chart, "Yes, but you must remember that taxes are squeezed from men and women, too."

Gaynor liked books and people (when they were not being hypercritical) about interchangeably, and his hold on the "submerged nine-tenths" of the population (as sociologists phrased it) was demonstrated strikingly when he reviewed the city's first Columbus Day parade from a stand at Columbus Circle. He had turned down a request for city funds to finance the celebration, whereupon a citizens' committee had raised all the money required. Thirty thousand marchers paraded, and Gaynor was kept busy doffing his hat in acknowledgment of the salutes.

On the opposite side of the circle spectators were held back by police. During a gap in the parade an old Italian fiddler darted across to the mayor's stand, and when a policeman moved to hustle him back, Gaynor called out, "What kind of a policeman are you? Leave him alone." The fiddler scratched out a tune and Gaynor tossed him a quarter. The other dignitaries on the stand followed suit, and the crowd cheered as the old man scrambled after the coins.

Another gap between the marching contingents occurring, a young chap standing on a pile of lumber yelled, "Let's go across and say how-de-do to the mayor!" The crowd surged forward, broke through the police line and swarmed around the reviewing stand. Reaching down and shaking hands, Gaynor said over and over, "I'm glad to see you," and to the men around him, "This is the best part of the parade."

"Viva Gaynor!" cried a man with a green velvet collar.

"Three cheers for the mayor!" echoed the chairman of the arrangements committee, and the cheers were given. Then, a band approaching, the crowd moved back quickly to the opposite side of the circle.

The next day the mayor addressed twelve hundred boys of "School City"—pupils at P.S. No. 114, at Oliver and Oak streets—and told them the ballot needed reforming, because "the big blanket ballot used in this state has a tendency to make the voter cast a straight party ticket." Upon Frank Perizzo being installed as mayor of "School City," Gaynor urged him not to lose heart if he found his popularity evaporating after being in office a while.

That Gaynor's "good days" were occurring more frequently was indicated by his remarks as he approved a bill giving women teachers equal pay with men. The harshest sort of criticism was being aimed at him for signing the bill, he told the delegation of women teachers, but that only reminded him of the big man whose little wife used to slap his face in public. When people asked why he let her, he said, "It doesn't hurt me at all, and it pleases Mary, so why shouldn't I let her have her way?"

Whether Gaynor had in mind the epithets being thrown at him by fusion members of his administration he did not say. A local election—for sheriff, surrogate, aldermen, and other minor officials—was coming up, and Prendergast and Mitchel were excoriating Gaynor and his appointees. Alluding to a statement made by Gaynor, Mitchel told a Carnegie Hall rally:

"I know there is a measure of respect due to a man who occupies the great office of mayor of the city. I know there is a measure of respect due to his years from a man of my years. But there are times when courtesy, good taste, and respect must be thrown aside in the interest of the people, and when a lie is deliberately uttered for the purpose of deceiving the people that lie must be nailed!"

Prendergast riddled most of Gaynor's appointments. Parks Commissioner Stover, he said, hadn't the brains to run a peanut stand, while the "mudlike lucidity" of some of the opinions written by Corporation Counsel Watson had to be read to be believed. McAneny was less bitter in his speeches, but he attacked the mayor's erratic course on the subways issue.

Throughout the campaign the only cool head seemed to be Gaynor's. The day after Mitchel's outburst at Carnegie Hall, the mayor waited forty-five minutes for his colleagues to show up at a Board of Estimate hearing. Then he observed that he had noticed in the newspaper that morning "that my associates were out late last night abusing me. I guess they haven't recovered from their efforts. Well, I can't wait any longer; I have something else to do in the way of official duties." And he adjourned the meeting.

About that time he gave his views in a symposium on what would happen if everybody told the truth for twenty-four hours. He said:

"It would produce a greater shock than an earthquake and possibly do more damage. Everyone would think, as now, that everyone was lying, and act accordingly. And you can see what mischief that would make!"

Critics ceased from troubling on the day the mayor attended the opening of the 1911 baseball world series at the Polo Grounds and saw the New York Giants down the Philadelphia Athletics, 4 to 3. As he came down the steps of the elevated, on arriving at the ball park, Gaynor encountered a group of newsboys, and taking one, Charlie Speranza, by the hand, he invited him to be a guest at the game. Given a front seat, the boy became frightened by the attention he was getting and retreated to a place found for him in the upper tiers. Gaynor grew so excited by the game he could hardly speak.

"Never saw anything like it!" he exclaimed. "Did you? I've seen some places where there was excitement, but nothing like this. I couldn't yell, because the commissioner of bridges took me to see all the bridges this morning, and it left my defective windpipe without a yell in it. I've a good notion to go over to Philadelphia tomorrow and see the game there. No, I can't, either; the Board of Estimate meets and I can't get away."

A sad event for the mayor and City Hall generally was the death of the little dog Spot, a mongrel that had made friends with Gaynor on the Brooklyn Bridge and had been adopted as the mascot of City Hall. Spot ate a cigarette snatched from the hand of an alderman who was petting him, and it proved fatal. Gaynor stayed in his office an hour after his usual quitting time to watch over Spot, and when the dog died he was much affected.

Another private grief was the death of the mayor's St. James crony, "Captain" DeMott. One bitter night DeMott was found half frozen in the roadside near Deepwells. Carried there, he died, and Gaynor paid for his burial in the village churchyard beside his wife. Later he erected a gravestone with an inscription reading: "Whatever God's will of me, may I be content."

As the year neared its close Gaynor's letters seemed to mirror a gentler mood than had been his for some time past. To a young Manhattan woman he wrote gallantly:

"I hope you will not be offended if I say that your handwriting is uninviting. I do love to see ladies write in a fine handwriting. It is more of an accomplishment in a young lady than a knowledge of chemistry."

A friend, Mrs. Charlotte Errani, of South Orange, New Jersey, got the jocose inquiry:

"What is the name of the 'old pelican' you asked me to appoint to the Board of Education? I think there is a vacancy coming on. Is she a loyal woman? Does she stand by her husband? Or has she any husband?"

Not so humorous but just as succinctly all-sufficient was the mayor's letter to George Frederick Alberga, of Manhattan:

"Dear Sir: I am very glad to receive your letter and your poem. The poem is very fine but your advice is very bad."

Gaynor was highly amused when he was asked to decide a newspaper contest on "How to Boil an Egg." He gave his decision with a will:

"And so I am to decide this great question, how to cook an egg and how long to cook it? First you must get the egg, a fresh egg. But where are you going to get it? That is the most difficult part of the question. It is a hard job. Call in someone else to decide that. Consult the hens. Hens sing in the laying season, which some people seem to doubt. If you can get the egg while the hen is singing you will be sure it is fresh. And then about cooking it. I see you have brought it down simply to a question of boiling it. How to boil it? I decide that you can only boil it in boiling water. And how long? Why, that is easy to decide—as long as you like. If you want it as hard as a bullet, boil it thirty minutes. If you want it nice and soft, as soft as the pates of some people, you can only boil it a little while. On that head I decide in favor of the little girl who answered my question in school. She said that it would take six minutes—by which she meant that from the time she went to get the egg until she took it out of the pan cooked, six minutes would elapse. She was entirely right. And I suppose she also meant that you would put your egg in the water before the water boiled, and let the water heat and begin to boil with the egg in it. I decided that she was right in that also. If you let the water boil, and then throw the egg in, the shock is too great for the egg. You see I know a good deal about eggs and cooking eggs. I am just the right one to decide the egg question."

The mayor heartily approved a suggestion advanced by Professor Henry Fairfield Osborn, of the Museum of Natural History, that nature study should not be dropped from the curriculum of the public schools.

"I am very much struck with one remark you make," the mayor wrote, "that hundreds of thousands of our children never see a living wild animal or bird. But I have several times gone much further than that. There are a very large number of people in this great city, larger than most people have any idea of, who have never seen a calf or a pig. We provide wild animals for them to look at, but not domestic animals. If I had my way we would have domestic animals for the people here to see. I am certain that a sow with a litter of pigs would be more intensely interesting to most people than any wild animal. And cow and calf, mare and colt, and so on, would also be most interesting. Is there any natural sight so interesting as a litter of pigs nursing?"

In addressing four hundred Methodist ministers in December of 1911 he discussed sectarianism, the Bible, sociology, intemperance, and clerical sensationalism, among other things. Although from the publicity received by clergymen who opposed him it sometimes seemed that Gaynor had no friends in the city's pulpits, the opposite was true. Many clergymen of many churches were among his outspoken supporters, and when he appeared before the Methodist preachers he received an ovation. His topic was, "Is the Ministry Helpful to Good Government?" and his answer emphatically was that it did help.

"And I include all denominations," he added, "excluding a minister here and there who has not the love of Jesus in his heart. You Methodist ministers have always been helpful to good government. I don't mean that you have dabbled in politics. But whenever a great moral issue comes up you are always ready to aid it. . . .

"In years gone by a good many of us have been struggling to magnify the differences in the denominations. Now we are trying to minimize them. Dear me! The Bible is exactly the same in the original. There is only one Bible. The difference is in the translations. I can think of only one great difference, and that is between 'penance' and 'repentance.' We are all trying to do right, and we are all just as God made us. If some of you ministers said things as plain as Jesus did you would have headlines in the newspapers bigger than have been seen so far. He did not hesitate to say, 'Ye generation of vipers' and 'Ye whited sepulchers.' . . .

"I suppose you preachers have some discouraging times. If I

had the right to advise you I would say do not be discouraged. You can not do everything. Leave something for those who come after you. Some people try to stop a man overnight from drinking a glass of liquor. Some have nothing in their heads but vice. I don't know why. . . . We have to deal with all things, but we have to do it in an orderly way."

That year 1911 also produced an exchange of letters between Mayor Gaynor and a clergyman which was as much talked about, argued, laughed over, and praised as any single letter the mayor wrote. It concerned the vexatious subject of beards. One day the mayor picked out of his tray of "incoming" letters the following piteous appeal written by the Rev. Basil N. Kerbawy, pastor of St. Nicholas Greek Orthodox Church in Brooklyn:

"Most Honored Sir: I want to know if it is a crime to wear a beard? I suppose this may appear to be a foolish question to you, but to me it means a great deal. I am the pastor of the St. Nicholas Greek Orthodox Church in Pacific Street, and my profession calls for the wearing of a beard. When I go out on the street the boys and young men mistake me for a Jewish rabbi and insult and assault me.

"They often throw decayed vegetables at me. If I were a rabbi would that be an excuse for loafers to assault and insult me? I am a citizen, and as such should be protected from assault.

"I have borne the insults and assaults patiently up to last Saturday night, when an incident occurred that made me lose all patience. I was alighting from a car at 73rd st. and 13th avenue, Brooklyn, when a little loafer hit me with a decayed vegetable, which I believe was a more than ripe tomato. This exhausted my patience. I went for the lad, who, luckily for him, escaped.

"Hoping that you will do what you can for me and gain for me the protection I deserve, I am, sir, very respectfully, Basil N. Kerbawy."

This desperate appeal received Mayor Gaynor's immediate attention, and he replied:

"Reverend and Dear Sir: Your letter informing me that as you walk about the city visiting the homes of your parishioners people apply opprobrious names to you, and throw empty cans and rubbish at you, is at hand. You ask me, 'Is it a crime in the city of New York to wear a beard?' No, it is not. I wear one myself and nobody ever takes any notice of it. How is it they take notice of your beard? Have you trimmed it in some peculiar way, contrary to the Scriptures? For you know the Scriptures say, 'Ye shall not round the

OPEN FOR ENGAGEMENTS
Mayor Gaynor did not enroll under any party emblem at the primaries.

Dec. 7, 1911

corners of your beards, neither shalt thou mar the corners of thy beard.' Yes, if they assault you, and throw cans at you, you have a right to defend yourself to the last extremity; but if you find it necessary I will have a detective go around with you for a few days until we arrest some of those who are wronging you. Are you certain that it is your beard which is the cause of the trouble?"

In almost the same breath, the mayor dictated a philosophical disavowal of the numerous persons named "Gaynor" who were claiming kinship. In answer to a newspaper query from Saginaw, Michigan, the mayor wrote conclusively:

"Dear Mr. Swart: The woman whom you mention is not my

niece. I have no nieces anywhere. Of late years there has been a growing number of people who claim to be my nieces, nephews, uncles, aunts, etc. I do not see what is the matter with them. Maybe someday they will all be disowning me."

The year ended with the mayor handing a Christmas present to that hardy band of music devotees, the standees at the Metropolitan Opera House. The gift was in the form of Gaynor's approval of an amendment to the city ordinance regulating theaters, exempting the Met from the restrictions on the number of standees allowed.

And the *New York Tribune*, one of the mayor's most constant critics, was favored by a ray of good humor from the sunny soul at City Hall in the form of New Year's musings, summed up:

"We must have a little philosophy in us, and then we are not disturbed by what mean people say or do."

ONE WAY TO END A GARBAGE STRIKE

———————◼•◯•◼———————

> *For those who are entering upon the greatest*
> *of all struggles must not shrink, but must be*
> *ready to endure stripes.*
>
> ——EPICTETUS

Dᴜʀɪɴɢ ᴛʜᴇ ᴀʟᴛᴇʀɴᴀᴛᴇ sᴘᴇʟʟs of fine and stormy weather that marked 1911 Mayor Gaynor had ridden out one gale that centered upon what a later generation of sociologists would term his "labor relations." These he coped with, as he coped with every issue, in his own way. As for his lifelong attitude, it might be called "prolabor," but "propublic" more. And the law was the law, to be respected and observed by both sides in any labor dispute. In a letter to union officials he had put his feeling about supporting organized labor with customary forcefulness:

"My views about union labor are too well known to be repeated at this time. If you have kept track of things you must know that. I do not believe in people beginning to talk about how much they are in favor of union labor about election time. Acts count for more than words. Such talk when an election is coming is cheap."

In longhand he had added to this typed communication:

"Some people are great friends of labor on one day of the year, namely, election day."

From his early days as a lawyer, and all through his tenure as a judge, Gaynor had shown sympathy with labor in its struggle to achieve equable treatment. His basic philosophy on the subject he expressed in the phrase "distributive justice." He explained this once to a group of bankers:

371

"The prosperity of a country does not depend wholly on the total product of the country. It depends even more largely on a just distribution of that product among all who contributed by their work to produce it, whether the work was mental or physical. I should define distributive justice as the highest production the community is capable of consistent with the mental, moral, and physical health and growth of its members, accompanied by a just distribution of the total product among those who produce it. I do not mean by that share and share alike. I think when we are all being paid alike each one of us would do just as little as we could, wouldn't we? All ambition and emulation would be gone. The mother of excellence is competition. I mean distribution according to the capacity of each, whether that capacity be mental or physical or both. Distributive justice also means that those engaged in the production shall be otherwise fairly dealt with—that they shall not be forced to work an undue number of hours, that they have proper machinery, and of all things that they be paid for the injuries which they receive in their work . . . especially from the dangerous machinery of our times. Until you have distributive justice you will not have a contented society."

Gaynor actively favored child-labor laws, workmen's compensation, and laws regulating the working hours of women and those engaged in hazardous occupations. In a celebrated letter to the mayor of Columbus, Ohio, he endorsed the principle of universal old-age pensions, saying:

"Here in this city we are empowered at our discretion to retire on an old-age pension all old persons who have been in the city employment for thirty years. We also have old-age pensions for several of our departments. For example, our street cleaners. . . . And we are soon to have such a law for all our city employees. Why should not the same rule apply to all industrial workers? . . . Distributive justice requires that it shall come to pass. The old workers should not be turned out to die or live in distress or go to the poorhouse, nor should the maimed and hurt."

This viewpoint was so far in advance of even enlightened public opinion at the time that Gaynor was constantly called a "radical"; he often recalled the time when, for advocating such measures, he had been called a socialist and an anarchist—"especially by newspapers that did not know what socialism was." Inherently conservative, Gaynor was always receptive to fresh ideas. He refused to be fettered by the past when a better way was pointed out, and people who worshiped the past simply because it was old aroused his scorn. As far back as 1896 he had told the Brooklyn Educational Association:

"We may get instruction from the past, to a great extent, as to what we should avoid, and to some extent as to what we should follow; but the argument that those who have gone before us must have been wiser than we are and that what is ancient must be right, which we hear constantly, is absurd. No one correctly informed as to the past can take a morose or desponding view of the present. Has not mankind advanced from the beginning? As Sidney Smith said to those who were always appealing to the ancients, 'We are the ancients'; and so we are, for the human race grows older all the time."

Socialism Gaynor considered visionary and based on fallacious reasoning, but the right of socialists to propagate their doctrine by all peaceful means he defended strictly. To a woman who was exercised about the inflammatory street orators he wrote counseling:

"Free speech is best. Let them say what they like. If they say something good it will have wings. If they say something worthless it will fall for lack of wings."

During his first year in office the mayor had been confronted with several labor disputes, in the course of which he enunciated the policy of his administration, which was to preserve order in the streets while remaining absolutely neutral. This in itself was in effect prolabor, because the police had notoriously been employed to protect the interests of employers. When the express-wagon drivers struck (for an eleven-hour working day, in place of the twelve and sixteen hours they had been working), Gaynor notified the companies that the police would "preserve the peace and prevent violence, [but] of course you are aware that by law they can not favor either side to the strike."

He tried to reduce the strong-arm tactics widely used against strikers by calling in the badges of some thirteen hundred special policemen—men sworn in as city policemen, and then hired out to private employers. Such quasi-official peace officers had been extensively used against strikers, and for this reason among others Gaynor took steps to suppress the whole system, except for a few special guards farmed out to banks. In letter after letter to prominent employers, Gaynor went to great pains to explain the reasons for his

action, which was widely misunderstood and criticized. He told
A. Sulka, of the haberdashery firm, for instance:

"It is contrary to the first principles of government to put a
public officer in the pay and under the command of private individuals. If such a special policeman should commit an unlawful
battery against a person, at the instance of his employer (and of
course he would have to obey the orders of those who paid him), the
city, and not the employer, would be liable for damages."

In the express drivers' strike, as in a simultaneous walkout by
taxicab drivers, Gaynor did finally consent to act as an intermediary
between the parties, for the purpose of bringing them together
only; and in each case, when an agreement was reached, he saw to it
that it was lived up to scrupulously by both sides.

Bias against labor unions he combated steadily. A Connecticut
attorney was lectured:

"Your letter shows a very great hostility to labor. I share no
such hostility. Labor has as much right to organize as capital has.
What would be the condition of labor today had it never organized
and asserted its rights?"

An alarmed employer in Battle Creek, Michigan, was given an
even more pointed rejoinder:

"You display a most lamentable lack of knowledge of the facts
for an intelligent man. . . . I fear you are a mere hater of workmen
who try to organize for their own protection. I notice that your company is well organized."

But striking for frivolous reasons, and strikes against the
public welfare, Gaynor refused to countenance. This he made plain
when the engineers on the municipal ferryboats agitated against the
dismissal of the service's chief engineer, who had been suspended,
tried, and discharged for cause by regular civil service procedure.
The engineers demanded that Mayor Gaynor review the case, and
sent a delegation to City Hall to back up their demand. Unluckily
for them, while they waited in the anteroom they talked truculently
about striking unless they got satisfaction. Word of this was relayed to Gaynor, and when the group was finally ushered into the
mayor's office he was in an equally truculent mood. The slightest hint
of attempted coercion caused Gaynor to bristle, and he listened to
the delegation coldly. Then he told them that their grievance would
be looked into, but only in due order.

"Are you under the impression that I have nothing else to do
except this one thing?" he asked, looking them in the eye. "It is
stated to me by persons who heard you that your coming to me is

under threat of a strike. Now, if that is so, go back and strike. There will not be one of you who strikes who will ever be employed by the city again while I am here as mayor. If you have left a paper with me with a grievance in it, it is going to be looked into. But as for this strike, you should go ahead and strike right now if you want to and not bother me, and then I will not look into the thing at all. If you want me to look into it, just go away."

When the leader interposed that he had been promised a decision, Gaynor exploded:

"I shall take up the case as soon as I can, and I am not going to have you coming here while I am doing it."

The chief engineer, he went on, had been tried and dismissed by "an orderly and legal proceeding, and it is the height of impudence for anyone to interfere with that procedure except in a legal manner. But if you tell me there has been some mistake or inadvertence by the commissioner of docks, I am willing in the interests of justice to review the case. If you are not satisfied with that, all I can say to you is 'good day.' "

The delegation withdrew muttering, and four days later received the mayor's report saying:

"The engineer was tried for neglect of duty and dismissed. This was a regular, legal, and orderly procedure, and he has redress in the courts if any injustice was done to him. I find that no injustice was done to him. If it be true that you have made statements that unless he be restored you will strike, then you are all guilty of insubordination and should be dismissed from the city service. I shall have Commissioner Tomkins inquire into that matter. If you want to strike, do so just as quick as you like. It is well for you to understand that you are employees of the City of New York, with the shortest hours and the highest pay known in this country, and that you are subject to the laws and regulations which exist for the government of the city and its employees. Anything counter to these laws and regulations on your part is insubordination, which will not be tolerated, and we do not propose to tolerate it."

Under civil service rules, insubordination was grounds for dismissal; and nobody doubted that Mayor Gaynor, unpledged and unbossed, with a lifetime reputation of meaning just what he said, would if necessary execute the law to the letter.

There was no ferry strike.

A more serious challenge to the public welfare arose in the autumn of 1911. Collection of the city's refuse—ashes and garbage

—had been the subject of chronic complaints, and in an attempt to minimize the discomfort caused by the messy operation the street cleaning department had resorted to making the collections at night, when the streets were comparatively empty and there were few pedestrians to be showered with clouds of dust from the ash cans. The arrangement was not to the liking of the drivers of the dump-carts, and light-sleeping householders were annoyed by the clatter of the cans on the sidewalk.

Gaynor tried to counteract the complaints of the latter by a campaign of letter writing. Mrs. W. N. Hogenkamp, who lived at 113 West 131st Street, was hardly mollified when she ripped open an envelope from City Hall and read:

"Dear Madam: When they used to collect the ashes and gar-bage in the day time I received innumerable complaints of the ashes flying in people's faces and of the disagreeable smells. For that reason we adopted the method of collecting them at night. Now you ask me to go back to the day collection. We have no intention of doing so. I am wholly unable to understand how the removal can keep you awake at night. In my block—and there is a large club immediately opposite my house—the wagons are not present more than five, or at the outside ten minutes, and they make very little noise at that. I am very sorry if you are disturbed, but there is no way for me to do away with the removal of ashes and garbage."

The protest lodged by J. C. Boody, of Lincoln Place, Brook-lyn, was dealt with more tersely:

"Your letter is at hand, and I make no complaint of its terrible contents. May I say to you, however, that the carts can not be in front of your place as long as fifteen minutes each night."

Early in July rumblings of rebellion among the dumpcart drivers and collectors became audible and Gaynor swung into action. He wrote officially to Edwards, the street cleaning commissioner, as follows:

"It is said that a few men are fomenting discontent and trying to bring on what is called a strike. If any of the employees of the department strike, strike their names from the rolls immediately and never take them back. The city pays its employees well, and trusts them well, but the city will know how to protect itself against any effort of coercion. We are even now trying to get a pension law for the department.* You will be able to get all the men needed; and

---

* Shortly after the date of this letter the law was passed and a pension system established for the department.

remember that if the civil service list should be exhausted you may employ whom you see fit. I have received some letters complaining of the removal of garbage at night, which are evidently inspired by employees of the department. Let it be understood thoroughly that such removal is to be continued."

An uneasy quiet succeeded this ultimatum until Wednesday, November 8, when a delegation headed by William H. Ashton, of the International Teamsters Union, called on Gaynor and warned that a strike would be called forthwith unless he rescinded the order that the streets be cleared of refuse and garbage before daybreak. The mayor listened and said "No." Then he dictated a new directive to Commissioner Edwards:

"In regard to the threatened strike of the drivers and garbage collectors of your department, be so good as to notify them at once by general order to strike just as soon as they see fit. And see to it that not one of the drivers gets back into city employment again. We can get along without them. It will inconvenience the householders for a few days, but they will stand it patiently. Let the contract system be resorted to if necessary. The city pays the men of your department the highest wages for the shortest hours; and in addition a pension law was passed for them. If they think they can make the city conform to their dictation by striking they will find themselves grievously mistaken. The city's business has to be done as the charter prescribes, and no strike can force it to be done in any other way. The city is not in the position of a private employer, and able to make any terms with its employees it sees fit."

This letter was read to the drivers and collectors at roll call that night and again the next morning. Except for about a hundred men, all walked out—about twenty-five hundred. The press was told by their business agent, George Prescott, that the real reason for the men's aversion to handling garbage at night was that it was un-American—"it's a Parisian innovation."

In accordance with Gaynor's instructions, on Thursday Edwards began to hire temporary replacements, the charter permitting the city to employ persons not on the civil service lists for a maximum of three days. On the lists there were about a hundred men qualified as drivers, but there were seven thousand listed as laborers, a very close classification. In groups, these were given a simple test to demonstrate that they could drive a horse, and before nightfall two thousand had qualified. Arrangements were made to give them a modified oral examination that would meet civil service requirements, and four thousand more were summoned to be tested the next day.

Meanwhile, the refuse began to stack up in the streets, along fashionable avenues and in ghetto alleys alike. A few collection carts remained out, escorted by police, and violence was forecast. The next day it erupted. Bricks were hurled from rooftops onto the carts and one driver was killed. There were many fights between strikers and their sympathizers and the police. Men hired in nearby cities to replace strikers began to pour in and were bedded down in the department stables. The weather turned warm and health department inspectors warned of an imminent threat of disease from the heaps of moldering vegetables and other noxious rubbish, and the newspapers flaunted in bold type the wording of the penal code that made it a misdemeanor to commit any act "injurious to the public health . . . or for the perversion or obstruction . . . of the due administration of the law."

In response to questions, Mayor Gaynor made his stand perfectly clear:

"The city officials are not trying to 'break' any 'strike.' The drivers of the ash and garbage wagons have quit their jobs and their places are being filled by others. They are not to be taken back. There is a great misunderstanding on this head. The commissioner could not take them back if he wanted to. He can employ such men only from the civil service list. When men in the city departments quit they are struck from the payroll and their employment by the city is at an end. Their places then have to be filled from the civil service lists. None of these men can ever be employed by the city again unless they undergo civil service examinations and get on the eligible list again. That the civil service board would ever permit them to get on the list again is not conceivable. None of them will get back."

Prescott, the strikers' spokesman, softened his stand that day to the extent of volunteering the information that the men might consent to work at night during the summer, but never in the winter. He appealed to the public to repudiate the mayor and "end this madness." Gaynor stuck by the law.

The next day, Saturday, garbage collection almost ceased. The normal daily haul in Manhattan was six thousand cartloads; that day five hundred and six loads were chalked up, and at 5 P.M. all work was suspended, after a boy had been killed by a flying brick. Violence broke out sporadically more or less all over town. Ashton, the Teamsters leader, sent the mayor a conciliatory letter asking him to arbitrate. This was forwarded to Gaynor at his home, since he had not come to City Hall that day. The letter was ignored.

On Sunday the outlook seemed ominous, and reports circulated that the National Guard was to be called out to quell rioting. A bomb was hurled into a squad of policemen and two men were injured. Ashton told the strikers that the mayor probably would mediate the strike in the next day or two.

Instead, on Monday two thousand men reported for work and the heaped-up refuse on the sidewalks began to diminish. Outside of occasional stone throwing there was no violence. Gaynor walked through the East Side and expressed satisfaction at the progress being made and appreciation of the cooperative spirit of the people. The weather had turned cold again, and the health menace was lessened.

Ashton appeared at City Hall that day but Gaynor refused to see him. Instead, he sent word:

"Tell Ashton I don't want to see him and never want to have anything to do with him. The drivers who quit work are not in the employ of the city. The department is being reorganized. It may take considerable time, and I am certain the householders of the city will be patient. The breaking in of the new men is no easy job, but it has to be done."

Ashton left in a rage, threatening to bring about a general strike that would "tie up everything in New York City." But the Teamsters executive council declined to sanction such action, and that day, Tuesday, four thousand men were at work clearing away the tons of accumulated rubbish. Six days after the start of the walkout the movement collapsed, and the next day street cleaning operations were back at normal.

Gaynor was bitter about the episode. He had been especially irritated by the rumor that the military was being appealed to. He wrote to a businessman who in the midst of the turmoil had made some rather silly suggestions:

"Your letter is in error in some particulars. The men who quit work . . . are not two-thirds non-citizens as you state. On the contrary, they are all citizens either by birth or naturalization. So your advice to deport them has no foundation. Nor do I intend to call out the military. This is not a government of military force. It is a free government. We call out the military only in case of dire necessity, that is to say, when the regular civil authorities are unable to put down tumult. Do you not understand this? I do not like to have people write me to call out the militia and shoot people down. A mayor of New York would have to forget himself to do a thing like that except in the last extremity. I hope the time is far distant when it will be necessary to call out troops to shoot anyone down. Ours is a government of law, and the military power has to keep its hands off until the regular agencies of civil government are unable to preserve order."

As soon as the strike ended, pressure was brought to bear on Edwards and Gaynor to take the strikers back. A delegation of aldermen made a strong appeal for reinstatement. They got no satisfaction. Gaynor told them:

"In the first place I would not do it if I could, and in the second place it so happens that I can not do it. Those who have been taken on from the civil service list to fill the deserted places can not be discharged except according to the law, which you know as well as I do —that is to say, they have to be brought up on charges and allowed an opportunity to explain. The men that we have taken on have been guilty of nothing. On the contrary, they have saved the city. And the men who are out are out. I know of no way by which I could take them back if I wanted to, and I am very certain that I do not want to. Now that is the whole case, and I will not add a word to it."

He told Monsignor John J. Barrett of Brooklyn that the garbage men "just quit. It was one of the meanest things I ever knew, especially after what I had done for working people in their strikes and other ways. They seem to be absolutely without gratitude or decency."

In strict compliance with the law, notices were posted that the strikers would be given individual hearings on the charge of failure to report for work, and their formal dismissal would follow. Edwards was besieged by appeals, but in the end nearly eighteen hundred were let out permanently. Privately, Gaynor rebuked Edwards for giving out "foolish interviews" on the subject, and reminded him that "the work of reorganization should be done quietly and not through the newspapers."

The mayor's sense of outrage did not grow less with the passage of time. Months afterward he was sending out letters similar to these:

"Your leaving the stable and quitting work was an act of

SITTING TIGHT
Mayor Gaynor—You can't scare me!   *Nov.* 15, 1911

treachery on your part. I guaranteed protection to every one of you. I do not wish to have anything to do with you."

And to the wife of a striker:

"Your husband quit work without any cause whatever and I can do nothing for him. He treated the city very shabbily."

The notion that one should not treat "the city"—that is, the public, the entire community—shabbily was novel then to some of its employees, and remains novel still.

A year later James Creelman, whom Gaynor had made chairman of the Civil Service Commission, sent the mayor a query that mirrored Gaynor's abiding sense of betrayal of the city's welfare by the street cleaners. Under civil service rules, the dismissed men were becoming eligible for reexamination and placing on the eligible lists, and Creelman desired guidance as to the policy to be followed in considering such applications. His letter read:

"I would not trouble you in the matter were it not for the fact that this question involves something deeper than mere disobedience. When 1,872 public employees, acting in concert, refuse to do their lawful duty, with the deliberate purpose to paralyze the city government in performing a function necessary to the health and comfort of the public, such conduct has the character of a mutiny. These employees were the servants and subordinates of the community as a whole, and the obvious purpose of their refusal to work was to create a condition of things so perilous to the public safety that the municipal government might be expected to surrender its authority to direct the conditions of their work."

The Civil Service Reform Association in this instance voted the mayor a resolution of gratitude for handling the crisis efficiently, "all within the civil service rules." But to Gaynor the demonstration of the supremacy of the community's interest and welfare was the paramount victory. In reply to a question put some time later by the *Tribune*, he hinted obliquely at the satisfaction he drew from having vindicated this principle. The *Tribune*'s question was: "What is your idea of heaven?" Gaynor's reply:

"Thus far in my life I have been too busy to try to get a fixed idea of what heaven is. Just now I have no wish for anything at all except to do all I can for the people of the City of New York. I suppose that if I do my best it will be recognized in heaven in some way, and that is entirely satisfactory to me."

SO THIS IS THE WHITE HOUSE

*To make everyone as good as we think
we are is a hard job.*

—GAYNOR

THE MAYOR OF NEW YORK who would please everybody had not materialized in William J. Gaynor, though that was what he, like his predecessors and successors, was clearly supposed to be. Hot or cold, he felt the blast of the citizenry's indignation over the fact that things were as they were, and not as each individual fancied they ought to be. Had you a gripe or a grouse? Write to Gaynor, was the answer in the years from 1910 on.

One cold winter day, on arriving at City Hall on foot after a brisk stroll across the bridge, the mayor noticed a rear door was closed. He called a janitor and ordered all doors to be kept open to insure proper ventilation. Then he retired to his own office (where he had had installed an oversize steam radiator, in place of the mere fireplace Mayor McClellan had relied on) and dictated a word of hearty advice to a Brooklyn complainant, who had written *his* grouse, as follows:

"Your letter complaining that the streetcars are not heated sufficiently to keep you from freezing to death, and asking me to see that they are heated, is at hand. It is my opinion that the heat in the cars most of the time makes them very disagreeable and unhealthful. So far as I am concerned, I wish they were not heated at all. Your statement that at least five thousand persons die every year from cold in the streetcars seems to me a great exaggeration. Suppose you stay out of the cars and walk back and forth for a month. I will warrant that at the end of that time you will not care much about heat in the cars, and that moreover you will not feel like finding fault with everybody and everything in the world."

If 1910 was Mayor Gaynor's year of triumph and tragedy, 1912 was to prove his year of greatest distress and defeat. The trouble would center in his administration of the police department. Since installing Waldo as commissioner, the mayor had virtually been running the police force himself. Waldo was a subordinate completely to his liking—honest, capable, and prepared to take orders unquestioningly and never act on his own initiative. Because of his enormous credulity, the new commissioner quickly came to be regarded in the force as a sort of glorified Boy Scout, running the mayor's errands and ready to believe any cock-and-bull story; but to Gaynor, to whom a total regeneration of the police was a cherished objective, Waldo was in every way admirable.

The year started with the mayor cracking down on the use of plainclothesmen as decoys for ensnaring "wayward women," which was the mayor's compassionate term for prostitutes. These men were not detectives, but patrolmen out of uniform, and Gaynor had forbidden their further use. He was incensed, therefore, when an auditing of the department's bills disclosed that his order was being ignored. To Comptroller Prendergast he wrote vigorously:

"I have this day issued an order to the police department forbidding that any member of the department should take women into hotels or rooms and have them strip or expose themselves immorally, or that any member of the force should be ordered to do the like. I have heretofore given oral instructions to the same effect, but they seem not to have been understood or carried out. There will be no more bills like the present ones showing that abuse. As for sending men into gambling houses, I suppose that is necessary. It does not present the same question of decency and morals which the sending of men with women into private rooms does. The bills for going into gambling houses and expending money there up to a certain point should be paid. I have talked with the police commissioner about it, and I do not quite see how we can get along without that kind of evidence. I am returning the bills herewith by messenger."

Then in a handwritten postscript he added, in order to be perfectly fair:

"Maybe you should pay the other bills with the consideration that they cease to come on."

Another misuse of the police—the detailing of numerous squads to weddings, receptions, and other private functions of a purely social nature—Gaynor was finding it harder to eliminate, and he was forced to write to Commissioner Waldo sternly:

"My attention is called to the statement in several newspapers here that policemen, and even a large number of policemen—some newspapers saying as many as 69—attended the Peace Dinner by your direction last Saturday night at the Waldorf-Astoria. Were any policemen sent to this dinner?

"I also saw it reported recently that the President [Taft] was given no police protection when he came to the city. Is this true, or did you furnish the head of the United States detective force the usual number of men? I have no doubt that both of these newspaper statements are false, but I prefer to have a record made of the matter. I particularly do not wish to have it belled all over the country that we sent policemen to stand over a dinner of gentlemen."

Nothing concerning the police department escaped the mayor's vigilance, and he resented the slightest implication that his reforms were not taking hold. Critics were brought up short with notes like the one fired back at a Dr. Eugene P. Hoyt, who had spoken about the "third degree" in vague but horrified language:

"Dear Sir: I shall read your interview, but I confess I do not know what the 'Third Degree' in the police department is. If you mean forcing people to give evidence against themselves, I can inform you that I permit no such thing in the police department, and that no such thing exists. I fear you are speaking of past years."

This tendency to accept conditions as they appeared to the mayor's intense inner vision, however discordant that might be with the way other people saw them, was becoming more and more pronounced in Gaynor, especially on his frequent "bad days."

But happier moods engaged the mayor, too, and during the opening months of 1912 he regained much of his former vitality, at least for short stretches of time. The dry cough still plagued him, but the paroxysms had stopped, and his tongue was being successfully drilled to overcome the difficulties in clear articulation. Occasionally Gaynor now made a speech, with good effect, although he confessed to a friend that he was forced "to pay the penalty for several days" after each effort.

One address he gave with satisfaction was at the dinner of the city's engineering staff on January 6. He was astonished to see so many assembled—four hundred and eighty of them—and exclaimed in mock dismay, "Now the taxpayers must see where the money goes!" He had brought along a thick, heavy, black book, and holding it up, explained:

"I have here Julius Frontius' 'History of the Roman Waterworks,' which I picked up this afternoon. They did some things in those days the same as we do now, only I think we do them better. They had their troubles, too, with contractors, and so on. There is here a letter to the governor of Saldae, explaining the recall of an engineer named Nonius Datus, who reported that everything connected with the building of an aqueduct through the mountains had gone wrong, and he blamed it on the contractors, just as we do today.

"On January 31 the tunnel under the Hudson River will be joined in the middle. On that date Waldo Smith [engineer in charge] will take the mayor, the water commissioner, and certain other officials through the tube, and it will be a great celebration. I don't mind," he addressed the chairman, "if on that day I do look down the neck of a bottle. I don't say that I'll drink, but I will look down the neck of a bottle. It will be a celebration worth remembering—the consummation of one of the greatest engineering feats in history."

On the appointed day the mayor, sheathed in oilskins and rubber boots, pulled the switch that set off the blast-through in the great tunnel at Storm King, and then, eleven hundred feet underground, standing in the aqueduct that would carry pure Catskill water to the city, he told a secret:

"After I was elected but before I took office a delegation headed by an engineer of repute waited on me. They declared it to be a demonstrated fact that no aqueduct could be built under the Hudson and that therefore water could not be obtained. I said to them if we could not get it under the river we would get it over. . . . The cross-section of this tunnel is seventeen feet. The largest Roman aqueduct, so far as I remember, was five feet by three. I say this for the benefit of those who are always saying that the days of the past were better than those of the present. These persons do not appreciate anything under their noses, but are always looking backward to find something better."

Gaynor's impatience with stand-patters, mossbacks, and old fogies came out when he went to Albany to address the state agricultural association in the Capitol:

"This country is not going to the dogs," he said. "We love to grumble and growl and like to hear people talk calamity, but things are not so bad after all. They are much better than when I was a boy."

Daily doses of astringent but salutary common sense were dished out in the flood of mail that crossed the mayor's desk. A Yonkers woman in quest of a husband was advised:

"Dear Madam: I regret to say that I do not know anyone to recommend to you as a husband. You can doubtless make a better selection than I can, as you know the kind of man you want. Of course it may be very hard to find him, but no harder for you than for me."

A man who resented his arrest for spitting on the Brooklyn Bridge got a promise and a scolding:

"I shall look into your case, but I could never understand why boys and men will go around spitting. Why should boys and men spit any more than girls and women? Did you ever think of that? What is the use of being so nasty?"

The suggestion of a Brooklyn innovator for thinning out the rush-hour crowds at Brooklyn Bridge met with no favor, the mayor advising:

"The only remedy for the congestion at the Brooklyn Bridge is more space, and more accommodation. . . . Your suggested remedy, namely, for the police to arrest those who crowd others, would not work, I fear. . . . I have very little faith in the police trying to make people observe good manners."

The mayor was cool, also, to the proposal advanced by Seth Low and others that water meters be installed in every household to discourage the waste of water. Gaynor felt that would merely discourage bathing, saying:

"If the heads of houses had to pay for water according to meter, they would be uneasy every time their wives and children took baths, for such is human nature. The result would be discomfort and uncleanliness."

Again the solution, he said, was not to use less water, but to provide an inexhaustible supply. To this logical inversion Seth Low had no reply.

Two letters that gave nationwide entertainment dealt with the question of growing vegetables all of one size, and with ways to balk chicken thieves.

A purchasing agent for the city informed the mayor of his chagrin when the Department of Charities rejected the carrots he sent them because they were of assorted sizes. Responded farmer Gaynor:

"I must say I deem the condition that the carrots be of one size as whimsical. What difference does it make whether they are of uniform size or not? They may look nicer, but will taste no better either to men or horses. You would have to have a good many acres of them to cull out any considerable number of the same size. But maybe they think there is some way of growing carrots all of the same size. And the condition that your new cabbages be white in the head is another extraordinary notion. New cabbages are rather green. Late cabbages get white in the head after a while. I fear those who rejected your vegetables never raised either cabbages or carrots or anything else. Try them again, and see what they say. How would it do if we send them all out on a farm for a year or so that they may learn at least the difference between their knee and their elbow about vegetables?"

The other complaint was from a Staten Island farmer, who wrote in positive fury demanding better protection against the raids on his chicken coop. He received the mayor's sympathy but little encouragement otherwise, in these words:

"My hen roost on Long Island has also been entered. You say there are sixty-five policemen in your precinct and demand more. Down my way there are only four constables in a territory about ten times as large as yours, with a population not much less. It is pretty hard to keep chicken thieves out of chicken roosts by policemen. However, I will see what can be done for you and your neighbors. Can you not induce your chickens to roost higher?"

Gaynor was amused when the farmer, a Scotsman, failed to see any humor in this suggestion and wrote back a scathing denunciation of the way affairs were administered in New York City.

Small wonder that a New York woman ("born on Washington Place") living in exile in Georgia wrote that she read her hometown newspaper enthusiastically to keep up with the sayings and doings of the mayor.

"He certainly is New York's sensible, common-sensible, big-minded grandfather, unruffledly taking care of the children all the time. His handling of the unruly and the foolish is a joy, and he handles! He'd make a President such as we have not had since Lincoln—better in some senses."

The mayor's letters were matched and even overmatched by his miscellaneous activities. Driving himself to regular weekend collapses, he touched all bases. Thus in January he ordered the license bureau to revoke the permits of dance studios that were teaching the new "ragtime" dances—the "turkey trot," the "bunny hug," the "dip," and the "grizzly bear." At the same time he conducted an effective campaign to clean up the city's employment agencies, which for years had operated as virtual procurement centers for houses of prostitution. He took time to apologize personally to a newsboy, Isidore Waltzer, whose photograph had been posted in the "rogues gallery" with the label "general thief," although he had never been convicted of any offense.

Then he was providing more public bathhouses at Coney Island, and carrying on a hard fight to break up a racket operated by the city's pawnshops, which refused to surrender to their rightful owners stolen articles that had been pledged by the thieves or a fence, unless the claimant paid the amount of the loan and interest. The law positively forbade this, the mayor reminded the police, the magistrates, the license bureau, and many of the victimized persons directly, and in time the practice was stamped out.

In between such activities, Gaynor toured the parks on Sundays and was heartened to see so many people at play in them. He gave his approval to the formation of a pedestrians' club with a distinguished membership, and challenged them to a walking match from New York to the eastern tip of Long Island, ninety miles away—a challenge that was not accepted.

In the conduct of the routine business of his job Gaynor ridiculed the rule laid down by the municipal explosives commission that the men who set off dynamite blasts must speak English. "Silly," said the mayor. "A regulation that is impossible, it seems to me; these blasters are generally foreigners." And he spurred along the chief magistrate's crackdown on smokers in the subway, observing that "some passengers insist on having partly smoked cigars between their fingers and in their mouths, and when spoken to defiantly say the cigar is not lighted. An unlighted cigar smells worse than a lighted one."

An attack on Parks Commissioner Stover, launched by Henry Bruere of the Bureau of Municipal Research, Gaynor fended off, saying in the injured tone and assuming the faraway gaze that often accompanied his blasts:

"I have nothing to say about Mr. Bruere because I do not deem him an honest reformer."

Gaynor would not desert a friend, although he found it difficult to overlook the shortcomings of some of his appointees. He insisted on taking complete responsibility for the actions of his subordinates, and when they came under fire he upheld them. Privately he could and did chide the errant for their mistakes. Stover had become a problem in particular, for he was unsuited to bear the pressures of office. Now and then a confidential message would be dispatched from the mayor's office to straighten out the inept commissioner, and although fatherly in tone, these clearly indicated Gaynor's displeasure. One read:

"I meant to say one thing to you yesterday, but I refrained. It is better that I put it in writing. You are too dilatory, and put things off unnecessarily. The best way is to decide things one way or the other and do them promptly. The complaint of your dilatoriness is general. I say this to you frankly for your own good, and I wish to help you all I can."

The parks commissioner was given another nudge shortly thereafter, the mayor writing him:

"I do not see how we can delay any longer in the matter of appointing a superintendent for Central Park, and I desire to hear from you about that also forthwith. . . . There is no use, Mr. Commissioner, some of these things have got to go faster than they have been going of late. When, also, are the bad places on the roads in Central Park to be repaired? I am receiving daily complaints of them."

But against public criticism the mayor stoutly defended Stover. One critic was ticked off:

"When I receive a letter saying something is 'outrageous,' and using similar adjectives, I always mistrust that the complaint amounts to much. I drove through Central Park last Sunday and I know your letter is a gross exaggeration. There are some places where the driveway needs to be repaired, but there is no such condition as you mention."

When his commissioners failed to come up to expectations, instead of dismissing them Gaynor quietly installed experienced, able men as deputy commissioners, and allowed them to carry on the business of their departments efficiently.

"Dear Madam: It is a hard job to decline the invitation of even one girl to dine, and when you are invited by 3,657 girls, it is altogether impossible to decline."

So wrote Mayor Gaynor to Miss Ada Becker, president of the Washington Irving Association of New York, in 1912, a Presidential election year, when he was also receiving invitations that were not merely social. Politics was very much to the fore, with Theodore Roosevelt planning his "Bull Moose" bid for a third term and slugging away at President Taft on the speechmaking circuit.

Mayor Gaynor thought little of this exhibition; the noise seemed to him excessive for the issues involved. To a West Virginian the mayor wrote confidentially:

"You hit the nail right on the head. . . . All this talk we are hearing should count for nothing. I confess I do not know what the debate between Mr. Roosevelt and Mr. Taft is. Do you understand it? Mr. Roosevelt was President for seven years. Just what did he 'do' about the tariff or any other living issue? He caused a lot of suits to be brought to break up business concerns, and Mr. Taft has continued the same policy. . . . It is easy to talk, and be flippant, but . . . again, what has been done? Has the tariff been modified? Has favoritism in freight rates been stopped? And so I might go on."

In the Democratic camp the discussion was all of candidates, and already Woodrow Wilson, recently elected governor of New Jersey, was barnstorming the country in grim pursuit of the Presidential nomination. Gaynor turned away from such undignified self-advertisement. Although Colonel House had sponged the mayor's name from his slate, Gaynor continued to be spoken of favorably in numerous quarters, especially after Bryan, titular leader of the party, included Gaynor in his list of the four or five most acceptable possibilities. Early in 1912 a definite boom was started to make Gaynor the Democratic choice at the convention in June.

The episode, which would occupy many columns of newspaper space as it unfolded, can be summed up concisely. Gaynor at heart did not want the nomination. He said so repeatedly, although neither friends nor foes nor the political pundits on the sidelines cared to believe him. True, under badgering and pressure, at times he seemed willing to "play along," and issued cryptic pronouncements; but from first to last he made no slightest effort, and was content to let matters take their course, in confidence that the boom would die aborning, and so it did.

Gaynor's public statements could not have been clearer or more emphatic. On January 9 he replied to harassment by newspapermen by handing them a written statement:

"I am not a candidate or aspirant for any office. I would give a good deal to be left alone. All I want is to try to be a fairly good mayor. Beyond that I have no desire or ambition. Is not the office of mayor of this great city, with the powers vested in it, as important as that of President? It is a far more difficult one to fill. . . . I am certain that if this Presidential bee could be got into my head it would impair my efficiency as mayor, and of all things I do not want that to happen."

This statement of attitude he repeated, just as emphatically and clearly, again and again during the ensuing months. He told two thousand women teachers who cheered him as "our next President":

"Don't! Just leave me alone. Don't put that bee in anybody's head. That has spoiled too many useful men in this country already. I have no illusions. . . . I am simply a very humdrum, matter-of-fact, everyday man, working just like you. And I am content with what I have to do. Now, don't try to make me discontented."

When admirers announced the opening of a Gaynor-for-President headquarters in New York, the mayor wrote that while "of course I have to recognize that you are free to do as you see fit, nevertheless if you consult my wishes you will not do this thing."

He was much in demand as a political speaker when the battle lines began to be more closely drawn. Invitations poured into City Hall from all parts of the country. These Gaynor parried tactfully by referring to his wound and loss of voice, but the widespread interest in him was undeniable. At home, what speeches he did make at political gatherings were scanned for significances that were not there.

When Calvin Tomkins, acting as a friend addressing a friend, sent his best wishes for the mayor's securing the Presidential nomination, Gaynor replied equally frankly:

"The good wishes you express I am grateful for, but I do not suppose that I am in it. I have kept aloof from the matter, and the order of the day seems to be that if you want a thing you must fight for it."

That, then, was the touchstone. Gaynor was naturally combative; throughout his life, anything he really wanted to obtain he was more than ready to fight for; he even, out of sheer exuberance, sometimes got into fights that did not concern him. His disinclination to fight for the Democratic nomination was the most convincing proof of his indifference to the nomination itself. And also, there was his own awareness that he was not well, that he was tired, old, and ailing.

What the mayor now and then did say politically had the usual effect scandalized upon politicians, especially when he let himself go impromptu. Wilson was the target of one devastating attack. It occurred at a dinner of the Democratic Club, and Gaynor and Wilson were seated within a few feet of each other. There was nationwide agitation at that moment against the "trusts"—holding companies —and New Jersey's laws were notoriously lenient toward these popularly pictured predatory monsters of wickedness; in fact, four-fifths of all the "trusts" in the nation were organized under New Jersey's indulgent legislation. Wilson had been denouncing the "trusts," just like his Republican opponents, in speeches outside his state, although as governor he had not lifted a hand to repeal the laws allowing them to flourish in New Jersey. Gaynor went directly to this discrepancy between talk and action. Reading from manuscript, he said bluntly:

"If the people of New Jersey want 'trusts' broken up—and their complaints are heard even across the Hudson River—they have only to elect governors and legislators who will carry out their will" —here he paused and interjected—"and stay at home and do it."

The effect was electric. Wilson sat stony-faced, while Gaynor went on to say that he hadn't heard any governor asking for repeal of New Jersey's "trust" laws, and added bitingly:

"We must not lay ourselves open to the charge of being demagogues."

Straying again from his manuscript, he remarked that if there was any more contemptible beast than a demagogue, he hadn't seen it, and continued relentlessly:

"After all, everybody knows better than anybody; that's a lesson some statesmen won't learn. There are statesmen who are now roaming all over the country. I, too, have been asked to roam, but I can't, for I have no time. I don't know who would perform my duties if I did. I don't see how they do it. They weren't elected to it."

The speech got great applause but not from Woodrow Wilson. And so did Gaynor's speech to a booksellers' convention in which he ridiculed the "sham battle" the politicians were waging.

"You haven't heard any of them say, 'Repeal the statutes under which "trusts" are organized,' " he said. "But they pass statutes to organize 'trusts,' and then the national government, after the 'trusts' are organized, brings suit to break them up. Did you ever hear of such nonsense?"

To a Philadelphia supporter Mayor Gaynor gave his views on the backing and filling of the politicians who were beating the bushes for votes.

"Might I say to you," ran the letter, "that what we most need in this country now is for our public men and statesmen to discontinue loose talk, and speak with exactness on public questions, and without regard to what effect they may think the truth may have on their own future. To try to advance in the field of politics, and in the attainment of office, by loose or false statements, is despicable. What we need is that our public men, instead of loosely crying out all sorts of evils, should put their finger exactly on the thing, and define it, and hold it up and show it, so that everyone of average intelligence may see it and understand it. Those who are not willing to do this should hold their peace."

To an inquiry from Richmond, Virginia, regarding his availability as a Presidential candidate, the mayor wrote, again with a side glance at the barnstormers:

"I could not possibly neglect my duties here by going about the country as a candidate for another office. I fear that is being done altogether too much already. I have the most difficult office in the country on my hands, and am very anxious to administer it fairly well."

So determined were the political forecasters to detect in every utterance of Gaynor's some veiled political significance, or some clue to his own stand on the nomination, that even when he wrote a letter on howling tom-cats, this was pounced upon as a political manifesto in disguise. A sleepless citizen of Brooklyn, beset by midnight yowls, piteously beseeched Gaynor for relief, and the mayor responded:

"I regret to say that I have so many official duties pressing upon me that I can not just now devote any time to tom-cats, as you request by your letter. There are a few in my neighborhood, but I go to sleep and let them howl. It amuses them and it doesn't hurt me. But some say it is the pussy-cats that howl, and not the tom-cats. How is that? We must not kill Tommy for the sins of Pussy. And, also, remember that the 'female of the species is more deadly than the male.'"

While the city was laughing over this epistle launched into the

night, and which decidedly cast suspicion upon the mayor's ear for
music, the *New York Herald*, spearheading the Gaynor-for-President drive, proclaimed that in ninety-six words Gaynor had scored
a bull's-eye on office seekers who were "dashing wildly over the
country looking for a crisis that could not be found." And the agitation to nominate this humorist went on.

That spring the annual "crime wave" was puffed up in the
newspapers, and Gaynor had relatively little to say in rebuttal, for
he was kept in bed with a severe attack of *la grippe* (or influenza,
as a later medical generation would name it). He did manage to
glance over a report from Police Commissioner Waldo stating that
the records contained no evidence of any startling increase in crime,
and to reply:

"Your letter giving me the statistics of crime since September
1, 1911, and the corresponding statistics for the last two years,
showing that there is now no unusual amount of crime in the city, is
at hand. This is all very true, but you must remember you can not
prevent the proprietors of ragbag newspapers from inventing a
wave of crime whenever they feel disposed to do so for the sake of
sensation and the circulation of their newspapers. They would be
willing to bring any infamy on the city for the sake of increasing
their circulation. But do not be disturbed by that. Intelligent people
understand it thoroughly."

As soon as the doctor permitted, the weary mayor went to
Atlantic City with Mrs. Gaynor for two weeks of rest. He reached
the resort looking worn and frail, and while there suffered a humili-
ating experience.

Several times Gaynor had sought to induce the New York physicians who had attended him in St. Mary's Hospital to send him
their bills, and they had declined to do so. The Hoboken surgeon,
Dr. William A. Arlitz, however, did submit a bill for $7,500. In
addition, his assistant asked $2,000. This Gaynor termed ridiculous.
Meanwhile, the legislature had authorized the city to pay the medical expenses of the assassination attempt, as an action due to "the
dignity of the community." Gaynor had signed the bill only after
making clear that his New York doctors had stubbornly refused to
present their bills and "they say they never will." He also pointed
out that the act would apply to the case of any city employee who
should suffer a similar misfortune.

The five New York doctors thereupon sent their bills to the

city; so did the Hoboken pair. The largest amount asked by any
New York physician was $5,500. The Board of Aldermen, in ap-
proving the bills, accepted the figures submitted by the New York
five, but cut the sums awarded to Dr. Arlitz and his assistant to
$2,500 and $500, respectively.

"I won't accept it!" Dr. Arlitz protested. "I am as big a man
in my locality as any of the New York doctors in theirs."

Full of belligerence, he retained a collection lawyer, who bided
his time until Gaynor entered the state of New Jersey, and in Atlantic City a process server handed the mayor a summons in a suit for
the full amount. The act occurred in the lobby of the mayor's hotel,
in view of scores of people.

Dr. Arlitz's action was bitterly condemned. The Sisters at St.
Mary's wrote the mayor, their "esteemed friend," in distress, and
disclaimed any responsibility for the suit. Several prominent New
Jersey attorneys requested the privilege of defending the action
without fee. Eventually the case went to trial, and Dr. Arlitz won
a judgment of $5,800. Gaynor bore the embarrassment in silence.

A second moral defeat added to Gaynor's tribulation at this
time—the spring of 1912. This was the culmination of the long-
pending libel suit brought against Gaynor by former Police Commissioner Bingham. The *Herald* had once commented that "Gaynor
plays the letter-writing game above the table. Every letter carries
his signature. And he is willing to accept the consequences of whatever he writes." The time had come to take the consequences of those
letters which Gaynor had written to Mayor McClellan during the
Duffy case uproar. These formed the basis of Bingham's suit, and
although Gaynor had invoked every legal technicality to stave off a
trial, the time arrived when no further delay was possible; and just
as the case was due to go before a jury, Gaynor settled it by publishing a profound apology and paying Bingham an undisclosed sum
of money. The action was applauded generally, but it was an undignified position for the city's mayor to be in.*

The brevity of life, and the imminence of death, had much

---

* Gaynor's embarrassment had been made worse by the incorrigibility of young
Duffy himself. Arrested several times for minor rowdyism, and helped each time by
the mayor, who found him jobs and tried to straighten him out, the youth at length
was sent to serve a term in the reformatory. With unwonted generosity, the New
York newspapers generally refused to throw his protégé's delinquency in the
mayor's teeth.

occupied Gaynor's thoughts since the shooting. There remained so much to be done, and the time was so short. Again and again in his letters occurred the phrase, "I have no future, I have only a present."

In April, when the sinking of the *Titanic* with loss of fifteen hundred lives shocked the nation, Gaynor was plunged into somber reflections, and on the night before the *Carpathia* reached New York with the survivors, he sent back to Dr. Finley the Marcus Aurelius that the latter had sent to St. Mary's Hospital months before. On the flyleaf the mayor had written:

"Consider the great universe, of which thou art only a speck, as governed by fixed laws, and be therefore content in all things, and especially to die at any time, and abide by God's will of thee, whether of individual future life, or dissolution into universal mind and matter."

In an accompanying note he added:

"My mind is all the more impressed with this now, for I have spent much of the day in considering of those who went down . . . and preparing to take care of the survivors of that awful catastrophe on their arrival here tonight."

Gaynor had lost friends in the disaster, including Isidor Straus and his wife, who perished together.

In this emergency the mayor acted with tact and energy. He ordered the police commissioner to exclude photographers from the dock where the dazed survivors would land. "Also rope off a large space on the outside for the protection of these unfortunate people from all sources of interference from photographers or anyone else. We owe it to them, and let it be carried out strictly."

In cooperation with the Lord Mayor of London Gaynor launched the relief fund for the victims' families, and at a memorial meeting for the Strauses held in Carnegie Hall he spoke movingly of that devoted couple. Their death was a personal grief to the mayor, felt the more keenly because of the death, a year before, of Abraham Abraham, another major steadying influence.

But the round of the mayor's activities was not interrupted by private griefs. After the "crime wave" had been replaced in the newspapers by more timely topics, Gaynor thanked the police force for "the fidelity of every one of them to duty during the recent weeks when there has been a combined effort by gamblers, corruptionists, and certain newspapers in this city to create insubordination and neglect of duty."

That year Gaynor opened the baseball season at Ebbets Field, and was angered when far more tickets were sold than the grounds could possibly hold, resulting in a near riot. Baseball was, in fact, his hobby. He was constantly buying baseball outfits for small boys who wrote that they were unable to afford a bat or mitt of their own. A letter from the mayor, shown to Lieutenant Kennell at the door, admitted these callers to the mayor's office, and few departed without the equipment they had come in hope of.

The perennial complaints about children playing in the streets brought the standard rejoinder, although in order to do no complainant an injustice the mayor sometimes visited the district complained of to verify conditions for himself. The lengths to which he would go to be perfectly fair were extraordinary. More than one letter reporting his personal observations carried a handwritten postscript:

"We must be patient with the children."

Some complaints met with a rougher reception. A resolution regarding subway routes passed by the Flatbush Taxpayers Association was rebuffed at City Hall with a curt if not insulting, "Permit me to say that I consider the resolution as very silly."

By contrast, an appeal that Gaynor addressed to a Brooklyn judge on behalf of the foreman of his St. James farm, who desired to become a naturalized citizen, was a model of urbanity. It read:

"The bearer, Mr. Junge, is my farm foreman, and a very prudent, intelligent, and wise man, though not glib, to say the least. He is able to 'hold his tongue' in all the languages without the least difficulty, which is more than can be said of most of us in St. James. He wants to be made a citizen. When he applied for citizenship before, he was rejected for not knowing how many members composed the House of Representatives. I could not help sympathizing with him, as I did not know the number myself. His calm German sense and judgment, as unerring as the crack of doom, seem to me far more important, especially as he has a good German education."

Always swift to register his admiration of the intelligent, industrious immigrants crowding the tenements of New York's East Side, Gaynor spoke in their defense repeatedly, taking special issue with prying uplifters. Dr. Parkhurst, of course, was one of these, and the mayor told the Motion Picture Exhibitors League of America:

"Some people are altogether too good for this world. The quicker they are translated the better. I know one of them here who in his imagination lives in the sky all the time. I think at the north-east corner of the Milky Way and the Aurora Borealis is his house. And from what I know of him I am sure that up there he has his head out of the window most of the time, meddling with other people's business."

A Brooklyn citizen who urged that the city manufacture ice to supply it free to those too poor to pay for it during the summer months was told plainly:

"When you ask [the advocates of the scheme] where all these poverty-stricken people are, they tell you they are on the 'East Side.' I deny it. I have made myself very familiar with the East Side. The people of the East Side are not a lot of paupers, by any means. There are no more paupers there, relatively, than in other parts of the city. They are an industrious, honest, and prudent people. They are well fed and well clothed. Their children are healthy and clean. Did you ever go into the schools down there and see these fine children? This eternal talk about the poverty of the East Side is annoying. . . . The people of the East Side are getting tired of hearing this thing of their poverty and wretchedness and vice. A lot of people are collecting money and living on this false notion about the East Side."

This whole area of reforms and reformers was proving to be strewn with booby traps for the impulsive, outspoken mayor. Temperamentally he was unable to work in harness with other vigorous natures, and more and more he had come to suspect the motives of those who identified themselves with reform organizations—"bone hunters" and "hypocrites," he called them, intent not on promoting the general welfare, but on imposing their own narrow views on the community by force and willy-nilly. Many of the objectives of the more conscientious reform groups Gaynor also held, and some he had carried to fruition, and he would continue to do so. But the proponents personally he would rebuff with intense rudeness, and to them there seemed perversity in his attitude; they could not understand it, and resented it just as intensely.

One incident that would prove detrimental to Gaynor was his conflict with William Jay Schieffelin, president of the public-spirited and politically potent Citizens Union. Gaynor had often been at odds with that organization; politically he considered it mainly a pious fraud. Schieffelin particularly got on the mayor's nerves because of his pomposity, and the temptation to shy stones at a pompous figure had been Gaynor's since his country boyhood.

In an acrimonious exchange of letters, Schieffelin had been

urging the revocation of a streetcar line's franchise in Queens, and
the mayor had refused, intimating that Schieffelin must have some
axe to grind. The latter replied huffily, and Gaynor hit back with:

"I conclude from your letter that you either have a personal
interest in the matter or represent someone who has. . . . In fine, I
do not care to hear from you on any subject."

This letter Schieffelin returned to City Hall as "unworthy of
your office. If matters of public concern can not be communicated
to you without receiving insult in return it is time the citizens of
this city knew it, and I shall take pains to see that they are properly
informed on the subject."

This declaration of open hostility caused consternation among
Gaynor's friends, for the only base of support the mayor could
reasonably count on was Schieffelin's group—the reform element.
The regular parties, at least through their leaders, were simply
sweating out four lean years of Gaynor, devoutly hoping to unseat
him at the next election. Without the backing of the reform element,
Gaynor would be hopelessly isolated.

Far from exhibiting contrition, the mayor went out of his way
to stir up resentment in another quarter—union labor—by publicly
stigmatizing the officials of the hotel workers' union as "misleaders"
and "low, mean men." The trouble arose out of the union's attempt
to disrupt an official dinner being given for the officers of the visiting
German fleet. The city had extended the invitation, and the officers
were the city's guests. The union's waiters were on strike, and at the
last minute an attempt was made to prevent the serving of the dinner at the Waldorf-Astoria. A disturbance was created inside the
hotel, to the scandal of the mayor, and forty-eight strikers and
sympathizers were arrested. Magistrate Corrigan leniently fined
them a dollar apiece and turned them loose, while the mayor published a scathing letter he had sent to the union heads, accusing
them of "meanness to the mayor and through him to the whole city."

This outburst, coming on the eve of the Democratic convention
in Baltimore, did nothing to brighten the mayor's prospects for
snaring the Presidential nomination. But a widely published incident in this connection did draw favorable attention to Gaynor at the
last minute. This was his swift release to the press of a telegram
sent to him by the leader of the Tennessee delegation to the convention, indicating that a canny outlay of money could boost his
chances. A Southern newspaper, getting wind of the action, recounted it in outline without naming names, and queried Gaynor as
to its authenticity. Back came his immediate confirmation:

THE DOMESTIC BOOM
Pussy Cat, Pussy Cat, where have you been?

July 4, 1912

"I do not see why your newspaper conceals the man's name. The newspapers up here did not conceal his name nor his telegram to me, but published it in full. His telegram is as follows: 'Dresden, Tennessee, June 15, 1912. Mayor William J. Gaynor, New York. As you know the Tennessee delegation to National Convention at Baltimore is uninstructed. Today was appointed assistant sergeant-at-arms of the convention and will have charge of the Tennessee delegation. Some of the rural delegates have not sufficient funds to get to the convention. If you can assist me to get some of these delegates to get there and in case your name comes before convention will make it of interest to you. Answer at once at Dresden, Tennessee. L. E. Holloday.' This is the whole case."

Gaynor's answer to the egregious custodian of the Tennessee delegation also was published. It went by telegraph:

"You will not be in charge long. Your moral perceptions are too inconspicuous."

Meanwhile, a committee of the mayor's friends—amateurs and inept, none with political experience—put up a foredoomed fight at Baltimore for a few days; but there was no likelihood of success, and after a dog fight among themselves the delegates nominated Woodrow Wilson.

Gaynor received word of the result without turning a hair. He had never varied from his daily routine and had never given the

MAYOR GAYNOR—I KNOW OF NO GAYNOR BOOM

June 19, 1912

"SO THIS IS THE WHITE HOUSE"

May 31, 1912

slightest encouragement to his well-meaning but interfering friends.

One of the few positive results of the flurry was to give occasion to the mayor to express some of his views of the Presidency and its responsibilities, and also of the responsibilities of an ex-President. To Ray L. Perkins he wrote:

"I am inclined to think that a six-year term for the President would be about right, and that he should not ever again be eligible for the office. A man who has been President is revered by all the people without regard to party. For that reason if he amounts to anything intellectually and morally he can be a great teacher to the whole country. People will listen to him and heed him because they know he has no political aspirations and that his words are disinterested. I know of no position on this earth greater than that of an ex-President as a teacher. He can do more good that way than by being President again."

Life went on, and so did Mayor Gaynor's correspondence—terse, jaunty, epigrammatic, acrid, or blistering, as the occasion inspired. William Jay Schieffelin ("that man always signs his full name," said the mayor) came in for periodic jabs, and other letter writers sometimes got an answer that they had not bargained for.

A poetaster who forwarded from Dobbs Ferry a religious poem was thanked by the mayor and provided with this thought to chew on:

"With those who find themselves only able to believe in God, without believing other things, there should be no quarrel. Everyone can say that he believes in God, and in His benign rulership of the universe. If some of us find it difficult to believe anything further I am certain God does not condemn us. Why then should anyone else? Some people say they do not believe in God even. No one can sincerely say that."

Another letter on the same subject breathed the spirit of ecumenicalism half a century before the churches embraced it. Replying to a New Jersey man, Gaynor counseled:

"Your letter, with the newspaper clipping, is at hand. The clergymen, and church members, to whom you refer, no doubt thought they were Christians, but they were not Christians. They did not have a spark of Christianity in their whole being. Jesus did not denounce anyone who believed in God, or who was, as it is expressed among us, and by you, a 'Unitarian.' I do not see how anyone can say he does not believe in the existence of God, but when it comes to believing more than that, or to embellishing that great fact with minor things, I can see how many of us may not be able to extend our belief that far. We can only believe as much as God gives us light to believe."

Why he himself believed in God he told Dr. Christian F. Reisner, pastor of Grace Methodist Episcopal Church, West 104th Street:

"You ask me, 'Why do I believe in God?' Because I can not help it. I simply know there is a God, and that settles it with me. I have absolute confidence in Him, and am willing to submit to whatever He wills in respect of me. You also ask, 'What good comes from reading the Bible?' An immense deal of good. It soothes you and makes you content and charitable. I might add that it educates you and gives you a good literary style."

But Gaynor was never too preoccupied with high thoughts, or too irritated, to smother the stone-shying impishness that some letters provoked him to. Herman Ridder, the publisher, who was heading a committee to organize a Fourth of July celebration, was rejoiced one day to receive the following from the mayor:

"I am enclosing to you a letter of Mr. Zerban, who suggests the ringing of bells on the Fourth of July. I like to hear bells, and a good many other people do, while a good many people do not like bells at all."

In the familiar bold handwriting was a postscript:

"If we can not do any better, how would it do to ring a lot of bells under his window at midnight?"

Mr. Zerban himself received the mayor's lukewarm endorsement of his proposal in a letter ending:

"There are very queer people in this world."

That was a phrase often in Gaynor's mouth. To him the world was a perpetual surprise, and by no means always an agreeable one.

SUMMER LIGHTNING

———◼◦◯◦◼———

*The voice of one citizen who is intelligent,
sober, and earnest is worth all the noise
and clamor that was ever heard.*

——GAYNOR

INDICATIONS THAT A STORM of more than moderate violence was
about to burst around Gaynor's head might have been detected by
acute observers about this time. The mayor had been demonstrating
his capacity for raising up enemies needlessly, and his rasping irritability had grown worse as his health fluctuated. At times it appeared
that his judgment was deteriorating, too, although this was shown
only erratically and fitfully; on most subjects his views were sound.
His doctors found that he was suffering from hardening of the ar-
teries, and this resulted in growing mental inflexibility. Sixteen
years on the bench had accustomed Gaynor to deciding matters with
the force of law, and seeing his decisions carried out; the habit
was hard to shake, and indeed he did not try to break it. This judicial finality of judgment was more and more resented by those who
were willing to cooperate with him, but found themselves rebuffed
when they attempted to offer dissenting views.

A natural tendency among those unable to grasp the complexity
of Gaynor's impulses was to cast doubt upon his sincerity. To the
conventional mind it was simply inconceivable that any man should
be indifferent to the prospect of possible election to the Presidency.
Gaynor's words and actions in that situation were put down to dis-
simulation and trickery; and from suspicion of his political sincerity
it was only a step to suspicion of his sincerity in every respect. Yet

Gaynor was never more sincere than in his contrariness and quixotism. To those close to him this had gradually become apparent, and at various times they tried to convey to others the strangeness of the mayor's character as they saw it themselves. During the Presidential agitation, the mayor's secretary, Robert Adamson, had tried to correct a misconception that had gained currency in parts of the South. The editor of the *Savannah Press* had remarked editorially that Gaynor was rather small-bore in politics; and Adamson, himself from Georgia, wrote to his colleague in Savannah a revealing analysis of Gaynor's uniqueness.

"A friend of mine has sent me a clipping from the *Press* entitled 'Gaynor and Tammany,' which, after quoting an extract from the *Macon News*, makes this comment on the part of the *Press*," Adamson's letter read: " 'Mayor Gaynor is at most an excellent politician. The Democratic party wants something more than that light pine timber.'

"The mayor, like all men of positive opinions and character, has encountered a great deal of abuse and is used to it, and expects it, but it is very rare . . . that such an erroneous statement as this has ever been made about him.

"Whatever the mayor is, he is not a politician. Whatever his enemies have said about him, they have not made that charge. . . . I have had a pretty wide acquaintance with public men of the country for the last twelve years, and I can say emphatically and sincerely to you that Mayor Gaynor gives less thought to the political effect upon himself for his future than any man I have ever known in public life. In fact, I think it is about the last thing he thinks about.

"The truth about him is that he is the despair of all practical politicians who think he ought to do this thing or that thing. They say he neglects too many chances to play to the galleries. He happens to be one of those old-fashioned kind of men, who merely says in plain and peculiarly pungent and interesting English just what is in his mind and lets the consequences take care of themselves."

A man with this habit was bound to run afoul of prejudices and hostilities, and he on his part had prejudices of his own, none of which exceeded his prejudice against professional reformers. How, to his way of thinking, these pseudo-reformers operated he had explained in a magazine article:

"We have also a large number of 'leading citizens' who call themselves reformers as each election draws near, and talk reform, although they never do anything. . . . The usual way is to 'appoint' a committee to take charge after the movement has got under full headway. Who the actual appointers are is observed by very few. . . . This committee in turn forms an executive committee of a small number, and in this executive committee the reform movement becomes locked fast, and its direction and fate are settled. . . . Some good, safe, sane, and incompetent man is nominated, and, it may be, elected. He goes into office with the high hopes of the community, but turns out to be a failure, and every honest voter soon perceives that he is duped."

Such reformers, Gaynor thought, had "neither the length, breadth, or thickness, mentally speaking," to be effective. And since the method of procedure he described almost exactly fitted the way the Citizens Union operated, Gaynor's target was not hard to guess. So mutual mistrust had been developed on both sides in Gaynor's relations with his quasi friends, and these, in a pinch, were conditioned to turn against him actively.

The *New York World*, which had broken sharply with the mayor over the subway proposals, published an estimate of the mayor at this time that was widely copied and quoted. The *World* admitted that on the whole Gaynor had proved probably the best mayor New York had had during living memory, and then went on:

"If anybody chooses to say that Mr. Gaynor is irascible and irritable in his discussions of public affairs, we shall agree with him; but we are aware of no provision in the constitution of the state or the charter of the city which asserts that the mayor of New York must be sweet-tempered and gentle and lovable. Mr. Gaynor is rather difficult to get along with at times and we are glad that we have no personal relations with him; but these infirmities do not greatly concern the public welfare."

Still, when proof was demanded, instances of an evident intention to insult were few in Gaynor's manifold communications both private and public. Since the exceptions sometimes involved persons of prominence, they became talked about, and some of the mayor's most egregious defiances of good taste were sheer acts of political suicide. That made no difference to Gaynor.

That Gaynor bore as patiently as he did with intrusions on his carefully economized time and energy was remarkable, in view of his waning health and his natural irritability. He was hardly to be censured for answering a complaint from Donald F. Ayres of Brooklyn in the same vein in which the complaint was written, since he took the trouble to answer it at all:

"I am enclosing to you a letter of the police commissioner. Please return it to me. I fear your letter impressed him as it did me, unfavorably. Of course he does not relish being told that Flatbush is a 'Bushwackville' under his management."

And Mrs. Belle Zimmerman of Brooklyn may have felt offended by the succinctness of the letter she elicited, although obviously she had provoked it:

"Dear Madam: I will not believe that any such message came back from Fire Headquarters as 'Oh, let it burn,' until you give me some proof of it. I do not believe a word of it."

And of the thousands of one-sentence letters that streamed from the mayor's hands, most brought comfort, reassurance, and companionship to obscure recipients. Letter after letter said merely, "Your photograph has been removed," and each meant that another victim of the "rogues gallery" injustice had obtained redress. Hundreds of messages said no more than "Your complaint will be attended to," and each of these brought an awareness of the mayor's concern to some unregarded, perplexed human being. Hundreds of messages read simply, "I thank you for your encouraging letter," or, "It was good of you to take the time to write me."

The Brooklyn Heights Railroad Company (which Gaynor as a judge had excoriated) took no offense at receiving this from City Hall, despite its curtness:

"I am enclosing five cents to pay my fare on car 1380, Fulton line, this morning, as I found myself without money after entering the car."

Nor could John Brown, of Richland, Oswego county, reasonably protest against this full, positive, and comprehensive answer to his question:

"Dear Sir: No, I do not want a bear."

These were flashes of summer lightning during the dog days of 1912, portending a storm. Gaynor plodded conscientiously, day by day and hour by hour, through the incoming mail—sifting and answering the petitions, protests, silly questions, denunciations, and vapid praise that seemed never to cease.

A dossier bulged with protests against the alleged desecration of the Sabbath by the playing of lawn tennis, baseball, and other games in the city parks.

Pushcarts were a perennial headache: some wanted more, some wanted fewer, some wanted none at all; some wanted them parked on one side of the street only, some on both sides of the street, and some wanted the streets barred to peddlers altogether. Gaynor appointed a commission to thresh out that difficulty.

Complaints came in about "mashers," about overworked horses, about a "revolting ballet at the Hippodrome, called 'Cleopatra,' " about chickens kept in a tenement house, about bad meals in hospitals, about Coney Island swindles, and about the din of steamboat whistles when Cunard liners sailed early in the morning. Gaynor dealt with them and reached into the basket for more.

Letters written in German, in Italian, in Yiddish, and many in the most basic English.

"What are you doing? There is a dead horse in the street on Park Row in plain view of your window in City Hall."

Or more emphatic:

"They say Edwards is All Right—Waldo is All Right—YOU are ALL RIGHT—nevertheless there is a *dead cat* in the street for two days between B'way and Mercer St."

And mailed from Hartford, Connecticut:

"To Hell with your administration! Billy, youre N.G."

These were spillings from the mailbag during the dog days of 1912, so hard on canines, cats, horses, and mayors. And they were acknowledged, sometimes cuttingly, sometimes genially, sometimes gratefully and at length. Especially when (rare occurrence!) a *sensible* letter arrived on the subject inseparable from July—the annual mad-dog scare. It was with genuine enjoyment that the mayor replied to such a letter from Rosebank, Staten Island:

"I am very glad to receive your letter about dogs. I have heard a good deal about mad dogs all my life but have never seen one, nor did I ever see anyone who saw one. Did you? I am very glad to receive your sane letter on the subject, for I receive a great many of the other kind. Many people hate dogs. An old friend of mine, Genl. Philip S. Crooke, said in my hearing to a man who said he hated dogs: 'I hate every man who hates a dog.' The muzzling of dogs has been so long the practice that it is hard to eradicate."

And at the height of this silly season an unsavory gambler was shot down in a blaze of Broadway lights—and in a flash the whole town caught the madness and fear ran wild in the streets.

CASTLE ADAMANT

———————◖○◗◖————————

*Falling back, they began to shower stones on
Don Quixote at such a rate that he was quite
unable to protect himself with his buckler,
and . . . Sancho planted himself behind his
ass and with him sheltered himself from the
hailstorm that poured on both of them.*

—DON QUIXOTE

O F ALL THE REFORMS he had carried out, none was as close to
Gaynor's heart as his struggle to eliminate graft from the police
department. The saloon graft he had all but wiped out, as the saloon
men themselves gratefully testified. A bartender for thirty-five years
in different parts of the city volunteered that he had never known a
time "when the laws were so nearly enforced in their intent as they
are today. Mayor Gaynor has done away with the collector who
used to come around from 'the man higher up.'"

But a secondary effect of this drying up of the saloon graft,
running to millions of dollars yearly, had been to force the unscrupulous members of the police force—especially the old-timers, who had
by no means been purified, as Gaynor knew—to look elsewhere for
their "rake-off." Gambling and prostitution were the chief sources
levied upon.

Herman Rosenthal was a flashy, greedy, loudmouthed braggart
of the East Side who had been a gambler by trade most of his adult
life. In the underworld of crime he was a minor figure, although back
in 1910 he had been one in a delegation of gamblers who called on
Mayor Gaynor at City Hall to protest against their spoliation by

policemen—allowed to operate only after payment of extortion money. The scene was one of the strangest ever witnessed at the mayor's office, inasmuch as running gambling houses was itself illegal. Gaynor was merely impressed that the group was "the worst gang of men I had ever seen," and they got no satisfaction from him.

From time to time thereafter the mayor received reports of police grafting on gambling establishments, and the name of Lieutenant Charles Becker had cropped up as implicated in this black-mail. Under Commissioner Waldo, Becker had been placed in command of the headquarters or "strong-arm" squad, charged with the suppression of gambling. Gaynor had turned over the complaints, as they came in, to Waldo for investigation. On September 8, 1911, a memo had gone from the mayor's office to the police commissioner saying, "I enclose to you a letter of Mr. Lynch concerning Charles Becker of the headquarters squad." Waldo had referred such communiqués to Becker, and the latter, without undue effort, had always succeeded in demonstrating his innocence of wrongdoing. In this respect Waldo was naïve, and Gaynor had accepted his assurances that all was well.

Rosenthal, meanwhile, had tried to escape paying the police blackmail, and his places of operation, one after another, had been raided and shut down. At length, bowing to necessity, he had entered into an agreement with Becker himself to obtain immunity from police interference, and the lieutenant provided capital to set up a gambling house at 104 West Forty-fifth Street, just off Times Square. Becker was to receive twenty percent of Rosenthal's profits.

For a time the business prospered, but during the early months of 1912 complaints against the prevalence of gambling establishments became so numerous that Waldo ordered Lieutenant Becker to crack down. At about the same time (according to Rosenthal's subsequent story) Becker demanded a larger percentage of the profits, a demand that the gambler indignantly refused. In retaliation (again according to Rosenthal), and in order to "make things look good" for himself, Becker raided the Forty-fifth Street house, smashed furniture and equipment, and posted a policeman in the building to prevent its reopening.

This violation of both their agreement and his home infuriated Rosenthal. He was not a discreet or brainy man, and he applied to a magistrate for an order to eject the policeman. The magistrate declined to act, and thereupon Rosenthal unwisely confided his troubles to a reporter, young Herbert Bayard Swope, of the *World*, accusing Lieutenant Becker. Swope got the gambler to put the facts into an affidavit, in which he divulged the whole "system" of organized police corruption. When word reached the underworld that such an affidavit had been sworn to, Rosenthal received advice through the grapevine to clear out of town. But he ignored the warning. The *World* published an edited version of Rosenthal's affidavit, omitting Becker's name. The lieutenant, however, showed up at the *World* office and requested to see the affidavit. He read it calmly and handed it back with the assertion that it was "a pack of lies." And Rosenthal received another warning to clear out of town.

Swope then induced District Attorney Whitman to listen to Rosenthal. Whitman was not impressed by the garrulous gambler; nevertheless, he consented to take Rosenthal before the grand jury and let them judge of the validity of his accusations. Rosenthal was told to meet the district attorney at the latter's apartment in the Madison Square Hotel, at the corner of Madison Avenue and Twenty-sixth Street, on the morning of July 16, and they would go together to the grand jury rooms in the Criminal Courts Building downtown.

Early in the morning of July 16—at about 2 A.M.—Rosenthal was in the dining room of the Hotel Metropole, on Forty-third Street just east of Broadway, a center of the Tenderloin night life, when a messenger brought word that somebody outside wished to speak with him. The gambler walked out under the brightly lighted canopy at the hotel's main entrance, and was shot down by four gunmen, who jumped into a slow-moving automobile and made off.

From then on events exploded. Awakened by Swope, District Attorney Whitman hastened to the morgue and encountered Lieutenant Becker already there, glowering at the bullet-riddled corpse. Whitman learned that at the time of the murder seven policemen had been within a hundred feet of the hotel entrance, one actually in the dining room, only a few feet away. None of these had interfered, nor had any of them managed to get the correct license number of the getaway car, although it had moved deliberately along Forty-third Street toward Sixth Avenue, where it turned north in front of the Hippodrome Theater and disappeared. At police headquarters Whitman found a bystander who had jotted down the correct license number, and oddly enough, when he brought it to headquarters, had been promptly locked up.

The next morning the *World* published Rosenthal's affidavit
in full, together with all the baffling aspects of the murder, and the
city was swept by hysteria. Was it possible that criminals, in league
with a corrupt police force, really ran the city, with immunity even
to commit murder? In distant Queens and Gravesend, householders
suddenly shivered at the sight of the familiar cop on the beat. The
apparent apathy, if not complicity, of the police as the case developed seemed to point to the most sinister conclusions.

The killers' car was traced, and several suspected accomplices
and material witnesses were locked up; but these either surrendered
voluntarily, or were brought in by the staff of the district attorney,
while the police seemed helpless. The newspapers as a unit cried out
against the suspicious listlessness of the police. Let Mayor Gaynor
act, was the demand.

For a while, no word came from City Hall, and the hysteria
grew. The newspapers screamed for action. "WHO IS THE MAS-
TER—THE PEOPLE, THE MAYOR, THE POLICE, OR
THE GAMBLERS?" demanded the *Herald*, which saw "the foun-
dations of law and order" being shaken. "Public opinion puts this
murder fairly up to the police. Until they catch the murderers,
until a good case is made out against them, there will be a taint on
the entire city administration. If it is true that, first, the police are
banded with the evil class, and, second, banded together for mutual
protection under secret oaths for the perpetuation of a 'system' that
has only graft as its motive, no man's home, no man's property, no
man's life can be regarded as safe."

In a second manifesto on the same page the *Herald* asked,
"WHAT WILL THE MAYOR DO? He has been liberal in his
views regarding an 'open' city. It looked like common sense. He was
supported in this theory. But, alas! it has been a theory. What do
we find in practice? The underworld taking possession. . . . New
York has in a night gone back from the 20th century to the 16th.
. . . Our hardheaded mayor may now take his head out of the sand
and recognize things as they are. Or he may make a few remarks in
classical prose about this being a mere incident in modern life or
the result of the heat. But it will not do for him to say that the police
force is above suspicion or that the call for reform of the police is
mere 'hysteria.' Hysteria! The feeling of outrage, of insecurity, of a
great civic crisis that has spread through the community is neither
hysteria nor frenzy. It will soon become cold and calculating specu-

lation whether the administration can cope with the situation or whether some other agency must be appealed to."

This from a newspaper which only a few weeks before had been proclaiming that Mayor Gaynor, out of all the people in the United States, was the man best fitted to be President! The turnabout was a measure of the city's upheaval.

In his affidavit Rosenthal had told of meeting Becker at an Elks Club dinner, where they had sat at the same table, and on the day the *Herald*'s overwrought editorials appeared, the mayor, in his first statement since the murder, alluded to this. In a formal communication to Police Commissioner Waldo, Gaynor instructed:

"Please have Lieutenant Becker and Policemen James White, Charles Foy, and Charles Steinhardt [members of Becker's squad] before me at this office at 11 o'clock tomorrow morning. After the precautions we have taken and all we have devised and done to do away with the long-standing and deep-seated grafting in the police department, it is very discouraging to have these Rosenthal accusations bandied about. To be sure he was a miserable outcast against whom you and your predecessors had been contending. . . . Those who killed him will be found, no doubt, and their motives disclosed. . . . I can not understand why Lieutenant Becker should sit down with such a scoundrel. That he did seems to be admitted. . . . Rosenthal and his associates were the worst gang of men I [have] ever seen. That is why I am so greatly surprised that Lieutenant Becker should sit down to dinner with any of them, or associate with them in any way."

This letter stunned the city. That the mayor should raise a point of social propriety when the question was one of murder! What had happened to Mayor Gaynor? Where was that famous "subjunctive of command" which formerly had been hurled against patrolmen accused of nothing worse than clouting a citizen? Where were the phrases that everyone expected to issue from City Hall— "Let him be suspended and tried forthwith"—"Let him be tried and if guilty dismissed"?

What had happened to the mayor was understandable, though not in the current mood of the city. He had always been sensitive to adverse criticism, and once he had decided in his own mind that an outcry was mere "clamor," probably selfishly inspired, his resistance to it had been adamant; nothing could force him to yield. "Clamor" meant coercion, to the mayor, and that would always arouse implac-

able opposition. His long-continued illness had increased this tendency to resist pressure. Gaynor's doctors knew that he was suffering
from myocarditis, an inflammation of the heart tissues for which the
standard treatment was rest and mental tranquillity, and neither of
these was within Gaynor's reach.

Also, in the outcry against the police Gaynor saw a threat to
the progress he had made in purifying and uplifting the force. He
had brought about an improvement in police manners and morality.
The change was not complete, and he knew that it was being perti-
naciously fought by some men influentially placed inside the force;
these men, in fact, he believed to be the prime instigators of the
outcry against his administration. He knew that the police were not
all sold to lawbreakers, but realized that a few members of the force,
mainly holdovers from previous regimes, had not foregone their
graft. This faction he was weeding out gradually by means of disciplinary action and retirement. Now to allow all his gains to be
denied and dashed aside by "ragbag" newspapers and a misled
public was more than he could bear. His pride as well as his sense of
justice was stung and he reacted stubbornly. His motivation was one
of preserving faith in himself and his ideals and in capability of
action; psychically one of self-preservation. If what newspapers like
the *Herald*, and others even more violent, were saying was the truth,
then Gaynor's lifetime of endeavor had been blotted out, and as an
individual he had been exposed as a futility and a sham. His common sense told him he was not.

In obedience to command, Lieutenant Becker did appear before
the mayor and denied all Rosenthal's accusations. But instead of
being suspended pending investigation and possible trial, he was
merely transferred to desk duty in a remote precinct of the Bronx.
In answer to Waldo's request for instructions the mayor told him:

"No, do not suspend [Becker] and put him on trial without
evidence to justify his conviction and dismissal by you. Let his case
be carefully investigated and all the facts ascertained. Do not bend
a single bit to clamor, and especially to the hired press agents of
the gamblers with whom you are at war, and those corrupt newspapers which have been all along and now are at the service of such
gamblers and against you. But they can not hurt an honest man.
One of the chiefest duties of public officials is to remain cool and
keep their heads in time of clamor and indiscriminate newspaper
accusation, and go on in the steady performance of their duties. I

feel certain that the force under you will remain steady, as they have
done in the other times of clamor and lying in the last two years. . . .
Rest assured that the mayor will stand with you against these corrupt scamps now trying to defame you and break you down in the
splendid work you are so systematically doing in the police department. . . . You have the hardest police situation in the world to deal
with. We have in this city the largest foreign population of any city,
and a large number of them are degenerates and criminals. . . .
The published names of everyone connected nearly or remotely with

**WE ASSURE OUR EXCELLENT MAYOR THAT NO POLICEMAN WILL
EVER AGAIN DINE WITH THIS DISREPUTABLE GAMBLER**

July 20, 1912

REFORMING THE POLICE *July* 20, 1912

Rosenthal and his murder show them to be of this same class of
foreigners to which he belonged. . . . Even if it should turn out that
Lieutenant Becker . . . deceived and betrayed you, I should still
have in mind your unimpeachable honesty and the splendid work
you have done, and excuse and sustain you. . . . No doubt the assassins will be arrested and no doubt the complicity of Lieutenant
Becker will be revealed if it does exist. Let us proceed in order. . . .

"Do not feel that I am expecting more of you than is possible.
I well know that you can not wholly suppress gambling, especially
among these degenerate foreigners to whom I have referred, any
more than you can wholly stop larceny or murder. . . . You may be
thwarted by raillery, and abuse, and political investigations, and
clamor, and the corruption of some members of your force (for they
are fearfully tempted), but remember that these are annoyances
and crosses that we must bear as best we can, while, conscious of our
integrity and good motives, we go on doing the best we can. It is

now nearly two years ago that I was asked to give up this onerous and grinding office of mayor and enter on a comparatively easy one [the governorship]. I thought it all over. I saw all of the rough road ahead, and the times of clamor and trouble. But I decided to stay and stick it out. I want you to feel just like that and do the best you can, and be cheerful and content. . . . In the many things I have to do I shall always try to devote some time to sustaining you and helping you all I can."

There is nothing more maddening to an excited person than a

TRAILING FOR THE CONFESSIONS
Never do anything in a hurry, Commissioner.

July 21, 1912

CATCHING THE MURDERERS

July 27, 1912

man who keeps his head. Such was the public's reaction to this homily from the mayor. Was it philosophy or bullheadedness that prompted it? Some suggested plain insanity. Yet the mayor was not alone. He received many, many letters of commendation, and as the weeks went by these swelled to a stream.

Meanwhile, the controversy raged. Whitman openly accused the police force of complicity in Rosenthal's "rubbing out," their motive being to prevent him from "squealing" to the grand jury. The murderers were identified, four hoodlums with the highly decorative names of Whitey Lewis, Lefty Louie, Dago Frank, and Gyp the Blood. Whitman conducted a man hunt from Arkansas to the Adirondacks, and on every street corner Becker was spoken of openly as the man who had procured Rosenthal's slaying. The public feeling alternated between revulsion and ridicule. A correspondent signing himself "Amphytrion" asked the *World*, alluding to the summer homes of Becker, Boss Murphy, and Mayor Gaynor:

"Please ascertain whether Lucullus Becker dines tonight with Lucullus at Far Rockaway, or with Epicurus Murphy at Good

Ground, or with Epictetus Gaynor at St. James, and notify Commissioner Waldo."

The newspaper cartoonists outdid themselves in lampooning the trusting mayor and his supposedly inane police commissioner; but the demands for Waldo's removal Gaynor understood were really attacks upon himself, and he did not yield an inch. Describing Rosenthal as a man without a shred of credibility (yet he was Becker's sole accuser), Gaynor maintained that "no honorable man the world over would accept his word to the injury of a beast, let alone a man." District Attorney Whitman struck back with intimations that the mayor must bear responsibility for the murder and the conditions that led up to it.

"Herman Rosenthal," said Whitman, "was to come to my house with his wife that Tuesday morning to supply me with evidence of a corrupt alliance between the police and lawbreakers of this city. He was butchered in the most brilliantly lighted street in New York . . . in a block literally swarming with policemen. Notwithstanding their presence, there was not a semblance of an effort to apprehend the murderers, and the pretext of pursuit is so silly and transparent that it ought not to deceive a ten-year-old child."

Gaynor was incensed when reporters followed him to St. James, even after he had made plain that he had no further public announcement to make. His temper snapped at this invasion of his cruelly needed weekend of rest and he ordered the intruders to "get off my front porch!" A reporter showed his press card as identification, but Gaynor stormed, "I don't know you, you don't know me. Now get off my porch!"

"But, Mr. Mayor—" the reporter expostulated.

"Damn, damn, get off my porch!" shouted Gaynor. "I don't know you! I have nothing to say! Get!"

Since there were dogs around, the reporters elected to "get."

But the scandal would not go away, and on July 29 Whitman arrested Becker on a charge of first-degree murder. Several witnesses and accomplices had consented to "squeal" in return for immunity from prosecution, and they told in detail how Becker had ordered Rosenthal's execution by hired gunmen, and had handed the killers $1,000 each on the street near the Metropole after the crime.

Becker was picked up by two detectives from the district attorney's office while on duty in the Tremont police station in the

Bronx. After he had been taken away, his precinct captain called
police headquarters and broke the news to Waldo. In a few minutes
a notice was posted on the headquarters bulletin board announcing
Becker's suspension from the force. His indictment by the grand
jury obviously had been on evidence of a convincing nature, but
that evidence had not been procured by the police; it had been procured by the district attorney's staff, working in opposition to the
police, whose integrity and efficiency Gaynor had so stubbornly defended.

Becker's indictment and arrest precipitated a cloudburst of
bitterly adverse criticism upon both Waldo and Gaynor. The police
commissioner started several suits for libel, and the *Herald* commented acidly:

"GET OFF MY PORCH!"   *July* 30, 1912

THE DUNCE CAP   *July* 31, 1912

"It would seem to be time for our excellent mayor to write another letter and our amiable police commissioner to bring a few more libel suits. The entire city administration could not find enough evidence in the Rosenthal case to suspend from duty one police lieutenant, but the district attorney, a county official, has succeeded in having one indicted, arraigned for complicity in murder, and held without bail."

Said the *Evening Post:* "We can not ask Mayor Gaynor to detest the criminals, but New Yorkers are certainly within their rights in expecting their mayor to come forward at such a crisis and display the qualities of a leader of public opinion."

The *New York Times:* "The bewildered and discouraged citizens of New York have the satisfaction of knowing that 'something has been done' . . . at last."

The *Atlanta Constitution* put it fervently: "Thank God Woodrow Wilson was nominated for the Presidency, and not Gaynor!"

Pulpit orators took up the cry. Mourned the Rev. George Starkweather Pratt, of All Saints Anthon Memorial Episcopal Church:

"In these days in our city there has come a sense of weariness and disturbment, if not despair. We have lost confidence in the police, in the courts, and the judges. The whole community has lost confidence on account of this unspeakable corruption."

But none, clerical or lay, quite equaled the diatribe poured out by Rabbi Stephen S. Wise. Since three of Rosenthal's killers were Jewish, the rabbi interpreted Gaynor's allusions to "degenerate foreigners" as a slur upon all Jews. He excoriated the mayor's "manifesto, whose rambling and discursive character might be attributed to an unconscious imitation of the Epictetan model. . . . After days of silence, which have seemed a veritable desert amid the innumerable oases of the mayor's epistolary fertility, the long-awaited word is uttered. Instead of sober and searching utterance we have an angry squeak. . . . Resort is had to that last refuge of the infirm temperament, wholesale and blustering abuse. . . . If one could bring one's self to judge it as the serious utterance of a serious person one would say that the mayor's outpouring was an intolerable insult to the intelligence of the people of New York. . . .

"If the public still refuses to be befuddled by his shrill and vulgar outburst he is quite ready to divert public attention from the assassination and all that it may mean by seeking to inflame and poison the public mind against the whole class to which the victim belonged. Any artifice will serve the purpose of this master of the craft of studied irrelevancy. . . . Deeply though I deplore that there be some Jews base enough to descend to the gambler's calling and kindred forms of criminality, no subsequent sophistication or mystification on the part of the mayor will serve to explain away his indictment of a whole people in the words, 'this same class of lawless foreigners to which he belonged.' Ignoring for the moment the unethical, injudicial, inflammatory character of these words, one wonders chiefly how the arch quibbler will reconcile them with the nauseatingly flattering references to every 'class of foreigners' which have illuminated his campaign speeches before and since his election. . . . The mayor bids his subordinate at the head of the police department 'be cheerful and content.' Some of us who are citizens of New York are neither cheerful nor content. . . . As to the citizenship of New York, tempted to abhorrence of the mayor's inept and infirm stand in the presence of a civic crisis, Epictetus has a word of counsel: 'Pity him rather.' "

Wise's attitude was hotly resented by many New York Jews, who were aware of Gaynor's admiration of their people, exhibited over the years in many of his closest friendships. Maurice Goodman, a lawyer, hastened to assure the mayor that "I sincerely regret the unwarranted and ill-timed attack on you by one of my co-religionists—a preacher. . . . Not one of the many persons I have spoken to believes you conveyed or intended to convey the impression that the Jews are a criminal class. Your record refutes any such imputation; and yet, at a time like this, a minister attempts to raise a racial issue!"

Gaynor was more than a match for the fulminating rabbi in the slugging bout that followed. To many letters similar in tone to Goodman's he replied in words fewer than his adversary used, but more deadly. To David Bernstein he wrote:

"I have no ill-feeling against Rabbi Wise. Of course I have observed in common with the rest of the community that he is without charity or truthfulness, although a preacher and teacher. But I have to remember that he is a mere rhetorician, and you know that rhetoricians are proverbially uncharitable and untruthful. The mouths of all of them are crooked, to use an ancient phrase, and you can not expect truth or charity to come from a crooked mouth."

To L. E. Miller, editor of the *Warheit*, Gaynor wrote similarly:

"I have your letter with regard to Rabbi Wise. Yes, I know he has made several very uncharitable and untruthful attacks on me. But I bear him no ill-will. He is a clergyman, and it is always a painful sight to see a clergyman with no charity or truth in his heart or soul. He has never lent me a helping hand. He has studiously tried to thwart me and do all the injury he can. I do not know why, except that it is his nature. . . . But if you see him tell him that I bear him no ill-will whatever. I have had to work hard as mayor to accomplish things which I set out to do. That he has not offered me his hand concerns him more than it concerns me, and that is also true of what he says of me."

To a Wall Street broker went the message:

"I thank you very much for your kind letter. You seem to be

NOTHING DISTURBS ME MUCH

"Of course it (the situation as to Becker) has greatly disturbed and morti-
fied the Commissioner, for he is a young and sensitive man. As for
myself, while I am not without feeling, nothing disturbs me much."—
Mayor Gaynor in a letter, dated August 16, to the editor of the Long
Branch Record.

Aug 22, 1912

under one strange error. I have not said a word about the Jews. I
called attention to the fact that those connected with the murder and
with gambling were 'degenerate foreigners.' That list is not entirely
made up of Jews by any means. Of course I know that no decent
Jews would defend criminals of their race any more than any other
criminals. You must have got the notion that I said something about
Jews from Hearst's lying newspapers."

Finally, to sum up Rabbi Wise comprehensively, Gaynor told a
fellow New Yorker:

"Your letter about Rabbi Wise, who you say is not a rabbi at
all, is at hand. The particulars you give of him are quite interesting. But I fear you take such blatherskites too seriously. He is a

man of vast and varied misinformation, of brilliant mental incapacity, and of prodigious moral requirements."

Apprised of these letters, as he was by numerous well-wishers, Rabbi Wise retorted:

"The citizenship of New York is growing weary of letters postmarked 'City Hall.' The only letter that we ought to have the patience and the willingness to read is a letter of resignation."

POLICE POLITENESS

Dec. 22, 1912

GAYNOR TO THE BOY SCOUT
Everything is all right, Becker is all right, you're all right, I'm all right.
There is no gambling, Rosenthal isn't even dead. Everything is all right
except the blackleg newspapers.

July 27, 1912

Nor did Gaynor neglect to state his case with cogency and calmness, as he had in previous crises. For a time, under the deluge of abuse, his public correspondence dwindled, but privately his pen was kept busy in justification of his course. And little by little the number of persons who were willing to listen and weigh the facts increased. In one comprehensive letter, to the editor of the *Daily Record* of Long Branch, New Jersey, the mayor stated the facts as he viewed them:

"As soon as I became mayor I began with one department after another to rid it of politics and graft, for they go hand in hand. In

"HE'S GOOD ENOUGH FOR ME!"
The System—"Well, Old Sport, I'm good enough for the Judge, you are good enough for me."

Sept. 11, 1912

that work I have received neither the aid nor the good will of the people who make the most noise in this city in the way of accusations and protestations of virtue. I have no reason to complain of that. I never expected their good will, much less their aid. I think I have succeeded pretty well in eliminating graft from the city government. Graft had been deep-seated here for over 40 years in most of the departments, if not in all of them. I think it will be admitted that I have driven graft out of nearly all of them. I have even been fortunate enough to take most of the graft out of the police department.

"The matter of stopping graft in connection with gambling and the like is an awfully difficult task. . . . We tried to cope with this . . . by narrowing the contacts of the department with the sources of that graft. I could see no other way. We narrowed such final contact down to a single point, namely, to the commissioner himself, and a special squad under him. And yet now we find that one of the three lieutenants of that squad was taking graft. . . . Of course it has greatly disturbed the commissioner, for he is a young and sensitive man. As for myself, while I hope I am not without feeling, nothing disturbs me much. I of course expected that cases of graft would develop. The police force as a whole is good. I hate to see the whole force abused for the derelictions of one or a few. But they know . . . I will stand by them."

This letter elicited hoots of ribaldry from the cartoonists.

Gaynor grew neither more nor less bitter and immovable. To a message of sympathy from Supreme Court Justice A. T. Clearwater, of upstate Kingston, the mayor wrote with feeling:

"My dear Judge Clearwater: In the largest mail of encouragement which I have received since I became mayor I find your letter. It was very good of one of your eminence, and not a resident of this

BETWEEN THEMSELVES
Mayor Gaynor—What did you get into this mess for? Didn't you know I was reforming you?

Sept. 13, 1912

"NOTHING DISTURBS ME"

Sept. 12, 1912

city, to take the time to write me such an encouraging letter. . . .
You speak of what you call the 'tremendous opposition and astounding abuse' to which I have been subjected, and say that you do not see how I stand it, or preserve your (my) serenity, as you express it. I have to do the best I can. The clamor and false statements of vicious persons and newspapers no doubt hinder me some, but I have to overlook them and go right along. Every morning I just forgive everybody and then take up the work where I left off the day before and go right on. How else could I do it? In the din of clamor and falsehood I often repeat to myself the saying of Marcus Aurelius: 'There is but one thing of real value, namely, to cultivate truth and

justice, and to live without anger in the midst of lying and unjust men.' That makes me content. I do not seek the good will of degenerate newspapers. The good will of intelligent and honest men is what I desire.

"The job of preventing scoundrels from bribing the police, and the police from taking bribes from scoundrels, is a difficult one. I

THE FATALIST
"Don't be disturbed, Commissioner. I regard this sort of thing as inevitable.

Feb. 17, 1912

hope I have succeeded largely, and I hope in the end that I shall succeed entirely. After 40 years of graft and corruption, and of rulership over the police by dishonest, lawless, and ignorant men, it is not an easy thing to bring about a better order of things. I was not at all surprised when it was found that Lieut. Becker was taking graft. That is nothing new in the police department. It would have been nothing new if the police commissioner himself were found to be taking graft, according to the past history of that department. But I have a police commissioner who is incapable of taking graft. And I have an able and honest man at the head of each of the other departments of the city, and reform and good work are being done all the time. Conscious of this nothing can disturb me, although I may be to some extent baffled by the opposition of criminals and degenerates. If I am ever inclined to feel discouraged when these are joined by people who believe themselves righteous, but never give me a helping hand, a moment's withdrawal into my inner self makes me patient again, and able to see again in the complexities of things

HEAR NO EVIL SPEAK NO EVIL SEE NO EVIL.

AT THE CITY HALL

July 30, 1912

only the slow working out of God's will. And letters from men like you, and good women, make me know that we are not working in vain."

That was the mayor's side of the story, and while propagating it diligently he scattered his philosophy about the kindred subject of prostitution, for which he admitted he had no solution except to preserve "outward order and decency." To Dr. William Robinson, of Mt. Morris Park West, he observed:

"It was very good of you to write me so encouraging a letter. I am also glad that you have the correct distinction between vice and

DISPOSED OF
Mayor Gaynor—The police scandal! Tush! A mere bagatelle. It didn't even surprise me.

Nov. 15, 1912

crime. There are persons in the community who think the mayor and the police can deal with vice in the same way that crime is dealt with. Indeed, there seem to be a great many people who are not aware of the fact that fornication is not a crime."

And to W. D. Breaker, of Duane and Hudson streets, went more pertinent observations:

"Dear Mr. Breaker: I thank you for your intelligent letter. You express the truth that government rises no higher than its source. If the people generally are corrupt their government will be the same. I am doing all I can to free all the departments of the city from graft and corruption. I have a splendid man at the head of each, and the city government is in no particular under the con-

THE DEAD LINE   *April 5, 1911*

trol of any outside organization or influence. As you say, it is entirely natural to expect cases of graft to crop out in the police department or elsewhere. I was not a bit surprised when the case of Becker occurred. I was looking for some such thing to happen. But I am gratified to be now satisfied that there was no general system or conspiracy of which he was one. He worked mainly by himself. Bank presidents, trustees, and business heads default and graft, and we have to expect the like in the government of the city now and then."

No, the mayor was not alone, although if one judged by the newspapers one would never know it.

MUTINY IN THE FORECASTLE

————————◖o◯o◗————————

*Almost everybody who goes into politics be-
gins by making a stump speech. They think
that is the way to do it. Only later do they
find out that stump speeches have nothing
to do with politics.*

—HENRY H. CURRAN

THE BECKER-ROSENTHAL SCANDAL, with its successive disclosures
of seamy secrets, had shaken the city too deeply for the mayor's
words to take effect. By the majority of the press and public, during those hot weeks of July, August, and September, 1912, fright-
ening conjectures were being made, and a mass meeting at Cooper
Union gave expression to the community's dismay. The mayor did
not attend, but District Attorney Whitman was cheered when he
laid the responsibility for the crisis squarely at Gaynor's doorstep.
Resolutions were passed pledging unlimited support in running
down Rosenthal's killers and in cleaning out the police department
of whatever infestations lingered there. William Jay Schieffelin
placed the resources of the Citizens Union at Whitman's disposal,
while John D. Rockefeller, Jr., sent a check for $5,000 with a pledge
of as much more as might be required to "end graft in New York."
And long after the initial shock had worn off, and justice had
triumphed, the scandal would remain a political rally cry.

Through all this, an energetic young alderman, Henry H.
Curran, was taking steps, with a few colleagues on the fusion side,
to investigate the "breakdown" of the city's police system separately

from any action by the district attorney. Curran was honest, intense, and idealistic. The Board of Aldermen was in recess for the summer, but Curran collected signatures to a request to the mayor to reconvene the board for the purpose of carrying out a thorough study of the situation. The reception he received from the mayor, when he presented this petition, was decidedly cool. Gaynor was faintly disdainful toward the eager young alderman, unresponsive and distant, and the interview ended without his consenting to issue the call. But Curran was determined, and he brashly wrote an open letter to the mayor serving notice that a court order would be sought to compel him to act. Tremendously in earnest, Curran "spoke right up" and told the mayor:

"You enjoy asking people questions. I want to ask you a few about this Rosenthal case. You said we are just trying to embarrass you. Will you tell me how it will embarrass you? . . . You puzzled me badly again when you said we would 'stultify' ourselves if we undertook this investigation. Just how do we stultify ourselves by doing that?"

Then came the real reason for Curran's vehemence:

"You said one other thing as we passed the time of day that placed 'a positive and immediate duty' upon yourself. In complaining of the Board of Aldermen you pointed to a basketful of papers on your desk and said that you had had there for some time an affidavit that a member of the Board of Aldermen had taken a bribe of $500 for giving out a privilege for a bootblack stand or some other kind of stand. Will you tell me what that has to do with your duty or ours in the Rosenthal case? Why did you mention it? Was it a threat? . . . I make this demand upon you as the mayor of this city. Act now on the affidavit or tell us why you don't. Let us have the facts."

Three days later Gaynor reluctantly convened the aldermen, who voted $25,000 to finance the inquiry. Before they could get the money, this appropriation would have to be approved by the Board of Estimate, where it was expected Gaynor would vote against it. To everyone's surprise, he did not, and the inquiry was launched, with Emory S. Buckner as the investigating committee's counsel. Curran was chairman. He suspected that Gaynor was planning to start a backfire to kill the investigation before it could gather headway, and he was outraged when the mayor, while addressing a gathering of newsstand owners, complained that he had been trying for two years to get the aldermen to cooperate in stamping out the graft in licenses, and had got nowhere. Curran thought it ominous that the mayor added:

"The thing I came here to say to you is that it seems now opportune for us to take it up again. I intend to write another message to the Common Council. There is so much talk about graft now perhaps they will listen to me. All we need in this case is a simple amendment of the ordinance by striking out the words 'with the consent of the alderman of the district.' It's as easy as turning your hand over. It's not like trying to stop gamblers and scoundrels from corrupting the police and others. That is a tremendous job, but this job is an easy one. I have no doubt that this graft, one of the lowest and dirtiest in the city, will be done away with this fall."

Boiling mad, Curran made clear that he was in total agreement with Gaynor in urging that the aldermen should have nothing to do with issuing licenses, and he warned the mayor that this counterattack would fail, saying belligerently:

"I know the temper of my colleagues, and we are not going to be blocked or hampered or thwarted by any circuitous move from the other end of City Hall."

As the date for the hearings to start approached, rumors spread that Gaynor still planned some tactic that would discredit the inquiry. He was invited to be the first witness. The day arrived, and somewhat nervously the committee convened. For half an hour it waited.

Then a letter was handed to the chairman. It was from the mayor. He acknowledged Curran's invitation to testify, and declined it in words that stung:

"Your letter makes it necessary for me to speak plainly to you, as much as I regret to do so. I can not ally myself with you in any effort to discover wrongdoing in the police department. I have devoted much of my life to efforts to lift government up and make it respectable and honest, and I intend to continue that work, but I have never allied myself with anyone who was not himself above reproach. I have called attention to the miserable grafting carried on by members of the Board of Aldermen in respect to the licensing of the newsstands and the like throughout the city. . . . I do not see how I can expect the police to be honest when they see on every hand that even the aldermen of the city are taking graft personally, or enabling corrupt go-betweens to do so. . . . My attention has also been called to the fact that you have of late several times published

VACATION TIME

Alderman—Mr. Mayor, I have come to ask you to investigate the police.
Mayor Gaynor—Go away! You are trying to embarrass me. It's your move, Commissioner.

July 29, 1912

statements regarding your visits to this office which are very far from being truthful. That is another reason why I do not wish to have any relations with you. If the committee wants any facts of me, let it subpoena me, or notify me to attend, and I will do so and give such facts. Beyond that I will not go."

The session adjourned in turmoil, and Curran immediately fired back his rejoinder:

"So far as your maliciously false statements concern me they will be taken care of in the libel suit which I have instructed my attorneys to bring against you."

CAN YOU BEAT IT?

Sept. 11, 1912

It was fortunate that Curran did not know at that time that Gaynor had been trying, through his own investigative agencies, to find some turpitude in Curran's record, and had met with failure. Curran was honest. This seemed incredible to the mayor, and when confronted with the fact, he protested, "How can he be honest? He's an alderman. Tut, tut!"

Curran did sue for $100,000 and the suit stuck. And the press had more grim comment to make.

The next day Gaynor responded to the committee's "notification" to testify by appearing promptly at the time mentioned. The aldermanic chamber was crowded, floor and gallery, when Curran took his place on the rostrum as presiding officer. He looked self-consciously solemn. Gaynor entered briskly, followed by his inseparable bodyguard, Lieutenant Kennell. He was greeted by applause from the floor, but paid no attention. He did not glance toward Curran, and not once during the session would a flicker of recognition pass between the men. Going directly to the witness chair, the mayor shook hands with Alderman Dowling, the Democratic minority leader in the board, and then slid into his seat with an air of resignation. Gazing straight ahead, he held up his hand and repeated the oath as Curran administered it. Then the battle opened. It would go on for two and a half hours, waged between the young and ambitious Buckner, as committee counsel, and the veteran mayor.

From the outset it was plain that Buckner was overmatched. He was punctiliously polite, and remained deferential even when he was insistent; but the advantage was clearly with Gaynor.

During the first hour the mayor's cough seemed to bother him; frequently he put his hand to his throat as if in pain. At such times his voice became barely audible. Later, when he warmed up and interpolated speeches into the record, defending his actions, defending Commissioner Waldo, giving his opinion of the number of hypocrites in New York City, scoring professional reformers, speaking up for the workingman who took a glass of beer on Sunday, quoting St. Augustine, and now and then giving a critic a dig, like a cat striking out unexpectedly with a forepaw—at such times his voice rang out and the applause was almost continuous. It was evident that the mayor relished the applause, though he took no notice openly.

Buckner suggested, in question form, his own understanding of how the police department was run, and got the patient reply:

"If you understand it that way, you can say so. I have not said so."

Buckner wanted to know whether there was any means by which Waldo communicated with the mayor "other than by letters or other than by speaking to you." The mayor murmured:

"I know of no other way in which he could communicate except by writing or speech."

When requested to give his opinion on a certain matter, Gaynor replied that he had been called to furnish facts, not opinions, and if the committee did not care to ask for facts, he would retire: "I might as well be plain with you."

"Do you think that your system [of administration] was defective?" Buckner pressed, and got back:

"I do not tell you what I think at all. I came here to produce facts."

Pressed to state the degree of personal attention he gave to police department affairs, Gaynor answered pleasantly:

"I have answered all that I intend to. I have a commissioner at the head of each department. I appoint a man that I have thorough confidence in, and I guess the whole community says I appointed a good lot of them, too. This government, good or bad, is in my possession, and not in your possession or the possession of anybody else outside of the mayor's office."

About the anticlubbing order . . . Buckner kept trying to get Gaynor to admit that some policemen had misconstrued that rule and in consequence had failed to make proper arrests. "Did you ever hear—" began the counsel.

Gaynor: "I don't think it makes any difference whether I heard it or not. If I were to go by what I hear from the newspapers and cutthroats of the city, the newspaper proprietors and others, I would vacillate every hour of the day. But I pursue my own course, even in the boiler shop of the city, now, with every onetime convict or newspaper proprietor or whoever wishes attacking me. I have not varied an iota up to this time, and I hope I shall not until I get through."

Buckner: "But has it been called to your attention that the policemen misunderstood your attitude on clubbing?"

Gaynor: "I don't care whether it has been or not; I know it is not true. I know I corrected the whole evil and I know the whole city thanked me for it. That is what I know. They do not club boys and defenseless people in this town now, not after the first month I was mayor, nor smash in doors without a warrant, either."

Buckner wanted to know whether the publication of Gaynor's letters about disciplining policemen had been bad for the force's morale. Gaynor's reply was sharp:

"I know of no such thing; neither do you. . . . I have never written a thing that I was unwilling to see published. I guess the whole world knows it."

Buckner: "You misunderstand me."

Gaynor: "I understand you very well."

Buckner: "You would not be willing to assist the committee [by your opinion] after your years of police study?"

Gaynor: "You say that; I don't. If there be any matter of opinion you want of me, it ought to be furnished in advance, and if necessary I will put it in writing for you. I might give opinions here offhand which tomorrow I would not be satisfied with; but if I can have a day to sit down and think it over, I suppose I would express my opinion to you or to anybody that I had enough respect for to express an opinion to."

Leaving that, Buckner asked Gaynor to state his policy in regard to police force appointments and promotions.

Gaynor: "Why, everybody knows: when I became mayor you couldn't get on the force without paying for it. Don't you know that? [Applause and laughter.] You couldn't get appointed captain without paying $15,000 to $17,500. Don't you know that well enough?"

Buckner: "I want it in the record."

Gaynor: "The record? Why, it is in the record of this whole community, and you can't take it out of their minds, either. I have absolutely stopped it all, and you know it. I don't know why I should be badgered about it here."

Buckner: "I hope you do not think I am trying to badger you, Mr. Mayor?"

Gaynor: "Oh, I have to make allowance for your zeal and everything, and I am willing to do that."

Applause and laughter greeted this, too, and Buckner asked whether Gaynor had put that policy into effect as soon as he became mayor.

Gaynor: "No, I did one thing at a time, and I have several things to do yet if you people will give me a chance to work them out."

Asked whether his motive in ruling that appointments to the police force and promotions in it must be made in numerical order from the top of the civil service list was to eliminate political favoritism, the mayor replied emphatically:

"And the payment of money. When you have the first man on the list he doesn't care for Murphy or anybody on earth, only those who put him at the top. That is what I did it for. I did not propose to be mayor and have someone else run the city. If it is run badly here is the man [indicating himself] that is responsible. Right here. Just look at me. If it is run badly I am to blame."

Buckner: "But you are willing to have the police commissioner run the police department?"

Gaynor: "Sure. He does run it, and run it well, too. He recently met with a great misfortune. One of his own staff was found to be a grafter, and every dog in the community is at his heels now. That don't change me a particle, not a particle. . . . My experience in the police department is that those who do their duty best have the most enemies and the most people to bark at their heels, and I happen to know that personally myself as mayor."

After several questions about police routine which he said Waldo could answer, he couldn't, the mayor grew impatient:

"You have been asking me over and over. It is not on honesty. It is for scandal. It so happens that I have a reputation in this community, and you can't scandalize me. I was engaged in purifying the government here long before you came in sight."

Again laughter and applause swept the room, and Curran rapped for order, while Buckner explained:

"We are trying to find out who is the head of the department."

Gaynor: "You are not holding an inquiry here to find out who is the head of the police department. You had better read your call there."

Buckner: "We think it might be beneficial."

Gaynor: "You are holding an inquiry to see if the police department is violating the law and not doing its duty. But I see now you are holding an inquiry about me—poor me. I'm not afraid of it, but still I have lots of things to do."

Turning to the saloon graft and Gaynor's action to halt that, Buckner asked whether the mayor had said that the police were taking two to three million dollars a year from the saloonkeepers.

Gaynor: "I don't know whether I ever made that statement or not. I know the way they were treated and blackmailed was absolutely infamous under the regime I came into. I know I put an end to it all. I know that any liquor dealer who pays now is a fool, and I don't think they do."

What was the means he adopted to stop this abuse?

Gaynor: "I do not allow the police force to go into the saloons right and left and collect graft—to put down a dollar on the bar and get $19.95 change from that after buying just a glass of beer."

Buckner veered to the sale of liquor in back rooms on Sunday. Did Gaynor think the law was being enforced in that respect?

Gaynor: "I suppose as much of it as can be. . . . I have told everybody, without any bones at all, that to prevent all of the people of this city drinking on Sunday is an impossibility, and every sane man knows it, and I am not willing to be a hypocrite for one minute about it. If you gentlemen think you can prevent everybody in the city from drinking, I turn the job over to you gladly. All the clubs in the city are open and in full blast, aren't they, where the rich people go, and they swig whisky and wine all day? Do you think you can do that, and that the poor people won't drink anything on Sunday? The thing is preposterous. Every club of rich men in this town is open on Sunday, and they are drinking from morning to night, and you know it as well as I do, and yet raise a row in the city here because I don't prevent every poor man in the Bowery and everywhere else from drinking."

A salvo of applause burst from the audience, and Curran rapped helplessly for order. Gaynor went on:

"I don't care two cents for these people. Some of them are even selling drugs down on the East Side and destroying the people of the East Side—some of these great reformers here. And I shall have great occasion soon to tell some of them, in place of meddling with everything, just to take that matter in hand and keep their dirty drugs out of the East Side—their cocaine and their morphine and their poisonous drugs, which are sapping the health of these people, and yet they get up and twit me because somebody is drinking a glass of beer on Sunday."

Buckner interposed: "Our only interest in the excise question is the interest of grafting."

Gaynor: "I know your interest. Your interest is to make some scandal about it, but it so happens that I have lived here so long that you can't do it a bit, not a bit. [Applause.] I believe you have been here three years, Mr. Buckner, if I understand it. I don't twit you for that. I came here when I was a boy, too. [Laughter.] But I know that I have some reputation in this community that this committee can not affect in any way whatever."

Laughter welled up again, and Curran rapped the gavel and attempted to speak, "The chairman would—" But the mayor kept right on, ignoring him, and speaking in a loud, clear voice:

"This examination is all unseemly from first to last. I came down here to tell you any fact about the police department, any disobedience of law there, and I see that it is turned into an examination, that it is intended to embarrass the mayor of this great city. You had better work with me in place of trying to embarrass me."

"I hope you do not think that, Mr. Mayor—"

"I think it, and I know it, too."

"I am trying to ask you if you can—"

"Oh, I know what you are trying to do. I wasn't born this morning at all. [Laughter.] I've dealt with hypocrites for a long time."

The questioning turned to the control of prostitution, and Gaynor explained at length his inability to do anything except to try to minimize this immemorial evil.

"We have to deal with it the best way we can under the law," he said, "and put it into the hearts of people, or men, not to ruin women; and as to the merchants and storekeepers and manufacturers, to put it into their hearts to pay women wages that don't drive them on the town and into vice. But for a man to pay a woman three dollars a week and then accuse me and say there are too many prostitutes in the city of New York is infamous, and there are people here who are doing just that thing."

This declaration was applauded stormily, and Curran looked stern but did nothing, while Gaynor continued with a tribute to "the regular ministers and priests of this city that have helped me infinitely. They have been patient with me, they have conferred with me, they have listened to me, they have helped me. While the few little miserable fellows, notoriety seekers with nothing in their hearts except uncharity and the wish to do me and others evil—they tried their best to frustrate me and annoy me, and do all that they could to make every difficult task more difficult yet. . . . I have needed help, but I have not got it from the people who have been nagging at me in the city. They have not disturbed me any at all, not a bit, but I believe there are more hypocrites in this city than on the whole face of the world outside it."

For two and a half hours the unequal duel kept up, Gaynor playing to the gallery and the crowd responding. Buckner failed to elicit anything helpful to the committee. It was clearly the mayor's round, and at the close, although the committee and counsel sagged with fatigue, Gaynor seemed good for another hour. Only once did he betray intense feeling. That was when the questioning turned to Charles Becker.

"Becker!" the mayor broke in. "I hate the sound of the name! I hope I never hear it again!"

This passage at arms the press generally reported respectfully. Not so the Hearst newspapers; they brushed the encounter aside as something stale. "Change your act!" was their jibe, and Hearst's gifted cartoonists made the most of it.

The storm was not over. For months it would continue to beat upon the mayor, through successive waves of disclosures. Charles Becker was tried, convicted, and sentenced to die. Rosenthal's murderers were caught and convicted and given death sentences. Several grafting policemen, including four of high rank in the force, were exposed, tried, and sent to prison. Through it all Gaynor went about his business with punctuality and energy and thoroughness, never retreating one inch in his defense of Waldo. Addressing the men's club of Central Baptist Church, Amsterdam Avenue and Ninety-second Street, on "Law Enforcement in New York," he said:

"I have, at all events, at the head of the police, a man . . . absolutely incapable of taking a wrong dollar or doing a wrong thing with anybody. . . . They call on me to throw him overboard to the wolves. But until somebody can show me something wrong in Mr. Waldo, if anybody has to be thrown out of the sleigh to go to the wolves, I would jump out myself. And while this pack of wolves was eating me up, poor Waldo would get away, wouldn't he? But I have a notion he would come back and help me. I don't think he would go away at all."

CHANGE YOUR ACT
  This is the third attempt of the hunted gamblers to break down the police administration inside of two years through their paid press agents.—From Mayor Gaynor's letter to Commissioner Waldo.

Aug. 13, 1912

FATHER KNICKERBOCKER—WHAT! HERE, TOO!

Mayor Gaynor, in denouncing those who do not agree with him in his address in the Fort Washington Reformed Church, compared himself to a hunted man seeking sanctuary from the mob.

Sept. 26, 1912

And before the International Congress of Applied Chemistry, where he was introduced as "the man holding the hardest job in the world," Gaynor assented, adding:

"I didn't need to come here to be told my job is a difficult one. I knew my job was a hard one before I took it. And I also knew that the harder I might work to do it right, the more abuse and less thanks I should get in some quarters of the City of New York. . . . There are some newspapers here such as you have never seen elsewhere. Some of them, of large circulation, have type six inches high, and not content with such type, they have to use red ink. They must think our skulls are so thick that nothing else will penetrate them with the commonplace thoughts they seek to convey."

The tone of the press continued adverse. After Gaynor's appearance before the Curran committee the *New York Tribune* bitterly suggested that "Mayor Gaynor calls the aldermanic inquiry scandalous, but his own conduct is the only scandal in sight." And the *Evening Post*—staid, judicious, temperate—deplored that "from the very beginning the mayor has taken a wrong attitude. It is all a matter of approach. A ringing utterance that he would devote all the powers of his office to ferreting out the criminals and purging the police department, if it took his last ounce of strength, and a frank offer to cooperate with the district attorney or anyone else, would have set him right with the people. . . . A blaze of frank, honest indignation is what is called for—an announcement of no quarter to wrongdoers. There has not been a trace of this at City Hall."

To the *World* the mayor seemed obsessed with the notion that "Rosenthal was killed merely to annoy him and discredit his administration." And the *Herald* regretted that, by a perversity that he seemed unable to control, the mayor had "with furious energy alienated friends and well wishers by the tens of thousands. It is a pity; it is too bad."

But when a woman friend since boyhood worried lest he might lose his head in the crisis, he replied jauntily:

"I have been keeping my head all these many years, have I not? Is it therefore fair to assume that I will continue to do so?"

And he went on turning an unflinching face to the united condemnation. He conceded nothing. Even while cautioning Commissioner Edwards that reports were coming in charging graft in the street cleaning department, he challenged George Sylvester Viereck, the publicist and editor, on the same subject:

"If you know of any graft in the street cleaning department you are the man I am looking for. If you do not, but only wish to deal in generalities, you are not the man I am looking for. We have too many like that running loose around here."

That Gaynor suffered under the opprobrium was evident to those around him. Henry Bruere would recall the mayor presiding over the Board of Estimate during those tumultuous days, silent in his isolation, "thinking up bitter, clever things to say." Yet the very vehemence of the feeling against him was creating a countertide. At the peak of the controversy the Bureau of Municipal Research, which frequently had been at odds with the mayor, reported on the

latest progress registered in the city departments under Gaynor's
direction—abatement of slaughterhouse nuisances, better schools,
early work on the 1913 budget, and a brilliant success of the municipal milk stations during the recent summer, which had supplied
fresh milk to fifteen thousand babies, of whom only two had died,
whereas the mortality rate previously had been staggering. The
bureau's report stressed that in spite of the police furor "New York
is making citywide strides never before equaled by this or any other
American city." And all this under the direct administration and
control of Mayor Gaynor.

This testimonial from an exacting and impartial critic pro-

THE MINUTE MAN OF 1912

Aug. 3, 1912

OUR PATIENT MAYOR

"I kept saying to myself each day, 'Now you must be patient. A bad thing has happened. But you must take it as an incentive to work harder than ever to accomplish what you have set out to do. Bend to God's will of you and be content'."—Mayor Gaynor.

Sept. 21, 1912

duced an effect, and gradually the pendulum of public favor swung toward the mayor again. His outpouring of personal letters also served to correct popular misconceptions. A smile takes the heat out of anger, and who could resist the mayor's rejoinder to a dweller in the Bronx who had forwarded a quotation from Aristophanes' "The Knights" on the belaboring which public men must expect:

"Dear Mr. Fingalton: Among the many letters of encouragement which I am receiving nowadays yours is a gem. It was good of you to take the trouble to let me know what Aristophanes had to say on the subject. I do not know whether Hearst or his crowd ever heard of Aristophanes. I should judge not. If they find out what he said they will probably proceed to do him up the same as they do me. I can stand it if they can. But I do not know whether Aristophanes can. What do you think?"

In the midst of the hullabaloo, the mayor gave a long-distance hiker heading for San Francisco a message of greeting to Mayor Rolph of that city, in which he admitted that "if I had time I would go with him. It would do me good. They knock me around pretty hard here now and then, if not all the time, and some days I feel as though a long walk would just suit me—the farther away the better. But the next day I feel right and content again."

To a man who forwarded a reformer's recommendation that the problem of controlling vice be solved by segregating it in a "red light district," went:

"Ask him what he thinks about segregating virtue. It would be an easier task."

By Christmas of 1912, so restored was the mayor's equanimity, he could write to a little girl in Mississippi:

"Dear Emelie: Your letter directed to Santa Claus, New York City, has been delivered to me, since you also wrote my name and address on the corner of the envelope. You tell me all your troubles and poverty, and how you hope that something will be in your stocking on Christmas morning. I should not be a bit surprised if that happens. I wish I could have Santa Claus put something in every little

I AM CONTENT

stocking in the land. But why did you not write to the Reverend Dr. Parkhurst, or the Reverend Rabbi Wise, instead of to me? Do you not know even way down in Mississippi that according to their own statements they are the good men here, and that I am a bad one?"

A second note to "Dear Emlee," as the name proved to be, written some time later, read:

"You write thanking me for the work basket. I also sent you a doll. Did you receive that?"

At Christmas time, even the irascible mayor could harbor no uncharitable thoughts toward anybody, or so he told a correspondent who had urged him to bear and forbear:

"You advise me to 'pay no attention to Dr. Parkhurst' and harsh people like him. When did I ever pay attention to him or them, or even to the Reverend Rabbi Wise, except now and then to say a jovial word or two about them, to make them feel good?"

THE WINDS OF LONELINESS

---◦◯◦---

*There is less misery in the world than
some miserable people think.*

—W. J. GAYNOR

"WHEN A MAN OF strong or violent character is right he is monumentally right," stated the *World* as 1912 closed, in reviewing the hectic events since July. "When he is wrong he is monumentally wrong. The mayor of New York is a case in point."

The *World* found Gaynor to have been monumentally wrong.

Not all New Yorkers joined in this verdict. In a letter that reached the mayor's home just after New Year's Day a different sentiment was expressed, one perhaps more representative of the general judgment. The letter was unsigned, but came from a Brooklyn man (later identified),* and it read in part:

"This letter is not addressed to the mayor of New York but to a man who came under my notice about the time of the John Y. McKane troubles, and whose career I have followed since with the curiosity of one who has had more amusement in studying the character of his fellow men than could be obtained in any other way. My interest has varied from intense anger at some of your views to that of equally hilarious ridicule of others, intermixed with a decided respect for many. Of late there has been added the sympathy that comes from every man of red blood to a plucky fighter.

"A few days before New Year's I happened to be sitting in a Flatbush Avenue car going down Livingston Street when you en-

*G. Hanscom.

454

tered and sat down opposite me. This was the third time I had happened on the same car with you and the mere study of your face
interested me and gave me the impression of an intensely lonely
man. . . .

"As an organization Republican I neither voted for you nor
sympathized with your policies, but . . . I have gradually fallen
in with your views of city government and especially with your
pertinacity. . . . I begin to feel it in my bones that . . . the Democratic party will turn to you as its candidate for mayor again. I
simply desire to say that if it does, my own leaders will have to be a
good deal wiser in the selection of their candidates than they have in
the past, to prevent me from voting for you. . . . As I have said, this
little note is in the nature of a New Year's card and to indicate that
there are many sane citizens who believe in you and that you are
not as lonesome as you may seem."

Yet even this heartening letter concluded wryly:

"But what are we to believe when your own private secretary is
said to have applied for an increase of salary on the ground: 'You
know what I have to stand'?"

Gaynor's growing tendency to affront well-wishers needlessly
was estranging some of his truest friends. His confidential secretary,
a woman lawyer who had been appointed a year previously with a
fanfare of publicity, resigned in a condition of incipient hysteria—
brought on, she excitedly wrote the mayor, by "worry and the fact
that there is no retiring room for the women in your office. Now you
tell me I take too great liberty in using your washroom in your
absence. . . . I have attempted repeatedly to have a place assigned
for our use, only to be laughed at and told that I was 'trying to run
City Hall.' The men, of course, are taken care of in this respect, and
I submit it is a matter as important for women as for men, if not
more so."

James Creelman, who had fought the mayor's battles loyally,
was finally driven to rebel by Gaynor's caustic interference. The
mayor respected and was fond of Creelman, and he received the
latter's letter of resignation as chairman of the municipal civil
service board with dismay. Protesting that he was "astonished," he
replied:

"The things which you recite are new to me. They never came
under my cognizance in any way whatever. . . . As to your statement
that I became cold and averse in my official relations with you, I do
not know what to say of it. You never told me any such thing, and I

am very certain that I never had any such feeling toward you. On the contrary I value your work highly. You are in a state of complete misunderstanding, and I very much regret that you should write me such a letter. It is a very great injustice to me. . . . I think you should talk this matter over with me. . . . I try to be patient under all difficulties, and to give my commissioners full swing, and I have given you full swing, and your associates. What I regret most is for you to say that I have been in any way cold or distant toward you. I fear that feeling arises out of the state of your health. . . . It is due to me that you talk these matters over with me. At least I think so."

The pain caused by Creelman's "injustice" was apparent in every line of this concerned reply. But Creelman had been hurt too deeply, and Gaynor appealed to him again: "If you really must go, let us sit down and fix a date as far ahead as possible." And added with his pen: "No, I will not *announce* your resignation and I trust you will not do so." A week later, reluctantly yielding to Creelman's insistence, he sent word: "I regret your retirement very much, but of course I can not keep you under the circumstances. . . . Yes, we must sit down to dinner in a few days."

The fact was that the cord of Gaynor's physical endurance was being stretched too tightly. His physicians protested against his overworking himself, but he paid little heed. Often these days he would be forced to lie down several times during the course of an afternoon, too weak to sit at desk or table. He carried on, but his increasing debility, fight it as he might, combined with inherent infirmities of character, exaggerated and emphasized by his chronic illness, was carrying him into untenable positions with more and more frequency. Privately, in personal conversation, or when alone with his thoughts (as in composing a letter), his perceptions were lucid and just and his responses genial. To a fellow dog fancier he might write exuberantly:

"Your account of the puppies made my mouth water. I would like to see them. Next week some day I will run down and get the puppy which you are so good as to keep for me. I do not know what name to give him. I suppose the family will give him some nickname, anyhow. I had a notion to call him 'Piccadilly.' 'Post Nati' would not be bad. It is the name of a great law case, involving the question whether persons born in Scotland after the union of England and Scotland were by the fact of birth naturalized as Englishmen."

But a collaborator and personal supporter like Ernest Harvier, who, Gaynor said, could come up with advice two and three times in a day, would be treated with biting scorn in a petty dispute over the cost to the city of manure purchased for use in the parks. Harvier, no countryman, persisted in calling it "fertilizer," whereas to farmer Gaynor it was plain "manure" and "well-rotted manure" at that. In despair, Harvier at length wrote allegorically to his perverse friend:

"My dear Judge: I have been rereading 'King Lear' and the first act reminds me very strongly of one feature of your administration. Lear, every inch a mayor, persisted in recognizing as well-wishers all those who at heart opposed him, and he denounced those who manifested toward him their good will and friendship. Cordelia he disinherited, and Kent, the only real 'politician' and the most clear-headed man at court, for expostulating he exiled. . . . But Cordelia and Kent were his only supporters and proved so in the extremity."

Gaynor was not put out, but refused immediately to admit the analogy. He must read *King Lear* again, he replied, "and see how much I resemble him; but you of all men have no reason to say that I don't like and trust my friends."

At the start of 1913 Gaynor won widespread commendation for his veto of an ordinance regulating motion picture theaters, to which had been attached a censorship clause. In a message to the Board of Aldermen that was worthy of his finest judicial opinions he made a ringing defense of the freedom of speech and publication. Since the pressure brought to bear in favor of the censorship provision had been intense, Gaynor's resistance again displayed his courage and refusal to be swayed by stridency. Later he obtained passage of a similar ordinance without the censorship clause.

A personal humiliation at this time was his last-minute settlement of Alderman Curran's libel suit. Gaynor had resorted to delaying tactics, but the case finally came up to trial date, and in the nick of time the mayor published an ample apology and Curran dropped the action. No money was paid, Curran explaining that the suit had been brought solely to clear his name, and that was accomplished with the mayor's retraction.*

A fresh involvement, little comporting with the dignity of the

---

* In later life, when chief magistrate of New York City, Curran paid Gaynor generous praise, calling him "a rare, resourceful character . . . a great mayor. He made mistakes. They all do. But he did much good, wisely and with insight . . . and he was his own master."

mayor's office, arose when Ralph Pultizer, son of Joseph Pulitzer, who had died in 1911, swore out a complaint against Gaynor charging him with criminal libel. Gaynor had said in a speech that the elder Pulitzer "amassed a fortune of $50,000,000 by blackmail and indecency," and Ralph Pulitzer came angrily to the defense of his father's memory.

These setbacks did not dampen the mayor's ardor for fighting. He seemed, in fact, to grasp at excuses for arguments and invite battle. And yet he retained his humor and liveliness, so far as his strength stood by him. At the annual banquet of the Sons of Oneida he gave New Yorkers an amusing insight into country customs, and incidentally into the softer side of his nature. Recounting the last visit he had made to "Skeeterboro," about five years previously, he said that he had found none of the old families in the neighborhood except his school chum, Bill Griffiths.

"He is still alive and he runs a threshing machine," the mayor reported. "And I went down to the little village cemetery, and I went over the stile, and went through the tombs, the modest tombstones, and there I saw all these names. Most of them were sleeping there. I would not like to say I knelt down, but I certainly was greatly affected. . . .

"I will tell you what happened as I was going along the road and I just came to the first lot of my father's farm. . . . I met a man on the road. I couldn't be mistaken. I went to school with him, but he doesn't live in Skeeterboro now, he lives a little way off. . . . I knew it was Tom Phillips as soon as I saw him. And I bade him good day, and he bid me good day, and spit more or less tobacco juice on the road, and we sat on the fence and talked, and he told me finally he was in much trouble. He didn't know who I was—I was then a justice of the Supreme Court—and he said he was in much trouble, and I says, what is it? Well, he says, not long ago I went down to Oriskany one Saturday night and I got rather high. We never said 'drunk' up there. We always said we 'got high.' . . . And he said a chap down there, I got into a fight with him, and he gave me a good licking. Oh, he says, he beat me bad. Well, I says, what of that? Yes, he says, but he came up here about a month afterwards and I met him on the road and I went for him and I gave him a good licking. So I says, what of that? That is an everyday occurrence up there, or used to be. Well, he says, he wasn't satisfied, but he went up to Rome [the county seat], to the district attorney, and got me indicted. He says, I have thirteen children, and I think he said, ten

MAYOR GAYNOR—"NO LAW!" COME DOWN HERE! I CAN LICK
BOTH OF YOU!

Jan. 30, 1913

cows. And he says I see no way except to sell a couple of cows and
hire a lawyer to defend me, and that goes pretty hard with me. I
talked it over with him and we finally parted. He didn't know who I
was, but when I got home to Brooklyn I sat down and wrote a letter
to the district attorney at Rome and told him poor Tom's case and
the trouble he was in, and it is needless to say that Tom didn't have
to sell his two cows to hire a lawyer. He was fortunate enough to
meet a lawyer on the road. I wrote the district attorney and told him
about some of the ancient customs up in that county. I told him the
whole story as Tom gave it to me, but I wrote also in the letter that
when I was a boy up there such things as that never happened; that
if a fellow got licked he never went up to Rome to indict anybody,
for we had an ancient custom among us that before we entered into

a fight we always said, 'Say no law and I'll lick you.' Then if the other fellow said 'No law' that meant that the law was off, and however the battle went there was to be no lawsuit and no indictment. I said to him in my letter that I didn't know whether Tom observed this ancient custom or not, but however it might be I hoped he would be as lenient with him as possible. But that was the custom when I lived up there. When we wanted to battle we said to the other fellow, 'Say no law and I will lick you,' and if he was brave enough he said, 'No law,' and then we had it out, and settled it right there, and there was no law afterwards.

"I would like to have that custom down here. If we had it there are two or three fellows down here that own nasty newspapers, and I would like to have it out with them on that basis. I don't want to boast, because I am growing old, but I think I could do them up. They may think they can do me up with their dirty pens, but I think I could do them up the other way. I think I have sand enough left in me for that, and it wouldn't require much either, to tell the truth."

Taking their cue from this, the satirists soon had the town laughing, although Pulitzer, Hearst, and some others were not amused.

ONE O'CLOCK AND NOTHING'S WELL

———————— |o◯o| ————————

> *"Thou are a great philosopher, Sancho," said
> Don Quixote; "thou speakest very sensibly; I
> know not who taught thee. But I can tell thee,
> there is no such thing as Fortune in the world,
> nor does anything which takes place there, be
> it good or bad, come about by chance, but by
> the special preordination of heaven. . . . I did
> my best, I was overthrown; but though I lost
> my knightly honor, I did not lose nor can I
> lose the virtue of keeping my word."*
>
> —DON QUIXOTE

EARLY IN 1913, after three years of crimination and recrimination, of misrepresentation, bad temper, and scandalous personal abuse, the long, bitter struggle over subway relief for the suffering taxpayers was brought to a tempestuous close. For weeks Gaynor had virtually dropped out of the negotiations, which were carried on mainly by McAneny and William R. Wilcox, chairman of the Public Service Commission. The final solution was embodied in a dual contract, or contracts, with the Brooklyn Rapid Transit (BRT) and Interborough Rapid Transit (IRT) companies, by which they furnished half the construction capital for extension of their existing lines, and in return were given relatively short-term leases to equip and operate the entire system. The agreement added one hundred and forty-seven miles of track, gave new service to the Bronx, Queens, and Brooklyn, and established a five-cent fare throughout.

At the last minute opposition flared up, spearheaded by John

Purroy Mitchel, with the backing of Hearst. Gaynor, Prendergast, and McAneny thereupon took to the stump to rally public support, charging that Mitchel and Hearst were maneuvering to keep the subway issue alive for use in the coming mayoral campaign. Gaynor wrote letter after letter and spoke throughout the city in denunciation of such obstructionism for political advantage, and finally the contracts (filling a book six inches thick) were signed on March 19, 1913. Gaynor hailed the settlement as the greatest accomplishment of his age, and the greatest industrial feat in the world, not excepting the Panama Canal. The ultimate cost would be close to $325,000,000.

"The city will operate the roads some day, no doubt," he forecast, "but I do not think that it is ready yet. If in ten, fifteen, or twenty years it wishes to do so, the contracts are there in writing."

At a banquet given by a citizens' committee to celebrate the signing Gaynor was in a cheery mood. He praised all who had had a hand in the work, wryly remarking that his colleagues and he were "so used to being abused that this is a strange sight to us." For himself, he claimed no credit, though he had been honored, as head of the city, to sign the contracts.

Only Mitchel, who sat at the speakers' table as a member of the Board of Estimate but did not speak, was not mentioned.

Directly after this event the mayor, impatient of delay, responded to the prodding of a restive correspondent by agreeing that "it is now time to get our minds on something else. . . . Let us therefore cease our jollification over what has been done, and the praising of those who were in the doing of it, and proceed to the actual work of construction."

While this last battle was being won, the mayor was also pushing through an ordinance abolishing the privately exploited taxicab stands before the leading hotels and throwing the curb space open to all public vehicles. This move, coupled with a scaling down and standardization of meter rates, was assailed bitterly by the monopolists affected, but it was a stride toward making it possible for New Yorkers to flag down a cab anywhere.

In-between times the mayor sat for his portrait (he liked the finished painting) and also for a portrait bust (which he "vetoed," to the sculptor's indignation), and brightened up the formalities when the first 220 workers in the street cleaning department retired under the new pension provisions. He reviewed the men at the department's stable at East Seventeenth Street and Avenue C, and when one of them, Michael Faughlin, bragged that he was seventy-six and had never missed a day in twenty-two years, the mayor retorted:

"You don't look it and I don't believe it!"

"Well," came the challenge, "it's up to you to come out on the sidewalk with me and try a wrestle or an Irish jig, and I'm telling you right here and now that I can clean you up, Your Honor, for fair. They tell me you need cleaning up."

Gaynor laughed and responded:

"You're all right! You are still able to fight, and that's a good sign."

Then he shook hands all around, joshing a widower who said he was planning to get married again, and was cheered as he left.

After a period when it appeared that the Curran committee would expire for lack of sensational disclosures, a parade of noxious characters—madams and panders—was passed through its witness box and testified to police corruption in connection with gambling and prostitution. Some of the cases dwelt upon dated back eighteen years. A report was then compiled by the fusion-elected majority of the committee, blasting conditions in the police department and calling on the Board of Aldermen to request Gaynor to remove Commissioner Waldo; and if the mayor refused, to appeal to the governor to act. The committee mustered enough votes to adopt this section of the report, but then was unable for some time to get a quorum together to pass on other sections.

Gaynor predicted that the aldermen would never ratify the report and accused the majority of inventing "wicked and willful falsehoods."

"Poor, miserable little scamps!" he exclaimed. "All cobhouses fall down at the first jar, and down comes this cobhouse of sensation, lying, and scandal!"

At a loss over "cobhouse," the reporters learned that it was the name given to the houses country boys built with corn cobs, and which invariably collapsed before they were completed.

Assuming that air of meek resignation which often accompanied his worst strictures, the mayor went on:

"But what is the use of mentioning it? I have suffered all this nagging now for three and a half years without manifesting any annoyance, and don't wish to manifest any now. It is my good for-

"SUBMISSIVE TO WHATEVER HAPPENS"

June 5, 1913

tune to be of a disposition which is submissive to whatever happens.
I am always able to say, even when the worst happens, that I am
content, since everything comes along at the will of Providence."

The aldermen did reject their committee's recommendations,
and Gaynor showed less resignation when he appeared before a
legislative committee headed by Senator Robert F. Wagner (of
which Franklin D. Roosevelt was a member), and claimed for the
police department credit for virtually everything that had been
accomplished in the Rosenthal case. As for graft still lingering in
the force:

"When I came in as mayor the graft was fully organized in this
town, and it had been so, in fact, for twenty-five years. During that
twenty-five years the heads of the police, one after another, went out
millionaires. . . . I want to know who is going to get rich from the
police now. . . . The great work the police have done in that respect
ought now to be written. And it will be written as soon as the people
of this city are ready to listen, and not be carried away by the lying
headlines of a few corrupt newspapers."

It appeared that the city was beginning to listen: the police force, it was acknowledged, was not universally rotten. This turn in public feeling was caught by the press; the *Herald*, for instance, which a few weeks previously had been attacking the mayor for saying that conditions were not as desperate as they were being represented, now sang a different tune, to wit:

"We are a-weary of the monotonous abuse heaped on this imperial city of the West. At home and abroad the press seems to delight in painting the picture of this city as sordid. . . . Always an evil word, never the true side of the picture! A gambler is murdered . . . and lo! the city and all its guardians are held up everywhere as rotten and corrupt. But five lives have been claimed by justice as the price, and the procession of unworthy bluecoats has already started toward prison. . . . An 'arson trust' is uncovered, and again the story spreads that only in this city can banded firebugs

ALAS! POOR NEW YORICK!

Nov. 1, 1911

I DID IT ALL.

New York Herald, February 28, 1913

exist. But the firebugs have already begun to lockstep toward Sing Sing."

The tide was turning: Gaynor was becoming popular again, and in this election year, when a mayor was to be chosen, that was significant. Yet precisely when politicians began to walk circumspectly, Gaynor permitted himself the most appalling candor.

A critic whom he detested quite as much as he abhorred Dr. Parkhurst and Rabbi Wise was a crusading Brooklyn clergyman, the Rev. William Sheafe Chase. This gentleman, who preferred to be addressed as Canon Chase, was preternaturally galled by the sight of people enjoying themselves on Sundays in the city's parks and the back rooms of neighborhood saloons. His complaints against the iniquitous laxity of the police were continuous, and he never spared the mayor. Canon Chase called at City Hall with a delegation to protest against these Sunday violations and was introduced to Mayor Gaynor formally. Gaynor refused to touch the canon's extended hand. Putting his own hands behind him and backing off, as if from an adder, he barked:

"You're no canon! You're no canon! You're only a popgun!"

Dr. Parkhurst, who in point of sanctimony and chiding of the mayor was no less continuous than Canon Chase, drew periodic fusillades from City Hall that were relished by the public, if not by Parkhurst himself. When the doctor sent Gaynor an "open letter" which he had first released to the newspapers, the mayor hit back:

"Sir: Your letter of March 24th is at hand. I have no notion that it is written to me in good faith. In fact, everyone will perceive that it is a dishonest letter. . . . Hereafter when you wish to utter conscious falsehoods concerning me to the public, do not take the dishonest method of writing a letter to me, when the letter is not meant in good faith at all."

Almost any excuse served for giving Dr. Parkhurst a knuckle rap. A citizen who complained of the clanging of the great clock in the Metropolitan Life tower, on Madison Square directly across the street from Parkhurst's church, received a mede of sympathy from Gaynor, to this effect:

"Dear Mr. Davis: You complain to me of the clock on the Metropolitan building. You want me to stop it. You say it strikes 4 times on the quarter, 8 times on the half, 12 times on the three-quarters, and 16 times on the hour, making 40 times every hour, or 210 times from 8 a.m. to 12 noon every day. I am sorry for you. But really does the clock make as much noise as Dr. Parkhurst does? You know we all have to bear with something, and I am willing to bear my share of it."

Persons who interfered with the legitimate recreations of others felt the sting of the mayor's lash quicker than anybody else. After spending years in trying to teach the police the limitations of their power, Gaynor was stirred to fury by an incident in Queens, and he wrote to Commissioner Waldo:

"It seems that the inspector and captains over in Queens borough assume to close up ball games on Sunday. Is it possible [in the summer of 1913] that you and I are not understood by these leatherheads about this matter yet? If necessary I must advise you to go over there yourself next Sunday and put an end to this business. If I am here I shall go also. Just think of a mounted officer going into a ball field and straddling the home plate with his horse and putting an end to the game in that way. Let him be taken away from there whoever he is. If there be a reason for stopping it we must do it in a decent way. But I know of no reason why they should be interfered with so long as they do not set up public games and charge admission therefor. *That is the law.* I want a full report on this matter and I do not wish to have a recurrence of scenes like this. If the inspector and captains who are doing this are doing it on the theory that boys and men can not play ball on Sunday I want them removed at once from the borough and put in some place where they can do no harm."

The public, reading this, wondered where this refreshing forthrightness had been during the Rosenthal furor.

Yet almost in the same breath the mayor could write to Moses Tannenbaum, who was exercised about the peril to pedestrians of the long hatpins used by women:

"Dear Mr. Tannenbaum: I fear I have no power to prohibit the ladies from having stick pins in their hats. Suppose you try the Board of Aldermen. They seem to be able to do almost anything. I must confess that I never saw anyone hurt by a lady's hatpin, but since you say so, and since the Prefect of the Rhone Department has issued an edict against ladies' hatpins, I suppose they must do much slaughter. But is it altogether seemly for a man to get his face so close to a lady's hatpin as to get scratched?"

Nevertheless, he conscientiously referred the citizen's alarm to Bellevue Hospital, and received back a formal report that the records showed only two instances of wounding by hatpins, and in both cases the injury had been to the wearer, and not to a bystander.

And then there was the curious matter of the grasshoppers and the broom corn crop, laid before the mayor of New York City by a sharecropper of Yalton, Oklahoma. Gaynor replied:

"Dear Sir: Your letter, asking me to assure the broom manufacturers that the grasshoppers did not eat up the broom corn crop in Oklahoma, as is reported in the newspapers, is at hand. I do not know why the grasshoppers should eat up the broom corn crop when there are so many other things much more juicy and satisfactory to their palates. I am therefore quite ready to believe you, and I shall pass the word around among the broom manufacturers, if I can. Perhaps the newspapers will do it, although it is very hard to get some of them to contradict their own stories. It detracts from the notion of their infallibility. However, we have some newspapers here that are just as ready to contradict themselves as to contradict anybody else. They daily contradict in their morning edition what they say in their evening edition, and in the evening what they say in the morning."

When a preacher in West Medway, Massachusetts, took Gaynor

to task for the rigor of his language, the mayor responded with the innocence of a frisking lamb:

"I thank you very much for your kind letter and the newspaper clipping which you enclose. That about my being an irritable and warm-worded man makes me laugh, as I suppose everybody knows that I have been rather reticent all my life."

Gay as might still be his correspondence, on occasion, the mayor's actions were increasingly showing his age. This came out in his sudden invasion of the field of sumptuary regulation, a matter which he had heretofore left to the influence of the church and school, deeming it outside the scope of police authority. The target of the moral crusade which the mayor undertook was the "disgusting" new steps that had the city dance-mad—the "turkey trot," "grizzly bear," "dip," "bunny hug," and variations. The town was on a dancing spree, and dance halls, cafés, and cabarets were thronged day and night. The "tango tea" had been introduced to cater to the afternoon crowds, and every night on Broadway resembled New Year's Eve.

All this carousing must stop, Mayor Gaynor decided, and he caused Police Commissioner Waldo to order all cabarets and dance halls where alcoholic beverages were served to close at 1 A.M. promptly, exactly as the excise law required, and stay shut and locked until 6 A.M., the legal opening hour. And this time there was to be no back-room or side-door subterfuge: locked meant locked. Waldo was instructed to show no favor in executing the edict.

To the night hawks the action seemed so out of keeping with Gaynor's well-known toleration of "innocent enjoyments" that it seemed incredible, and the night the order went into effect produced scenes of disorder along the Great White Way.

Just before 1 A.M. Inspector Dwyer of the Tenderloin district entered Churchill's cabaret, on Broadway at Forty-seventh Street, with a squad of men, and climbing up on the orchestra stand announced that at one o'clock the place would be closed and everybody must leave; those resisting the order, he said, would be arrested. He was greeted with catcalls and boos. A scrimmage followed, with policemen pushing and dragging Churchill's customers out to the sidewalk. Women's purses were left on tables, dishes were broken, and at the height of the tussle Captain Jack Churchill, the proprietor, yelled, "Watch out for your pocketbooks!" infuriating Dwyer.

THE MAYOR'S EARLY CLOSING ORDER
"Cease guzzling!"

March 27, 1913

Similar scenes were enacted in other late-night spots; but the police saw that every "turkey trotter" was evicted, and the doors of the establishments were locked shut.

The mayor was vastly pleased with Waldo's report of "mission accomplished." Said he:

"I think the commissioner and his men did the job well last night. This all-night guzzling and vulgarity is at an end in New York forever, I hope. I see the worst of the proprietors say they are going to the district attorney to make graft disclosures. Good! Let them go and tell everything. If any of them paid graft it hasn't saved them. They threw it in the waste basket."

All this seemed so unlike the liberal-minded Gaynor that the city could only laugh in astonishment. But the mayor was in earnest. He drafted and sent to the legislature a bill creating a "morals board" for the city that would guard against any renewal of the "lascivious orgies going on in the so-called 'respectable' places." The startled grand jury looked into the situation, and while deploring the prevalence of "tango teas" failed to indict any of the promoters of these "lascivious" goings-on.

"Why didn't they hold their tongues?" snapped the mayor. "It is their business to hand down indictments if they find anything wrong, and not to make presentments and scold. . . . They come in after it is all over and make a sputter."

Amid much confusion (helped by Gaynor's mistakenly calling the degenerate tango the "tangle") three judges of the Court of General Sessions heard the complaint against one all-night restaurant owner, Thomas Healy, who had been arrested for violation of the liquor law, when he was serving only food after 1 A.M. The judges ruled unanimously that Healy had violated no law and set him free.

Gaynor, who never stood in awe of judges, brushed this action aside and ordered Waldo to enforce the curfew at Healy's the same as at every other place. Healy felt secured by the court's ruling and the next night kept open.

Inspector Dwyer then tried a new strategy. Entering the crowded restaurant at 1 A.M. he ordered everybody out. Nobody budged, whereupon Dwyer locked the doors and said they would stay locked until 6 A.M. The crowd laughed. Improvising skits and lampooning bluecoats whiled away the time, but after an hour the fun began to sour. A crowd having gathered outside, Dwyer stepped out to disperse this mob, whereupon his captives by twos and threes

OUR PURITAN MAYOR

April 5, 1913

slipped down to the basement, under pretext of going to the wash-rooms, and escaped through a service door. Dwyer's temper was not sweetened when he found the birds had flown, and the next evening he provided scenes that the Tenderloin would long remember.

When Healy's customers refused to leave at 1 A.M., Dwyer and his huskies threw them out. Women were carried out kicking and screaming, men were slugged and if they resisted were tossed into waiting patrol wagons. Tables were overturned, glassware smashed, food trampled into the carpet, and checks left unpaid. At the height of the uproar, Inspector Dwyer came face to face with District Attorney Whitman, at a table with a party of celebrities, among them Richard Harding Davis.

"ONE O'CLOCK AND ALL'S WELL"   *April 9, 1915*

THE MAYOR OF OLD N'YORK,
HE HAD TEN THOUSAND MEN;
HE MARCHED THEM UP THE HILL ONE DAY,
AND HE MARCHED THEM DOWN AGAIN.

April 1, 1913

"Get the hell out of here!" bellowed Dwyer. Then recognizing Whitman, he tried to apologize, but Whitman retorted, "I refuse to accept an apology from a man of your make-up!"

In the morning Healy swore out a warrant charging police oppression. The hearing was before Magistrate Deuel, who heard both sides and dismissed the case, after scolding the police for their actions and warning that any repetition would be dealt with severely—"no courtesies, such as parole," for instance. Dwyer looked worried, for the district attorney was intimating that if anybody was prosecuted for the riot it probably would be the police.

Gaynor's rout was complete. Bitterly he notified Commissioner Waldo that it would be useless and impossible for the police to enforce the law when the district attorney was "advising and upholding" resistance to it—even though, he repeated, "as all the city knows, many of [these] places . . . were turned into places of all-night orgies, drunkenness, and shamelessness."

Whitman, he charged, had gone to Healy's "with a retinue of trained and brilliant writers to write him up, and of flashlight photographers to take his picture in heroic attitudes, and at one o'clock in the morning joined a mob which had been collected by concert to forcibly resist the police in doing their plain duty."

Yet on the evening of the disorder, so Stoical was the philosophic mayor, he had driven out to Coney Island, and strolled along Surf Avenue, unrecognized until spotted by an acquaintance of years gone by—Frederick K. Lundy, a Democratic district leader in Brooklyn who had been a close ally of John Y. McKane. Since the McKane trial Gaynor and Lundy had not spoken to each other. Now Lundy impulsively stepped forward and put out his hand. Without hesitation the mayor grasped it, and the two men chatted for a while. Then Gaynor took Lundy into a photographer's booth (where the barker was another old-time Brooklyn acquaintance) and had their picture taken together.

The picture was printed in the newspapers, and again the riddle was asked—what would the mayor do next? The *Brooklyn Eagle* had the best answer to that conundrum:

"Give it up." *

---

* A curious echo of Mayor Gaynor's flareup of Puritanism, and also of his paternal feeling for the community and his sturdy defense of New York City's good name, was provided surprisingly in 1926 by New York's gayest, most night-clubbing mayor, James J. Walker. Speaking at a luncheon given in his honor by the Cheese Club on April 27 of that year, Mayor Walker replied to quips about his many appearances at public luncheons and dinners, then launched into a defense of his announced desire that night clubs close at 3 A.M.

"As to the dinner business," said Walker, "I go to them because I feel that the chief magistrate of this town should continue to be one of the family over which he presides, and not remain aloof or aloft . . . It is true that the Jimmy Walker of yesterday was known along Broadway as a patron of the theaters and the cabarets. . . . But there is an hour in the early morning when in some of these resorts an orgy takes the place of clean entertainment. There is no demand on the part of respectable and decent people for such places, which at seven or eight o'clock in the morning disgorge crowds of men in evening dress and women in flaming cloaks and finery, which they flaunt in the faces of workmen on their way to their jobs.

"A reformer is a terrible thing, but I believe in a certain amount of reform in respect to conditions like these. I don't believe in outsiders coming to New York, which is the cleanest city on the face of the earth, and behaving in such a manner as to make it appear that New York is a Sodom or Gomorrah."

This Gaynoresque pronouncement, coming from a mayor of a totally different stamp, the *New York Times* deemed worthy of its front page, under a two-column headline:

"Walker Criticizes Night Club Orgies at Dawn."

"I HAVE BEEN MAYOR"

———————o◯o———————

*Forward, then, Sancho my friend, let us go
to keep the year of our novitiate in our
own country, and in that seclusion we shall
pick up fresh strength to return to the by me
never-forgotten calling of arms.*

——DON QUIXOTE

THE TIME OF MAYOR GAYNOR's retirement from office—or of his
reelection—was approaching. That year, in the midst of the final
struggle to get the subway contracts signed, James J. Gallagher
had died in the New Jersey Hospital for the Insane; Gaynor had
never filed charges against him. The memory of that tragic August
day when Gallagher's bullet had ended one epoch and opened another, more tangled one in Gaynor's career was much in people's
minds in August, 1913, as the political pot seethed again. The question overshadowing all others in the coming election was, what
would Mayor Gaynor do? That he would do something was sure,
and that whatever he did would vitally affect the campaign was
certain, but the *Herald* merely stated the obvious when it declared
that "no wise man will attempt to predict what the mayor will do."

In three and a half years Gaynor had managed to alienate practically every vestige of organized political support. The reform
element had been snubbed too often to have any liking for him;
the Republicans wanted no part of "Tammany's mayor"; and the
starved Democratic machine shuddered at the thought of prolong-
ing the agony. Except for independent support, the mayor was

isolated. Ernest Harvier, indefatigable adviser, outlined for Gaynor his vulnerability with bland frankness:

"My dear Judge: Lucullus was a good soldier as well as a good general, and one of the reasons why he defeated Mithridates and was able on his return to Neapolis to enjoy life, participate in banquets and distribute largesse was that he looked after his soldiers when they were on the firing line, and Mithridates didn't. On one occasion, Mithridates left his army to shift for itself in disaster, but Lucullus stuck close to his legions and they did to him. In this (in public view here) you resemble Mithridates, for there is not a settlement worker, uplift reformer, civic center planner, or municipal roustabout who will not be against you in November, irrespective of any concessions you have made or recognition given. Without organized Democratic support outside of Tammany no candidate can be elected . . . this year, and citizens' committees and businessmen's leagues are mere paper, politically. . . . 'Save me from my friends' must be recalled by you."

Then Harvier added a surprising remark:

"One of the most candid and impartial of those whom I have found to speak of the good things in your administration to approve is William M. Ivins."

Ivins in Gaynor's camp! Who, then, were his friends and who his enemies?

Gaynor made no statment. But when some of the same over-zealous admirers who had led the Presidential drive the year before began to form "Gaynor clubs" to work for his reelection, the mayor asked them to desist.

He went his usual rounds. He opened the baseball season at the Polo Grounds, marching across the field in full view of the crowd and receiving a lusty cheer. A possible foretaste of political activity was seen in his making a "moving talking picture" by the "Kinetoscope"—a moving picture film synchronized with a voice recording on a wax cylinder—at the Edison studio in the Bronx. Technicians said his voice "fairly bit into the record." Shown in vaudeville houses around the city, the film, in which the mayor discussed his administration, won applause, and speculation arose as to whether Gaynor planned to seek reelection and campaign by means of filmed talks, instead of personal appearences.

Gaynor himself paid no heed to the election talk, but found time to cover a wide assortment of other topics. Critics of New

York's municipal architecture he took to task sharply, bidding them look at the Public Library, the Municipal Building, and the Woolworth tower, all recent structures, for proof of the city's superior artistic taste. And with the advent of summer he launched a vigorous campaign against littering the streets and parks. He set up a committee, headed by the well-known banker-citizen, George W. Perkins, to devise a model pension system for all municipal employees. Corporation Counsel Watson got a reminder to appoint "a respectable commission" to carry out the task of condemning property for the new North River piers (not "little people . . . who would drool over the matter for months or years, and then soak the city two or three times the value of the property"). And the mayor cited with jubilation the increase in the number of marriage licenses issued in June, compared with the same month the year before. ("Bully! The more the better.")

The mayoral letter file was brightened by an exchange of views with a poultry fancier on the subject of White Orpington hens; Gaynor found them disappointing, and thought egg dealers all "more or less tricky." Then there was his commiseration with a citizen whose repose was shattered by the morning cock-a-doodle-do of a nearby rooster.

"Dear Sir," wrote the mayor, "You complain that your rest is disturbed by a neighboring rooster that crows every morning at sunrise. He must be a strange rooster. Does he not crow at midnight also, like all other roosters? Or it may be that you are too fast asleep at midnight to hear him. Do you not know that every rooster in the world crows at midnight, so that like Daniel Webster's British evening drum beat, the midnight crow of the rooster continually circles the earth? 'Loud swells the note of Chanticleer,' says the poet in admiration. But you do not like the note of Chanticleer, and I shall have to see what I can do to make him keep his mouth shut at sunrise. I shall see what the Board of Health can do with him. Suppose we get someone to 'goozle' him."

But on the subject of running or not running for a second term in office, Gaynor spoke in oracles. Numerous letters and statements issued from City Hall, but they fell short of clarifying his intentions. These pronouncements included:

"I have not said that I am willing to run again for mayor. All that I have said is that I do not think any party will nominate me. . . ."

"I think it is unlikely that any party would nominate me, as I have not permitted the government to be used in the interest of any party. . . ."

"I am perfectly content to step down and out whenever the people of the city are through with me. I have had four years of hard work and much detraction and abuse. I hope that everyone is beginning to see that I have in my plodding way done something. . . ."

Such statements could be interpreted as one wished; and even when in a formal communication to the public Gaynor reviewed his position, he managed to skirt the direct question: would he or would he not run for reelection if nominated? Political pundits puzzled over the cryptic sentences:

"I have no party back of me. I have not heard a word from leaders of any party. I do not suppose there is any party or organization that would nominate me. . . . No political organization made me. I never belonged to any to start with. Nor can they unmake me, I hope. . . . I bear the marks of physical and moral assassins on me, and I am perfectly content to go on carrying them with me to the end. . . . Sometimes I think I ought to be nominated by the so-called fusionists. Have I not carried out what they have been pretending to demand for years and years? Let them stand up and answer that. . . . I could have tried to build up a party of my own. I did not do that. I am glad I did not do it. It is true that I have no party back of me. That is often an uncomfortable position to be in. But I am satisfied."

The fusion leaders, quarreling among themselves, were united only in agreeing that they wanted no dependence on a mayor who impugned their sincerity and delighted in exposing their shortcomings. And though there appeared indications that Boss Murphy still considered Gaynor the best vote-getter in sight, the Democratic district leaders were unanimous in their detestation of the man who had let them down so abysmally. "Big Tim" Foley, Murphy's second in command, speaking for them all, said succinctly:

"I will say this for Mayor Gaynor: he did more to break up the Democratic organization than any other man ever has in this city."

The truth was that Gaynor yearned for reelection as a vindication of his administration. But he kept his longing to himself. His friends, foreseeing no party endorsement, were anxious to run him independently, and petitions were circulated to test his popular strength. This activity was directed by Jacob Schiff and Herman Ridder; Gaynor neither helped nor hindered it. The fusionists, in angry confusion, at length yielded to the persuasiveness of John Purroy Mitchel and handed him the mayoral nomination. Still Gaynor said nothing, but went about his affairs, making news in divers ways, none of them positively political. But he watched the developing situation closely, especially among the Democrats.

One hot August night, in the midst of the hubbub, the mayor showed up at a band concert in Battery Park. He strolled to a bench, and remarking a group of children dancing in time to the music, called one small boy over to him. Taking him on his knee, Gaynor asked the child his name. Michael Donovan, four years old, said the boy.

"Michael Donovan!" the mayor repeated. "Why, that's an Irish name, and when I saw you keeping time with the band I thought you were Italian."

"But that was an Irish tune," called over Father M. J. Henry, pastor of the Immigrant Home for Irish Girls, who occupied the next bench. "It's the good old stirring piece called 'As Long as the Shamrock Grows Green.' "

Gaynor gave Michael a quarter, and the boy ran to the ice-cream cart. The other children asked where he had got the money, and he told them, "From the old man with the whiskers there." In a minute Gaynor was surrounded, and he passed out quarters from a purse open in his hand as long as the supply lasted.

Word spreading that the mayor was in the park, soon three thousand tenement dwellers had deserted their fire escapes to say hello to his honor. At the close of the concert, Gaynor shook hands with the conductor and complimented him on his choice of program.

"I like music of this kind at a place like this," he said, "and the people like it. Of course, I suppose this band can play classical music when the occasion arises, but this music was splendid."

(The numbers the mayor liked had included "Snooky Ukums," "In My Harem," and "Here Comes My Baby Now.")

Getting into his automobile, Gaynor then took Father Henry and the Tammany alderman and the leader of the district on a tour of the downtown streets.

Shortly after this, the mayor added another word to the city's vocabulary when he called the quarreling fusionists a "mingle-mangle committee." This floored the reporter who was interviewing him, and Gaynor impatiently interjected:

"Why, just read one of honest old Hugh Latimer's sermons to the king and you will find out what it means. It's good English. I can't stop to play dictionary with you."

The dictionary revealed that "mingle-mangle" was an old word for the stuff fed to swine, whereupon the feeling against Gaynor in fusionist circles reached a boiling point. But the cartoonists had a merry time, the *Herald* picturing Gaynor as a bristly porcupine snarling, "Don't mingle-mangle with me!" *

Finally, meeting in Boss Murphy's private dining room at Delmonico's, the Democrats made their choice of a mayoral candidate. But first the assembled district leaders spent several hours in congenially tearing Gaynor to shreds. Murphy ordered supper served at 11 P.M. and the cursing kept up until 4 A.M. Then former Supreme Court Justice Edward E. McCall was handed the nomination over his protest, and in obedience to the party's command he reluctantly accepted. Throughout that verbal lynching, Murphy was said to have been the only person present who spoke a kind word for the mayor; but Murphy always had a sneaking regard for a man who would not be bossed.

When it thus became definite that both parties had ditched the mayor, Gaynor's backers prepared to incorporate as an independent party and name him their candidate. The newspapers tried hard to get Gaynor to say whether he would accept such a nomination, and under extreme pressure from the City Hall newsmen the mayor finally yielded. On Friday, August 22, just before leaving his office for a weekend at St. James, he dictated a formal statement:

"To the Staff of City Hall Reporters: I do not know just what to say in answer to your written request. But there is one thing I can say to the whole city. I have not turned the city, or the rent payers or the taxpayers of the city, over to the spoliation of anyone. I have not turned them over to the spoliation of any organized band who make that their pursuit in life, and whose smug and sleek faces and figures are standing evidence that they wax rich and fat by

---

* *Mingle-mangle:* A mixture; a mess of mixed food for swine. Chiefly in contemptuous or disgusted use, a confused medley (of things or persons).

    Latimer, 3rd Ser. bef. Edw. VI—"They say in my contrye, when they cal theyr hogges to the swyne troughe, Come to thy myngle mangle, come pyg." 1549.
    —*Oxford English Dictionary*

ROBINSON CRUSOE

June 6, 1913

filching by this cunning way and by that the taxes paid into the treasury by their industrious and respectable neighbors. The rent-payers and taxpayers may now turn themselves over to the spoliation of such people if they want to. I am able to say that I have not done it. Whether I am to run again depends entirely on the wishes of my fellow citizens. I have had a pretty hard time for four years to hold my own against all comers, and against every corrupt influence, but I have been mayor.

"W. J. GAYNOR."

Having sent this to the reporters' room, the mayor picked up his hat and walked out of his office. In the anteroom he was besieged by newsmen begging for amplification. Calmly Gaynor replied:

"If you will only quote me on what I wrote over my own signature, and not mangle it or pervert its meaning, I will be very much obliged. There is nothing more to say."

But that day a leader in the movement for an independent nomination passed the word that Gaynor had agreed to run, if the movement seemed strong enough.

Commented the *Herald:* "Let the battle proceed!"

A SEA CHANGE

So I awoke, and behold it was a dream.

— PILGRIM'S PROGRESS

WHILE THE CITY SWELTERED in August heat, the mayor remained unapproachable at St. James. Twenty thousand signatures had been obtained to petitions to enter him as an independent candidate; only his formal consent was lacking. Still he hesitated. He was aware of the hazard of attempting to buck the regular party organizations, especially the Democratic. But in the Republican ranks there was a strong feeling against Mitchel, who was disliked by the conservatives as too brassy, too overreaching, too reformist for their taste; he was the fusion's choice, not theirs. Gaynor waited to see whether, as seemed possible, the Republican party convention might break the fusion alliance and perhaps nominate himself. The fusion leaders desperately strove to head off the threat. The whole political picture was dominated by Gaynor's baffling silence. Even his lieutenants in the city heard nothing from him.

This silence was not merely strategical. Directly after reaching Deepwells Gaynor had been brought low by a violent recurrence of the old coughing and retching, and for the time being he was incapacitated.

For weeks the reporters had noted that he seemed to be near the limit of his strength. All summer he had struggled against weakness, some days leaving City Hall so drained that his chauffeur had to help him up the steps of his home. Not for many weeks had he walked across Brooklyn Bridge, and at the Montauk Club, where he had been taking his meals while the family was in the country, the waiters observed that he barely touched his food. Usually he dined alone, preoccupied and irritable. He confided to a friend, "Nothing would please me better than to have a year to myself."

Adamson knew of the crisis at St. James and was worried, but on August 28 he received a telegram saying:

"Am up and everything seems natural and right. Had a bad attack. Send down stenographer."

The stenographer came and the mayor dictated a few letters, including one to his son-in-law, J. Seward Webb, Jr., in which he divulged his intentions:

"My dear Seward: I am very glad indeed to receive your letter, and I thank you for your willingness to help. I had no disposition to enter into the contest again, but since there seems to be a respectable number who desire me to run, I shall do so."

Another letter went to Louis Wiley, business manager of the *New York Times*, and in this Gaynor gave one of his few detailed accounts of the agony he had endured recurrently since the shooting. He wrote:

"I have been down for a day or two, but am up today, and will be all right tomorrow. I suppose you guess what the trouble is. My right lung, pneumogastric nerve, and stomach have taken it into their heads that by combined and violent effort they could succeed in casting this 'fishhook' out of my throat, which that bullet lodged there. But as in their former occasional attempts, they succeeded in casting everything out except the 'fishhook,' and have completely done themselves and me up in the bargain. And now the sore and exhausted lung, nerves, and cords, and stomach have to be bathed and soothed for a day or two to get them into shape again. The attack of mechanical retching and vomiting lasted over twelve hours. You can imagine the condition I was in at the end. My lung and stomach are so sore that I can hardly speak or swallow. It is good that these attacks are so rare. But we must all have our cross, and I am willing to bear mine. These members of my body which try to do this thing now and then are just as foolish as people you and I know who want something done all at once which can only be done gradually and little by little. But they won't have it that way. And so to work they go, might and main, to do it all at once by violence, with the result that instead of doing it they do much harm and mischief and exhaust themselves. I will be all right in a day or two."

That day Adamson let it be known that Gaynor would run as an independent candidate, and that he would accept the nomination on the steps of City Hall.

The fusion camp was thrown into consternation, and proposals were excitedly advanced to drop Mitchel and substitute Gaynor; only in that way, it was argued, could Tammany be beaten. Mitchel hurried back to the city from the Adirondacks, where he was vacationing, and after a hard fight managed to squelch this revolt. It was then announced by the Gaynor League, which had been incorporated as a separate party, that the nomination ceremony would take place on Wednesday, September 3. For its emblem the new party chose a shovel, symbolizing the start on new subway construction.

Invalided at Deepwells, Gaynor was philosophical. In a luncheon conversation with Hyde he lifted a bit the veil that shrouded his motives. With Hyde he could be more open than he could be with almost anyone else, and on this occasion he was surprisingly candid. Hyde was shocked by the mayor's feebleness; Gaynor had to lie down for half an hour before he could sit at table. Why, Hyde wondered, should Gaynor, with his wealth and at his age and in his physical condition, engage in another political dogfight, as the mayoral campaign was bound to be?

"I do it because I like the excitement," was Gaynor's answer, his eyes flashing the glint of the born fighter.

Hyde thought that with his means Gaynor could buy some less exhausting form of excitement, but the judge shook his head impatiently:

"You can't buy the excitement you get in the mayor's chair, and if I didn't have the means I couldn't afford to hold the position. I find that it costs me a great deal of money to be mayor."

Then he told an anecdote:

"You know, they say I never smile, but I want to tell you that I had some excitement recently when I came across a man who smiles less than anyone I ever met. You see, when you are up there in the mayor's office they are all the time handing you someone. It is a visiting count, or a grandee of some kind. These people pay you a formal call of a few moments and then you must pay a call in return. When you go to call on them, there are always a lot of officious people about, and just after you have paid your respects someone suggests, 'Let's have a dinner.' I always have to say 'Yes' to such a proposal, and then later I get the bills to pay.

"Well, the last person they presented to me was a Japanese admiral. He is the man who smiles less than any other man I ever met. I tried four days to get him to smile, and spent a lot of money in the attempt. I talked statesmanship, books, authors, war, travel, and everything to this admiral for four days, and never a smile. Finally, near the close of the fourth day, while at dinner, I said to him in desperation, 'Were you seasick when you came over this time?' Immediately a smile spread over his face, and he made reply. I had him at last!"

"What did he say?"

"It was a remark between friends and not to be repeated," Gaynor answered, smiling to himself at the recollection.

Wednesday, September 3, dawned intensely hot, and by noon a perspiring crowd of five thousand had assembled in City Hall Park for the Gaynor acceptance formalities. Squads of supporters had come marching in formation; one contingent of nearly a thousand marched across Brooklyn Bridge carrying shovels on their shoulders. Three bands pumped out martial airs simultaneously, and the three hundred policemen keeping traffic lanes open were very, very polite.

Gaynor reached the Hall at 10:30 with his son Rufus. In the anteroom a reception committee and the heads of the city departments were waiting. When the mayor entered, they gave one glance and were appalled. The change from Gaynor's usual dapper, confident appearance was shocking. Instead of his firm tread, he shuffled through the room, head down, darting glances from side to side. This was a mannerism with him, and ordinarily these glances were keen, indicative of his desire to notice rapidly who was present; now the movement of his head was mechanical and his eyes were inexpressive. Most startling of all was his attire: he who had always been so spruce and correct in matters of dress wore a rumpled, untidy gray suit and a limp straw hat entirely out of keeping with the occasion.

Passing into his inner office, the mayor rested there until the signal came to emerge on the portico. A chair had been placed in the shade, and Gaynor sank into it gratefully. Then the speeches began. Herman Ridder, Jacob Schiff, and R. Ross Appleton, chairman of the Gaynor League, paid the customary compliments and extolled the achievements of the Gaynor administration. In the stifling heat, the speakers' voices came faintly, and few in the crowd heard them distinctly. There was a little cheering, not much. Gaynor had written out his acceptance statement. When Appleton handed him a beribboned, gilded shovel, the mayor stood up and posed with it, then passed his statement to Adamson to read for him. It said:

"I accept. What you do this day shall become memorable. You are teaching the intelligent people of this city how they may nominate their candidates for office, if they see fit, and have the spirit, and not submit to having candidates imposed on them by a little coterie of men who follow politics as a dishonest trade, and have no other visible means of support.

"How different this vast and impressive scene is to the little scene which occurred in a room at Delmonico's one night a week ago. There sat at a table eight men to decide who might run for mayor and other offices. They were all of one stripe, and of a kind fit even to cast lots on the garments of the city. Let me read their names to you, lest you have forgotten them:

"Charles F. Murphy,

"John H. McCooey,

"Thomas Foley,

"Philip Donahue,

"Edward E. McCall,

"John Fitzgerald,

"Arthur Murphy,

"John Galvin.

"There was no room for anyone except themselves. None of you were invited. None of you were allowed to make a suggestion. But here today, all the different people of the city, and their representative men, have a voice:

"Mr. Chairman, in presenting me with this shovel you stated that the meaning of it was that the work of constructing the subways was to go on vigorously. It means far more than that. It means that the people of this city are going to shovel all of these miserable little political grafters into one common dumpheap."

Suiting action to the word, the mayor made several scoops in the air with the shovel, then waved his hat solemnly while the crowd set up a ripple of cheering.

In a concluding demonstration, the delegations flung down their shovels in a heap around a sign reading, "Way down under these shovels lies the body of C.F.M.," and enumerating the Tammany leader's political transgressions.

The reaction in the various political camps to Gaynor's formal entrance into the competition was one outwardly of bravado, and inwardly of quaking. "Bathetic," was the official scoff at fusion head-quarters. "Big Tom" Foley growled, "The old rogue is in his dotage." Mitchel sneered that Gaynor was only a "Tammany decoy . . . permitted to float out, or be hauled in, just as Mr. Murphy and his Delmonico 'board of strategy' deem advisable." Several Tammany stalwarts (young James J. Walker among them) charged that by naming eight Irish Catholics as his villains he was "bringing religion into politics."

But in reality the politicians were neither indifferent nor disdainful; they were worried. Ran the *Tribune*'s headline: "Politicians Pause at Shadow of Gaynor." What Gaynor was offering to do, judged by every rule of practical politics, seemed impossible; but Gaynor had done the impossible before. He was, in fact, impossible altogether—certainly impossible to predict. The test, of course, would lie in how much of the vague "silent vote," how much bedrock support among the mass of people, he commanded. This was anybody's guess, and even a man as ready to risk predictions as Ernest Harvier admitted he was at sea on this subject. Harvier headed a splinter group of independent Democrats, and after they had been polled on their preference for mayor he reported to Gaynor:

"My associates have no good reason to be favorable to your administration, but on the vote taken on August 15th, twenty-two of the thirty-five districts in Manhattan and Bronx declared in favor of your administration. It is proper to add, as I can truthfully, that in no single instance during the present year have you taken my advice on any political matter."

In plain truth, the politicians were baffled. In the fusion camp the rules were hastily rewritten to allow fusion nominees to accept endorsement by the Gaynor League, and McAneny and Prendergast prepared to do so. Mitchel angrily held aloof.

In Gaynor's ranks the question was whether he could conduct a campaign in his physical condition. He was certain that he could, and reassured his aides that all he needed was a brief rest to regain his vigor. It was guessed that he might campaign by means of letters rather than speeches, and his supporters thought that would be effective: as a letter writer he was unbeatable.

Surprise followed surprise. The day after he accepted the independent nomination, Gaynor and Rufus sailed for Europe aboard the White Star liner *Baltic*. Their intended departure had been kept secret, and at twenty minutes before sailing time Lieutenant Kennell and a detail of police accompanied them to the pier. As Gaynor walked slowly up the gangplank he looked wan and frail. Halfway up he waved to the police escort to fall back, and only Kennell accompanied him on board. A trained nurse was being taken along as medical attendant; the three would occupy an $800 luxury suite, the Hearst newspapers would point out. Shaking hands with Kennell, Gaynor promised, "I am coming back a well man." Then the whistle blew and Kennell said good-by.

The mayor had left with Adamson a message explaining his departure:

"Yes, I am going to take a couple of weeks' vacation. I can not possibly get any privacy on land, so I am going to spend two weeks on the ocean, where nobody can get at me. . . . Murphy and the chaps that sat down with him at Delmonico's the other night and guzzled and abused me until their faces were red were ready to cut me up, I am told, and yet I never did anything to them except what tended to make them look respectable. . . . The McCooeys and the Foleys and the Murphys and the Donahues and the whole bunch have had four lean and hungry years. I have had no time to quarrel with them. I simply went on and did my work and kept their hands out of the public treasury."

To Creelman and a few others the mayor had confided that when he returned he intended to "tell the whole damnable story" about Tammany and its allies. He had named men high in official life and called them "of a piece with Rosenthal."

The day after the *Baltic* steamed out of the bay a wireless message came to the *Evening Mail*, in response to its request:

"The rent-payers and taxpayers of New York City will not throw the government of their city into the hands of an outside king grafter. Nor will they throw it into the control of a vulgar gang of grafters, all of one stripe, such as met at Delmonico's. Give them the shovel. No king, no clown shall rule this town. That day is gone forever."

Clear enough in wording, yet cryptic in its allusions, it was the last oracle of Mayor Gaynor.

What phantoms of illusion or regret, what surges of indignation on behalf of the exploited, what admonitions to self that "charity is everything," what thirst for combat coursed through Gaynor's mind as the *Baltic* plowed eastward can only be surmised.

Most of the time he spent alone, reading, or sunning himself on deck. Adamson's last service had been to hunt up a copy of Emerson for shipboard reading; Emerson had always been a favored author, and this book Gaynor opened frequently. He walked a good deal. The other passengers respected his wish for privacy and did not intrude, but he found a companion in a little boy, with whom he made his morning promenade, hand in hand, chatting pleasantly. With Rufus he was cheerful and lively, and his strength and appetite improved steadily.

On September 12, as the *Baltic* approached the coast of Ireland, Rufus went to call his father to luncheon, served in their suite. Ten minutes before, the mayor had marked on the menu card brought to him by the steward the dishes he wanted. As Rufus came up to the still figure wrapped in a deck chair he thought his father was sleeping. But on shaking him gently he realized that it was not sleep. In private and alone, death had come to William J. Gaynor.

AND THEN—

Merit and good works is the end of man's
motion; and conscience of the same is the
accomplishment of man's rest.

—BACON, *Of Great Place*

THE MAYOR'S DEATH, occurring so remotely and inopportunely,
startled and shook the city. The event threw the already muddled
election prospect into still wilder disorder, but for the time being the
city at large put aside calculations and mourned, on a scale and
with an intensity that surprised itself. The avalanche of praise that
poured from the press was the more striking because of the condemnation which the mayor had so often undergone by the same newspapers. It seemed that the composers of the panegyrics dwelt almost
gloatingly on the faults of Gaynor, in order to lend brilliance to his
elements of greatness, truncated though these had been by the
unlucky assassin's bullet. The New York *Evening Sun*'s eulogy set
the tone when it stated:

"In every sense of the word, William J. Gaynor has been the
mayor of this town. Mistakes he made; who does not? Errors of
judgment stand forth, added to errors of temper; but who is guilt-
less? But above and behind them looms the great bulk of his wise
decisions, his unhesitating courage, his independence, which alike
defied dictation and repulsed those who sought to bribe him with
false popularity and empty praise, or coerce him by undeserved
calumny."

The *World*, long since turned against the mayor, recalled that during Gaynor's first year in office the city had witnessed "a revolution in the administration of New York's affairs"; and reminded New Yorkers that for that achievement alone, even if he had done nothing else, Mayor Gaynor deserved to be remembered gratefully.

Gaynor's personality, seen at such close range, remained an enigma, it was generally felt, and his impact upon the course of political life was actively debated. So was the apparently magnetic attraction he had for the electorate. The *Nation's* best "short answer" to this question was to point out that William J. Gaynor was "the most interesting man in New York," and that he had interested people on all levels with equal facility.

The *New York Herald's* obituary stressed Gaynor's invincible independence, saying:

"Yes, he *was* mayor.

"One of the strangest characteristics of the man . . . was that he was no man's man but his own. His opinions were his opinions. *His politics were his own politics.* His virtues were his own virtues. His failings were his own failings. His successes were his own successes. His life was just what he made it. Positiveness was one of the ruling traits of this great figure. . . .

"At the time of his death Mayor Gaynor was perhaps the most conspicuous public man in America. He was made so by no party, sect, or race, but by William J. Gaynor. Stripped of the petty things which go with every strong individuality, he stands out, now that death has taken him, as a gigantic man, whose successes were mental, whose failings were temperamental.

"New York never had a mayor who was so pervasive of the the public presence. When he took the stage there was no other actor on it. A scholar, a philosopher, and a dreamer, he was at the same time a man of initiative and a terrible antagonist. No friend who differed with him was safe from the lash of his pen or tongue, and no enemy when conquered could find a finer comforter. The mayor was charming in his own inconsistencies. He had no greater admirers than his enemies. His swiftness to combat was Homeric. He seemed to fear neither man nor devil, and yet he was a lover of peace. The scourge of his wrath fell upon the sycophant and the charlatan, and the breadth of his mind took in especially the weak and the lowly, giving a liberty of view which at times staggered his intimate friends.

"Mayor Gaynor's public services have been many and they

have been notable. They lasted over many years, and as a builder he left more hammer marks upon the municipal structure than any other man now living within the five boroughs.

"Yes, he *was* mayor!"

Though few spoke publicly of it, the knowledge that Gaynor's death could probably be traced to the effects of Gallagher's bullet lay uneasily on people's consciences. The *Nation* did allude to that contributing cause, and admitted that that bullet, "in all human probability, never would have been fired but for the mayor's firm refusal to conduct his office on the spoils principle."

Alone, William Randolph Hearst's *Journal* and *American* passed over Mayor Gaynor's death in contemptuous silence; not one word of tribute or regret appeared in their editorial columns.

The city was determined that its farewell should be commensurate with its sense of bereavement. The wish was anticipated abroad; when the *Baltic* docked at Liverpool, the mayor's body was borne in solemn state to the Town Hall, where it lay for twenty-four hours on the catafalque which had recently served for the funeral of King Edward VII. Then, aboard the *Lusitania*, the casket was started on the voyage home.

On September 19 the *Lusitania* passed through the Narrows. The mayor's body was removed quietly and carried to the family home in Brooklyn, where a simple service was held for the relatives and a few friends, while the honorary pallbearers, headed by ex-President Taft, waited in the Montauk Club across the street to convey the coffin to City Hall.

Two hundred mounted policemen clattered before and after the hearse as it passed down Flatbush Avenue and across the familiar bridge. Along the entire route traffic had been halted, and the stillness, except for the jingling accoutrements of the mounted escort, was eerie.

At City Hall the plain metal casket was placed upon a bier in the rotunda, where Lincoln's body had lain, to remain there all the following day. "A wilderness of flowers" filled the hall, though only one spray, of purple asters, rested on the open casket—the gift of Lieutenant Kennell. On either side five firemen and five policemen maintained constant guard, and draped across the foot of the coffin was the flag of the mayors of the City of New York.

Rain was falling when the doors of City Hall were opened at eight o'clock the next morning. Five hundred persons already were waiting, and in a few moments the number swelled to a thousand. The first person admitted was a crippled bootblack who worked on the city's ferries. By nine o'clock nearly fifteen thousand persons stood in the shuffling line extending for more than two miles along the wet pavements. Marshaled by hundreds of policemen, the double file stretched from the Municipal Building at Chambers Street, along Park Row to Broadway, down the east side of Broadway to Bowling Green, crossed Broadway there and continued north on the west side of Broadway to Chambers Street, where it crossed over to City Hall Plaza. There it entered the front door of City Hall, filed past the coffin, and emerged by the rear door.

All afternoon the line never grew shorter, though rain fell steadily; the upper half of the Woolworth tower was completely blotted out by mist. Into the night the people of New York filed patiently, silently, past the coffin and took their last look at the still face. The enigmatic eyes were closed, the privacy which they had guarded so rigorously now inviolable. At midnight the doors were shut, with twenty thousand still in line.

The next morning the coffin was carried down Broadway to Trinity Church through a throng of one hundred thousand silent spectators. The jam on lower Broadway was so dense the hearse could hardly push through. Thousands looked down on the scene from skyscraper windows on either side, and the roofs of the lower buildings were crowded. Only the clatter of the escort's horses and the soft tolling of Trinity's bell as the hearse approached broke the stillness. The list of notables crowding every inch of space in the church filled column after column in the newspapers.

There remained only the final journey—across the bridge for the last time, past tens of thousands of silent citizens who lined Brooklyn's streets, and out to Greenwood Cemetery. People who remembered the outpouring for Abraham Lincoln's New York funeral said that in size and solemnity the crowds exceeded even those of 1865.

A NOTE ON SOURCES
AND ACKNOWLEDGMENTS

The principal source availed of in preparing this biography is the voluminous *Gaynor Papers* in the Municipal Archives of the City of New York. This immense collection covers mainly the four years of Mayor Gaynor's administration. Comprised in it are letters personal and public, official reports, messages, letters received, and a mass of miscellaneous memoranda. Since it has never been thoroughly catalogued, any estimate of the number of items it contains can be only a guess, but by rough calculation the total can scarcely be less than 100,000, and it may run as high as 150,000. There are perhaps 40,000 to 50,000 letters personally signed by Gaynor, while his three secretaries wrote perhaps twice that number on his behalf.

For providing facilities for mining this rich vein of information, both as to Mayor Gaynor's activities and as to his motives and insights into his character, heartiest thanks are extended to Mr. James Katsaros, administrator of the Archives, and to his entire staff, who so cheerfully and efficiently cooperated with the demands of the research over a protracted period of time. Without such help and the availability of this material the book would have been impossible.

A second major source of information about Mayor Gaynor is the files of the New York newspaper press. Few public men have supplied as much, or as lively, newspaper copy as Gaynor did, both before and during his mayoralty; hence few have been so extensively documented, day by day. To follow the course of this reporting, affected and colored as much of it was by the strong political bias of some of the newspapers, was tedious, but productive of a cross-section of attitude that gave depth to the outline of the man and his activity.

The periodicals of the day also furnished many sidelights on Gaynor, especially as he was viewed outside New York City.

Still another source of major importance was comprised in the memoirs of persons who knew or worked with Mayor Gaynor, preserved in the Oral History Research Office of Columbia University. Dr. Louis M. Starr, director of the office, and his able assistants are particularly thanked for their generous help in this research, as well as for specific contributions of fact and quotation.

Mayor Gaynor's Brooklyn connections were traced through the morgue of the defunct *Brooklyn Daily Eagle*, now in the possession of the Brooklyn Public Library. Mr. Roy D. Miller, Jr., chief of the History Division of the Brooklyn Library, most generously placed these records at the author's disposal.

Two previous studies of Mayor Gaynor have been of assistance as guideposts in writing this account. One is Mortimer Smith's biographical essay, *William J. Gaynor*, excellent within its limits, and the other is William R. Hochman's unpublished doctoral dissertation titled, *William J. Gaynor: The Years of Fruition*, an examination of Gaynor and his actions in reference to the municipal reform movements of his time. Dr. Hochman has placed all later students of the *Gaynor Papers* under a debt of gratitude by his courageous start on a systematic organization of that immense collection.

Of Mayor Gaynor's children, two were surviving at the time of the writing of this biography. One of these, Mrs. Dudley G. Bird (née Ruth Gaynor, the mayor's youngest daughter), kindly furnished personal recollections, while Mayor Gaynor's granddaughter, Mrs. Frederick Wynne, recounted family traditions with wit and acuity.

None are more warmly thanked for their cooperation throughout the long task than the staffs of the New York Public Library, the Brooklyn Public Library, the New York Historical Society Library, and the workers in the library of the short-lived *New York World Journal Tribune*.

PRINCIPAL WORKS CONSULTED

———————◖◦◉◦◖———————

Newspapers
New York Morning Advertiser
New York American
New York Globe
New York Herald
New York Journal
New York Evening Mail
New York Press
New York Sun
New York Evening Sun
New York Evening Telegram
New York Times
New York Tribune
New York World
New York Evening World
Brooklyn Daily Eagle

Periodicals
Albany Law Journal
American Heritage
American Magazine
American Mercury
Bench and Bar
Century Magazine
Collier's
Current Literature
Current Opinion
Good Housekeeping
Harper's Weekly
Independent
Literary Digest
Municipal Affairs
Nation
North American Review
Outlook
Pearson's Magazine
Review of Reviews
World's Work

ALGER, GEORGE W., "Mayor Gaynor and the Police," *Outlook*, January 1, 1910
ALLEN, FREDERICK LEWIS, *The Great Pierpont Morgan*. Harper, New York, 1949
ANGELUS GABRIEL, BROTHER, *The Christian Brothers in the United States 1848–1948*. D. X. McMullen Co., New York, 1948
ARMSTRONG, HAMILTON FISH, *Those Days*. Harper, New York, 1963

ASBURY, HERBERT, *The Gangs of New York*. Knopf, New York, 1927

———, *Sucker's Progress*. Dodd, Mead, New York, 1938

"The Attempt to Assassinate Mayor Gaynor," *Outlook*, August 20, 1910

"The Austerity of Judge Gaynor," *Current Literature*, August, 1909

BARRETT, JAMES W., *Joseph Pulitzer and His World*. Vanguard, New York, 1941

———, *The World, the Flesh, and Messrs. Pulitzer*. Vanguard, New York, 1931

BELMONT, ELEANOR ROBSON, *The Fabric of Memory*. Farrar, Straus & Cudahy, New York, 1957

BENT, SILAS, *Ballyhoo*. Boni & Liveright, New York, 1927

BERGER, MEYER, *The Eight Million*. Simon & Schuster, New York, 1942

———, *The Story of the New York Times 1851–1951*. Simon & Schuster, New York, 1951

BLAKE, EUPHEMIA VALE, *History of the Tammany Society*. Souvenir Publishing Co., New York, 1891

BREEN, MATTHEW P., *Thirty Years of New York Politics*. Privately printed, New York, 1899

BROUN, HEYWOOD, and LEECH, MARGARET, *Anthony Comstock*. Albert & Charles Boni, New York, 1927

BROWN, HENRY COLLINS, *From Alley Pond to Rockefeller Center*. Dutton, New York, 1936

———, *Valentine's Manual of Old New York*. Valentine's Manual, Inc., Hastings-on-Hudson, 1916–1924

BUTLER, RICHARD J., and DRISCOLL, JOSEPH, *Dock Walloper: The Story of "Big Dick" Butler*. Putnam, New York, 1933

BUTT, ARCHIBALD W., *Taft and Roosevelt: The Intimate Letters of Archie Butt*. Doubleday, Doran, Garden City, 1930

CARLSON, OLIVER, and BATES, ERNEST SUTHERLAND, *Hearst, Lord of San Simeon*. Viking, New York, 1936

CERVANTES SAAVEDRA, MIGUEL de, *Don Quixote*. Translated by John Ormsby. Heritage, New York, n.d.

CHAFETZ, HENRY, *Play the Devil*. Clarkson N. Potter, New York, 1960

CHAMBERS, WALTER, *Samuel Seabury: A Challenge*. Century Co., New York, 1932

CHURCHILL, ALLEN, *Park Row*. Rinehart, New York, 1958

CLEWS, HENRY, "Address delivered at Memorial Meeting in Commemoration of the late William Jay Gaynor," Cooper Institute, New York, September 13, 1913

COHEN, JULIUS H., *They Builded Better Than They Knew*. Messner, New York, 1946

CONNABLE, ALFRED, and SILBERFARB, EDWARD, *Tigers of Tammany*. Holt, Rinehart & Winston, New York, 1967

CRANE, MILTON, ed., *Sins of New York*. Boni & Gaer, New York, 1947

CREELMAN, JAMES, "Municipal Non-Partisanship in Operation," *Century Magazine,* August, 1910

———, "Unpledged Candidate," *Century Magazine,* September, 1910

CURRAN, HENRY H., *Pillar to Post.* Scribner's, New York, 1941

DAVIS, ELMER, *History of The New York Times 1851–1921.* New York Times, 1921

DAVIS, RICHARD HARDING, *Adventures and Letters of Richard Harding Davis.* Edited by Charles Belmont Davis. Scribner's, New York, 1918

"The Death of Mayor Gaynor," *Literary Digest,* September 20, 1913

DELMAR, VIÑA, *The Becker Scandal—A Time Remembered.* Harcourt, Brace & World, New York, 1968

DITMARS, CHAUNCEY L. C., "Judge Gaynor of St. James," *Long Island Forum,* March, 1939

EISENSTEIN, LOUIS, and ROSENBERG, ELLIOT M., *A Stripe of Tammany's Tiger.* Robert Speller & Sons, New York, 1966

ELLIS, EDWARD ROBB, *The Epic of New York City.* Coward-McCann, New York, 1966

EPICTETUS, *The Discourses and Enchiridion,* translated by Thomas Wentworth Higginson, Black, New York, 1944

FOWLER, GENE, *Beau James.* Viking, New York, 1949

FRANKLIN, BENJAMIN, *Autobiography.* Heritage, New York, 1951

———, *Poor Richard's Almanacks.* Heritage, New York, 1964

FURNAS, J. C., *The Life and Times of the Late Demon Rum.* Putnam, New York, 1965

GANS, HOWARD S., "In the Matter of the Lawlessness of the Police—A Reply to Mr. Justice Gaynor," *North American Review,* February, 1903

GARDINER, ALEXANDER, *Canfield.* Doubleday, Doran, Garden City, 1930

GAYNOR, WILLIAM J., "The Arrest and Trial of Jesus," *Albany Law Journal,* August, 1888

———, "Books and Reading," *Independent,* November 21, 1912

———, "A Government of Laws, Not Men," *North American Review,* February, 1903

———, "Lawlessness of the Police in New York," *North American Review,* January, 1903

———, "Libel in England and America," *Century Magazine,* October, 1911

———, "The Looting of New York," *Pearson's Magazine,* May, 1909

———, *Mayor Gaynor's Letters and Speeches.* Greaves Publishing Company, New York, 1913

———, "The New York Subway Situation," *Outlook,* July 30, 1910

———, "The Pleasures and Profit of Walking," *Independent,* June 1, 1911

———, "The Problem of Efficient City Government," *Century Magazine,* August, 1910

———, "Water, Dirt, and Railroad Public Highways." Speech at National Rivers and Harbors Congress, Washington, D.C., December 7, 1911

"Gaynor's Work as Mayor," *Collier's,* August 20, 1910

GERARD, JAMES W., *My First Eighty-three Years in America.* Doubleday, Garden City, 1951

GOLDBERG, ISAAC, *Tin Pan Alley.* Ungar, New York, 1961

GOLDEN, HARRY, *Ess, Ess, Mein Kindt.* Berkley, New York, 1967

———, *Forgotten Pioneer.* Fawcett Crest, New York, 1966

GRIFFIN, HENRY F., "Mayor Gaynor and His Work," *Outlook,* August 20, 1910

GRISCOM, LLOYD C., *Diplomatically Speaking.* Literary Guild, New York, 1940

HALE, WILLIAM BAYARD, "Gaynor, Mayor of New York," *World's Work,* July, 1910

HEATON, JOHN L., *Cobb of "The World."* Dutton, New York, 1924

———, *The Story of a Page.* Harper, New York, 1913

HOCHMAN, WILLIAM R., "William J. Gaynor: The Years of Fruition." Unpublished doctoral dissertation, Columbia University, 1955

HOLLEY, MARIETTA, *Samantha at Coney Island.* Christian Herald, New York, 1911

HOUSE, EDWARD M., *The Intimate Papers of Colonel House,* Arranged by Charles Seymour. Houghton Mifflin, Boston, 1926–1928

HUGHES, RUPERT, *The Real New York.* Smart Set Publishing Co., New York, 1904

JOHNSON, C., "A Talk With Mayor Gaynor," *Harper's Weekly,* February 25, 1911

KAHN, E. J., Jr., *The World of Swope.* Simon & Schuster, New York, 1965

LANGFORD, GERALD, *Alias O. Henry.* Macmillan, New York, 1957

———, *The Richard Harding Davis Years.* Holt, Rinehart & Winston, New York, 1961

Low, BENJAMIN R. C., *Seth Low.* Putnam, New York, 1925

LUNDBERG, FERDINAND, *Imperial Hearst: A Social Biography.* Equinox Co-operative Press, New York, 1936

LYNCH, DENNIS TILDEN, *"Boss" Tweed.* Boni & Liveright, New York, 1927

LYON, PETER, "The Master Showman of Coney Island," *American Heritage,* June, 1958

———, *Success Story: The Life and Times of S. S. McClure.* Scribner's, New York, 1963

MANDELBAUM, SEYMOUR J., *Boss Tweed's New York.* Wiley, New York, 1965

"Mayor Gaynor: An Estimate of His Administration," *Outlook,* August 20, 1910

"Mayor Gaynor and Hearst," *Collier's,* October 8, 1910

"Mayor Gaynor Shot by an Assassin," *Independent,* August 18, 1910

"Mayor Gaynor's Appeal Against the Yellow Press," *Century Magazine,* December, 1910

"Mayor Gaynor's Appointments," *Outlook,* January 22, 1910

"Mayor Gaynor's Letter," *Independent,* September 29, 1910

"Mayor Gaynor's Letters," *American Magazine,* January, 1913

"Mayor Gaynor's Public Career," *Nation,* September 18, 1913

"The Mayor Who Wrote Letters," *Independent,* September 18, 1913

McAdoo, William, *Guarding a Great City.* Harper, New York, 1906

McAdoo, William Gibbs, *Crowded Years.* Houghton Mifflin, Boston, 1931

McClellan, George B., Jr., *The Gentleman and the Tiger: Autobiography,* Edited by Harold C. Syrett. Lippincott, Philadelphia, 1956

McGurrin, James, *Bourke Cockran.* Scribner's, New York, 1948

Madison, Charles A., *Critics and Crusaders: A Century of Protest.* Holt, New York, 1947

Marcus Aurelius, *Meditations.*

Martin, Edward Sandford, *The Life of Joseph Hodges Choate.* Scribner's, New York, 1920

Mitgang, Herbert, *The Man Who Rode the Tiger: The Life and Times of Judge Samuel Seabury.* Lippincott, Philadelphia, 1963

Morgenthau, Henry, *All in a Lifetime.* Doubleday, Garden City, 1922

"A Morning With Mayor Gaynor," *Literary Digest,* February 10, 1912

Morris, Lloyd, *Incredible New York.* Random House, New York, 1951

———, *Not So Long Ago.* Random House, New York, 1949

Myers, Gustavus, *History of the Great American Fortunes.* Random House, New York.

———, *History of Tammany Hall.* Boni & Liveright, New York, 1917

———, *Ye Olden Blue Laws.* Century Co., New York, 1921

Nevins, Allan, *Abram S. Hewitt.* Harper, New York, 1935

"The New Mayor of New York City," *Independent,* November 25, 1909

"New York's Subway Policy," *Municipal Affairs,* June, 1901

Nock, Albert Jay, *Memoirs of a Superfluous Man.* Harper, New York, 1943

Northrop, William B., and Northrop, J. B., *The Insolence of Office.* Putnam, New York, 1932

O'Connor, Richard, *Courtroom Warrior: The Combative Career of William Travers Jerome.* Little, Brown, Boston, 1963

Older, Mrs. Fremont, *William Randolf Hearst, American.* Appleton-Century, New York, 1936

Parkhurst, Charles H., *My Forty Years in New York.* Macmillan, New York, 1923

Pilat, Oliver, and Ranson, Jo, *Sodom by the Sea.* Doubleday Doran, Garden City, 1941

Pink, Louis Heaton, *Gaynor, The Tammany Mayor Who Swallowed the Tiger.* International Press, New York, 1931

"The Police Policy of Mayor Gaynor," *Outlook,* January 1, 1910

PUSEY, MERLO J., *Charles Evans Hughes.* Macmillan, New York, 1951

REID, S., "Tell It to Gaynor," *Independent,* August 18, 1910

Reports, New York State Supreme Court, Vols. 6–49, 1894–1905

Reports, New York State Supreme Court, Appellate Division, Vols. 110–134, 1905–1909

RIORDON, WILLIAM L., *Plunkitt of Tammany Hall.* Knopf, New York, 1948

ROVERE, RICHARD H., *The Magnificent Shysters.* Grosset & Dunlap, New York, 1947

SEITZ, DON C., *The James Gordon Bennetts.* Bobbs-Merrill, Indianapolis, 1928

————, *Joseph Pulitzer, His Life and Letters.* Simon & Schuster, New York, 1924

SHACKLETON, ROBERT, *The Book of New York.* Penn Publishing Co., Philadelphia, 1920

"The Shooting of Mayor Gaynor," *Current Literature,* September, 1910

"The Shooting of Mayor Gaynor," *Harper's Weekly,* August 13, 1910

SLOAN, JOHN, *John Sloan's New York Scene.* Edited by Bruce St. John. Harper & Row, New York, 1965

SMITH, ARTHUR D. HOWDEN, *Mr. House of Texas.* Funk & Wagnalls, New York, 1940

SMITH, MORTIMER, "Mayor Gaynor: A Political Maverick," *American Mercury,* October, 1949

————, *William Jay Gaynor,* Regnery, Chicago, 1951

STARR, LOUIS M., "Joseph Pulitzer and His Most Indegoddampendent Editor," *American Heritage,* June, 1968

STEFFENS, LINCOLN, *The Autobiography of Lincoln Steffens.* Harcourt Brace, New York, 1931

————, *The Shame of the Cities,* Sagamore Press, New York, 1957 (Reprint)

STILL, BAYRD, *Mirror for Manhattan.* New York University Press, 1956

STOKES, I. N. PHELPS, *The Iconography of Manhattan Island.* Robert H. Dodd, New York, 1915–1928

STONE, MELVILLE E., *Fifty Years a Journalist.* Doubleday, Page, Garden City, 1921

"The Sudden Death of Mayor Gaynor," *Current Opinion,* October, 1913

SULLIVAN, MARK, *Our Times.* Scribner's, New York, 1926–1935

SWANBERG, W. A., *Citizen Hearst.* Scribner's, New York, 1961

————, *Pulitzer.* Scribner's, New York, 1967

SYRETT, HAROLD C., *The City of Brooklyn, 1865–1898.* Columbia University Press, New York, 1944

VAN WYCK, FREDERICK, *Recollections of an Old New Yorker.* Liveright, New York, 1932

WEINSTEIN, GREGORY, *The Ardent Eighties, and After.* International Press, New York, 1928

WELLING, RICHARD, *As the Twig Is Bent.* Putnam, New York, 1942

WERNER, M. R., *It Happened in New York.* Coward-McCann, New York, 1957

———, *Tammany Hall.* Doubleday, Doran, Garden City, 1928

WHITLOCK, BRAND, *Forty Years of It.* Appleton, New York, 1930

———, *The Letters and Journal of Brand Whitlock.* Edited by Allan Nevins. Appleton-Century, New York, 1936

WILLEMSE, CORNELIUS, *Behind the Green Lights.* Knopf, New York, 1931

———, *A Cop Remembers.* Dutton, New York, 1933

WINKLER, JOHN K., *W. R. Hearst, An American Phenomenon.* Simon & Schuster, New York, 1928

———, *William Randolph Hearst, A New Appraisal.* Hastings House, New York, 1955

WOODIN, GLENN W., "Contributions of Mr. Justice Gaynor to the Law of Libel and Slander," *Bench and Bar,* July, 1917

INDEX